Following the Nez Perce Trail

Following the Nez Perce Trail

A Guide to the Nee-Me-Poo National Historic Trail
with Eyewitness Accounts

Cheryl Wilfong

Second edition, Revised and Expanded

Oregon State University Press
Corvallis

The paper in this book meets the guidelines for permanence and durability of the Committee on Production Guidelines for Book Longevity of the Council on Library Resources and the minimum requirements of the American National Standard for Permanence of Paper for Printed Library Materials Z39.48-1984.

Library of Congress Cataloging-in-Publication Data
Wilfong, Cheryl.
  Following the Nez Perce trail : a guide to the Nee-Me-Poo National Historic Trail, with eyewitness accounts / Cheryl Wilfong.— 2nd ed.
      p. cm.
  Includes bibliographical references and index.
  ISBN-13: 978-0-87071-117-6 (alk. paper)
  ISBN-10: 0-87071-117-2 (alk. paper)
 1. Nez Perce National Historical Trail—Guidebooks. 2. Nez Perce Indian Buffalo Trail—History. 3. Automobile travel—Nez Perce National Historical Trail—Guidebooks. I. Title.
  F597.W75 2005
  917.96'8504—dc22

                    2005022602

Oregon State University Press
500 Kerr Administration
Corvallis OR 97331-2122
541-737-3166 • fax 541-737-3170
http://oregonstate.edu/dept/press

Table of Contents

Acknowledgments to the 2nd edition

Thanks to the Maker of My Path, which wasn't quite ready to let me detour off the Nez Perce Trail despite the fact that I had just given away all my books, files, and photos to the Resource Center of the Colville Confederated Tribes.

Thanks to Mary Elizabeth Braun, acquisitions editor at Oregon State University Press, who asked me to update this book. Since I procrastinated in answering her, Jim Court of custertours@juno.com provided the next impetus for me to get back in the saddle to revise the directions in this book. The group who was "following the Nez Perce Trail" with Jim and Virginia suggested specific changes. Thanks particularly to Tom King, who rode shotgun beside Jim and GPSed every intersection.

Thanks to Charlie and Margaret Moses for updating me with contacts and for tuning me back in to the Trail.

Albert Andrews reminded me that some Nez Perce have never been in favor of national recognition of the Nee-Me-Poo Trail. Thanks to Frank Andrews for the tour of Nespelem. Jewie Davis asked me to include Fort Spokane. Thanks also to Agnes Davis, Mark Davis, Leah Conner, and Paul and Ruth Wapato. Thanks to Adrian Holm, librarian, who lent the photos in this book back to me.

Thanks to Nez Perce National Historical Park rangers Diane Mallickan, Tim Nitz, and Robert West. Thanks to Otis Halfmoon for keeping after me about including citations; they are posted on my Web site, www.nezpercetrail-guide.com.

Jim Magera provided his usual excellent tour of the Bear Paw Battlefield and Blaine County.

Sandi McFarland reminded me to focus on women and children and allowed me to use the Nez Perce Trail map on my Web site. Thanks to Clark Whitehead of the Lewistown BLM.

Researcher extraordinaire Larry O'Neal shared loads of Kansas and Oklahoma historical documents with me and gave me a tour of Miami County. Thanks to Matt Novak for the Fort Leavenworth tour, and to Kelvin Crowe for amplifying my knowledge of Fort Leavenworth.

After I drove 8,000 miles (including all the Intrepid routes) in five weeks, my sister Dona Fuller provided me a home away from home on the far edge of Nez Perce country and within sight of where L.V. McWhorter ran sheep in the 1930s. My brother-in-law, Jim Fuller, updated the Bismarck section, and my nephew Calvin Fuller GPS'd Fort Abraham Lincoln.

Thanks to my sweetie, Bill McKim, who kept the home fires burning and chopped and split enough wood to keep us warm during the winter while I was at the computer.

Thanks to all the fans of the first edition of this book, including members of the Nez Perce National Historic Trail Foundation.

Acknowledgments to the 1st edition

Thanks to my dad, Ralph Wilfong, for being my patron during two years of this project. I am thankful for the support of my sister, Dona Fuller, who paid my bills, read me my mail over the phone, and was my daily contact for the nine months I was on the road. I am grateful to Tracy and Tammy Wilfong, Cindy Gorman, and Chad Wille for their companionship on the trail.

Thanks especially to Grace Bartlett, Ralph Space, and Stu Connor, whose historianship inspired me. Bill Lang articulated several points I felt strongly about. Thanks to Frances Brenner, Eileen Bennett, and LeRoy Anderson for their helpfulness and local research. Thanks to Jim Dolan of the National Forest Service for his cooperation and for access to maps of the Trail. Thanks to all my friends who read and re-read chapters, especially Lani Wright and Connie Woodberry.

I honor Soaring Dove and Wabun, guides for the two vision quests I undertook while writing this book.

How to Use this Book

Are you about to turn the page and skip this part because it looks like instructions and because you'd really rather be reading about the Nez Perce? Spending just a few minutes to scan these pages will save you several minutes on the road later. These explanatory notes will help make your experience of the Nez Perce Trail a richer, more rewarding experience.

Much of the actual Trail traveled by the Nez Perce and their horses is not easily accessible to the modern-day traveler in a four-wheeled vehicle. The official Nez Perce (Nee-Me-Poo) National Historic Trail includes many back roads, jeep trails, ranch roads on private lands, and hiking trails. In some places the Trail cuts across country where no trails at all are shown on today's maps. So the routes recommended by this guidebook get as close to the actual Trail as practical.

What Type of Traveler Are You?

On the road, as in life, there are usually several different ways to get from where you are to where you want to be. When you're traveling, your vehicle determines, to some extent, the roads you feel most comfortable on. A switch-backing, narrow, dirt road may not be a good place to drive an RV, for example, while someone in a four-wheel-drive vehicle might enjoy that very same road.

With these variations in mind, this historical guide for travelers offers two and sometimes three different ways for getting from point A to point B. Whether you drive a car, a recreational vehicle, a truck, or an SUV, you'll find a route this fits your style of traveling. These various routes are defined here as **Mainstream Traveler, Adventurous Traveler**, and **Intrepid Traveler**.

The Mainstream Traveler

For people in a hurry and for campers hauling trailers or driving large recreational vehicles, the Mainstream Traveler is the route to follow. These roads are paved, unless otherwise noted, and are usually state or federal highways. The Nez Perce themselves avoided most major thoroughfares, so the Mainstream route will frequently be some distance from the actual Trail. Nevertheless the Mainstream Traveler will gain a general sense of the terrain the Nez Perce rode through.

State highway maps will provide sufficient back-up road information for the Mainstream Traveler when used in combination with this guidebook.

The Adventurous Traveler

For the traveler who likes to drive on back roads occasionally, the routes recommended for the Adventurous Traveler will, in many cases, provide a closer glimpse of the trail taken by the Nez Perce. These county dirt or gravel roads can be traveled easily by cars during the summer months. Mileage is indicated for the Adventurous Traveler because these roads tend to bypass cities and towns—and therefore, gas stations.

Forest Service or Bureau of Land Management (BLM) maps are recommended for the Adventurous Traveler, although a Gazetteer also will usually serve. Each travel section suggests the maps that are relevant to that particular excursion. See Appendix 1 for sources of these maps.

The Intrepid Traveler

If you enjoy narrow, bumpy roads that are out in the middle of nowhere, the Intrepid Traveler routes will take you there. Many of these roads are as close to the Nez Perce Trail as you can get without going by horse or foot. Thus, these routes will often give the traveler a first-hand sense of the Trail. Occasionally these are roads with grass growing in the middle of them. Just in case a wrong turn is taken, the Intrepid Traveler should not mind turning around in the sagebrush, since wide spots in the road or junctions with other roads may be minimal. While four-wheel-drive is not a necessity for these roads in good weather, a vehicle with a higher clearance is recommended. In inclement weather, inquire locally about road conditions before proceeding.

Forest Service and Bureau of Land Management (BLM) maps are highly recommended for the Intrepid Traveler. Especially for Intrepid Travelers who have the urge to "just see where that road goes," a Forest Service or BLM map expands your personal touring opportunities well beyond the scope of this guidebook. The names of the required maps are noted in each travel section. A Gazetteer does not contain sufficient detail for the Intrepid Traveler. See Appendix 1 for sources of maps that contain quite a lot of information and are also inexpensive.

Mileage is indicated for each leg of the journey to enable the Intrepid Traveler to plan refueling stops.

All Travelers Should Know:

Special considerations are noted for all travelers where appropriate. Such notes include some minimal seasonal road condition information as well as reminders to fill up on gas. The best time of year to follow the Trail is the same season the Nez Perce traveled it—June through October. Almost all Intrepid Traveler Roads and many Adventurous Traveler roads are closed by snow from the first snowfall in November until snowmelt sometime in May.

This book is designed to be used in conjunction with an accommodations guide. Each state publishes its own accommodations guide, from which you can select your kind of overnight lodging. (See Appendix 1.) Private organizations such as AAA also publish travel guides that are aimed at particular tastes. When planning your overnights, take into consideration that campgrounds and motels can be far apart and not immediately adjacent to the Trail.

For a first-hand experience of the Nez Perce National Historic Trail, contact the Appaloosa Horse Club. (See Appendix 2.) Each summer, the Club's week-long Chief Joseph Trail Ride covers about 100 miles of the Trail. Over the course of thirteen summers, the entire 1,170-mile Trail is completed.

Traveling the Trail with Respect

To the Nez Perce, the land where their ancestors are buried is sacred. More than one hundred of their people died on this four-month journey. Nearly three hundred more died in exile. While this fact contributes to the poignancy of the story, the death of so many of their people is a matter of great sadness. Traveling this Trail is, in a sense, traveling on the graves of Nez Perce people. The Trail is sacred land. Please be respectful.

Artifact-hunting and grave-robbing are illegal in Oregon, Idaho, Montana, and Wyoming.

Travelers Joining the Trail for Just a Few Chapters

Very few people travel the Nez Perce Trail from beginning to end in one continuous trip. Even avid Trail buffs can usually manage to retrace just a segment or two at a time. The structure of the chapters is intended to ease your entry onto the Trail.

The Story

This section at the beginning of every chapter gives an overview of the events that are detailed later in the chapter. Travelers joining the route along the way can catch up on the story of the flight of the Nez Perce by reading the condensation provided by the one- or two-page **The Story** at the beginning of the chapters preceding the place where you join the Trail. For example, readers starting this book in Yellowstone National Park, which is Chapter 9, should take a few minutes to read **The Story** section of Chapters 1 through 8.

Travel Plan

The one-page travel plan in each chapter summarizes the various legs of the journey. Using this page as a reference point, you can select the routes you wish to take.

Directions

Although the Nez Perce Trail chronologically goes from west to east, not everyone is able to follow it in that order. Accordingly, north, south, east, and west are used as directions to assist people who are following the Trail "backwards."

Distances between towns are figured from the center of town. Mileages are rounded down to the nearest 0.1 mile. Still, not all odometers are created equal, so you may have to use your judgment.

Federal highways are designated by a US preceding the number (for example, US 12). National Forest roads are designated by an NF preceding the number (for example, NF 46).

Eyewitness Accounts

Soldiers and settlers whose lives were touched by the Nez Perce War knew that they had been eyewitnesses to history. Many of them wrote letters, journals, reminiscences, manuscripts, articles, books, or reports on the most memorable event of their lives. The quotes used in this book, complete with creative spelling and colorful grammar, are drawn from these first-hand accounts.

The Nez Perce side of the story is meager by comparison. The fact that it exists at all is because Lucullus V. McWhorter,[1] a Washington state rancher, spent 30 years gathering Nez Perce versions of the events. His books *Yellow Wolf* and *Hear Me, My Chiefs!* are as close as most of us can get to the Nez Perce side of the story.

xii

1. *Voice of the Old Wolf: Lucullus Virgil McWhorter and the Nez Perce Indians,* by Steven Ross Evans, tells the story of how McWhorter collected the Nez Perce stories.

This historical guidebook relies heavily on these eyewitness accounts of events that happened during the flight of the Nez Perce. The author of each quote is identified by one or two words that define his or her role in regard to the conflict. Because about eight hundred Nez Perce and two thousand soldiers participated in the campaign, trying to figure out who did what where and when can be very confusing. If you would like to know more about a particular person, see the **Cast of Characters** in Appendix 3 for a brief biosketch.

Some of these quotes were written within a day or two of the event they describe; others were written twenty to sixty years later. Because information written at the time of the event is likely to be more accurate than recollections recorded some years later, dates have been included on items written contemporaneously with the event.

Truth has many faces. Frequently, quotes describing the same situation don't quite jibe with each other. In fact, the points of view can be uncomfortably different. The reader is placed in the position of a historian, sorting through the facts to determine just where the truth lies.

Language of the nineteenth century was laced with racial slurs. Words such as "squaw" and "half breed" are pejorative terms but have been kept as they occur in diaries, manuscripts and letters of that era.

For Further Reading

While each chapter ends with a recommendation of books for further reading relevant to that particular chapter, several good books cover the entire flight.

Yellow Wolf, by L.V. McWhorter, is the account of one young Nez Perce warrior. This simple, readable account is so direct and personal that it grabs the reader's attention.

Chief Joseph and the Nez Perces: A Photographic History, by Bill and Jan Moeller, provides beautiful half-page color photos that illustrate the landscape as the brief text narrates the day-by-day history of the 1877 war.

In *Children of Grace*, Bruce Hampton skillfully leads the reader through history by providing thumbnail stories of most of the participants in the 1877 conflict. Very easy and interesting to read.

Jerome A. Greene has thoroughly researched and written *Nez Perce Summer, 1877: The U.S. Army and the Nee-Me-Poo Crisis.*

I Will Tell of My War Story: A Pictorial Account of the Nez Perce War, by Scott Thompson, looks closely at a booklet of drawings made by an anonymous Nez Perce veteran.

Mark Brown approached *The Flight of the Nez Perce* from a unique perspective: He used only source material that had been written within a few days of the actual event. Although this approach—and his own military career—skew the focus of the book in favor of the military, his conclusions sometimes bear out the Nez Perce side of the story.

The weighty volume, *The Nez Perce Indians and the Opening of the Northwest*, by Alvin Josephy, thoroughly covers the history of the Nez Perce from their first contact with white people—Lewis and Clark, in 1805—to the Nez Perce War of 1877.

Hear Me, My Chiefs!, McWhorter's other book of Nez Perce accounts, is dense reading but an invaluable and unique source.

Western historian David Lavender has written a very readable history, *Let Me Be Free: The Nez Perce Tragedy*.

Intrepid travelers who can't get enough detail can read *Dreamers: On the Trail of the Nez Perce*, in which Martin Stadius tells the 1877 story side by side with his own pilgrimage.

American Girl has produced an excellent series. *1764: Meet Kaya: An American Girl* by Janet Shaw is the first of the many Kaya books for ages seven and up. Naturally, Kaya has her own horse.

Soun Tetoken: Nez Perce Boy Tames a Stallion is for intermediate readers, ages nine to thirteen. During the 1877 conflict, boys had the important job of herding the horses.

The September 1990 issue of *Cobblestone: the history magazine for young people* is devoted to the Nez Perce. Written for grades four and older.

Chief Joseph: Thunder Rolling Down From the Mountains, by Diana Yates, is for ages twelve and up.

"I Will Fight No More Forever," by Merrill Beal, is a basic text on the events of 1877 that is easy to read, objective, succinct, and historically accurate.

Chief Joseph of the Nez Perce is an epic poem written by Robert Penn Warren.

For those people who prefer the readability of novels, Terry C. Johnston's *Lay the Mountains Low* covers the period June 20 to August 9, 1877.

While some of these books or other recommended books may go out of print, used books can easily be found and bought on the Internet.

Chapter 1

The Wallowa Country

Home of Chief Joseph's Band of Nez Perce

La Grande, Oregon, or Walla Walla, Washington, to Lewiston, Idaho

We came from no country, as have the whites. We were always here. Nature placed us in this land of ours....—Yellow Wolf[1]

I have no other home than this. I will not give it up to any man. My people would have no home.—Chief Old Joseph

If we ever owned the land we own it still, for we never sold it. In the treaty councils the commissioners have claimed that our country had been sold to the Government. Suppose a white man should come to me and say, "Joseph, I like your horses, and I want to buy them." I say to him, "No, my horses suit me, I will not sell them." Then he goes to my neighbor, and says to him: "Joseph has some good horses. I want to buy them, but he refuses to sell." My neighbor answers, "Pay me the money, and I will sell you Joseph's horses." The white man returns to me and says, "Joseph, I have bought your horses, and you must let me have them." If we sold our lands to the Government, this is the way they were bought.—Chief Joseph

There is abundant room for Joseph's band on the present Nez Perce reservation.... Joseph's band do not desire Wallowa Valley for a reservation and for a home.—Gov. L. F. Grover, July 21, 1873

We have plenty, and we are contented and happy if the white man will let us alone. The reservation is too small for so many people with all their stock.
—Chief Joseph

The Story

The deepest canyon on the continent, the most perfectly formed glacial lake in the world, beautiful alpine mountains, rolling hills covered with grass—the Wallowa is magnificent country. Since time beyond memory, Nee-Me-Poo, the Nez Perce people, had lived on this land. The Creator placed the Nez Perce here together with the trees, the mountains, the fish, the birds, and the animals. Yet today, very few Nez Perce live in the Wallowa country.

Chief Old Joseph, Chief Joseph's father, signed the Treaty of 1855, which, among other provisions, guaranteed the Wallowa country to the Nez Perce. He did not sign the Treaty of 1863, which shrunk the Nez Perce Reservation by ninety percent and excluded the Wallowa. The five bands whose chiefs did not sign the 1863 Treaty became known as the nontreaty Nez Perce.

Chief Joseph became the civil chief of the Wallowa band after the death of his father, Chief Old Joseph. In his own language he was named Heinmot Tooyalakekt, which means Thunder Traveling to Loftier Mountain Heights. (Photo courtesy of Montana Historical Society.)

Although he had been one of the first two Nez Perce converts to Christianity in 1838, Chief Old Joseph was so incensed by the "thief treaty" of 1863 that he not only tore his copy of the treaty to shreds, he also destroyed his Nez Perce translation of the Gospel of Matthew. He knew the time was coming when whites would be pressing his people for their land.

> *The Wallowa valley...is a fine country.... Let the white man travel through it, and, while doing so, eat your fish and partake of your meat, but receive from him no goods or other presents or he will assert that he has purchased your country.*—Chief Old Joseph

Chief Old Joseph died the same summer that the first white settlers arrived in the Wallowa valley–1871.

The man known to history as Chief Joseph succeeded his father as the head of the Wallowa band. Joseph's brother, Ollokot, who was two years younger, became the war chief of the band. During the next six years, Chiefs Joseph and Ollokot counciled and talked to settlers, agents, commissioners, and military men as they stated their case again and again and again. The Wallowa country was their home. They had not sold their home. In 1873 President Grant signed an executive order setting aside half of the Wallowa country for the Joseph band. In 1875 he rescinded the order.

Friction between the nontreaty Nez Perce and the settlers increased, and in May 1877 the ultimatum came: the Wallowa band and the four other nontreaty bands had to leave their homes and move onto the reservation within thirty days.

> We were raising horses and cattle—fast race horses and many cattle. We had fine lodges, good clothes, plenty to eat, enough of everything. We were living well. Then General Howard and Agent Monteith came to bother us.
>
> I had seen twenty-one snows when they came. They told us we had to give up our homes and move to another part of the reservation. That we had to give up our part of the reservation to the white people. Told us we must move in with the Nez Perces turned Christians.... All of same tribe, but it would be hard to live together. Our religions different, it would be hard. To leave our homes would be hard. It was these Christian Nez Perces who made with the Government a thief treaty [of 1863]. Sold to the Government all this land. Sold what did not belong to them. We got nothing for our country. None of our chiefs signed that land-stealing treaty. None was at that lie-talk council. Only Christian Indians and Government men.—Yellow Wolf[2]

Chronology of Events

c. 1786	Tuekakas, also known as Chief Old Joseph, is born.
1805	Lewis and Clark arrive in Nez Perce country. They leave their horses in the care of the Nez Perce and are given canoes and directions for traveling down to the Pacific.
1834	Benjamin Bonneville and his fur traders struggle through Hells Canyon in December and are befriended by Nez Perce. They meet Looking Glass Sr.
1836	Henry and Eliza Spalding establish a Presbyterian mission at Lapwai, Idaho.

3

1838	Tuekakas camps near Lapwai, converts to Christianity, and is given the name Joseph.
1840	Chief Old Joseph's infant son, the future Chief Joseph, is baptized as Ephraim.
1853	Washington Territory is established, dividing the Nez Perce homeland into two parts.
1855	Isaac I. Stevens, governor of Washington Territory, negotiates a treaty with the Nez Perce reserving 7,000,000 acres of Idaho, Washington, and Oregon.
1859	Congress ratifies the treaty of 1855.
1860	Gold is discovered on Nez Perce land.
1863	Chief Lawyer signs the Treaty of 1863, shrinking the Nez Perce Reservation to 700,000 acres.
1871	Chief Old Joseph dies.
	The first settlers arrive in the Wallowa Valley.
1873	President Grant signs an executive order granting half the Wallowa Valley to the Nez Perce.
1875	President Grant rescinds his 1873 executive order.
1876	Wilhautyah is killed in the Wallowa. His murderers, McNall and Findley, are acquitted.
November	A five-man commission meets with Joseph, but the two sides fail to reach a settlement. The commission's report recommends that the nontreaty Nez Perce be moved onto the reservation.
1877	
3–15 May	At a council between the nontreaty Nez Perce and General Howard at Lapwai, Howard gives the ultimatum that the nontreaty Nez Perce must move onto the reservation in thirty days. Joseph, White Bird, Husishusis Kute, and Looking Glass pick out their allotments on the reservation.
31 May	The Wallowa band crosses the Snake River at Dug Bar.

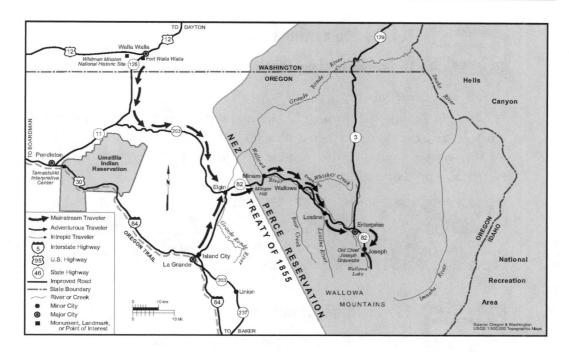

Getting to the Beginning of the Nez Perce Trail

Bounded to the east by Hells Canyon and to the south by the Wallowa Mountains, there are only a few ways to get to the beginning of the Nez Perce (Nee-Me-Poo) National Historic Trail at Wallowa Lake in Oregon: from LaGrande, Oregon, to the west, from Walla Walla, Washington, to the northwest, from Clarkston, Washington, to the north or from the southeast along the Imnaha River.

Since this guide exits the Wallowa country by going north to Clarkston, entry into the Wallowa country will be from LaGrande or Walla Walla.[3]

Travel Plan

La Grande, Oregon, or Walla Walla, Washington, to Wallowa Lake

Mainstream Traveler	Adventurous Traveler	Intrepid Traveler
La Grande to Elgin *or* Walla Walla to Elgin	follow Mainstream	follow Mainstream
Elgin to Wallowa Lake State Park	follow Mainstream	follow Mainstream

5

For the Mainstream Traveler
La Grande to Elgin, Oregon
Oregon Trail

The Oregon Trail passed through La Grande, at the edge of Nez Perce country. The Nez Perce capitalized on these pioneers by trading some of their fine horses for the worn-out cows of the west-bound settlers. Within a decade the Nez Perce had a herd of hundreds of cattle.

> In La Grande, turn east on Oregon route 82. From the junction of Interstate 84 and Oregon 82 (exit 261), it is 19 miles to Elgin.
> Continue with the Mainstream Traveler in Elgin.

For the Mainstream Traveler
Walla Walla, Washington, to Elgin, Oregon
Walla Walla

In the early 1850s, surveying crews were at work in the West searching for the best route for an east-west railroad. Isaac I. Stevens, governor of Washington Territory, directed the survey for a feasible route through the Northwest. Although North-South politics in Washington, D.C., meant that a northern railroad route would not be approved, the needs of the future were becoming clear. To promote the area and pave the way for settlement, Indian title to the land would have to be extinguished. In 1855, Governor Stevens began making treaties in the Puget Sound area. By May he had worked his way east; the Nez Perce took their turn at negotiating with this dynamic young man.

Twenty-five hundred Nez Perce, Yakama, Cayuse, Umatillas, Wallawallas, and Spokans gathered at old Fort Walla Walla in Washington Territory (near present-day Wallula, twenty-nine miles west of Walla Walla). Governor Stevens' plan was simple: put the Nez Perce, Cayuse, Wallawallas, Umatillas, and Spokans together on one reservation and put the rest of the Columbia River tribes, including the Yakamas, together on another. The Americans native to this land were not pleased with the idea of being grouped together with their neighbors on a small plot of ground.

Considering Stevens' scheme, the Nez Perce actually fared rather well in the council of 1855; they ceded very little of the land they considered theirs. This fact was one of the enticements that led all the Nez Perce chieftains to sign a

From 1853 to 1857, Isaac I. Stevens was governor of Washington Territory, territorial Superintendent of Indian Affairs, and director of the northern Pacific Railroad Survey group. (Photo courtesy of the Library of Congress.)

treaty reserving seven million acres to their people. The area included a sliver of southeastern Washington, the Wallowa country of north-eastern Oregon, and a chunk of central Idaho from the Palouse River to south of the Salmon River.

One provision of the treaty stated that the agreement would not take effect until Congress had ratified the treaty and the Nez Perce had received the promised payments. In fact, the Treaty of 1855 was not ratified by Congress until four years later, and the first payments to the Nez Perce did not arrive until November 1862. But twelve days after the Nez Perce had signed the treaty, a notice was carried in the Oregon newspapers declaring "the country…is open to settlement…. This notice is published for the benefit of the public." Legal or not, Nez Perce land was now considered open.

West of Walla Walla, at mile marker 330 on US 12, turn south to the Whitman Mission National Historic Site.

Whitman Mission

In 1831 a group of three Nez Perce and one Salish journeyed east to St. Louis, where they met with Captain William Clark, whose memory was revered among the Nez Perce. No one in St. Louis spoke Nez Perce, and it was widely assumed that these four warriors were seeking "The Book of Heaven." The circuitous and eventual result of their visit was that missionaries were sent to the Nez Perce and to their neighbors, the Cayuse. In 1836, Henry and Eliza Spalding built their mission at Lapwai, Idaho, while Marcus and Narcissa Whitman settled near Walla Walla.

Converting the nomadic, stock-raising Nez Perce to a settled, agricultural, monogamous, Christian, English-speaking life was not an easy task. Spalding and Whitman both became frustrated; they competed with the Catholics for Indian souls; they felt isolated; and the relationship between them was backbiting and ill-tempered. In order to prevent the missions from being closed, Whitman traveled east in 1842 to speak with the Mission Board of the Presbyterian Church. When he returned in 1843, he came with a wagon train of a thousand emigrants following the Oregon Trail.

The response to the missionaries was mixed. The religious Nez Perce had been curious about the religion of the white man. Assuming that religion was the source of the white men's power, they at first welcomed Spalding. But as the years went on, the cultural change demanded by the church was too great. On the other hand, it was obvious that the Nez Perce could not compete with the power of the Americans. The missionaries' relationships to the Cayuse and Nez Perce deteriorated. Several times Whitman and Spalding were ordered to leave Cayuse and Nez Perce land. Still they remained.

The river of settlers flowing past the Whitman mission and through their homeland worried the Cayuse. When an epidemic of measles swept through the tribe in 1847, the frustration and anger of the distressed Cayuse erupted. Whitman's skills as a doctor had no curative effect on measles. The Cayuse response was the same as toward a shaman whose powers have gotten beyond his control—Whitman was murdered. The Nez Perce held Henry and Eliza Spalding as hostages against a potential invasion by American soldiers. They were ransomed a month later and taken to safety in the Willamette Valley of Oregon. The Spaldings' mission to the Nez Perce had ended.

8

By watching their friends and relatives, the Cayuse, the Nez Perce learned many valuable lessons. An army of citizen volunteers seeking retribution invaded the Cayuse, Palouse, and Nez Perce countries. All attempts at peace failed because the commanders of the volunteers were bent on fighting Indians

Stevens, standing in the center wearing light-colored trousers, speaks to the assembled Nez Perce, Cayuse, Wallawalla, Umatilla, Palouse, and Yakama. (Photo courtesy of Washington State Historical Society.)

and refused to talk peace. Initially the Americans skirmished indecisively with Cayuse and Palouse a few times. But after a while they were unsuccessful at locating the Cayuse, who had escaped to the mountains. The Superintendent of Indian Affairs confiscated Cayuse land, which was then distributed to the volunteers. Two-and-a-half years later, five Cayuse leaders, not the murderers, sought to end their exile and harassment by having a council with the settlers near Walla Walla. The five were arrested, tried for the murder of the Whitmans, and hanged.

Although their own showdown with Americans did not come until thirty years later, the Nez Perce did not forget how white people punished their enemies.

Returning to US 12, continue east to between mile markers 331 and 332. Following the signs for Fort Walla Walla, turn south on Wallula Avenue for 2.6 miles. At Rose Street, turn south for one block, then west on Myra for 0.8 mile. Turn in to Fort Walla Walla and bear left (clockwise) for 0.1 mile to a parking lot near the cemetery.

Fort Walla Walla Cemetery

As you walk into the cemetery, head to the tall obelisk, which commemorates the military dead from the White Bird battle. The two squat granite cubes list the dead soldiers from White Bird on June 17, 1877, and from Cottonwood on July 3, 1877.

> Leaving Fort Walla Walla, continue south on Myra for 0.3 mile to Washington highway 125. In 3.4 miles its name changes to Oregon 11. In 11.8 miles turn east on Oregon 204 to Elgin. (A side trip may be taken by continuing on Oregon 11 for 20 miles to Tamastslikt Interpretive Center on the Umatilla Reservation. Follow the signs.) Bypassing Weston, proceed 42 miles to Elgin.
>
> Join the Mainstream Traveler in Elgin.

For the Mainstream Traveler
Elgin to Wallowa Lake State Park, Oregon

> East of Elgin 8.5 miles, as the road rises to the altitude of pine trees, you come to the summit of Minam Hill between mile markers 28 and 29.

Minam Hill

This small rise in the landscape appears indistinguishable from the neighboring hills. But to the Nez Perce, the summit of Minam Hill marked the border between nations. The Treaty of 1855 defined the western-most edge of Nez Perce land as running north-south along this hill, which forms the divide between the Grande Ronde and Wallowa river drainages.

> *In order to have all people understand how much land we owned, my father planted poles around it and said:*
>
> *Inside is the home of my people—the white man may take the land outside. Inside this boundary all our people were born. It circles around the graves of our fathers, and we will never give up these graves to any man.*
> —Chief Joseph

The boundary referred to by Chief Joseph consisted of about seven posts located on the hill somewhere south of where Oregon 82 crosses Minam Hill today. Poles set in stone cairns marked the western edge of Nez Perce land, because Chief Old Joseph realized that settlers would enter his country from this direction.

> *We were troubled greatly by white men crowding over the line. Some of these were good men, and we lived on peaceful terms with them, but they were not all good.*—Chief Joseph

As you crest Minam Hill today, you enter the land that was originally the Nez Perce Nation.

> Continue traveling east on Oregon 82 for 16.5 miles on Oregon 82. Just as the highway crosses the river, Bear Creek flows into the Wallowa River, on the south side of the bridge.

Confluence of Bear Creek and Wallowa River

The excellent hay country of the Wallowa supported the Nez Perce herd of thousands of horses. Worn-out cattle, initially acquired from Oregon Trail pioneers in the 1840s, became the parent stock of a herd that prospered and multiplied into the hundreds. In Indian terms, wealth was measured by stock, and the Nez Perce were considered to be a rich people. Selling horses and cows to pioneers newly arrived in Oregon netted the Nez Perce a good supply of gold dust and greenbacks. The Nez Perce were well-to-do by any measure.

A dry season hit the Grande Ronde valley (La Grande area) in 1870 and 1871. When farmers ran out of hay for their stock, they naturally headed for the plentiful hay in the Wallowa. Once they arrived in this beautiful valley, they found other reasons to stay.

> *They were all so pleased with the country that they located claims on upper Prairie Creek. At that time it was a custom, and was usually all that was necessary to hold a claim, to lay a foundation of four logs and post a notice in the center describing the boundaries of your claim. It was respected by newcomers.*
>
> *The men located their claims one day and the next day began their work, some cutting logs, some hauling, and other laying the foundation. While thus in action a band of Indians called on them and informed them that the land belonged to the Indians and they must stop work and leave. The*

11

choppers saw the Indians and that there was a powwow and came to join the crowd. Then Indians then went to where they were chopping, got their axes, brought them out, gave them to the men and invited them to leave and do it quick as they could.... All praised the wonderful country and vowed to try again.—James W. McAllister (settler)

Settlers felt that they could make the land productive. After all, the Indians weren't using the land—they were just letting it go to waste, and they didn't even live there for eight months of the year. Tensions ran highest during the summer when the Joseph band came to their summer camp near the town of Wallowa. Their herd of thousands of "cayuse" horses roamed the valley, trampling grain fields and interbreeding with the "American" stock.

To smooth ensuing friction, the first council between the settlers and the Wallowa band was held in 1872 near where Bear Creek joins the Wallowa River.

On the 14th [of August] a council was held between the whites, numbering about forty, and the Nez Perce Indians to the number of forty or fifty, being those who are dissatisfied with the settlement of that section.... The whites were requested to leave the valley and take their hay with them.... The settlers did not understand that the valley belonged to the Indians and that they [the settlers] had permission to settle upon the lands, and also asked if the Indians intended to drive the settlers from the valley. The Indians stated that they had no such hostile intentions, but were friends of the white men, and wished to remain so, but insisted they should leave the valley.—Grande Ronde Mountain Sentinel, *August 24, 1872*

The crux of the issue was clear: both sides believed the land was theirs. And each side wanted the other side to leave.

You say your people are too well settled to be disturbed, and I say the Indians are too well settled to be disturbed. So it is better to leave the Indians alone.—Chief Joseph

The settlers believed the territorial imperative was theirs. After all, the government had bought the land from the Nez Perce by the Treaty of 1863, and the land had been surveyed in the late 1860s. The fact that the Wallowa band had not signed the treaty was a legal detail unknown to the settlers. It was a legal detail ignored by elected officials and military men.

The Wallowa band of Nez Perce lived well on their land. They were self-supporting and peaceful. But their land had been sold out from under them by what some might call a jury-rigged treaty council. Without the land, their horses and their cows would have no place to graze. Without their herds, the Nez Perce would be impoverished. Their land—which was their wealth as well as their heritage—had been legally conveyed to the United States government and thence to the new settlers. Although the Wallowa band had never agreed to the sale and was never paid for its land, the people had no recourse.

> Proceed southeast on Oregon 82 for 1.4 miles to Wallowa. In Wallowa, turn north on Storie Street for one block and then west on 2nd Street. The Wallowa Band Nez Perce Trail Interpretive Center, Inc. at 209 E. 2nd, is the interim location for this organization that seeks to restore a part of Nez Perce culture to Wallowa County. Their little museum has lots of information.
>
> Return to Main Street and proceed east on Oregon route 82 for one block. Bear east on Whiskey Creek Road for 0.3 mile. As soon as you cross the railroad tracks, turn north into the project site of the Nez Perce Wallowa Homeland Project, Nimipunim Wetes. The Tamkaliks Celebration is held here in mid-July.
>
> Returning to Whiskey Creek Road, continue east for 1.3 miles. Turn east on Evans Road. This paved road immediately crosses Whiskey Creek.

The Murder of Wilhautyah (Wind Blowing)

Farther up Whiskey Creek, two settlers murdered a Nez Perce man in 1876.

> *In April last there was some stray horses come into my neighborhood and three of them took up with my horses.... Two of them I took to be Indian horses & one to be a half breed, it having a white mans brand.... I feared they were stolen horses; I feared the Indians, when they removed them they would take mine with them which made me keep a vigilant watch for them.*
>
> *Some time in June I missed some of my horses, some of which had bee[n] raised on the range, one of which one had been ridden by my children to school on Monday.*
>
> *On Tuesday I went to look for my horses for my children to ride to school, but could not find those.... Afterwards on the same day I...found the ones they were used to riding.*
>
> *...I went farther and found an Indian camp; my suspicion that my horses were stolen were confirmed.*
>
> *I immediately returned to get assistance to search for my horses.... We, McNall and myself found an Indian casch.*

13

This casch found contained venison I told Mr. McNall we wold return home and get more help.... The next morning Mr. McNall and I returned to the casch, afer we had been there about an hour and a half I saw an Indian coming in from the woods.

...We then saddled our horses and went down to the casch, and spoke to the Indians. They asked to look at our guns.... They examined it very minutely before returning it.... One of them said his gun was broke and uncovered it to let us see....

....I then got off my horse and got hold of the gun leaning against the tree and told the Indians I believe they had stolen and we wanted them to go to the settlement until we had an understanding about the matter. They did not consent to go.... Then Mr. McNall brought a gun that was near him.... Then the Indian with whom I was talking to...arose and started toward McNall. The next thing I knew McNall called on me to shoot....

I then saw fire from his gun and heard the report; about the time of the report I cocked my gun and held it ready, waiting to see the result of the scuffle over the fun of McNall, resolved not to shoot until I saw our lives were in danger.

I noticed one hand of the Indians on the brich and the other on the barrel of McNalls gun, the muzel of the gun bearing on me, and I thought he would use McNalls gun to kill us.

I had decided not to shoot when I heart the report of my gun; I was not conscious of pulling the trigger.—A. B. Findley, September 21, 1876[4]

Three Indians started out to the mountains in search of game. After arriving where game was plentiful, they had little or no difficulty in procuring a reasonable supply, and, after caching it, returned to their homes, making an agreement before starting to return at a certain time and take it home. This being agreed upon, the three separated, and upon their return, two met at the cache about the same time. Feeling somewhat fatigued, by their trip, they dismounted to take a short rest, when two white men approached them in a rude manner, disarmed them, and asked one of the Indians whether or not he was the man that interpreted for Chief Joseph. The man answered him to the contrary.... The white man called him a liar, at the same time knocking the Indian down and abusing him in a brutal manner. The Indian's companion made no resistance or attempt to save him, but the third one of the party referred to, named Willatiah [Wind Blowing], arrived while the scuffle was going on, and made inquiries as to the cause of it.... Willatiah at once interfered in hopes to stop the white man from offering any further abuse, when suddenly the white man sprang on him. But Willatiah being a man of considerable nerve and strength, soon had the white man upon the ground, when the latter called to his companion to shoot the ————. The companion obeyed the command— Willatiah fell a corpse.—Duncan McDonald (Nez Perce reporter)

Findley's missing horses were found five days later, grazing at his home.

When I learned that they had killed one of my people I was heart-sick. When I saw all the settlers take the murderer's part, though they spoke of bringing him to trial, I told them that the law did not favor murder. I could see they were all in favor of the murderer, so I told them to leave the country.—Chief Joseph

Early in September, 1876...I received information that Joseph with his band of Nez Perces had appeared in the Wallowa valley and demanded the surrender of the two men McNall and Finley, accused of killing one of his Indians, and threatened, in case this demand was not complied with, to destroy the farms of the settlers therein, giving them a week's time to decide.... I at once directed...one company of cavalry to the scene of the difficulty, and...Lieut. A.G. Forse, commanding, was at once dispatched. He had an interview with Joseph, which resulted in his withdrawing his demand and threats, and a promise on the part of the military authorities that they would use their endeavors to bring the accused men before the civil authorities for trial.—Gen. Oliver Otis Howard

A. B. Findley and Wells McNall were tried at Union, near La Grande, and acquitted.

Although this murder was a unique occurrence in the Wallowa, it was not an isolated incident. According to Nez Perce reckoning, white people killed twenty-eight Nez Perce prior to 1877. Of the few whites brought to trial for murdering Indians, all were, like McNall and Findley, acquitted. Such injustice was hard to bear.

It seemed to me that some of the white men in Wallowa were doing these things on purpose to get up a war.—Chief Joseph

15

From the bridge over Whiskey Creek, proceed southeast on Evans Road for 0.9 mile. Then turn south on Baker Road. In 0.2 mile, after crossing the railroad, you will cross the bridge over the Wallowa. Somewhere along this next 1.2 miles, before crossing the Lostine River, is the area of Joseph's summer camp.

Forks of Wallowa and Lostine Rivers

Looking west from Baker Road, you can see the area between the junction of the Lostine and Wallowa rivers where the Wallowa band made their summer camp. The band circled their land throughout the course of a year. After wintering in the warmer canyons of the Grande Ronde or the Imnaha, they returned to summer camp here. In August and September they were at Wallowa Lake catching salmon. Then they moved up to fall hunting camps along Chesnimnus Creek before returning to winter camp. Of course, they might at any time go to visit friends and relatives among the Umatillas, the Cayuse, the Palouse, or other Nez Perce bands in Idaho. On occasion they may even have gone to the buffalo country of Montana and Wyoming to spend a season or a year there hunting buffalo and visiting their friends, the Crows and the Salsh. But the underlying pattern was a cycle of visiting different parts of their land in harmony with the cycle of the seasons.

During this circle of the seasons, within the circle of the land, in the circle of the village, within the circle of a tepee, Chief Old Joseph completed part of the circle of his life.

Soon after this my father sent for me. I saw he was dying. I took his hand in mine. He said, "My son, my body is returning to my mother earth, and my spirit is going very soon to see the Great Spirit Chief. When I am gone, think of your country. You are the chief of these people. They look to you to guide them. Always remember that your father never sold his country. You must stop your ears whenever you are asked to sign a treaty selling your home. A few years more, and white men will be all around you. They have their eyes on this land. My son, never forget my dying words. This country holds your father's body. Never sell the bones of your father and your mother." I pressed my father's hand, and told him I would protect his grave with my life. My father smiled and passed away to the spirit land. I buried him in that beautiful valley of Winding Waters. I love that land more than all the rest of the world. A man who would not love his father's grave is worse than a wild animal.—Chief Joseph

Old Chief Joseph was originally buried here between the forks of the rivers in 1871. After the Nez Perce left the Wallowa, his grave was twice robbed. His skull was stolen by a dentist in the first robbery and displayed in his office in Baker, Oregon. In 1926 Old Joseph's remains were moved and reburied at Wallowa Lake.

Continue south from the bridge over the Lostine River for another 0.5 mile to the junction with Oregon 82. Turn southeast onto the highway for 3.8 miles to Lostine.

From Lostine proceed south on Oregon 82 for 9.0 miles to the Visitor Center of the Wallowa-Whitman National Forest, which has maps and books as well as a few displays.

Another 0.1 mile will bring you to a historical marker overlooking the Wallowa Valley and Wallowa Mountains. Continue for 1 mile into Enterprise and another 6.3 miles into Joseph. South of Joseph 1.4 miles is the Old Chief Joseph Gravesite and Cemetery, where the Nez Perce (Nee-Me-Poo) National Historic Trail officially begins. However, before starting the Trail, you will probably want to continue driving around Wallowa Lake for 4.5 miles to Wallowa Lake State Park.

A wallowa is the tripod that holds one end of a fishtrap used to catch salmon. (Photo courtesy of Idaho State Historical Society.)

Wallowa Lake State Park

Nestled at the foot of the alpine Wallowa Mountains, Wallowa Lake State Park is a modern version of what has happened here for centuries. Camping, fishing, swimming, horseback riding, hiking, boating—these contemporary recreational activities were part of Nez Perce daily life.

Joseph's band of Nez Perce camped here at the south end of the lake in August and September to catch and dry salmon for their winter food supply. Wawamaikhal is the Nez Perce word for the month of August and translates as the time of salmon migrating to river headwaters to spawn.

The plentitude of salmon in those days is now beyond imagination. Stories abound from the pioneer era about walking across the river on the backs of fish, using a pitchfork to spear several salmon at a time, and one family pulling out enough fish in one net for their winter's supply of food. With the final damming of the lake in 1916, the fish were landlocked. The redfish, or "yanks," that live in Wallowa Lake today are descendants of those earlier sockeye salmon.

While some people believe the word *wallowa* means winding waters, it actually refers to the tripods that held the fishtraps stretched across the river.

After you have enjoyed the Wallowa Mountains and Wallowa Lake, return to the Old Chief Joseph Gravesite and Cemetery at the north end of the lake to begin the Trail.

The Nez Perce (Nee-Me-Poo) Trail

To follow this first chapter of the Nez Perce Trail in exact order would involve many miles of backtracking. For the convenience of today's traveler, the recommended routes in this chapter do not follow the chronological order of the official Trail. Rather, routes are suggested in an order that will minimize miles and backtracking.

When the Joseph band left its home, the people and stock crossed the Snake River at Dug Bar. Since vehicles are limited to crossing the Snake River at the bridge between Lewiston, Idaho, and Clarkston, Washington, this guide detours several miles off the actual route in order to cross the river. This detour gives the traveler an opportunity to see the country the Nez Perce claimed as theirs, the country they were forced to give up based on the "thief treaty" of 1863.

Chief Old Joseph was reburied at the foot of Wallowa Lake in 1926 after his grave at the fork of the Wallowa and Lostine rivers had been desecrated twice. (Photo courtesy of National Park Service, Nez Perce National Historical Park, Stephen D. Shawley Collection.)

Travel Plan

Wallowa Lake, Oregon, to Lewiston, Idaho

Mainstream Traveler	Adventurous Traveler	Intrepid Traveler
Wallowa Lake to Joseph	follow Mainstream	follow Mainstream
		Sidetrip Joseph to Dug Bar and return to Joseph
Joseph to Joseph Canyon Viewpoint	Joseph to Buckhorn Lookout	follow Adventurous
	Buckhorn Lookout to Joseph Canyon Viewpoint	Buckhorn Lookout to Joseph cave
Joseph Canyon Viewpoint to Fields Spring State Park	follow Mainstream	
Fields Spring State Park to Asotin	Fields Spring State Park to Joseph cave	
	Joseph cave to Asotin	follow Adventurous
Asotin to Lewiston	follow Mainstream	follow Mainstream

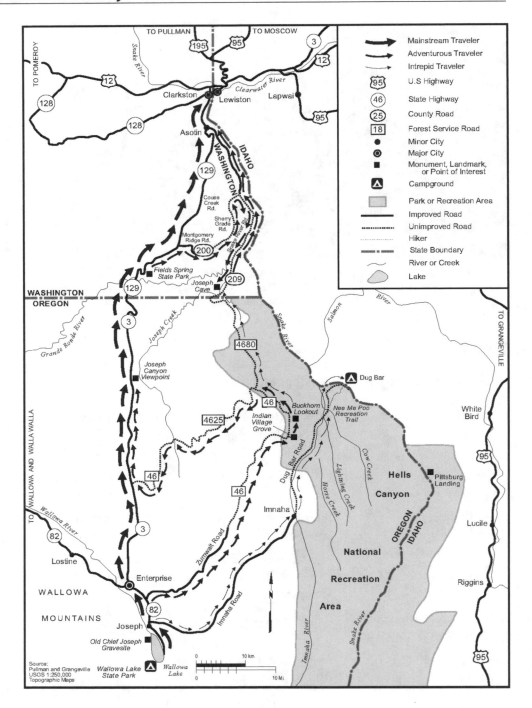

Source:
Pullman and Grangeville
USGS 1:250,000
Topographic Maps

For the Mainstream Traveler

Wallowa Lake to Joseph

Old Chief Joseph Gravesite

The Nez Perce (Nee-Me-Poo) National Historic Trail formally begins at the Old Chief Joseph Gravesite and Cemetery at the foot or north end of serene Wallowa Lake. The Joseph band of Nez Perce did not literally start their journey from this point. Rather, Old Chief Joseph's grave marks the symbolic beginning of the Trail.

Tuekakas was a young man when Lewis and Clark traveled through Nez Perce country. In middle age, he converted to Christianity and was baptized as Joseph. He is called Old Joseph to distinguish him from his famous son, Chief Joseph.

Old Joseph signed the Treaty of 1855, which set aside seven million acres for the Nez Perce Reservation. Eight years later, only a few headmen signed the Treaty of 1863, which relinquished more than six million acres, including the Wallowa. Old Chief Joseph did not agree with the Treaty and did not sign.

Old Chief Joseph's life spanned the era when the Nez Perce believed they and the United States co-existed as two independent sovereign nations. Chief Old Joseph's death presaged the realization that a foreign country—the United States of America—claimed dominion over the Nez Perce people and their land.

> *I learned then that we were but few, while the white men were many, and that we could not hold our own with them. We were like deer. They were like grizzly bears. We had a small country. Their country was large. We were contented to let things remain as the Great Spirit Chief made them. They were not; and would change the rivers and mountains if they did not suit them.*—Chief Joseph

Fittingly, the trail of the Nez Perce quest for freedom begins here at the grave of Old Joseph, a chief who retained his people's sovereignty as long as he could.

Follow Oregon 82 for 1.4 miles north into Joseph.

Joseph

The Wallowa County Museum on Main Street has a Nez Perce room with a synopsis of the flight, several photos, and many artifacts. The museum is open from the last weekend of May through the third weekend of September and is a good place to buy the local history books recommended at the end of this chapter.

The Nez Perce name for the area around Joseph was *hah-um-sah-pah*, which means "big rocks lying scattered around." Those big rocks that are strewn around here are part of a terminal moraine of an ancient glacier. When the glacier receded, it left behind the load of rocks it had bulldozed this far south.

Join the Mainstream, the Adventurous, or the Intrepid Traveler at Joseph.

 For the Intrepid Traveler

Sidetrip
Joseph to Imnaha to Nee-Me-Poo National Recreation trailhead

Miles: 52.0, one-way
Map: Wallowa-Whitman National Forest, north half
Special considerations: The Dug Bar campground has no water.

While the Joseph to Imnaha road is paved, the road beyond Imnaha is not. Inquire locally about road conditions on the Dug Bar Road before proceeding. The Imnaha to Dug Bar portion of the road is white-knuckle-producing enough in good weather; a driver will not want to contend with rain or mud or any other adverse conditions. A trip to Dug Bar will consume most of one day.

The Dug Bar road is not recommended for passengers with a fear of heights. Stories are told of drivers who have "frozen" on the road—not from cold, but from fear—and have had to be driven out by someone else.

On the positive side, this road provides a trip through spectacular country. Since Nez Perce bands wintered in Hells Canyon, the Grande Ronde Canyon, the Imnaha River Canyon, and the Salmon River Canyon, this trip will immeasurably expand the traveler's feeling for the homeland of the Nez Perce. The canyon terrain contrasts sharply to the rolling loveliness of the Wallowa valley. Much of this canyon country is still wild.

> In Joseph, turn east on the Imnaha Road. The paved road takes 29.2 miles to get to the town of Imnaha.

Imnaha

The historical sign here tells about the Wallowa band leaving from the Imnaha canyon. The fighting and the flight did not actually begin until a couple of weeks later, when the five bands of nontreaty Nez Perce were camped on Camas Prairie in Idaho in mid-June of 1877.

Two of the four roads leading out of Imnaha go to Hells Canyon. Both roads are about twenty-five miles long and both require at least four hours to make a leisurely round trip from Imnaha. The Dug Bar Road is the only road on the Oregon side that leads onto the floor of the canyon. The road to Hat Point leads to the canyon rim. It's a 5,706 foot drop from Hat Point to the canyon floor—a distance greater than the depth of the Grand Canyon.

> Turn north in Imnaha on the Lower Imnaha Road, which remains paved for the next 6 miles. It then becomes a one-lane dirt road with turnouts and is not appropriate for RVs or trailers. Plan to drive the remaining 19 miles in first or second gear, at a top speed of 20 mph. This narrow road has steep dropoffs to the side and no guard rails.
>
> 7.8 miles after the end of the pavement, the road levels out alongside the Imnaha River. Look back to the southeast to see Horse Creek Canyon.

Horse Creek Canyon

Horse Creek derived its name from the fact that several horses were found here after the Joseph band left in 1877. The horses were overlooked when the Nez Perce gathered up their stock prior to crossing the Snake River.

Imnaha Valley

During the winter, the larger Wallowa band broke into several small groups that wintered somewhere along the Grande Ronde or Imnaha canyons. The Nez Perce wintered in canyons such as this because they were relatively warm and free from heavy snow.

Prolonged camping in one spot scared away all the game, thus as spring came on, hunters went higher up in search of more meat. This cycle—of wintering on the floor of the canyon and following the snowline up the mountains in the spring—is the same one followed by the cattle in the Imnaha Canyon today, grazing during the summer on the plateau above the canyon.

23

> It is 6.4 miles to Cow Creek Bridge over the Imnaha River and another 0.4 mile to Cow Creek itself.

Cow Creek

The natural corral formed by Cow Creek Canyon is probably where the Nez Perce held their horses and cattle prior to crossing the Snake River. Perhaps the women tended the stock while the men and boys were out in the hills rounding them up and herding them here to Cow Creek.

> After the bridge over Cow Creek proper, the road becomes even narrower and rockier with grass growing in the middle. Beginning 0.8 mile past the little bridge, you can see Lone Pine Saddle in front of you. The Nee-Me-Poo National Recreation Trail, which is reached in another 1.8 miles, goes over Lone Pine Saddle to Dug Bar.
>
> Join the Hiker for the Nee-Me-Poo Recreation Trail or continue with the Intrepid Traveler on the road to Dug Bar.

For Hikers

Nee-Me-Poo National Recreation Trail

> **Miles:** 3.7, one way
> **Maps:** The Nee-Me-Poo National Recreation Trail brochure is more informative in its narration than in its map. The USGS quad, Cactus Mountain, does not show the trail, but it does provide the necessary topographical detail for the hike.
> **Special considerations:** The trail is not well marked.
>
> The trailhead is 2.6 miles past the Cow Creek bridge. Keep your eyes peeled for a post anchored in a pile of rocks. The trail terminus is about 0.2 mile from the Dug Bar campground. The road between these two points is twice as long as the 3.7-mile hiking trail. The most efficient course of action is to drop the hikers off at the trailhead while the driver continues along the road. It will take the driver about half an hour to reach the terminus of the trail, while it will take the hikers about two and half hours to get there. Because of the extreme heat in July and August, hiking is not generally recommended. Even June can be too hot for hiking.

While the trail is only moderately strenuous, a hiker should be confident of his or her direction-finding abilities, as the trail is marked by just a few signs.

Starting at the trailhead, N45° 47.458', W116° 44.181', the trail quickly begins to look the same as stock trails that parallel and weave in and out of the hiking trail. In fact, you are more likely to see hoof prints than boot prints on this trail. If you become confused, head for Lone Pine Saddle, marked by a lone pine, which can be seen from the road. After an elevation gain of 650 feet in 1.1 miles, the rest of the path is mostly downhill.

Begin by walking into the draw. At 0.4 mile you will walk by a survey corner marker. 0.15 mile farther on, cross a draw and then in 0.14 mile a barbed wire gate. Squeeze through another barbed wire gate in 0.33 mile.

At the top of Lone Pine Saddle, N45° 48.266', W116° 43.934', stands a post marking the National Recreation Trail. From here the trail parallels the road as it skirts ridges for the next mile or so. Then the trail heads toward another single pine as it begins to parallel a fence and climbs gently uphill to another saddle. At the top of this nameless saddle, the hiker has the first view of Dug Bar, a bench of flat land beside the Snake River.

From the gate at the top of the saddle, the trail becomes even more indefinite. Gravel acts like ball-bearings underfoot and keeps you sliding downhill. The trail terminus, N45° 48.657', W 116° 41.691', is on the northwest side of Dug Bar. Choose the path that will take you in that general direction.

The experience of hiking this trail will confirm to you why the Nez Perce did not generally use travois as did the Plains Indians. Instead, women used pack horses to carry household goods and food stores.

For the Intrepid Traveler

Nee-Me-Poo Trailhead to Dug Bar

Miles: 8.1, one-way
Map: Wallowa-Whitman National Forest, north half

The Dug Bar campground, with two or three primitive campsites, is 7.5 miles past the Nee-Me-Poo trailhead. If you are planning to camp, bring your own water as there is no potable water here. The campground lies at the lower end of Dug Bar.

The sign commemorating the Nez Perce Crossing stands at the upper end of Dug Bar. To get to the sign, drive through the gate and observe the courtesy of leaving the gate as you found it (open or closed). Continue 0.6 mile to the boat ramp.

From the Y by the outhouse, bear south (upriver) for 0.14 miles. Find the path that stays above the boulders to N45° 48.137', W116° 41.192'.

Nez Perce Crossing

The Joseph band crossed the Snake River here at the end of May. Today there are dams to control the spring flooding caused by rains and snow melt. In 1877, the river would have been running high at the end of May.

> *We gathered all the stock we could find, and made an attempt to move. We left many of our horses and cattle in Wallowa, and we lost several hundred in crossing the river. All my people succeeded in getting across in safety.*
> —Chief Joseph

Due to the raging spring runoff, people and horses landed perhaps half a mile or more downstream from their starting point. As you look across to the other side, it's pretty difficult to imagine just where the Nez Perce might have ascended a ridge to continue their journey east.

The Joseph band did not know they were actually leaving their homeland forever. They imagined they would be coming back to dig roots, hunt game, and care for the graves of their ancestors. Some stock was left behind unintentionally because all their thousands of horses and cattle could not be rounded up in just a couple of weeks. Settlers and rustlers appropriated the homeless stock, which the Nez Perce never saw again.

Return to Joseph and join either the Adventurous Traveler or the Mainstream Traveler there.

For the Adventurous Traveler

Joseph to Buckhorn Lookout

Miles: 45.1

Map: Wallowa-Whitman National Forest, north half

North of Joseph 2.9 miles on Oregon 82, a sign points east to Buckhorn Springs. When Oregon 82 bends west, turn east on Crow Creek Road for 5.1 miles. At the Y, turn east onto the Zumwalt Road. As you leave the hill country behind and enter the Wallowa-Whitman National Forest 23.9 miles later, this road becomes NF 46, Wellamotkin Drive. Wellamotkin was one of Old Chief Joseph's names and means "hair tied back in a sort of bun or knot at the top of the head."

Chesnimnus Ridge

The headwaters of Chesnimnus Creek and a few of its many tributaries are on the ridge just west of NF 46. The area along the Chesnimnus, a major drainage, was the site of the fall hunting camps of the Joseph band.

5.5 miles after entering the National Forest, turn east on NF 880 for 1.9 miles.

Indian Village Grove

A half-mile trail leads through a grove of ponderosa pines. This area was a spring camp, as attested by the scars on the trees. When winter food supplies ran out in March, before spring greens and berries ripened, the bark of pine trees could be peeled and the inner cambium layer eaten to fend off starvation.

Return to NF 46, and turn north for 2.8 miles. Turn northeast on NF 780 and pass by Buckhorn Campground. Then in 0.9 mile, turn southeast on NF 810 for 0.2 mile to Buckhorn Lookout.

Buckhorn Lookout

The magnificent view you see from Buckhorn Lookout is the parallel canyons of Horse Creek, Lightning Creek, and Cow Creek coming into the Imnaha Canyon. Off in the far distance is Hells Canyon. Intrepid Travelers who have

27

made the journey to Dug Bar may recognize this view, although they've seen it from a different angle on the Dug Bar Road.

The Nez Perce Trail travels from these heights down to the canyon floor. From Cow Creek, the northernmost canyon, the Trail goes up out of the Imnaha Canyon and crosses the divide leading over into Hells Canyon.

> Join the Adventurous or Intrepid Traveler at Buckhorn Lookout.

For the Intrepid Traveler
Buckhorn Lookout, Oregon, to Joseph Cave, Washington

Miles: 31.1
Map: Wallowa-Whitman National Forest, north half
Special considerations: Generally this route is closed by snow between November and May.

From Buckhorn Lookout, return to NF 46 and turn north for 7.3 miles. Then turn north on NF 4680, Cold Springs Road. This road leaves the Hells Canyon National Recreation Area in 12.5 miles and becomes a very narrow, rock-rough trail for the next 7.3 miles. But as soon as it crosses the Washington-Oregon border, it turns into a well-maintained gravel road called Asotin County Road 209. From the Washington border, proceed north for 4.0 miles to Joseph cave.
　Join the Adventurous Traveler at Joseph Cave.

For the Adventurous Traveler
Buckhorn Lookout to Joseph Canyon Viewpoint

Miles: 56.8
Map: Wallowa-Whitman National Forest, north half

From Buckhorn Lookout, return to NF 46, a well-maintained gravel road, and proceed northeast for 8.1 miles. At the junction with NF 4625, Chesnimnus Road, turn south. After 10.6 miles, dirt changes to one-lane pavement with turnouts for the next 9.6 miles.

Like a thread stringing the terrain together, Chesnimnus Creek, which began southeast of Buckhorn Springs, now runs alongside NF 4625. At the T where NF 4625 meets NF 46, Chesnimnus Creek meets Crow Creek to form Joseph Creek. Joseph Creek flows north from here and has cut the Joseph Canyon, which is the next sight to see. Turn south on NF 46, a dirt road, for 5.0 miles. It then becomes nice, two-lane pavement and, in 8.5 miles, junctions with Oregon route 3. Turn north on Oregon 3 for 15.0 miles to Joseph Canyon Viewpoint.

Join the Mainstream Traveler at Joseph Canyon Viewpoint.

For the Mainstream Traveler

Joseph to Joseph Canyon Viewpoint

From Joseph, continue north on Oregon 82 for 6.3 miles into the town of Enterprise.

Enterprise

The flat where Enterprise now stands was called *tom-mah-talk-ke-sin-mah*, which means white, fluffy, or alkali soil. Salt licks here attracted animals, and, in the spring, when food reserves were low, the animals attracted hunters. Then, small groups of Nez Perce families camped along Trout Creek. In addition to hunting, the families caught the spring run of salmon, building their fishtraps at the mouth of Trout Creek on the northeast side of town.

In Enterprise, turn north on Oregon route 3 for 29.6 miles to Joseph Canyon Viewpoint.

Continue with the Mainstream Traveler at Joseph Canyon Viewpoint.

For the Mainstream Traveler

Joseph Canyon Viewpoint, Oregon, to Fields Spring State Park, Washington

Joseph Canyon Viewpoint

The Nez Perce name for the Joseph Creek area was a*n-an-a-soc-um*, which means "long, rough canyon," an appropriate name for the two-thousand-foot-deep basalt canyon here.

A preview of coming attractions, this view of Joseph Canyon hints at the drama of the Grande Ronde Canyon, which it soon joins and which the highway will soon be descending. About fifteen miles farther down the creek, some families of the Wallowa band made their winter camp at the confluence of Joseph Creek and the Grande Ronde.

> Continue north on Oregon 3 for 13.2 miles. By the time the highway changes its number to Washington 129, you are winding down into a spectacular canyon in order to cross the Grande Ronde River. From the Washington border it is 13.5 miles to Fields Spring State Park.

Fields Spring State Park

Fields Spring State Park was a kouse gathering camp for Nez Perce. Kouse, of the Lomatium family, was an important staple in the Nez Perce diet. Kouse was the first root to be dug in the spring, and its parsnip-like taste of must have been a welcome relief from the dried roots, dried salmon, and dried and fresh meat of the winter menu. The tuberous roots were gathered during April and May. The common method of preparation involved drying the roots, then grinding them into a meal. Mixed with water, the meal was then formed into cakes and partly baked for storage. These cakes tasted like stale biscuits, giving the plant the name of biscuitroot.

> Continue with the Mainstream Traveler or join the Adventurous Traveler at Fields Spring State Park.

For the Adventurous Traveler

Fields Spring State Park to Joseph Cave

Miles: 37.1
Map: Asotin County

North of Fields Spring State Park 2.2 miles, turn east on the paved Montgomery Ridge Road, Asotin County Road 206. The pavement ends in 5.1 miles and the road becomes a wide, well-maintained gravel road for the next 6.4 miles. Follow the signs for Snake River and drive north on the Sherry Grade Road for 7.6 miles. As it descends into Montgomery Gulch by traversing the hillside, the Sherry Grade becomes narrower but remains relatively smooth, packed dirt. No guard rails stand between you and the kind of scenery usually reserved for Intrepid Travelers. After crossing a small bridge, this same road changes its name again to Couse Creek Road. At the T with Snake River Road, turn south. The road is paved for 3.3 miles, but then turns to gravel for the remaining 7.6 miles to the confluence of the Grande Ronde with the Snake. At the confluence, continue on the same road, which now turns west and parallels the Grande Ronde for 2.5 miles to a bridge. From the bridge over the Grande Ronde, drive south on Joseph Creek Road, Asotin County 209, for 2.2 miles to Joseph Cave. Just 0.2 mile farther on, is a wide spot in the road that can be used for a turnaround.

Return to Joseph Cave and continue with the Adventurous Traveler there.

For the Adventurous Traveler

Joseph Cave to Asotin

Miles: 27.6
Map: Asotin County

Joseph Cave

Approached from the south, a chimney-looking rock juts up on the west side of Joseph Creek, which flows alongside the road here. The entrance to a cave is screened by brush. Joseph Cave is supposedly the birthplace of Chief Joseph. It is on private land; request permission before you go exploring.

> Drive 0.9 mile north on Asotin County Road 209 to the confluence of Joseph Creek with the Grande Ronde.

Confluence of Joseph Creek and the Grande Ronde River

Joseph's band wintered at the confluence of Joseph Creek and the Grande Ronde. Here the low elevation plus the protection provided by canyon walls meant a warmer winter than in the high Wallowa Valley at the edge of the mountains.

> Continue north and east for 4.1 miles on to the Snake River Road to Heller Bar, one of the points of departure for jetboat trips going up the Snake River. From Heller Bar, proceed north on the Snake River Road for 22.4 miles, to the junction of Washington 129 in Asotin. Continue for 0.2 mile to Asotin Creek.
>
>   Join the Mainstream Traveler at Asotin.

For the Mainstream Traveler
Fields Spring State Park to Asotin

> From Fields Spring State Park, proceed north on Washington route 129 for 22.8 miles to the town of Asotin.
>
>   Continue with the Mainstream Traveler at Asotin.

For the Mainstream Traveler
Asotin to Clarkston, Washington

Asotin

On your way out of town, the road bridges Asotin Creek. Here, where the creek flows into the Snake River, eels abound. The Nez Perce called this area *hasotain*, meaning eel creek. The winter camp of the Looking Glass band, another nontreaty Nez Perce band, was located in this area.

The Asotin band of Nez Perce was visited by Lewis and Clark in 1805 and by Captain Bonneville in 1834. Both these accounts mention Apash Wyakaikt (Flint Necklace). His son, who was also named Apash Wyakaikt, was known to whites as Looking Glass, Sr. It is he who figured in the treaty councils of 1855

Looking Glass, Sr. (Apash Wyakaikt) wintered his band where the town of Asotin now stands. After his death in 1863, his son, Looking Glass (Allalimya Takanin), succeeded him in chieftainship of the band. (Photo courtesy of Washington State Historical Society.)

and 1863. Looking Glass, Jr. was designated as the leader of the nontreaty bands that fled Idaho in 1877.

Some jetboat tours leave from Asotin; others leave from Clarkston and Lewiston. If you would like the opportunity to see the **Nez Perce Crossing** and other interesting places along the river, Asotin is one place to find a ride upriver.

Continue north from Asotin along the Snake River on Washington 129 for 5.9 miles to downtown Clarkston and the junction with 12. Turn east on US 12, which crosses the Snake River in 0.2 mile and heads into Lewiston.

Join the Mainstream Traveler in Lewiston in the next chapter.

Snake River

From just west of Clarkston, down the Snake River to its junction with the Columbia lies the home territory of the Palouse Indians. Hahtalekin and Husishusis Kute (Bald Head) headed two small Palouse bands that went along on the flight with the Nez Perce. Hahtalekin's band lived at the junction of the Palouse and Snake rivers. The band of Husishusis Kute had their ancestral home at Wawawai, just west of Pullman.

These Palouse bands were closely related by marriage to the Looking Glass band. In fact, when General Howard ordered the nontreaty bands onto the reservation, Looking Glass insisted that the Palouse choose an area next to his on the reservation.

33

The Palouse and the Nez Perce were closely related tribes. They shared not only the same language family but also many customs. Lewis and Clark did not distinguish between them, as several other Euro-Americans also failed to do. The Palouse were therefore lumped in with the Nez Perce.[5]

A testament to the horsemanship of this tribe remains in our language today. "A Palouse" horse became the word *Appaloosa*.

For Further Reading

Grace Bartlett's *The Wallowa Country, 1867–1877* is an excellent book for the avid Nez Perce Trail buff. This book documents the era when both Nez Perce and whites claimed the land and lived here, relatively peacefully, together.

The booklet, "Wallowa: The Land of Winding Waters," also by Grace Bartlett, contains the origin of some Wallowa County place names and four articles about the Chiefs Joseph.

The booklet, "The Death of Wind Blowing: The Story of the 1876 Murder That Helped Trigger the Nez Perce War," by Mark Highberger, tells the story of Wilhautyah's murder on Whiskey Creek. Bear Creek Press has published several little booklets on Wallowa County history.

Into the Valley: A Homesteader's Memories of the 1870s, by James W. McAllister, gives a snapshot of the first whites to enter the Wallowa Valley.

From the Wallowas, by Grace Bartlett, contains more recollections by early settlers, some about their Nez Perce neighbors.

In mid-July a Tamkaliks Celebration is held in Wallowa, Oregon. Call 541-886-3101 for more information or visit www.wallowanezperce.org.

CHAPTER 2

Lapwai

Recipe for War

Lewiston to Cottonwood, Idaho

War is made to take something not your own.—Yellow Wolf[1]

There is a certain class who are afraid that there will not be an Indian war.—John Monteith (agent for the Nez Perce Reservation), March 19, 1877[2]

Please correct impression in Walla Walla newspapers that campaign against Joseph has been ordered.—Maj. H. Clay Wood, March 1, 1877

The white man has been drawing Nez Perces blood for many years. Our chiefs have put all their nerves between their teeth to keep peace with the white man.—Wahchumyus (Rainbow)

The Story

The routine that had been repeated hundreds of times across the continent was to be played out one more time: The U.S. government makes a treaty with the native inhabitants of the land. Before the treaty is ratified or the Native Americans receive payment, whites begin to settle on land the Indians still consider theirs. Inevitably, conflicts arise between individual whites and Indians, and, invariably, individual Native Americans are shot or raped. Sometimes, but not always, the Native Americans take revenge. The settlers feel unsafe and demand military protection. The media, in the form of newspapers, demand justice. The injustices perpetrated on the original owners lead to frustration and anger, doubled by the fact that the law and power are on the side of the whites. Any Indian uprising is met by the army. Eventually, the Indians always lose and are either sent to Indian Territory (Oklahoma) or are placed on reservations.

The first ingredients in this recipe for a war were on the table. The treaty was made and the land declared open to settlement, even though legally it was still Nez Perce land. The situation simmered for five years before the next ingredients were added.

35

Gold was discovered on the Nez Perce Reservation in 1860, and a town of two thousand sprang up overnight at Lewiston to supply the thousands of miners and prospectors who swarmed onto the Nez Perce land in search of *oro fino*—gold dust. A settlement clearly violated the treaty, but Chief Lawyer was willing to cede the area around Lewiston.

The impact of 18,000 white men on the Nez Perce along the Clearwater was tremendous. To maintain order, a fort was constructed at Lapwai in 1862, and another treaty council convened there in 1863. The government treaty-makers supported Lawyer as the head chief of all the Nez Perce. The Nez Perce themselves recognized no head chief of all the bands. Although a "president" makes perfect sense to the American federalist way of thinking, a "head chief" was utterly contrary to the Native American view of the world. Lawyer had ingratiated himself among the whites, but among the Nez Perce his standing as a chief was not as high as that of other chiefs.

The treaty of 1863 reduced the land reserved to the Nez Perce by ninety percent, leaving the tribe 700,000 acres contained within the borders of the present-day reservation. Chief Lawyer, whose home was within these boundaries, signed the Treaty of 1863 along with fifty other Christian Nez Perce men. Fifty-six chiefs had signed the Treaty of 1855, so the numbers appeared about the same. But some important names were missing on the second treaty, including Old Joseph, Looking Glass Sr., Toohoolhoolzote, White Bird, Big Thunder, Red Owl, and Eagle from the Light. These and several other traditional Nez Perce headmen were so disgusted with the council proceedings that they left before the council had ended. They did not agree to the treaty and did not believe they were bound by it. They did not imagine that anyone beside themselves had the authority to sell their land. The government representatives conveniently used their departure to further the treaty process.

The result of the Chief Lawyer faction signing a treaty for their land meant that their land would henceforward be considered the Nez Perce Reservation. Those who did not sign the treaty were left without recourse; thus an already existing division in the Nez Perce tribe was widened. The split between Christian and traditional Nez Perce was formalized into treaty and nontreaty Nez Perce. The war in 1877 and the resulting exile accentuated the gap. Returning from exile, many traditionals opted to go with Chief Joseph to the Colville Reservation, so that even today the Nez Perce continue to be divided among reservations.

As white people settled on land belonging to the nontreaty Nez Perce, the friction between the cultures increased, particularly in the Wallowas and in

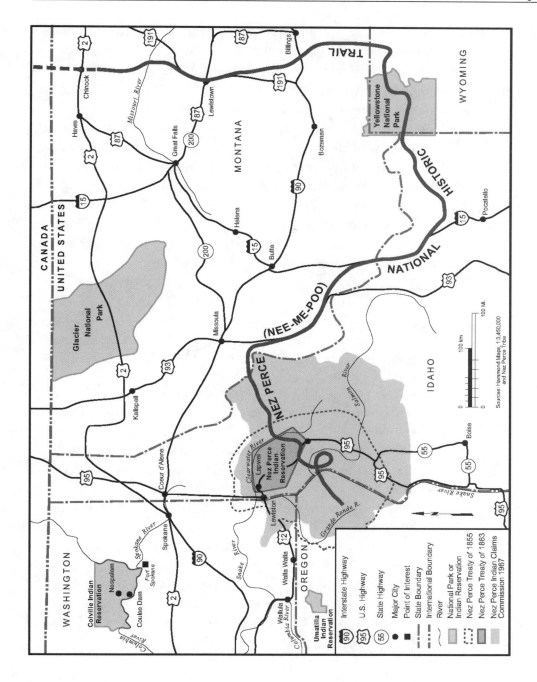

the Salmon River country. During these years, nearly thirty (or forty-seven, depending on which account you read) Nez Perce were killed by whites, yet the judicial system consistently found in favor of the whites. The major grievance of the nontreaty Nez Perce—that their land had been stolen out from under them—was never addressed. Ill feelings mounted.

A commission convened at Fort Lapwai in 1876 to make recommendations about the Nez Perce problem. Although a minority report held that Nez Perce title to their land had not been extinguished, four of the five commissioners agreed that the nontreaty Nez Perce must be forced onto the reservation.

A follow-up council was held at Fort Lapwai in May 1877 to carry out the recommendations of the commission. General Oliver Otis Howard spelled out the conditions: the nontreaty Nez Perce must be on the reservation within thirty days or soldiers would drive them on. Seeing that they had no realistic alternative, the nontreaty chiefs agreed to move onto the reservation.

Chronology of Events

1835	Henry and Eliza Spalding establish a Presbyterian mission at Lapwai, Idaho.
1847	Cayuse Indians kill Marcus and Narcissa Whitman at their mission near Walla Walla. To avoid danger, the Spaldings leave Lapwai.
1860	Gold is discovered on Nez Perce land. Lewiston springs up.
1863	Idaho Territory is created, dividing the Nez Perce homeland into three parts.
	Chief Lawyer signs the Treaty of 1863, shrinking the Nez Perce Reservation to 700,000 acres.
1867	Congress ratifies the Treaty of 1863.
November 1876	
	A five-man commission meets with Chief Joseph at Lapwai, but the two sides fail to reach a settlement. The commission's report recommends that the nontreaty Nez Perce be moved onto the reservation.
3–15 May 1877	
	A council between the nontreaty Nez Perce and General Howard at Lapwai results in the jailing of Nez Perce spokesman Toohoolhoolzote. Joseph, White Bird, Husishusis Kute, and Looking Glass pick out their allotments on the reservation. Howard gives the ultimatum that the nontreaty Nez Perce must move onto the reservation in thirty days.

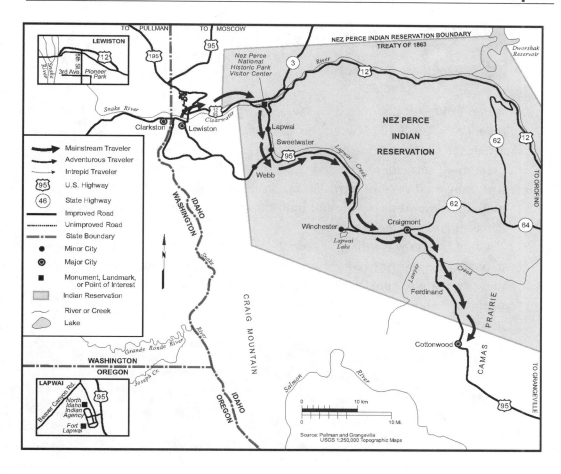

Travel Plan

Mainstream Traveler	Adventurous Traveler	Intrepid Traveler
Lewiston	follow Mainstream	follow Mainstream
Pioneer Park	follow Mainstream	follow Mainstream
Lewiston to Cottonwood	follow Mainstream	follow Mainstream

For the Mainstream Traveler

Lewiston

When gold was discovered in Pierce, sixty miles east of here, in 1860, the *tseminicum*, the land between the forks of the Snake and Clearwater rivers was a natural supply point. A town sprang up here almost overnight. Since a permanent settlement violated the terms of the Treaty of 1855, the town, at first, consisted only of tents. Soon, however, streets were laid out; lots were platted, sold and recorded; and buildings were erected, even though the Nez Perce still owned the land.

Chief Lawyer was willing to cede the land around Lewiston. Yet even Lawyer may have been surprised by the next step. Word came from Washington that a new treaty was required. Only eight years after the Treaty of 1855, this traditional people who had held the land in perpetuity for centuries were asked to sell still more of their land.

> From the US 12 bridge that crosses the Snake River and connects Clarkston with Lewiston, continue east on US 12 into Lewiston for 0.4 mile to the junction with 5th Street.
>
> Join the Mainstream Traveler for a sidetrip to Pioneer Park. Or continue with the Mainstream Traveler in Lewiston.

For the Mainstream Traveler

Sidetrip
Pioneer Park

> Turn south on 5th Street for 0.1 mile. Then turn sharply northeast on the extension of 2nd Avenue into Pioneer Park.

Rifle Pit

40

When news came that Nez Perce warriors had killed white people on the Salmon River, the people of Lewiston panicked. On the high vantage point of this hill, they dug rifle pits for their self-defense. At the southwest corner of the old Carnegie library is one of the rifle pits from that time.

Lawyer was designated as head chief of the Nez Perce Nation by U.S. government treaty makers in 1863. (Photo courtesy of Washington State Historical Society.)

Lawyer
Hakhal-tsostsot
Head Chief of the Nez Perce Tribe.

Lewiston has an organization of 60 men, poorly fitted for home duty and for cases of emergency.—The New York Times, June 20, 1877

Although the fleeing nontreaty Nez Perce bands never actually came closer than forty miles to Lewiston, the existence of the rifle pit here shows just how apprehensive the settlers were during the early summer of 1877. People in the Pullman-Moscow area, twenty miles north of here, built stockades. They were sure that the Nez Perce uprising was just the tip of the iceberg and that all the Northwestern tribes would soon be on the rampage.

Circle clockwise around the Pioneer Park on the one-way street. At 3rd Avenue, turn west for 1 block, then turn north on 5th Street and return the 0.3 mile to Main Street (US 12).

Join the Mainstream Traveler at Lewiston for the trip to Cottonwood.

For the Mainstream Traveler

Lewiston to Cottonwood

From Lewiston, follow US 12 east, out of town, for 6.7 miles to the border of the Nez Perce Reservation.

Nez Perce Indian Reservation

The boundaries of the Nez Perce Reservation you are entering today were defined by the Treaty of 1863. Those of you who crossed the border of the Nez Perce Nation as defined by the Treaty of 1855 in chapter one have an experiential sense of the difference between 7,000,000 acres and 700,000 acres.

The shrinkage of Nez Perce homeland did not end with the Treaty of 1863. The Dawes Act of 1887 allotted 160 acres to each Indian adult and 80 acres to each minor child. The remaining 542,000 acres of the reservation were then ceded to the government and opened to white settlement. Today, less than 90,000 acres of the Nez Perce Reservation remain in Nez Perce hands.

Where US 12 and US 95 diverge, 2.8 miles farther on, take US 95, across the Clearwater River, for 1.8 miles to Spalding, the Visitor Center of the Nez Perce National Historic Park.

Visitor Center, Nez Perce National Historic Park, Spalding

Nez Perce National Historic Park is a unique park because it is a collection of twenty-six historic sites scattered throughout Nez Perce, Lewis, Clearwater, and Idaho counties in Idaho, plus the Camas Meadows battlefield west of Yellowstone, two battlefields and Canyon Creek in Montana, four sites in Oregon, and four sites in Washington. At the Visitor Center, be sure to pick up a brochure of the park's sites. Browse through the exhibit room, which displays Nez Perce artifacts, and take time to see the movie or slide show, which is shown regularly in the theater. Many of the best books about the Nez Perce flight are on sale in the lobby. (For quick reviews, see **For Further Reading** on page xiii of the Introduction.)

After you leave the Visitor Center, continue 0.3 mile east, down to the picnic area to the see the site of the Spalding Mission.

Spalding Mission

Henry and Eliza Spalding arrived among the Nez Perce in 1836. Their colleagues, Marcus and Narcissa Whitman, set up a mission to the Cayuse near Walla Walla at the same time. After three years of intense missionary zeal and frustration, Spalding made his first converts—Chief Old Joseph and Chief Timothy. Old Joseph was baptized into the Presbyterian Church in 1838. His infant son, who was baptized by Spalding in April 1840 as Ephraim, was the future Chief Joseph.

Because Chief Old Joseph spent a lot of time at Spalding's mission, his young sons, Joseph and Ollokot, probably played and had their first contacts with white people here until 1847. As future chiefs of their people, they must have had a unique childhood, observing and experiencing the white man's ways until they were almost eight and six years old.

Henry H. Spalding and his wife Eliza arrived as missionaries to the Nez Perce in 1836 and built their mission on Lapwai Creek. (Photo courtesy of Smithsonian Institution.)

Twenty-five years later, when his home in the Wallowa began to be settled, Chief Joseph counseled and talked with his white neighbors to maintain peace and smooth out conflicts. He alone, of all the non-treaty chiefs, had a great deal of experience in talking and counseling with white men. His was the name most well-known to the general public, and the press incorrectly ascribed to him the brilliant maneuvers of the Nez Perce flight. This false assumption was confirmed when Joseph was one of two chiefs who surrendered. Regardless of the facts, legendary status followed Chief Joseph for the rest of his life. To this day, Chief Joseph remains a sympathetic historical figure about whom the public has a very positive image.

Stroll around the picnic area, which was, in the 1840s, the location of the Spalding Mission. Later, the agent for the reservation lived here in the cabin in the northwest corner of the park. In 1877 that man was J.B. Monteith.

Following the murder of fellow missionaries Marcus and Narcissa Whitman in late 1847, Spalding and his wife and children left the mission on January 1, 1848.

Originally called *Lapwai*, place of butterflies, the name was changed in 1898 to honor Spalding. Fort Lapwai was built three miles south of here on Lapwai Creek in 1862, and the name Lapwai stuck to the settlement that grew up around the post.

Leaving the Spalding Site/Visitor Center area, proceed south on US 95. 3.9 miles south of the Visitor Center, on the south side of Lapwai, turn west onto Parade Avenue to see the site of Fort Lapwai. Proceed 2 blocks west to the old parade grounds, then south 1 block and then west again. The duplex on the corner, west of the parade grounds, was officer's quarters.

Fort Lapwai

Although Fort Lapwai was a military post, it was not built to be a stronghold.

> *There is really no fort. There is a hollow square on the western side of the ravine; the Lapwai flows northerly, near the eastern slope of it. The usual officers' quarters are on the west, facing inwards; the barracks opposite; office on the south; guard-house, with its one sentinel walking up and down*

This 1876 photo of Fort Lapwai shows the officers' quarters on the west, the barracks on the east and the parade grounds separating them. The home of Emily and John FitzGerald (bottom, left of center) is marked with an X. (Photo courtesy of the University of Pittsburgh Press.)

Tuekakas or Chief Old Joseph was over sixty when Gustavus Sohon sketched his portrait at the Walla Walla Treaty Council of 1855. (Photo courtesy of Washington State Historical Society.)

in front, on the north, and the parade between. The post-trader's and laundress' houses are nearer the Lapwai; while the stables and other outbuildings are arranged a few paces outside the square and up the valley.—Gen. O. O. Howard

While this was still a new garrison, a council convened here that resulted in the Treaty of 1863. Only eight years had elapsed since the Treaty of 1855, but change was coming fast to this traditional people. With all the Nez Perce present, the treaty negotiators made their offer: Nez Perce lands would be reduced by ninety percent. Chief Lawyer, whose lands were contained within the new boundaries, agreed. Chiefs Big Thunder, Old Joseph, White Bird, Looking Glass, Red Owl, Eagle from the Light, and Toohoolhoolzote did not.

The debate ran with dignified firmness and warmth until near morning, when the Big Thunder party made a formal announcement of their determination to take no further part in the treaty, and then with a warm, and in an emotional manner, declared the Nez Perce nation dissolved; whereupon the Big Thunder men shook hands with the Lawyer men, telling them with a kind but firm demeanor that they would be friends, but a distinct people. —Capt. Currey[3]

45

Chief Old Joseph was so upset by the proceedings that he tore up his copy of the Treaty of 1855 and his Gospel of Matthew that Reverend Spalding had printed in Nez Perce over twenty years earlier. The bands who left the council without signing the treaty would henceforward be called the nontreaty bands. Their departure conveniently suited the purposes of the treaty negotiators. Since the nontreaty chiefs would never agree to the provisions of the new treaty, the obstacle of their objections was removed. The only men left to negotiate with were the Nez Perce who would agree. Fifty-one of the fifty-two men who signed the Treaty of 1863 were Christians. The chiefs who had left never could understand how their land had been sold by someone else. Land—much more than simply "property" to the Nez Perce—land—the mother of all living beings—land—their heritage, for centuries and even millennia—had been taken from them by "touching the pen." Incomprehensible.

For the next fourteen years, the nontreaty Nez Perce remained on their traditional lands—lands which, according to the Treaty of 1863, were now open to white settlement. In the 1860s, white people began moving into the Salmon River country. In the 1870s, the Wallowa country was surveyed and began to be settled. The inevitable conflicts between whites and Nez Perces mounted. In the Wallowa, Chief Joseph counseled with his white neighbors, asking them to leave because the Indians were there first. A company of soldiers was stationed in the Wallowa every summer to prevent conflicts. In the Salmon River country, nearly thirty Nez Perce were killed over the course of the years. While a few settlers acted neighborly, a vocal contingent wanted the nontreaty Nez Perce put on the reservation.

A report reviewing "The Status of Young Chief Joseph" sided with the nontreaty Nez Perce on the issue of the legality of the Treaty of 1863.

> *The nontreaty Nez-Perces cannot in law be regarded as bound by the treaty of 1863; and in so far as it attempts to deprive them of a right to occupancy of any land its provisions are null and void. The extinguishment of their title of occupancy contemplated by this treaty is imperfect and incomplete.*—Asst. Adj. Gen. H. Clay Wood, January 8, 1876

But in practice, whites were settling on Nez Perce land in larger and larger numbers. By 1876, the tension between the native residents and the new residents had become strained. The Secretary of Interior appointed a five-man commission consisting of General Oliver Otis Howard, Colonel H. Clay Wood, and three Easterners to settle the differences. In November 1876 they met here at Fort Lapwai.

General Oliver Otis Howard was the commander of the Department of the Columbia. As such, he was in charge of negotiating with the Nez Perce. (Photo courtesy of Idaho State Historical Society.)

Emily FitzGerald, wife of Dr. John FitzGerald, lived at Fort Lapwai. Her observations of the Nez Perce negotiations were recorded in her letters to her mother. (Photo courtesy of University of Pittsburgh Press.)

The negotiations stuck on a familiar theme: the Nez Perce did not understand the white man's law about why they were bound by a treaty they had not signed; the whites did not understand Nature's laws about the importance of the earth as the mother of all living beings.

> *The Creative Power, when he made the earth, made no marks, no lines of division or separation on it, and…it should be allowed to remain as then made. The earth was his [Joseph's] mother. He was made of the earth and grew up on its bosom. The earth, as his mother and nurse, was sacred to all his affections, too sacred to be valued by or sold for silver and gold. He could not consent to sever his affections from the land that bore him. He was content to live upon such fruits as the Creative Power placed within and upon it, and unwilling to barter these and his free habits away for the new modes of life proposed by us.… To part with the earth would be to part with himself.… He asked nothing of the President. He was able to take care of himself. He did not desire Wallowa Valley as a reservation, for that would*

47

subject him and his band to the will of and dependence on another, and to laws not of their own making. He was disposed to live peaceably. He and his band had suffered wrong rather than do wrong. One of their number [Wil-haut-yah] was wickedly slain by a white man during the last summer, but he would not avenge his death. But unavenged by him, the voice of that brother's blood, sanctifying the ground, would call the dust of their fathers back to life, to people the land in protest of this great wrong.—Gen. O. O. Howard

Dr. John Fitzgerald and his wife lived in one of the officer's quarters.

The Indian Commissioners departed on Wednesday without Joseph coming to any terms. They all got indignant at him at last and threatened him.... He said he was ready for them.... General Howard says Joseph has taken the course to make him lose all sympathy for him, and next summer, if the trouble in the Wallowa is brought up again, he will send out two men to Joseph's one—no matter how many he raises—and whip him to submission. Delightful prospect for us whose husbands will probably be in the fight, isn't it?—Emily FitzGerald (Army doctor's wife), November 19, 1876[4]

The objective of a negotiated settlement failed. The report prepared by the commissioners read like an ultimatum.

So long as Joseph and his band remain in the Im-na-ha Valley, and visit the Wallowa Valley for hunting, fishing, and grazing for only a short time in each year, we recommend a speedy military occupancy of the valley by an adequate force to prevent a recurrence of past difficulties between the whites and the Indians. Meanwhile the agent of the Nez Perces should continue his efforts to settle these Indians in severalty upon the land of the reservation that are still vacant....

Unless they should conclude to settle quietly...within a reasonable time in the judgement of the department, they should then be placed by force upon the Nez Perce reservation....

If these Indians overrun land belonging to the whites and commit depredations upon their property, disturb the peace by threats or otherwise, or commit any other overt act of hostility, we recommend the employment of sufficient force to bring them into subjection, and to place them upon the Nez Perce reservation.

The Indian agent [Monteith] at Lapwai should be fully instructed to carry into execution those suggestions, relying at all times upon the department commander [Howard] for aid when necessary.—Nez Perce Commission, December 1, 1876

Two months later,

The Department of the Interior, at Washington, issued its ominous instructions to carry out the recommendations of the November Commission to its agent [J.B. Monteith] at Lapwai, early in January, 1877....

Monteith sent friendly Indians to Joseph and the non-treaty Indians, and did all in his power to induce them to do what they told the commission they would not do; i.e., come on the Lapwai reservation.—Gen. O. O. Howard[5]

A couple of meetings were held during the spring as the pressure to move the nontreaty bands onto the reservation intensified. On May 3, 1877, and the days following, the final council with the nontreaty Nez Perce was held at Fort Lapwai.

I have been in a great many councils, but I am no wiser.—Chief Joseph

There is a big tent pitched on the parade ground, ...and in and around it, squatted on the ground, are about a hundred Indians in the most gorgeous get-ups you can imagine. General Howard and his aides, the Indian Agent, and several of the officers of the post in full uniform are inside talking with Joseph. The outside line of Indians around the tent consists almost entirely of squaws and papooses. —Emily FitzGerald (Army doctor's wife), May 4, 1877[6]

There came togethe the morning of the 3d about 50 Indians, mostly of Joseph's band....

One old "dreamer" lectured the interpreter, Mr. [Perrin] Whitman, urging him for the sake of coming generations, both white and Indian, to interpret correctly....

I saw that they were alarmed for their personal safety.

Friday, the 4th of May, the Indians came together again, very much re-enforced, part of White Bird's Indians and some others having come in....

Joseph simply introduced White Bird and his people, stating that they had not seen me before, and that he wished them to understand what was said.—Gen. O. O. Howard, May 22, 1877

49

Chief Toohoolhoolzote, whose band lived in the rough country between the Salmon and Snake rivers, spoke on behalf of the nontreaty Nez Perce. General Howard responded with what he thought was an open mind.

> *It is my usual manner, proceeding from the kindest of feelings, and from an endeavor to behave as a gentleman to the weakest or most ignorant human being.*— Gen. O. O. Howard

This patronizing point of view was understood very directly by the Nez Perce.

> *We have respect for the whites, but they treat me like a dog.—Ollokot, May 3, 1877[7]*

Unaware of the offensiveness of a paternalistic point of view, white Americans had no doubt that they knew what was best for Native Americans.

> *For in the interest of the Indian, in order to change his habits of life and render him speedily self-supporting, there is required…"patient and constant perseverance, instructing, correcting and reproving…. They are grown-up children…."—Nez Perce Commission, December 1, 1876*

> *You have no right to compare us, grown men, to children. Children do not think for themselves. Grown men do think for themselves. The government at Washington, "cannot" … think for us.—Toohoolhoolzote, May 4, 1877[8]*

The negotiations hit one cross-cultural snag after another. Americans, accustomed to a representative form of government, did not understand how insulting the idea was to people accustomed to self-rule. With some of the preliminary misunderstandings unresolved, the talk moved on to another substantive issue: the legality of the Treaty of 1863.

> *I have heard about a bargain, a trade between some of these Indians [the treaty Nez Perces] and the white men concerning their land; but I belong to the land out of which I came. The Earth is my mother.—Toohoolhoolzote, May 4, 1877[9]*

> *The Nez Perces did make such an agreement, and as the commission from Washington explained last fall, the nontreaty Indians being in the minority in their opposition, were bound by that agreement and must abide by it. —* Gen. O. O. Howard, May 4, 1877[10]

> *Then…Too-hool-hool-suit…rose in the council and said to General Howard: "The Great Spirit Chief made the world as it is, and as He wanted it, and He*

made a part of it for us to live upon. I do not see where you get authority to say that we shall not live where He placed us."—Chief Joseph

We listened to the oft-repeated Dreamer nonsense with no impatience.—Gen. O. O. Howard[11]

The second day of the council began with restating the crux of the issue from the Nez Perce point of view. This contrasted dramatically with what the whites thought the problem was.

Chief Toohoolhoolzote stood up to talk for the Indians. He told how the land always belonged to the Indians, how it came down to us from our fathers. How the earth was a great law, how everything must remain as fixed by the Earth-Chief. How the land must not be sold! That we came from the earth, and our bodies must go back to earth, our mother. General Howard stopped the chief. —Yellow Wolf[12]

I don't want to offend your religion, but you must talk about practicable things; twenty times over I hear that the earth is your mother and about chieftainship from the earth. I want to hear it no more, but come to business at once.—Gen. O. O. Howard, May 7, 1877

Chief Toohoolhoolzote *was* talking directly to the point of the business at hand.

"You ask me to talk, then tell me to say no more," Toohoolhoolzote replied. "I am chief! I ask no man to come and tell me anything what I must do. I am chief here!"—Yellow Wolf[13]

I answer, "You know very well that the government has set apart a reservation, and that the Indians must go on it...."
   The old man...asked, "What person pretended to divide the land and put me on it?"—Gen. O. O. Howard, May 7, 1877

General Howard answered sharp. "...I am telling you! Thirty days you have to move in!"
   "Yes, picking your own count!" our chief said. "Go back to your own country! Tell them you are chief there. I am chief here."
   General Howard was showing mad. He spoke sharply, "If you do not mind me, if you say, 'No,' soldiers will come to your place. You will be tied up and your stock taken from you."

Toohoolhoolzote answered, "I am telling you! I am a chief! Who can tell me what I must do in my own country?"

General Howard was now strong mad. He spoke in loud voice, "I am the man to tell you what you must do! You will come on the reservation within time I tell you. If not, soldiers will put you there or shoot you down!"

Chief Toohoolhoolzote did not become afraid. His words were strong as he replied, "I hear you!... I am a man, and will not go! I will not leave my home, the land where I grew up!"—Yellow Wolf[14]

I then...say, "Then you do not propose to comply with the orders?" He answers, "So long as the earth keeps me, I want to be left alone; you are trifling with the law of the earth." I reply, "Our old friend does not seem to understand that the question is, will the Indians come peaceably on the reservation, or do they want me to put them there by force?"—Gen. O. O. Howard

He [Toohoolhoolzote] declared in substance, "I never gave the [treaty] Indians authority to give away my lands.... The Indians may do what they like, but I am not going on the reservation!"—Gen. O. O. Howard, May 7, 1877

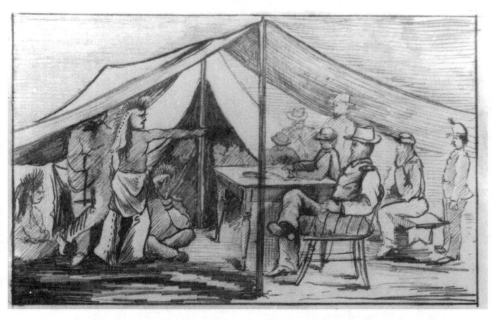

Toohoolhoolzote responds to General Howard in this sketch by Lieutenant Guy Howard. (Photo courtesy of courtesy of Dr. Norris Perkins.)

General Howard now called a soldier to come forward. He pointed to Toohoolhoolzote and ordered, "Take him to the guardhouse." —Yellow Wolf[15]

Chief Toohoolhoolzote was arrested for speaking his mind. —Chelooyeen (Bow and Arrow Case)[16]

All that hurt us. In peace councils, force must not be talked. It was just the same as showing us the rifle. General Howard was just pricking with needles. —Yellow Wolf[17]

Had General Howard created Toohoolhoolzote, the chief would have minded his orders and moved to the reservation. But it was otherwise and he had to remain where placed from his birth. The Flying Person was greater than General Howard, who might kill by gun and sword and destroy with fire, but that was all. The chief had to observe the rules and laws first given by the true Creator of all life. He was not scared at threats against his own body. He was not to tremble at death of any form. He was not to be scared at death of any form. He did not want war and had General Howard been more kind there would have been no war. —Wottolen (Hair Combed Over Eyes)[18]

Chief Toohoolhoolzote was held in the guardhouse for eight days while the council continued.

In a council next day General Howard informed us in a haughty spirit that he would give my people thirty days to go back home, collect all their stock, and move on to the reservation, saying, "If you are not here in that time, I shall consider that you want to fight, and will send my soldiers to drive you on."

I said: "...I cannot get ready to move in thirty days. Our stock is scattered, and Snake River is very high. Let us wait until fall, then the river will be low. We want time to hunt our stock and gather our supplies for the winter."

General Howard replied, "If you let the time run over one day, the soldiers will be there to drive you on to the reservation, and all your cattle and horses outside the reservation at that time will fall into the hands of the white men." —Chief Joseph

Why such hurry at that time of year? Time was not quitting, was not stopping! The big, swift rivers in full flood, much stock was sure to be lost in crossing. —Wottolen (Hair Combed Over Eyes)[19]

*This was language that hurt the Nez Perce feelings.... Guns must not be talked in peace councils. Only in war talks must arrows be spoken.—*Two Moon[20]

On May 8, 1877, Howard and his aides rode out with Joseph, Looking Glass, White Bird, and Husishusis Kute to choose the sites on the reservation where the chiefs would settle their bands.

*Joseph, ...White Bird, and Little Baldhead or the Preacher [Husishusis Kute], started out with the General to select homes for themselves. While riding around the country Howard had a few soldiers and an interpreter along with him. Howard said to White Bird, "What made you a chief? I am a chief because I lost my arm while fighting in big battles and fought bravely." Joseph and White Bird were surprised at these remarks, and said amongst themselves, "Howard is anxious for war."—*Duncan McDonald (Nez Perce reporter)

The council ended on May 15, 1877, with General Howard's final ultimatum: Be on the reservation in thirty days or else be driven onto it by soldiers. The chiefs had no choice. They left Fort Lapwai and went to their respective homes to prepare for the move.

The threat of reprisals by soldiers was severe. What the Nez Perce did not know, however, was that the soldiers were just about to have a morale problem.

The funds for the payment of the army have "run out," and that last, mean, rebel Congress refused to make a new appropriation for it. So, after this month, there will be no more money for poor army people until the next Congress meets sometime in the fall and makes a new appropriation. — Emily FitzGerald (Army doctor's wife), May 11, 1877[21]

A month later, when word of the Salmon River killings came, Fort Lapwai sprang into action as the base for the troops General Howard had promised to use to drive the Nez Perce onto the reservation.

Return to US 95 and turn south for 41.2 miles to Cottonwood. The highway follows Lapwai Creek to Winchester. Then halfway between Craigmont and Ferdinand, the highway crosses Lawyer Creek and enters Idaho County, the largest county in the state. Ascending out of the Lawyer Creek Canyon, you arrive on Camas Prairie. The luxuriant-looking farmland that extends for miles was once covered with bunchgrass. Those were the days when the prairie was dotted with some of the thousands of grazing Nez Perce horses.

Two miles after leaving the Nez Perce Reservation, the conflict begins. Join the Mainstream Traveler at Cottonwood in the next chapter.

For Further Reading

A collection of letters written mostly by Emily FitzGerald, *An Army Doctor's Wife*, gives a very personal view of the conflict between the military and the Nez Perce. Emily lived at Fort Lapwai and chronicled the councils leading up to the war. Her husband was one of the surgeons accompanying General Howard's troops, and the book contains some of his correspondence from the field.

The Nez Perce Nation Divided: Firsthand Accounts of Events Leading to the 1863 Treaty has collected every government document and many newspaper articles from 1858 to 1863. This tome makes fascinating reading for those interested in the background details of the War of 1877.

CHAPTER 3

Camas Prairie Loop

Where the War Began

Cottonwood to Grangeville, Idaho

The Indian war now raging in Idaho is to a certain extent, the result of the half-measure policy frequently adopted by the Government in its treatment of questions pertaining to the red man. The causes that led to the present outbreak have been presented for the consideration of the proper authorities several times during the past ten years, but no notice was taken of them until two years ago, when the usual do-nothing delegation was sent out to see what could be done with the grumbling savages. The result was also the usual one—a heavy talk, but no action. The Indians have been chafing ever since, and have threatened to drive all the white settlers from certain sections unless their wrongs were righted, but no notice was taken of their threats until they put them into execution by killing fifteen white settlers and wounding two women and one child.—Frank Leslie's Illustrated Weekly, July 28, 1877

No chief talked or wanted war.—Yellow Wolf[1]

The Nezperce war ought not to have occurred and would not had our government used a little more diplomacy. The Indians owned the country and had a right to it by reason of possession. One very old Indian who lived on White Bird Creek, a tributary of the Salmon river, who was reputed to be quite wealthy, asked me in regard to the government's order to compel all Indians to evacuate their homes and move to the reservation. I told him it was true. He said where he lived was his only home; that he had lived there a great many years; that his wife and child were buried there; that he could not live but a short time and he wanted to be buried there also. While making this statement he seemed very much affected and shed tears of genuine sorrow. I do not justify the Indians in going on the war path, but I sometimes wonder what their pale face brothers would have done under similar conditions. —Henry C. Johnson (Camas Prairie settler)[2]

My native country! You tell the government that I want my old home given back to me! I am now old and I want to die and be buried where my ancestors lived and are now returned to Mother Earth. —Chelooyeen (Bow and Arrow Case)[3]

We the undersigned residents of Salmon river, Idaho County, Idaho Ty., respectfully represent that we are sorely annoyed by the presence of a lawless band of Nez Perce Indians numbering about 200. They tear down our fences, burn our rails, steal our cattle and horses, ride in the vicinity of our dwellings, yelling, firing pistols, menacing and frightening our women and children and otherwise disturbing our homes. We therefore pray that measures may be speedily adopted to remove these from our midst, upon the reservation where some restraint, can be imposed upon their lawless acts, —and as the duty bound we will ever pray. —Salmon River, I.T. May 7th, 1877, (Signed) James Baker and 56 others.[4]

The Story

Although the town of Cottonwood is a couple of miles outside the Nez Perce Reservation, aboriginal Nez Perce country extended through the Camas Prairie, south past the Salmon River to about where Weiser, Idaho, is today, west to the Wallowa Mountains and east to the Bitterroots. The bands living near the Salmon River were not as well known to the American public as Chief Joseph's

57

Cottonwood as it appeared in 1889. (Photo courtesy of The Historical Museum at St. Gertrude, Cottonwood, Idaho.)

band in the Wallowa. In 1877, two nontreaty bands were native to this area: Chief White Bird's band lived along the Salmon River south of Camas Prairie, and Chief Toohoolhoolzote's band lived between the Salmon and Snake rivers. The inaccessibility of Toohoolhoolzote's territory meant that very few whites disputed Nez Perce ownership. On the other hand, white people were settling in the area claimed by White Bird's band, which includes the present-day towns of White Bird and Slate Creek. Feelings ran high because the White Bird band believed the whites were on their land and the whites believed the Native Americans were on their land. The ensuing tension resulted in a number of Nez Perce being murdered individually.

March 1875   Larry Ott killed Eagle Robe in a dispute over land. The grand jury returned no bill.

August 1875   Samuel Benedict killed Chipmunk and wounded another Nez Perce. Benedict claimed the drunk Indians were demanding admittance to his house. He himself had been accused, in the past, of selling liquor to Indians.

April 1877   Harry Mason whipped two Indians. A council of arbitration, made up of three white men, decided against the Indians.

The Nez Perce had not sought revenge for the deaths or the shame caused by the settlers.

In mid-May 1877 General Howard and Agent Monteith had ordered the nontreaty Nez Perce to be on the reservation by mid-June. Accordingly, the Joseph band crossed the Snake River at Dug Bar, headed east across the Joseph Plains, crossed the Salmon River, and went up Rocky Canyon to Tolo Lake. There they convened on June 3, with Chief Toohoolhoolzote's band, Chief White Bird's band, Chief Looking Glass's band, and two small Palouse bands headed by Hahtalekin and Husishusis Kute (Bald Head).

While the women gathered and prepared camas, the men counseled, the young men raced horses, and the children played. These were to be their last days of freedom, their last days of following the old ways. Underlying the light-hearted events was a current of tension. One thoughtless insult provoked the son of Eagle Robe to seek retribution for the murder of his father. Wahlitits (Shore Crossing) gathered his cousin and nephew, and together they left Tolo Lake on June 13. The trio that formed the first raiding party traveled as far south as Carver Creek, where they killed their first victim. While returning to the Tolo Lake camp, they stopped at John Day Creek and killed three more men.

When the word came to camp that the blood of white men had been spilled, Joseph's, White Bird's, and Toohoolhoolzote's bands of Nez Perce moved north from Tolo Lake across Camas Prairie to a place of safety on Cottonwood Creek. The Looking Glass and Palouse bands immediately returned to their home on the reservation, near Kooskia, in an effort to distance themselves from the trouble.

While tepees were being struck, a second raiding party of seventeen warriors was formed. All except one were members of White Bird's band who had suffered the greatest loss at the hands of white men. The long-held resentment had been uncorked.

Unfortunately, two families of settlers from Cottonwood, the Nortons and the Chamberlins, elected this precise moment to move to the safety of the stockade at Mount Idaho. On their way across Camas Prairie, the families met up with the second raiding party, who fired on them in the middle of the night. Two men and one child were killed outright and two other men were fatally wounded. The raiders then rode on toward White Bird, where they killed six more men and where one woman and her baby disappeared.

The next day, the Nez Perce camp moved south from Cottonwood Creek to White Bird. And on June 17, the first major confrontation between the Nez Perce and the army occurred. To everyone's surprise, the Nez Perce with their antiquated weapons easily routed the charging cavalry. After one bugler was shot and the second had lost his trumpet, the commanders could no longer communicate with the troops, and chaos reigned. The tired troops retreated, and the Nez Perce chased them for thirteen miles. The result of the Battle of White Bird was thirty-four soldiers killed and three Nez Perce slightly wounded. Additionally, the Nez Perce gained over sixty rifles and pistols.

In a sense, the victory sealed the fate of the Nez Perce. Their neighbors, the Cayuse Indians, had taken their revenge by murdering Marcus and Narcissa Whitman in 1847. When the perpetrators were turned over to civil authorities, they were summarily lynched. The Nez Perce now expected similar treatment if they surrendered.

> *The Indians say they know they will be hung if taken.*—Emily FitzGerald (Army doctor's wife), June 25, 1877[5]

> *All that has got to be done is to catch the leaders and hang them.*—Capt. Robert Pollock, July 22, 1877[6]

> *Some wanted to surrender to Howard, but they feared they would be shot or hung.*—Duncan McDonald (Nez Perce reporter)

With their now vastly improved supply of arms, the three bands crossed to the west side of the Salmon River. General Howard and his troops arrived on the east bank of the Salmon and were taunted by warriors daring them to come across and fight. Two days later, Howard and his troops finished crossing the river. By that time, the Nez Perce had traveled north through the Joseph Plains and were about to recross the Salmon. They then moved east across Camas Prairie, going by Cottonwood and then on to the confluence of Cottonwood Creek and the South Fork of the Clearwater River.

While the big Nez Perce camp of four hundred to five hundred people prepared to cross the open Camas Prairie, the warriors skirmished with a squad of 12 soldiers, killing them all. Two days later, the warriors again skirmished on the prairie near Cottonwood, this time with a group of 17 Mount Idaho volunteers. While the volunteers were under fire with no appreciable cover, 113 soldiers watched the action from their trenches at Cottonwood. General Howard's troops were only eighteen miles away but were once again stymied at the prospect of recrossing the Salmon River. Eventually they backed up and crossed the river at White Bird.

The war had begun. For the first time, but not the last, the Nez Perce had gained a comfortable lead and were a couple of days ahead of the troops pursuing them.

Chronology of Events

1875	Larry Ott kills Eagle Robe and is acquitted.
	Samuel Benedict kills Motsqueh and wounds Sarpsis Ilppilp.
1877	
April	Harry Mason whips two Nez Perce. A council of arbitration decides against the Indians.
31 May	The Wallowa band crosses the Snake River at Dug Bar.
3 June	The five nontreaty bands of Joseph, White Bird, Looking Glass, Toohoolhoolzote, and husishusis Kute converge at Tolo Lake for a council and camas-gathering.
13 June	Wahlitits, Sarpsis Ilppilp, and Wetyetmas Wahyakt leave the Tolo Lake camp to find Larry Ott.
14 June	Wahlitits and Sarpsis Ilpilp kill Richard Devine at Carver Creek, and Henry Elfers, Henry Beckrodge, and Robert Bland at John Day Creek. Sarpsis shoots Samuel Benedict in the legs.
	Upon hearing the news, the encampment at Tolo Lake breaks up. Looking Glass and Husishusis Kute hurry back to the

60

reservation. The other three bands flee to a place of safety on Cottonwood Creek.

The Norton and Chamberlin families leave Cottonwood for the safety of Mount Idaho at 9 p.m. Their wagons are attacked in the middle of the night. John Chamberlin, his three-year-old daughter Hattie, and Benjamin Norton are killed. Lew Day and Joe Moore are fatally wounded.

A raiding party of seventeen warriors kills James Baker, Samuel Benedict, and August Bacon in White Bird, and Harry Mason, William Osborne, and François Chodoze at Cooper Bar. Jack Manuel and his six-year-old daughter, Maggie, are wounded, and Jeanette Manuel is injured in a fall from her horse.

Ninety soldiers leave Lapwai at 8 p.m.

16 June	The Manuel house is burned. Perhaps Jeanette Manuel and her baby are inside.
17 June	The Battle of White Bird. Thirty-four soldiers are killed, and three Nez Perce are slightly wounded.
18 June	The Nez Perce camp moves to Horseshoe Bend.
19 June	The Nez Perce camp crosses the Salmon River.
26 June	General Howard's troops bury dead soldiers on the battlefield at White Bird. Jack Manuel is found alive.
27 June	Troops finish burying the dead.
29 June	Howard camps at Horseshoe Bend. Hunter buries Mason, Osborne, and Chodoze.
30 June	Howard's troops begin to cross the Salmon River.
1 July	Howard's troops finish crossing the Salmon River.
2 July	The Nez Perce cross the Salmon River at Craig's Ferry.
3 July	A scout and a squad of twelve men under the command of Lieutenant Rains are all killed near Cottonwood.
4 July	Nez Perce warriors and troops entrenched at Cottonwood skirmish throughout the day.
5 July	The Brave Seventeen, citizen volunteers from Mount Idaho, ride to the rescue of the troops at Cottonwood. One hundred thirteen soldiers watch from their trenches as Nez Perce warriors skirmish with The Brave Seventeen. Two volunteers are killed, and one is mortally wounded.
6 July	Howard fails to cross the Salmon at Craig's Ferry.
7 July	Howard recrosses the Salmon at White Bird.

61

Travel Plan

Mainstream Traveler	Adventurous Traveler	Intrepid Traveler
Sidetrip Cottonwood to William Foster's grave	follow Mainstream	follow Mainstream
Cottonwood to Wayside Exhibit Shelter	Cottonwood to Wayside Exhibit Shelter	follow Mainstream or Adventurous
Wayside Exhibit Shelter to junction of old US 95 and new US 95 via White Bird	follow Mainstream	follow Mainstream
Sidetrip Junction of old and new US 95 to Fiddle Creek	follow Mainstream	follow Mainstream
Sidetrip (cont'd) Fiddle Creek to John Day Creek	follow Mainstream	follow Mainstream
		Sidetrip John Day Creek cemetery
Sidetrip (cont'd) John Day Creek to junction of old and new US 95	follow Mainstream	follow Mainstream
Junction of old and new US 95 to Grangeville	*Sidetrip* Junction of old and new US 95 to Pittsburg Landing	
	Junction of old and new US 95 to Cottonwood	follow Adventurous
	Cottonwood to Grangeville	follow Adventurous

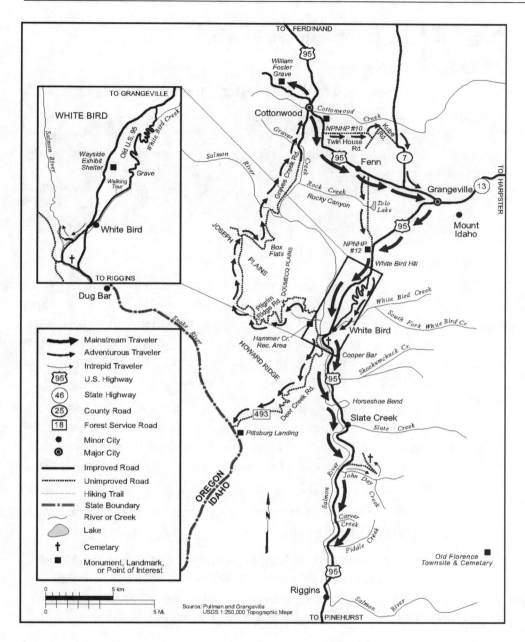

For the Mainstream Traveler

Sidetrip

Cottonwood to William Foster's grave

From the north junction of US 95 with Business 95 into Cottonwood, proceed south toward Cottonwood on Business US 95 for 0.4 mile. Turn onto the first street going north, East Street, for 0.4 mile. At the T by the cemeteries, turn west on Cottonwood Butte Road for 2.7 miles, to the grave of William Foster.

William Foster Grave

On July 3, 1877, William Foster and Charley Blewett were sent out from Cottonwood to scout for the Nez Perce. Meanwhile, a Nez Perce scout, Red Spy, was standing guard for the camp of the main party, which had recrossed the Salmon River. Having left General Howard far behind, the three nontreaty bands were now ready to venture out of the protection of the rugged Salmon River country and strike out across the open, level Camas Prairie.

> *Some squaw man had reported that the Indians had crossed the Salmon River at the mouth of Maloney Creek, and to verify that report Colonel Whipple sent a half breed Indian named Billy Foster and a young white man named Blewett out to make a reconnoiter.*—Luther P. Wilmot (Mount Idaho volunteer)[7]

Charley Blewett was one of the youngest members of the Walla Walla volunteer company, which had arrived on Camas Prairie ten days earlier.

> *On Sunday morning June 24th,...[we] got up early and started for Mount Idaho. We had all regretted leaving Charley but he wanted to stay and Colonel Whipple said he would look after him and take him into his own mess. He was a likeable boy.* —W. S. Clark (Walla Walla volunteer)[8]

Scouts Blewett and Foster got as far as the ridge to the north-northwest of the Foster grave. Red Spy shot Blewett. Foster attempted to rescue his partner but had to give it up and flee for his own life.

> *On Tuesday Whipple sent out Bill Foster and Charley Blewett as scouts to learn the whereabouts of the indians in the direction of Howards command at Craigs crossing of Salmon River They...had not proceeded far before they came upon a large band of horses driven by one indian—They soon saw*

three others in another direction They put their horses to their speed on retreat four being in advance he soon looked back and saw that his comrade had become unhorsed & seperated from him he sung out to him to take to the brush and he would try to catch the horse The horse took down the cañon and he could not overtake him—He then rode in haste to Whipples quarters [at Cottonwood].—Anonymous, July 7, 1877[9]

When morning came, I heard a gun report and the echo of a song. I saw a warrior on a horse and Indians all about him.... Seeyakoon Ilppilp [Red Spy], the mounted warrior, said, "Some white men almost kill me. I suppose scouts—two white men coming this way. They didn't look like soldiers."

The white men had seen him, Seeyakoon told us, as he was watching on guard away off from camp. They made for him. Seeyakoon jumped from his horse and dodged behind rocks. They fired at him. When they did that, he ran toward them, keeping hid by rock protection. He was not afraid! He killed one of them, shot him through the head. The other man got away.— Yellow Wolf[10]

Back at Cottonwood, a squad of ten men under Lieutenant Sevier M. Rains, along with Foster and another guide, rode out in search of Blewett. Red Spy had, of course, raised the alarm at the Nez Perce camp, and a party of warriors set out from there. They reached the top of the ridge to the north here, saw the military camp at Cottonwood, and fanned out in the two ravines above.

Lieutenant Rains had been told to keep to the high ground, but apparently became careless and came up toward this area in search of Blewett's body.

A bunch of about a dozen were out on the hillside.... Rainbow ordered that we go after these soldiers and we did so. We made the charge. The soldiers whipping their horses, fled for their lives. They struck the main hill or mountain. But it was no use! All were killed.—Two Moon[11]

My friends went after those soldiers, and I overtook them. There was shooting, and one soldier fell from his horse. Then another went down a little way from us. Soon a third fell; and another and another, not far apart, went to the ground. Some distance on, a man—maybe wounded—got down from his horse and was killed. I will not hide anything. That part of the fight was not long. Those six soldiers did not get up.

The remaining six soldiers ran their horses up a hill, maybe one half mile. Then they jumped off and lay among some rocks, and began shooting.— Yellow Wolf[12]

65

Two and a half weeks later, a war correspondent visited the grave of William Foster.

> *We then came upon a cluster of graves, five in number; then a single one containing the body of Foster, the scout. Such was the carelessness or laziness of the burying party, that even at this recent time his boots were sticking out of the "grave."*—Frank Parker (scout and war correspondent), July 21, 1877

The monument itself was erected in 1888 by popular subscription, with no one being permitted to give more than $1.

Charley Blewett's body wasn't found until almost seven weeks after the Rains massacre.

> To see the group of rocks where the last stand was made, continue west for 0.2 mile and turn north on Bogli Road. In less than 0.1 mile, look to the east to see one of the groups of rocks where the remaining six men of Rains' squad were killed.

Rains Massacre

> *Those soldiers were trapped. They had no show. When they began shooting, it was just like their calling, "Come on! Come on! Come on!" A calling to death.*
>
> *Our leader Pahkatos [Five Wounds], threw up his hand, and we stopped. The soldiers were shooting at Tipyahlanah [Strong Eagle, a decoy] in the canyon to their left. We dropped back out of sight, then circled the hill to the right. A little beyond the soldiers we dismounted. Some men stayed with the horses, and the others crawled toward the soldiers. I was one of the crawlers. The soldiers were still firing, but not at us. They did not see us, and we got close to them. I will not hide it. Those soldiers were killed!*
>
> *I was soon there with the others. One soldier was sitting up, leaning against a rock. He was shot in the forehead, almost level with the eyes. He had two other shots, through the breast, and he still lived. He washed his face with his own blood, and looked around. He made a clucking noise, a sound like that of a chicken. The Indians, hearing wondered! They asked one another, "What about him? He must be more like us!"*
>
> *...All stood around that soldier, many of them saying, "He cannot live. His body is too bad hurt."*

But one man thought differently and he said, "He can live if he wants to!"

"He is too many times shot," answered one. "Head too bad shot!"

Then one oldlike man named Dookiyoon [Smoker], who had a gun with flint to set the powder afire, spoke, "We shall not leave him like that. He will be too long dying."

With those words, Smoker raised his gun and shot the soldier in the breast. The bullet knocked him over, but he raised again. He sat there, still calling to his Power. Calling with that same clucking. He washed his face again with his running blood, and still looked around.

The warriors, all silent, said nothing. Then some of the them taunted Smoker about his gun, that it was not strong. Smoker reloaded and shot once more, but it did no good! The soldier still sat against the rock, still making the clucking of the hen.

While the warriors stood silent and wondering, one man stepped forward and knocked the soldier over with his kopluts [war club]. Others spoke to save him, but our leader said to us, "We have no doctor. Poor fellow! He is suffering. We better put him out of trouble."

When our leader made this talk, we all became one-minded. I then helped with my kopluts.—Yellow Wolf[13]

At Cottonwood I mounted to follow the warriors who went after the party of soldiers seen leaving their camp. My mother told me not to go but I wanted to see the fight. Two of us boys followed, and we came to a soldier who had been shot many times, in head and breast. He raised up and we heard him go "Kluk! Kluk! Kluk!"—Charley Kowtoliks (sixteen years old)[14]

The troops at Cottonwood watched the skirmish in dismay.

During the time that the scout reported and the time of our getting ready to start out, the Indians came within 1-1/2 miles of our camp intending to surprise us, but seeing our advance guard [Rains' squad] coming they lay'd in a ravine at the foot of Craigs Mountain, Idaho, and allowed our guard to ride into the ambush prepared for them, and killed them all. (Lt. Rains, Troop "L," and Pvt. Ryan, Troop "E," almost succeeded in making theyr escape by clearing their way through the Indians again towards us, but there were too many for those brave men.) We heard rapid firing for a few minutes, but seen nothing more of our guard. On our approach the Indians rallied on the Mountain, but they outnumbered us (three or four to One). Besides, it being after sundown, and only about 56 men in Skirmish line, (after No. 4's were taken out to hold horses). We had two good reasons not to give battle, so we formed a square around the horses, and retreated in good order (as they call it) to Cottonwood Rancho, some of the men growling because we did not attack the Indians, or look for our advance guard, but the more sensible ones guessed that either the guard were all killed or cut they'r way through to Ft. Lapaway. Anyway what was done, was right.—Pvt. Frederick Mayer, July 3, 1877[15]

We intented to bury the dead, and we did start to dig the graves, but before we could bury any of the men, the Indians attacked us, from the woods and rocks at the base of Craigs Mountain. They being undercover and we in the open field of course we had to retreat to Cottonwood, where we intrenched ourselfs quickly, but none too soon. The Indians surrounded us soon after, and kept up a steady fire until dark.—Pvt. Frederick Mayer, July 4, 1877[16]

There was fighting and we women came to a spring where we stood watching.

We left the spring only a little distance when one man...overtook me and said, "Your husband is left near the battle afoot. He has no horse."

I rode back leading a horse for Ollokot. When I came near he seemed under heavy fire. Ollokot came afoot, leading his winded horse. I met him and he advised me, "Be careful! Line your horses with the soldiers' firing! Do not stand broadside to them."—Wetatonmi[17]

A young man named Rains was killed last week. It was his first fight. He was a lovely boy. Mrs. Theller felt dreadfully about his death. He was the officer in charge of the party that found and buried Mr. Theller's body [at White Bird]. Rains had so marked Theller's grave that he would have no difficulty in finding it again, and now we don't know that it can be found. Mrs. Theller is so anxious to have the body.—Emily FitzGerald (Army doctor's wife), July 12, 1877[18]

Lieutenant Rains and the men of his command are now buried in the cemetery at Fort Walla Walla, Washington.

Turn around and return to Cottonwood. Continue with the Mainstream or Adventurous Traveler there.

For the Mainstream Traveler

Cottonwood to Wayside Exhibit Shelter, Nez Perce National Historic Park

Cottonwood

In June 1877 Cottonwood House was the only commercial establishment in Cottonwood. For the preceding fifteen years, it had served as a way station on the stage road from Mount Idaho to Lewiston. As such it was a hotel, saloon, and store all rolled into one. Built from lumber obtained from a nearby cottonwood grove, its large stables accommodated the number of horses used for hauling in those days. Benjamin Norton was the current proprietor of Cottonwood House, which he had bought from Joe Moore and Pete Ready.

> From the junction of US 95 with Business 95 on the north side of Cottonwood, proceed south 2.5 miles to the historical information sign at Nez Perce National Historic Park (NPNHP) site 10.
>
> Continue traveling southeast on US 95 from for 12.8 miles through Fenn to Grangeville.

Norton-Chamberlin Party

When news came on June 14 that three warriors had killed four white men on the Salmon River, the Nez Perce camp hurriedly moved north from Tolo Lake, just south of Fenn. The same day, a party of seventeen warriors headed south to do some more raiding. About halfway between Fenn and Grangeville, the Norton and Chamberlin families fleeing from Cottonwood ran into this group of warriors in the middle of the night.

> *It was on the evening of the 14th of June, 1877 that John Chamberlin drove up to our home at the Cottonwood House. He had with him his wife and two children and his wagon was loaded with household goods.... Lew Day came along about that time and told us that the Indians were on the warpath, and then went on up the Cottonwood hill. In a short time he came back, wounded by the Indians. He had been shot in the back, but managed to escape on his horse and got back to the Cottonwood House. My father (Ben Norton) and Joe Moore dressed his wounds as best they could.*
>
> *Since there were Indians on the mountain, the Chamberlins decided to make a run for Mount Idaho and begged us to go with them. We hurriedly finished packing a few clothes in their wagon, and shortly after dark started*

69

Tolo, for whom Tolo Lake is named, was a friend of people in Slate Creek. She rode from there to the mining community of Florence in the mountains to spread the news of murders committed by the Nez Perce raiding parties. (Photo courtesy of Idaho State Historical Society.)

out with the tired horses. Besides my mother and Mrs. Chamberlin and the two little Chamberlin children, there were in the wagon, Lynn Bowers, my mother's 18-year-old sister, the wounded Lew Day and myself. Father and Joe Moore rode ahead— Chamberlin was driving.

As I remember, we were getting along fine until the moon came up, and we were about five miles from the Grange Hall, when the Indians came running and firing from the direction of Tolo Lake. Father and Joe Moore galloped out to meet them but they were both wounded and their horses shot down. Then our team was shot down. Father and Joe Moore got back to the wagon; father got inside the wagon box with the rest of us, and Joe Moore and Lew Day got under the wagon and began shooting from behind the wheels. I think Moore was shot again before he got under the wagon and I'm sure Day was shot again. Moore died about six days later from his wounds, but Day lingered for two months before he died.

Then we all got under the wagon, the men firing, keeping the Indians away. Day was getting feverish and was begging for water. There was a jug of water in the back of the wagon box and father climbed up on the hub to reach it and there received his deadly wound. He fell to the ground. Later mother called out, "My God, I'm shot!" She was shot through both legs. Then, I think, Chamberlin stampeded. He insisted that he and his wife and the two little children leave the wagon and try to break through to Mount Idaho.

The moon must have gone down or been covered by a cloud, when the entire Chamberlin family left the wagon, but went toward Lake Tolo instead of Mount Idaho. They evidently ran right into the Indians, as we could hear shots, and the screaming of the children and Mrs. Chamberlin. We learned later that Chamberlin and one child was killed and the baby's tongue had been cut off.

Father was still alive and choked out that I should try to get away, but mother did not want me to go. Father said, "He'll be killed here anyway." He died a little while after I left. Lynn Bowers took off her heavy skirt so that she could run faster, and we both sneaked away toward Grange Hall, through the high bunch grass. Joe Moore kept firing until his ammunition was gone. I was found near Grange Hall by Frank Fenn and another settler found Lynn.

It was a terrible experience! —Hill Beachey Norton (ten years old)[19]

Most of that night I had been scouting over the prairie northerly and westerly for a distance of a mile or so from the Grange Hall which at that time comprised about all there was of the present city of Grangeville.... About one and a half miles northwesterly from the Hall, I detected some person crawling through the tall grass about one hundred yards away. I rode my horse toward the person whom I had thought to be an Indian skulking in the grass. Getting near I saw it was a white person and when within perhaps twenty paces he arose to his feet and clapped his hands, exclaiming "It's Mr. Fenn— It's Mr. Fenn," And I recognized him as Hill Norton, a boy who had attended school under my instruction the year before.

Mounting the boy on the crup behind me I started my horse on a gallop for the Hall.... Upon arriving at the Hall, I found some four or five men assembled there....

No time was lost in starting west over the stage road to find the survivors of the attack. Charles L. Rice, ...James Adkison, ...and I, just the three of us, rode off in a hurry to the scene of the attack.

Upon reaching the wagon and ascertaining conditions Charles Rice rode back some distance to a small gully in which there was some running water and filling his hat with water returned with it to allay the thirst of the suffering wounded. In the meantime, Jim Adkison and I busied ourselves stripping harness from the dead horses, unsaddling the saddle horses that had been ridden by Rice and Adkison and putting on them the harness taken from the dead animals. My horse was not broken to harness.

By the time Rice had got back to the wagon with the much needed water Jim and I had nearly finished harnessing the two horses we had fit for work. Practically at the same moment a large body of Indians appeared from the direction of Lake Tolo and not over a half mile away. There was no time lost in hitching the horses to the wagon.... The Indians were coming toward us at full tilt....

Mrs. Norton...was under the wagon shot through both legs and helpless. Her husband lay dead within a few feet of the wagon. We hustled Mrs.

71

Norton into the wagon in which there were already Lew Day, shot in three places, and Joe Moore, shot through the hip. Both died a few days later. We had no chance to pick up Norton's body because the Indians were almost upon us. I mounted the "off" horse and Rice mounted the "near" one and we started plying halter ropes as whips to urge the horses to their best speed. Adkison rode my saddle horse on that eventful trip.

Fortunately for us, from the point where the wagon had stood, there was a long, gradual slope in the direction of Grange Hall and our horses had no pull to make. All that was necessary was to keep them in the road and encourage them to win the race. There was encouragement aplenty for those halter ropes never "missed a lick." Before we reached the foot of the slope the Indians had appeared at the top of the hill and it seemed that they would surely overhaul us when he had to drag the wagon over relatively level ground. Just then, however, quite a large relief party hove in sight riding hard from the direction of Grange Hall.... The advance of the hostiles was checked and shortly, as the volunteer party drew nearer, the Indians turned about, abandoned the chase and enabled their prey to escape. —Frank Fenn (Mount Idaho volunteer)[20]

The second relief party returned to the scene of the attack.

We were not long in reaching the place where the Norton Party had been attacked. I was off to the right of the road and a few hundred yards from the wrecked wagon, when I saw some object not far from me. I rode up and there lay Johnny Chamberlain cold in death, and his oldest girl was lying on his arm. She too was beyond all earthly harm. —Luther P. Wilmot (Mount Idaho volunteer)[21]

Benjamin Norton, John Chamberlin and his three-year-old daughter Hattie, Lew Day, and Joe Moore were all buried in the Mount Idaho cemetery.

Bypass Grangeville and continue south on US 95 for 6.1 miles to the Camas Meadows sign, Nez Perce National Historic Park site 12. From here you can see Tolo Lake in the mid-distance. Read **Tolo Lake** on page 75.

Follow US 95 south for 2.9 miles from the Camas Prairie historical site sign. The White Bird summit marks the divide between Camas Prairie to the north and the Salmon River canyon to the south.

White Bird Hill

When news of the killings on Camas Prairie and the Salmon River reached Fort Lapwai, the response to the settlers' request for protection was immediate. Ninety cavalry men set out to find the Nez Perce. Forty-one hours later, with no sleep, they arrived at White Bird Hill. You have driven the same distance in a couple of hours or less.

Troops F and H, First Cavalry, therefore left Fort Lapwai for Mount Idaho at eight o'clock on the evening of June 15th....

We halted at Cottonwood long enough to cook coffee and unsaddle our animals for a roll and an hour's grazing and then proceeded across Camas Prairie to Mount Idaho, which we reached in the afternoon. We found the citizens armed and very much excited. In the course of the evening a delegation from the small town waited on Colonel Perry, urging him to move down to the Salmon River where the Indians were camped, and attack and punish them for the murders committed by them. Perry called the officers of the command together and after a prolonged conversation with the citizens, who professed to know the situation and strength of the Indians, claiming an easy victory, it was decided to make the attempt. The citizens were deceived in their supposed knowledge of Indian affairs as events subsequently proved.

We fed our men and horses and started at ten o'clock P.M. for the Salmon River, distant about twenty miles. We were now two days and on our second night without rest or sleep.... Half a dozen citizens accompanied us to act as guides and assist in the prospective fight....

We plodded along in the dark until about one o'clock in the morning when we reached the head of White Bird Cañon, where we made a halt until dawn. Colonel Perry ordered perfect quiet and under the circumstances no light of any kind was to be made, yet one man of his own troop lighted a match to light his pipe; two hours later that man paid the penalty of his disobedience with his life. Almost immediately the cry of a coyote was heard in the hills above us, a long, howling cry, winding up, however, in a very peculiar way not characteristic of the coyote. Little heed was paid to it at the time, yet it was a fatal cry to the command. It was made by an Indian picket on the watch for the soldiers who they knew were already on the march. Probably he had seen the light. The signal was carried by others to the camp, so that they were thoroughly prepared for our coming.—Lt. William R. Parnell

73

The troopers began their journey down White Bird Hill before dawn on June 17 from near here. Later the complaint was made that their cinches were not even tightened before they began their descent.

> *At 2 A.M. we were rousted out of what little sleep we could catch in the saddle where a halt without dismounting had been ordered. We were near entering the White Bird Canyon to make a surprise attack on the Indians at daybreak. But let me state right here, we were to have the surprise of our lives.—Sgt. John P. Schorr[22]*

Halfway between mile markers 228 and 227 was where Captain Theller's company was caught retreating from the White Bird battle.

> *Capt. Theller with six soldiers started to retreat and missed the trail which they had come and followed a stock trail that led up into the hills where it was so steep a horse could not carry a man. Here all were killed.—Luther P. Wilmot (Mount Idaho volunteer)[23]*

Continue descending US 95 for 2.0 miles, stopping at the overlook, which is a Nez Perce National Historic Park site.
   Continue with the Mainstream Traveler at the Wayside Exhibit Shelter.

For the Adventurous Traveler

Cottonwood to Wayside Exhibit Shelter, Nez Perce National Historic Park Site

Miles: 33.3
Map: Nez Perce National Forest

From the junction of US 95 with Business 95 on the north side of Cottonwood, continue traveling southeast on US 95. If you are expecting to continue following the Adventurous Traveler route for the remainder of this chapter, skip NPNHP site 10 at this time because you will be looping back to this point to pick it up in chronological sequence.
   It is 8.4 miles from Cottonwood to Fenn. Then, 0.8 mile southeast of Fenn, on US 95, at milepost 246, turn south on Lake Road for 2.9 miles to Tolo Lake.

Tolo Lake

It was a bittersweet time. Five nontreaty Nez Perce bands gathered at Tolo Lake in early June of 1877. The women dug and gathered camas bulbs. The young men were doubtless racing their horses. Some old people were gambling. Children were probably sneaking tastes of camas before it was ready and playing their games. This gathering was a time for preparing the winter food supply, but it was also a time for visiting, chatting, and gossiping with friends and relatives of the other bands. Over seven hundred people were camped around Tolo Lake during the early summer days of that year.

And the horses! Imagine a few thousand horses corralled in Rocky Canyon just south of the lake.

> *During that spring the Nez Perces gathered in camp at Camas Prairie.... It came June, and the Indians were having a good time gambling the bone game, horse-racing and different sports.*—Two Moon[24]

While the camas-gathering, racing, gambling, and playing were going on in the bright sunshine, the warriors, chiefs, and elders sat in a lodge and smoked and counseled: To go onto the reservation or not? There was really no choice. At the council with General Howard in May at Lapwai, the chiefs had agreed to move onto the reservation. What were their alternatives? Noncompliance would only bring the cavalry down on them. And the chiefs knew they stood no chance in prolonged combat with the U.S. Army. During the ten days at Tolo Lake, all the nuances, all the possibilities must have been heard and discussed.

> *Many of the Nez Perces came together in Rocky Canyon to hold a grand council.... This council lasted ten days. There was a great deal of war talk and a great deal of excitement. There was one young brave present whose father had been killed by a white man five years before. This man's blood was bad against white men and he left the council calling for revenge.*— Chief Joseph

By June 13, the chiefs were ready to move their people onto the reservation.

> *That same night the chiefs held a council, putting the question to one another, "Shall we mind General Howard and go to the reservation? Shall we bring out all our stock from the Salmon River country, everything else we have, all the property along the river? It will take quite a while to do this and the waters are at this time big!"...*
>
> *Some said, "We shall not have war," Other talks, "We may have war brought to us." Should we fight or not fight?...*

75

While having this council, someone called from the next tepee, "You poor people are holding council for nothing! Three young men have come from White Bird country, bringing horses with them! Horses belonging to a white settler they killed. Killed yesterday sun! It will have to be war!" —Two Moon[25]

The council ended abruptly.

Their camping ground was a little over a mile from my home…. And when the report reached camp it created a great commotion. Wickyups were torn down, stock driven in from all directions, and as soon as possible thereafter the women and children and also noncombatants were hustled off north about eight miles where they had a better place to fortify and give battle in case they were attacked, which was an impossibility as the few soldiers who were available were stationed at Fort Lapwai, distant forty miles, and no conveyance better than heavy freight wagons and the road were in bad condition from recent rains, which made rapid travel out of the question.— Henry C. Johnson (Mount Idaho volunteer)[26]

The Nez Perce were not the only ones who panicked at the news of the killings. In the community of Slate Creek, forty miles south of here, a stockade was hurriedly erected. Not a man could be spared to carry the news of the hostilities to the mining town of Florence, which was twenty miles southeast of Slate Creek, in the mountains. Tulekats Chikchamit (Betting and Dealing Cards) volunteered to be the courier. English-speaking tongues, unable to wrap themselves around all those syllables, simply called her Tolo. This pond is named for her, a heroine to the white settlers of those times.

A month after the Nez Perce had hurriedly left Tolo Lake, Rocky Canyon once again functioned as a horse corral. This time, the military was using it as a place to keep the horses taken from the Looking Glass band on July 1.

Six hundred and twenty two (622) Indian horses were receipted for by the Mt. Idaho Company. Please have the members of the Companies cull out such horses as are necessary for mounting the men, or other military purposes, and drive the balance into Rocky Canyon and kill them, reporting the number killed to me. People who have followed the operations and who belong to no company, but have picked up bands of Indian Ponies to enrich themselves should be deprived of them: if you with the two (2) vol. Cos. will take their ponies from them, put to use such as your Companies need and kill the remainder you will do a good service to your people and to me. — Gen. O. O. Howard, July 18, 1877[27]

Three red-caped warriors parade in camp. (Photo courtesy of Idaho Historical Society.)

A red-blanketed warrior and another warrior parading. During such a parade at Tolo Lake, Wahlitits' horse stepped on a woman's drying kouse roots. Her irritated husband said, "If you so brave, why you not go kill the white man who killed your father?" (Photo courtesy of Idaho Historical Society.)

The veiled reference to horse thieves referred to a particular volunteer company that had appeared on the scene as news of the Nez Perce uprising rippled out.

> *Bands of armed men, styling themselves volunteers, have every now and then come in a cloud of dust to our assistance.... One band of men from Washington Territory, who represented themselves as thirsting for Nez Perce gore, turned out to be a gang of organized horse thieves.*—Thomas Sutherland (war correspondent), September 10, 1877[28]

77

Volunteers companies from Lewiston, Walla Walla, and Dayton, Washington, rushed to Camas Prairie to fight Indians.

From Tolo Lake proceed south. In 0.3 mile, Lake Road crosses the head of Rock Creek and Rocky Canyon. Proceed on Lake Road for 3.4 miles as it continues south and then jogs east. At the junction with US 95, turn south for 0.7 mile to the Camas Prairie historical information sign.

Continue south on US 95. In 3.7 miles, at mile marker 230, turn east on old US 95 and follow it as it zigzags downhill. Although this road down White Bird Hill, with its many curves and 15 switchbacks, was quite an accomplishment when it was completed in 1921, the pavement is now broken in spots.

In 1.4 miles, note White Bird Creek to the east.

Cavalry Advance

About three o'clock that fatal morning, as we passed in single file along the side of the hill, a sad and pitiable sight presented itself to us. We discovered an unfortunate woman, whose husband had been killed by the Indians, concealed in the gulch below us with a little four year old girl in her arms.— Lt. William R. Parnell

Isabel Benedict had been wandering up White Bird Creek ever since her husband was killed two days before. For the rest of her story, see **Mouth of White Bird Creek** on page 91.

Proceed downhill for 5.0 miles to a tombstone on the east side of the road.

Soldier's Grave

The soldier was an old gray-headed sergeant, one who had no doubt, passed through many campaigns against hostile Indians. He was killed in as fair a duel as ever was fought.... They were probably 15 paces apart; the sergeant would fire and fall back a few steps, the Indian would fire and advance. Each combatant must have fired four or five shots before the sergeant was hit and fell.—Frank Fenn (Mt. Idaho volunteer)

Continue 0.5 mile to a pullout.

The Battle Begins

Captain Perry's troops advanced down White Bird Hill just a few hundred yards west of where the road runs today. Not until the advance guard topped the ridge south of here, where the lone hackberry tree stands, did they see the Nez Perce were ready and waiting for them. Ad Chapman, a volunteer, rode ahead to see the Nez Perce for himself and fired twice on the Nez Perce truce party. The battle commenced. The first casualty, Trumpeter Jones, was shot out of his saddle seconds later.

On the east side of the road, volunteers, led by George Shearer, advanced southward but were quickly driven back by the Nez Perce. Meanwhile, Companies F and H had dismounted just west of the road. With every fourth man acting as a horse holder, the horses were sent back 0.4 mile to about where the last two switchbacks in the road are. Afoot, Companies F and H advanced from just west of here up the ridge, where they were joined by the volunteers. While Captain Perry looked for a trumpeter, the line broke and retreated up the hill paralleling where the new highway runs today.

> Continue 0.5 mile to a gate on the north side of the road where you may take a walking tour of the battlefield.

White Bird Creek

South of the road, in this narrow little valley created by White Bird Creek, lived John J. Manuel and his family. The trio of the first raiding party stopped at his ranch to sharpen their knives on June 13. Two days later, the second raiding party of seventeen warriors halted here.

> *Our family consisted of my father and mother, sister, Julia, a baby brother 11 months old, grandfather and myself. With the exception of my sister, Julia, who was in school at Mount Idaho, we were all at home when James Baker and Patrick Price came to the house and told us that the Indians had wounded Mr. Benedict, and that we had better flee for our lives. They suggested that we had better go to Mr. Baker's stone cellar, about a mile down the creek and there leave the women while the men defended the place.*
>
> *We started immediately. I mounted a horse behind father, while mother and the baby took another horse. Grandfather and Patrick Price remained at the house. We had proceeded about half a mile on our journey when, looking at a hill we had descended, I saw several Indians coming toward us*

79

on the run, yelling and whooping at the top of their voices. "The Indians are coming," I said to father. Just as the Indians appeared we became frightened, as did our horses, at the noise. The latter stampeded, separating father from mother. The Indians opened fire on us with arrows, the first arrow striking my left arm near the shoulder. An arrow struck me near the back of the head and glanced and pierced my father's neck. An Indian who had only two cartridges, as we afterward learned, fired at father, at the same time, and shot him through the hips. The wound thru the hips caused him to fall from his horse, dragging me with him. We were at the top of the hill when we fell from our horse.

Father saw that our only chance was to roll down the hillside into the brush, and this we did, under a fusilade of rocks from the Indians. One rock broke father's little finger, and another struck me on the head. The redskins failed to follow us, doubtless thinking father had his pistols. Very foolishly we had left all weapons and ammunition at the house, with the idea of showing any Indians we might meet, that we were peaceable.—Maggie Manuel (six years old)[29]

I was furnished with a bow and a few arrows, and somewhere above White Bird we chased a white man who was mounted with a small boy [Maggie Manuel] behind him. I used an arrow drawn on the man but it struck the boy on the arm and he cried. When I heard that pitiful voice, I turned my horse and backed away. Not used to killing, it hurt my feelings to hear that little child crying.—Lahpeealoot (Geese Three Times Lighting on Water)[30]

Mother's horse threw her and the baby and in the fall one of her kneecaps was broken, and the baby injured. She said afterwards that some of the Indians took her to the house and promised not to molest her if she would give up the ammunition and a fine rifle that father had. She did this and was uninjured by her captors.

As soon as the Indians left the house grandfather and Mr. Price came in. Mother told them where we had crawled and grandfather came to us. He took me to the house, and left blankets, food and water for father.

That night all of us, including Mrs. Benedict, who came over after her husband's death, slept in the brush. Next morning Mrs. Benedict tried to persuade us to go up the creek and escape to the prairie, but mother and grandfather decided to return to the house, thinking the danger was over. Then too, mother refused to leave father in the brush, wounded and without aid. So we returned to the house, except Mrs. Benedict, who with her children started up the creek, where she was rescued.

Mother and I went to bed while grandfather and Mr. Price stood guard. Along in the forenoon Mox Mox [Yellow Bull] and a band of White Bird Indians, nearly all of whom we knew, as they had camped on a part of our place, came to our house. They ransacked it, but did not offer to molest us.

Being sick and exhausted from my wound, I fell asleep and didn't wake up until nearly dark....

I went to look for grandfather, but found instead Pat Price, with whom I remained in the brush that night. In the morning we were attacked by the Indians. Mr. Price decided to try a ruse.... He then proposed to the Indians that if they would allow him to take me to Mount Idaho he would return and give himself up. The chief agreed to this. —Maggie Manuel (six years old)[31]

Soon a person came to view and I recognized a white man. I saw on his left arm a child that he was carrying....

That white man nodded his head at me, a "how-do-you-do." The first words I understood him say, was "Will you kill me?" I answered, "No."

I had a gun, a rifle. I turned and walked to the three men smoking. Close behind me came the white man with the child on his arm.... When I approached near the smokers, the one facing me, Loppee Kasun [Two Mornings], an oldish man, sprang up pointing his gun ready to fire, trying to make a shot past me. One of the other men, all of them past middle age, spoke to Loppee, "Hold there! Do not shoot! Can you not see child in his arms?"...

The white man stood without speaking. I motioned him to the bushes. To beat it! Which he did!

When he reached the thicket, he turned again and nodded to me, then disappeared in the brush. I saw him no more. I now said to Loppee, "If you shoot the man, who can care for the child? Would you carry it?"— Whylimlex (Black Feather)[32]

I was barefooted and in my nightclothes. We traveled all day, Mr. Price carrying me part of the way.... Mr. Price fashioned a chair out of a drygood box, and with a piece of rope fastened it on his back. In this I rode to Mount Idaho. During all this time my left arm, which had been broken in my fall from the horse, hung limp at my side, as the older people in their excitement had overlooked it, not even fixing me a sling.

The day after we left our house the Indians burned it....

81

Father remained in the brush and the outbuildings for thirteen days, living upon berries and vegetables that he was able to secure from the garden. After suffering for five days from the arrow in his neck, he cut it out with his pocket knife and dressed the wound using horseradish leaves and water from the creek. His hip wounds were so bad he couldn't travel. Soldiers found him and brought him to Mount Idaho where he finally recovered. Grandfather came into Mount Idaho several days after Mr. Price and I arrived. —Maggie Manuel (six years old)[33]

Although in later years Maggie Manuel remembered having seen her mother and brother dead, her story was not corroborated by others nor were any bones found in the ashes of the house after the Nez Perce burned it. What actually happened to Jeannette Manuel and her baby remains a mystery. A tombstone was erected to her memory in the cemetery at Mount Idaho.

The raiding party passed through here on June 15; on June 26, John Manuel was finally rescued.

Next we left the ridge and went down on the bottom to Manuel's on White Bird. We went inside the gate and looked at the ruins of the fire. A few of the soldiers strayed down to the creek and what was their surprise to see sitting in a little shed, which the Indians had spared, a white man whom we all soon found to be Jack Manuel, whom we had reported as among the killed. He had been wounded in the back of the neck with an arrow and had also been shot in the hips. Our next task was to get him out and away to safety.

We soon fixed a pole in a broken buggy that was standing near and by fastening what spare ropes we had to the buggy and to the pommels of our saddles we succeeded in getting him away. Finding that we were not making headway fast enough our captain sent to Captain Miller for two pack mules which we soon had. Then, turning the pole into

One of the three red-coated warriors: Wahlitits, Sarpsis Ilpilp, or Tipyahlanah Kapskaps (Strong Eagle). (Photo courtesy of Idaho State Historical Society.)

shafts we soon got to camp where we turned Mr. Manuel over to his friends who were to take him to Mount Idaho the next day. It had rained all day and we had had a hard day's work. —W. S. Clark (Walla Walla volunteer)[34]

Indian Camp

During the White Bird battle, the bands of Joseph, White Bird, and Toohoolhoolzote were camped along White Bird Creek, in the home territory of Chief White Bird's band.

We moved over to White Bird Creek, sixteen miles away, and there encamped, intending to collect our stock before leaving; but the soldiers attacked us and the first battle was fought. We numbered in that battle sixty men, and the soldiers a hundred. The fight lasted but a few minutes, when the soldiers retreated before us for twelve miles. —Chief Joseph

Part of the reason so few warriors met the attackers was that kegs of whisky had been discovered in the stores farther down White Bird Creek.

I was drunk the night and morning of the battle as were a great many of the young men and even the older men. —Whylimlex (Black Feather)[35]

It was not yet the break of day when scouts came to the village with word that soldiers were coming. There was stirring in the tepees, warriors preparing to meet the soldiers before they could reach our camp. The sun was up when mounted soldiers were seen. Mounted warriors rode to flank the enemy while others hurried to the attack in front and near sides. I was on a horse but kept at a distance. Warriors rode one by one, scattered out in long lines. Soldiers were close together, and the first shots—one—three— came from them, then the clatter of shots fast and unbroken. Many soldiers went to the ground at the first volley, their horses rearing and whirling every way. Indians and soldiers are close together. The war-whoop is heard above the guns, and there was shouting from the soldiers. —Eelahweemah (About Asleep, fourteen years old)[36]

After seeing the battlefield close up, continue 2.0 miles into White Bird and turn east on the road that connects to US 95 in 0.4 mile. Turn north on US 95 and drive up the White Bird grade for 3.3 miles to the Wayside Exhibit Shelter, to see an overview of the White Bird battlefield.

Join the Mainstream Traveler at the Wayside Exhibit Shelter.

Jackson Sundown, a twelve-year-old horse-herding boy in 1877, is pictured here in 1918 dressed as a warrior who is "stripped as for war." (Photo courtesy of Nez Perce National Historical Park.)

For the Mainstream Traveler

Wayside Exhibit Shelter to White Bird

Battle of White Bird

Five warriors…had been sent out from the other [west] side of the valley as a peace party to meet the soldiers. These warriors had instructions from the chiefs not to fire unless fired upon. Of course they carried a white flag. Peace might be made without fighting….

From the north echoed a rifle report, and right away a white man on a white horse came riding swiftly south…. He did not look like a soldier. A big white hat, he was dressed more like a citizen. When he came closer, we knew him…. It was Chapman, called by the whites a squaw man! Having an Indian wife was why he had been friends. He and my uncle, Old Yellow Wolf, had lived in the same house, just as brothers. Now he was the first enemy we see. Changed, and trying to kill each other. It was he who fired the first shot we had just heard. Fired on our peace party.—Yellow Wolf[37]

84

Several, maybe twenty, soldiers followed close after Chapman. There was a bugler and when the party all stopped, this bugler rode a little ahead of them. He began calling orders on his trumpet. Otstotpoo [Fire Body] said to me, "You now watch! I will make a good shot and kill that bugler!"

He did make the long-distance shot, and dead dropped the bugler from his horse. Chapman and his soldiers whirled and rode rapidly away from there. They did not give Otstotpoo a chance for another shot. He had fired the first shot from our side and killed.... It was good to get the bugler who called the General's orders to his fighting soldiers.—Two Moon[38]

One bugler was dead, and the other one could not find his trumpet. With no means of communicating with the troops, confusion reigned among the soldiers.

Unlike the trained white soldier, who is guided by the bugle call, the Indian goes into battle on his own mind's guidance. The swift riding here against the troops was done mostly by the younger men.

All the warriors, whoever gets ready, mount their horses and go. — Weyahwahtsitskan (John Miles)[39]

This close-up view of the White Bird battlefield was taken in the early 1900s. (Photo courtesy of Idaho State Historical Society.)

A red-blanketed warrior (with an intriguing S.I.— Sarpsis Ilpilp?—crossed out) rides his war horse. (Photo courtesy of Idaho State Historical Society.)

> *The three men with me now began shooting. A long distance! I, with only bow and arrows, could do nothing.*—Yellow Wolf[40]

Only a few of the Nez Perce had rifles. Many were armed only with bows and arrows, muskets, or cap-and-ball revolvers.

> *The warriors charging the soldiers left flank were just a small force. Some of them middle aged and some quite past that time of life. They routed the volunteers from a rocky butte. Not all the warriors of this band had guns.*— Weyahwahtsitskan (John Miles)[41]

> *The few volunteers who went with us, saw but little of the fight. They were the first to break and run.*—Sgt. John P. Schorr[42]

> *Upon the first fire of the Indians the soldiers broke ranks and retreated and the officers could not rally them to face the enemy, that the Indians pursued them about 16 miles...firing constantly.*—Lewiston Teller, June 23, 1877

> *It is a bad mixup for the soldiers. They do not stand before that sweeping charge and rifle fire of the Indians. Their horses go wild, throwing the riders. Many of their saddles turned when the horses whirled, all badly scared of the noisy guns. Soldiers who can, remount, and many without guns dash away in retreat. It was a wild, deadly racing with the warriors pressing hard to head them off.*—Weyahwahtsitskan (John Miles)[43]

It was a wild battle and over quickly. Soldiers seemed poor shots. No Indian was touched by a bullet in all of this battle. In other parts of the field two warriors were light wounded but none killed anywhere.—Two Moon[44]

The soldiers do not hold for more than five or ten minutes. Now running from the battle, they are dropping like hunted birds.

   With other boys, I ran my horse as racing for about two miles. We kept near the warriors chasing the soldiers. About half way to the foot of the mountain, the horse of my brother, nine or ten years old, Teh-to-honet [No Leggins] gave out. He said to me: "Give me your horse!" I got off my horse. Soldiers were not far away and one was killed close by. His horse came running to us, where we were holding our cayuses. My brother made for that horse and took off the canteenus [pockets]. A six-shooter was in a scabbard, a "44", and he gave it to me. I then had two pistols. Another soldier was killed just ahead of us and I got his gun. I did not use it. I was too small to handle the rifle.—Eelahweemah (About Asleep, fourteen years old)[45]

I was drunk that night. Next morning they missed me, and I must have lain out all night in the bushes where one woman found me. My wife said to me, "What are you doing here? Everybody has gone for the fighting."

   "Where is my horse?" I asked her. "Tied out there; your best horse!" she answered. I jumped on my horse and hurried away without my weapon. Not all had guns and one must have taken mine.... I overtook an old Indian and I asked if he had my gun. He pulled out an old-time pistol with one bullet and the last powder and cap in place. I took it and went on.

   I came to a soldier thrown from his horse. Perhaps he was wounded. I rode up to him, but instead of receiving me and asking me questions, he pointed his gun and made to shoot me. As he raised his gun I drew the old pistol with its last bullet. I shot first and he fell backwards and did not move....

   I jumped to the ground and took his gun and belt of cartridges. I left the dead soldier the old pistol as a present. Laid it on his breast.—Husis Owyeen (Wounded Head)[46]

I was about twenty-one snows of age and unmarried when the war broke. The first battle was on Sapalwit [Sunday] early in the morning. Many of the young men were drunk but, never a whiskey drinker, I was cold sober.

   I had a rifle, an old-time musket loaded from the muzzle. Not a good gun for meeting soldiers with breech-loading army guns. In going to the place selected for the battle, no one warrior waited for another. So stripped for war, I mounted my horse and rode swiftly along with the strung out riders, some of them carrying bows and arrows only. Soon the soldiers started firing. After making the first shot with my old musket, I found that I had left the ramrod down at camp. Having no way to reload the gun I thought, "I will get a rifle somewhere!"

I was still holding the musket when about eight soldiers were surrounded. Because of lacking ramrod I missed firing at these soldiers. But they were all killed and I made for one of their guns.... I now had two guns and gave the musket to another man.—Tipyahlahnah Elassanin (Roaring Eagle)[47]

One of the things I meant to tell you yesterday was the active part the Indian squaws take in these fights our soldiers have had. They follow along after the men, holding fresh horses and bringing water right in the midst of all the commotion. Colonel Perry says that in the fight of White Bird Canyon, he saw one Indian...have as many as three changes of horses brought him by his squaw. See what an advantage that is to them. As soon as their horses are a little blown, they take a fresh one, and our poor soldiers have perhaps ridden their[s] fifty or sixty miles before the fight begins.—Emily FitzGerald (Army doctor's wife), July 12, 1877[48]

I downed one soldier, and then kept after the others. My wife runs to that fallen soldier, and while he was trying to get up on his knees, she unbuckled his cartridge belt from his waist. Taking it, she ran to another of the fallen enemies, and took a belt and a box of cartridges from him with this supply of ammunition, she came running back to me. I could use those cartridges in captured soldiers guns.—Two Moon[49]

The soldiers were now riding hard in an effort to escape with their lives. With the other warriors, I, Two Moons, and Otstotpoo [Fire Body] mounted our horses and set out chasing the soldiers.—Two Moon[50]

The Nez Perce pursued the soldiers for thirteen miles, to within four miles of Mount Idaho.

The whole force guarding the horses, Indians and whites, broke and ran, some for Mount Idaho and some for La Pwai, leaving the horses to run loose over the prairies.—The New York Times, June 20, 1877

Two Moon and his wife, Lets-Koho-Kateswehien. He was middle-aged in 1877. (Photo courtesy of MASC.)

With the assistance of Capt. Parnell, an old Crimean soldier, the scattered troops were rallied at the head of the grade, reduced to something like order, and marched into Mt. Idaho.—E. J. Bunker (Mount Idaho volunteer)[51]

One of the major gains of the battle was the improvement in the arsenal of the Nez Perce.

> *The chiefs held a council just below our village....*
>   *The chiefs said, "Bring all guns you take from the soldiers."*
>   *The guns were brought, and one man appointed to count them. He counted and reported, "Sixty-three guns!"*
>   *There were not so many pistols, and not much account taken of them. They were picked up mostly by women.* —Yellow Wolf[52]

After the Nez Perce scavenged the weapons, other scavengers were at work because the soldier's bodies were not buried until nine or ten days later.

> *The scene of the battle, as I viewed it, showed that there had not been any stand made after they were attacked; as here and there would be found a*

89

dead soldier, who had been overtaken and killed. There were a few instances which proved that some of the soldiers, after being unhorsed, got to some rocks and made a gallant fight before they were finally dispatched, as the empty shells lying around their dead bodies testified.

These dead soldiers were buried where they had fallen, as they were not in a state to be moved to a more suitable burial ground.—George Hunter (captain of the Dayton volunteers)

The burying, however, didn't happen until June 26 and 27.

The dead had been lying for about 12 days before General Howard's command came to bury them. By that time, through the effects of heat, sun, and rain, they were in such a state that when a body was lifted up or rolled over into his grave, his hair and whiskers would adhere to the ground, tearing off the scalp and skin, which gave to the uninitiated the appearance of their being scalped and caused the circulation of the rumor.—Lt. Albert G. Forse[53]

My own company buried eighteen of the thirty-three bodies which had lain ten days exposed to the elements, the hot sun by day, until they were swollen and changed into awful shapes, too dreadful for our eyes and olfactory nerves, so we had to run a distance every little while during the making of the shallow graves in the rocky soil with entrenching bayonets, and trying to find enough of our scarce blankets into which to pull the bodies for a semblance of decent interment.—Lt. Harry L. Bailey[54]

From the overlook, continue down the remaining 1,800 feet of the White Bird Grade in second or third gear, for 3.3 miles. After crossing the bridge over White Bird Creek, turn east and follow the paved road for 0.4 mile into the town of White Bird.

Join the Intrepid Traveler at White Bird or continue with the Mainstream Traveler there.

For the Mainstream Traveler

White Bird to the junction of old US 95 and new US 95

White Bird

Jim Baker, a seventy-four-year-old bachelor, had his homestead and orchard near the center of present-day White Bird. Just five weeks before, he had submitted a petition to General Howard complaining of the vandalism being committed by the Nez Perce. Because Baker's house had a stone foundation, he tried to talk the Manuel family into coming to the safety of his home, but he was killed by the second raiding party on June 15 between here and Manuel's house, two miles up the creek. His body lay along the roadside, where he fell, for a few weeks before a scouting party found it in late July. James Baker was buried at Mount Idaho.

> Continue west through White Bird on old US 95 or River Street. This road parallels White Bird Creek for the next 1.1 miles to its confluence with the Salmon River.

Mouth of White Bird Creek

One wonders why the first settlers were attracted to places like this where there is just about enough flat land for a house and a small garden. The advantage of being located at the confluence of White Bird Creek and the Salmon River must have outweighed the lack of flat land, for it was here that the Benedict homestead had been located since 1868.

Samuel Benedict's home doubled as a store. He had had at least one run-in with the members of White Bird's band.

> *Motsqueh [Chipmunk] was found killed near the mouth of White Bird Creek, where a mean white man kept a saloon store. Chipmunk was not reckoned a bad Indian and I do not know for what reason he was killed. He would not have done anything for which he should be shot to death. This saloon man was always robbing Indians by keeping change money coming to them when buying anything from him. He never gave back their change no difference if cents or dollars.*—Peopeo Tholekt (Bird Alighting)[55]

> *The first victim was a man who had a little store on the White Bird. They killed him but did not harm his family. It seems this trader had some*

91

The homestead of Samuel and Isabel Benedict was located at the mouth of White Bird Creek. Compare this photo to the scene now existing there. (Photo courtesy of Idaho State Historical Society.)

difficulty with an Indian and had killed him some time before. I was a member of the Grand Jury at Lewiston, when the case was brought before us, but from the evidence we judged the man not to blame and returned not a true indictment. This matter, however, had rankled in the minds of the Indians, and they sought revenge by killing him.—Frank Redfield (sub-agent of Nez Perce Reservation)[56]

The trio of the first raiding party found Samuel Benedict out looking for his cows when they rode by on June 14. Benedict had wounded Sarpsis Ilpilp [Red Moccasin Tops] in the incident mentioned above. Sarpsis Ilpilp now returned the favor, shooting Benedict in the legs. He played dead, and the warriors rode on. Two days later the second raiding party returned to the Benedict house.

I went into the garden for lettuce and onions for supper. On my return, I saw a body of mounted Indians approaching, and ran into the house, crying "The Indians are coming!" August [Bacon, a Frenchman] saw them, and taking up the gun, placed himself in the door. In the meantime, they had dismounted, and some were in the yard. They had their arms, and were painted.... My husband...told me to take the children and fly. I said, "No, I

92

won't leave you." He replied, "Think of the children, and save them!" I started, but on reaching the back gate, saw some Indians watching me from the hillside, and returned to the house....

Glancing into the front room, I saw August...and at the instant I looked, he fell backward into the house. I flew to the creek, and rushed with my children into the water. Crouching low among the reeds, we escaped their observation.... When all was still, I cautiously crept to the house under cover of the night. August lay just as I had seen him fall.... I could find no clew to my husband's whereabouts.... He was never found.

Covering August's body with a quilt, I left all that once was home, and set out with my little ones for Mt. Idaho, where my two older children were in school.... I hid in the daytime and traveled at night. On reaching the Manuel home, I went in and found Mrs. Manuel alone with her children. She showed me her knee, and told me what the Indians had done. I tried to induce her to go with me, but she said she would not leave her husband and father, who were wounded and needed her aid. I went on, keeping near the creek, not daring to approach the road. At the least sound, I would wade into the creek, stand still, and listen. When it would grow quiet, I would go on again. In this way, I at length reached Whitebird grade, and was in hiding among the rocks below the grade when the main body of the Indians passed down, the night before the battle. I heard them passing all night and dared not move. I could hear their children crying, and the squaws talking. I had eaten nothing for three days. The Indians had eaten every morsel in the house before they left, and I could not get even a crust at Mrs. Manuel's. We were almost dead with fatigue, hunger and exposure. My babe could not retain even the drop of water that little Frankie carried from the creek in the heel of its tiny shoe. That morning, about dawn, after the Indians had ceased to pass, I was rejoiced to hear the voices of white men [the soldiers] who were approaching my place of concealment, and sent Frankie to make our presence known.... They gave us something to eat.

I begged them to send us on to the Prairie. They said it would require a strong escort to do that with safety, and they had no men to spare, as they expected to engage the Indians in battle before they could cross to the south side of Salmon river with the settlers' stock. They left us and went on, with the promise to return in two days. They came in less than an hour, and in a hurry too, with, seemingly, the whole Nez Perce nation at their heels. They came—at first a few; then the way was lined with flying soldiers, and riderless steeds with turned saddles and flowing reins. As the poor animals *bounded past my hiding place, I could hear their hard-drawn breathings and feel the flecks of foam thrown from their nostrils....*

They seemed to have forgotten us, until one Charlie Crooks, a young man of Grangeville, said: "Halt, men, for God's sake! You are not going to leave that woman and her children! This is where we left them!" Springing from his horse, he reached the children one to each of two soldiers whom he succeeded in stopping on the steep hillside long enough to take them, and, catching up a flying horse that had left its dead rider behind, he lifted me into the saddle. Then, remounting, he rode off at a furious gallop before the fast approaching savages, telling me to cling tight and let the horse go. I hung to the saddle until it turned, then vainly tried to stop the animal by holding to the bridle. I was at length left on the road. Thankful that my children were saved, I again felt myself at the mercy of the Indians, who soon overtook me, and after robbing me, forced me to go back with them. An Indian tossed me on behind another mounted Indian, and they took me with them. They met some squaws, who compelled them to set me down. We were at the foot of the grade.—Isabel Benedict (White Bird resident)[57]

The warrior who carried Isabel Benedict on his horse told the story somewhat differently.

We now turned back toward camp lower down the White Bird. While going on the trail I looked back and saw a bunch of Nez Perces. They called to me, "Look ahead to the hillside. See what is coming toward you!" I looked. It was a white woman making her escape down the hillside. I rode to her. She made a sign that I do not kill her. I motioned her to get on the horse behind me. She did so and I turned back to the trail where the other Indians met me.... With the woman I rode on down the trail, but not in view of the camp. I continued along the hill out of sight of the rest of the people, down to the gulch where I stopped. I think she was scared when I told her to get off to the ground. I instructed her to escape with her life, and I shook hands with her. She went and I rode back to camp.—Husis Owyeen (Wounded Head)[58]

The ground was strewn with men and horses, who had fallen in the first furious charge by the Indians who so completely surprised and defeated Perry's troops.

The Indians were already stripping the bodies of men and beasts, securing arms, accouterments, etc. Saddened and disheartened, I again set out to climb the grade. I traveled all night, and just at dawn, reached a point near

Henry Johnson's place on Whitebird mountain. Seeing someone approaching, and supposing it to be an Indian, I hid in some willows near a straw stack.

Imagine my surprise and delight when I realized that it was a friend coming to my rescue. The soldiers had reported me as left on the road, and Mr. Ruby (Robie), he who had left his gun in care of my husband, hearing their story, and not being content to await the slow movement of the troops, had gone out to look for me. He took me in safety to Mt. Idaho. —Isabel Benedict (White Bird resident)[59]

August Bacon is buried in the cemetery a mile down the road. The body of Samuel Benedict was never seen again.

On June 26, General Howard camped at the mouth of White Bird Creek while his troops buried the dead on the battlefield.

Nothing in particular occurred this night, except that a young lieutenant mistook one of his guards for an Indian and shot him, while out relieving the guard. I think he killed his man. —George Hunter (captain of the Dayton volunteers)

Salmon River

It was distressing to see the beautiful homes that had been destroyed. —George Hunter (captain of the Dayton volunteers)

One year later, a Nez Perce warrior echoed a similar sentiment.

Then the places through which I was riding came to my heart. It drew memories of old times, of my friends, when they were living on this river. My friends, my brothers, my sisters! All were gone! No tepees anywhere along the river. I was alone. —Yellow Wolf[60]

Continue driving south on old US 95, which now parallels the Salmon River. It is 0.5 mile to a bridge over the Salmon. Continuing south, 0.2 mile past the bridge entrance is a large turnout on the east side of the road. Park here if you want to walk up to French Cemetery, in which some of the raid victims are buried.

From the road, angle uphill to GPS N45° 44.531', W116° 19.396'.

95

Cemetery

Three tombstones, enclosed by a metal fence, are in this cemetery located under a hackberry tree on BLM land. William Osborne, Harry Mason, François Chodoze, and August Bacon, all victims of the Nez Perce raiders, are buried here, although not all the graves are marked.

> *Having obtained permission from General Howard, I with a part of my company, went up the river a mile or two, to where one Mason and others [Osborne and Chodoze] had been killed and burned up in their cabins. My recollection is, that in all there were three killed and burned here. We collected all of the remains we could find (there was little left but the feet, which were incased in boots), and buried them.*—George Hunter (captain of the Dayton volunteers)

Continue on old US 95 for 0.7 mile to the junction with new US 95.

Join the Mainstream Traveler for the sidetrip to Fiddle Creek. Or join the Adventurous Traveler for the sidetrip to Pittsburg Landing or for the trip to Cottonwood via Pilgrim Ridge Road. Or join the Mainstream Traveler for the return to Grangeville.

For the Intrepid Traveler

White Bird to the junction of old US 95 and new US 95

Miles: 3.5

Map: Nez Perce National Forest

0.7 mile west of White Bird, turn north across a narrow bridge. Continue on this narrow access road about 0.5 mile to a pullout.

H. C. Brown's Store

While the raiders were at Benedict's, H. C. Brown, his wife, and father-in-law made their narrow escape. They were rowing across the river just as the Nez Perce warriors arrived at their store. After wandering for two weeks, they were discovered near Cottonwood. For the conclusion of this story, see **Cottonwood Skirmishes** on page 118.

The night of the 14th the Indians spent in debauchery at Brown's store, which they looted, helping themselves freely to the goods and liquors on the shelves. They remained until morning, when they started for the Mason ranch.—An Illustrated History of North Idaho

All the buildings on Salmon river from Brown's store below the mouth of White Bird up to Slate Creek were burned and all the cattle and horses driven off.—Lewiston Teller, June 30, 1877

Return to old US 95 and continue south for 1.8 miles to the junction with new US 95.

Join the Mainstream Traveler for the sidetrip to Fiddle Creek. Or join tthe Adventurous Traveler for the sidetrip to Pittsburg Landing or for the trip to Cottonwood via Pilgrim Ridge Road. Or join the Mainstream Traveler for the return to Grangeville.

For the Mainstream Traveler

Sidetrip
Junction of old and new US 95 to Fiddle Creek

This sidetrip traces the routes of the first and second raiding parties as well as the route of the Nez Perce immediately after the White Bird Battle. Follow US 95 south for 5.4 miles to Horseshoe Bend paralleling the Salmon River while you drink in eyefuls of the gorgeous canyon scenery. Ridges rise 1,000 to 1,400 feet above the road.

Wahlitits/Larry Ott Land

Look off to the west halfway between mileposts 218 and 217 as the river bends west and runs out of sight briefly. Eagle Robe and his son Wahlitits (Shore Crossing) cultivated the land west of the river.

Larry Ott, an old miner from Florence…asked the old Indian [Eagle Robe] for permission to build a hut on his land. This was readily granted. After a time, he asked for a piece of ground to make a garden. The Indian at first refused, finally granting him permission to enclose a small potato patch. Next year, he wanted to enlarge his enclosure for an orchard and vineyard. The Indian

97

*objected, Larry Ott insisted, and went into the woods to make rails on the
Indian's claim. The old Indian told him the land was his by right, and that
he must desist. Larry went ahead and commenced to haul out the rails. The
Indian seeing him with a load of rails, stepped out in front of his team and
shook his blanket at the horses. Larry drew a pistol and shot him from the
blind side.... Larry then fled to the river.... The old Indian lived nine days
after being shot.*

*This caused a great commotion among the settlers as well as the Indians.
They held a council of Indians and settlers to determine what to do. The
council was presided over by Whitebird on the part of the Indians. On behalf
of the settlers were Messrs. Norman Gould, Henry Elfers, Samuel Benedict,
and others. Gould told me that, in answer to all their offers or suggestions in
the way of settlement, Whitebird would say, "Give us Larry Ott." The council
broke up without arriving at any settlement. Things went on thus for a year
or more.* —Augustishee[61]

*The first day of March, 1875, Larry Ott, who lived on the south side of
Salmon River, had a quarrel with an Indian, which terminated in the death
of the latter. The grand jury had the killing of this Indian by Ott under*

*Larry Ott (Photo courtesy of Idaho
State Historical Society)*

Wetyetmas Wahyakt, later known as John Minthon, acted as the horseholder for Wahlitits and Sarpsis Ilpilp. He was the only member of the trio to survive the flight. His part in the initial raiding party did not become known until after his death in the 1920s. (Photo courtesy of National Park Service, Nez Perce National Historical Park, Betty Rudfelt Collection.)

consideration, and being unable to find sufficient evidence of guilt, brought in no bill.—Gen. O. O. Howard

When Wahlitits (Shore Crossing) left Tolo Lake with his cousin Sarpsis Ilpilp (Red Moccasin Tops) and his nephew Wetyetmas Wahyakt (Swan Necklace), his intention was to come here to kill Larry Ott and thereby avenge the death of his father. Larry Ott, however, was not at home. So the trio rode on.

From Horseshoe Bend, continue south on US 95 for 15.6 miles. Turn around at Fiddle Creek at milepost 201. Continue this sidetrip with the Mainstream Traveler at Fiddle Creek.

For the Mainstream Traveler

Sidetrip (continued)
Fiddle Creek to John Day Creek

Now, head north on US 95 for 1.5 miles. If you feel like you've driven a long way out of your way, imagine what the trip would have been like on horseback. Carver Creek is located about halfway between milepost 202 and 203. This stream is difficult to see from the highway. If your windows are open and you are driving slowly, you may hear it, however.

Carver Creek

When it became apparent that Larry Ott, the intended quarry, was not at his home near Horseshoe Bend, the trio that constituted the first raiding party continued south to Carver Creek. Here, on a small bar alongside the river, lived a former sailor, fifty-two-year-old Richard Devine, who had a harsh reputation. He set his dogs on any passing Indian, whether or not they were trespassing on his fenced field. He had also killed a Nez Perce woman, Dakoopin (Wounded Leg), for removing a white man's horse from her garden. Civil authorities overlooked this murder. But punishment eventually did overtake him late on the night of June 13. Leaving seventeen-year-old Wetyetmas Wahyakt (Swan Necklace) outside to hold the horses, the two warriors, Wahlitits (Shore Crossing) and Sarpsis Ilpilp (Red Moccasin Tops) entered Devine's cabin.

> *The two older of these young men met an old white settler, a bachelor, who was rather mean. Any time the Indians visited to have a talk with him, they were driven away. He killed one crippled man. The Indians never had done any wrong to him....*
>
> *They killed this white settler.... They took a stallion that he kept, and it was brought over to Camas Prairie to show what they had done.*—Two Moon[62]

Continuing north now on US 95, drive 6.0 miles to John Day Creek.

Richard Devine's cabin on Carver Creek has long since disappeared. This was the place where the first murder of a white by Nez Perce occurred on June 14, 1877. (Photo courtesy of Idaho State Historical Society.)

John Day Creek

He expressed his opinion, that if the Indians had commenced a war, it would have been Harry Elfers and the people at the ranch they would have killed.—Helen Mason Walsh[63]

Henry Elfers had located his ranch on John Day Creek. Elfers habitually sent his dogs to attack any passing Indians and at the same time warned off any native passersby with his rifle.

Elfers was an old enemy. He opposed prosecuting Larry Ott for killing Chief Eagle Robe; declaring openly, "He should not be prosecuted for killing a dog."—Camille Williams (Nez Perce interpreter)[64]

Early on the morning of June 14, the trio of Wahlitits (Shore Crossing), Sarpsis Ilpilp (Red Moccasin Tops), and Wetyetmas Wahyakt (Swan Necklace) laid in ambush waiting for Elfers to drive his stock to pasture on the plateau east of the highway.

The three men started down and arrived at John Day ranch early morning and staked their horses in oat field so the whites would be attracted to that direction so to be easy killing and it was. The owner, Henry Elfers first came and noticed the horses staked in the field. He came to the horses swearing. Sarpsis [Red Moccasin Tops] was about to jump up and shoot him, Wahlitits [Shore Crossing] told him to keep still, to let him come closer. When he was about a rod away, Elfers noticed a gun, turned and ran back. Wahlitits started after him and grabbed him and downed Henry. Then Sarpsis caught

101

Henry Elfers' ranch on John Day Creek was where the first raiding party killed Elfers, his nephew, and his hired man on June 14, 1877. (Photo courtesy of Idaho State Historical Society.)

up to them and shot Elfers dead.—Camille Williams (Nez Perce interpreter)[65]

After killing Elfers, they shot his nephew, Henry Beckrodge, and the hired man, Robert Bland. Then the three men took the finest of his horses, a rifle, and a handful of cartridges and headed north, toward the Tolo Lake encampment. Catherine Elfers was churning butter in the milk house while all this was going on and didn't hear the gunfire over the sound of the rushing creek. She even saw the Nez Perce threesome leave, but did not suspect anything.

Join the Intrepid Traveler for a sidetrip to the John Day Creek cemetery or continue with the Mainstream Traveler from John Day Creek.

For the Intrepid Traveler

Sidetrip
John Day Creek Cemetery

Miles: 1.2, round-trip
Map: none

Just before crossing John Day Creek, turn east on the narrow dirt road that runs alongside the stream. In 0.4 mile, turn sharply and steeply to the northwest and park. Walk through the gate and close it behind you. It is 0.2 mile up to the cemetery.

John Day Creek Cemetery

As you stand at the cemetery and look out toward the fields to the south, you may well be looking at the area where the three Nez Perce ambushed the three white men. Henry Elfers and Robert Beckrodge, who were killed in that field, are buried in this cemetery. Also buried here is Richard Devine, from Carver Creek, who was the first casualty of the Nez Perce war.

> *On the Salmon River a few miles above the mouth of White Bird Creek is the grave of a white man killed by Nez Perces at the outbreak of hostilities. The history of this case as told by a half-blood of good repute, is, that before the war, a young married Indian couple were met in their forest camp by this same white man, who, having the ascendancy in arms, subjected the woman to unwarranted indignities. For this was his life forfeited.—* Anonymous Nez Perce[66]

Return to US 95 and rejoin the Mainstream Traveler.

For the Mainstream Traveler

Sidetrip (continued)
John Day Creek to junction of old and new US 95

From John Day Creek, proceed north on US 95 for 5.1 miles. Just at the north end of Box Canyon, turn northeast onto the narrow, paved road that goes into the town of Slate Creek. Proceed along this old highway for 0.6 mile to the stream named Slate Creek.

Slate Creek

Before John and Caroline Wood settled on Slate Creek in 1862, this area was a traditional Nez Perce village site. Over the years, Wood had become a friend to the Nez Perce, helped, perhaps, by the fact that he paid the original Nez Perce owner for his land.

The second raiding party of seventeen warriors visited Wood.

> *Not all whites were against the Nez Perces. I know two men who lived up Slate Creek, who were our best friends....*
>
> *One of these men was Wood....*

103

Wood saw the Indians coming after they had killed some whites. He stopped them and said, "Tie your horses and come in. We will have a talk."

Chief Yellow Bull, Sarpsis Ilppilp [Red Moccasin Tops], Wahlitits [Shore Crossing] and others were in the bunch. They went into this white man's house as requested. Men, who were working for this man, got scared. They thought to be killed. The friendly white man spoke to Yellow Bull, "I know you people! For many years I have known you very well. Also, I know the actions of the whites toward you. The government is cheating you of your lands. You Indians have been enduring wrongs for many years. While you have remained peaceable, not so the whites. You have lost good horses and cattle by thieving white men. Miners have taken possession of your country, digging out your gold. Your people have been killed; many of them. Now you are making resistance. One thing I want to tell you. Stay here around Snake River. This is a rough country. Do not leave it! Here you will always have good food. Get ready! Meet the soldiers and fight them."

They then shook hands, saying good-bye. The white man spoke final words to them, "Boys, I hope you good luck!" —Red Elk[67]

The town of Slate Creek as it appeared in 1889. (Photo courtesy of The Historical Museum at St. Gertrude, Cottonwood, Idaho.)

104

Despite their friendship with the Nez Perce, the settlers were uneasy and built a stockade on the south side of Slate Creek.

The settlers congregated at Slate Creek...where a stockade was built enclosing the house and buildings of Mr. Cone. One of these structures was

Yellow Bull, a sub-chief of the White Bird band, led sixteen young warriors of the second raiding party on June 14, 1877. (Photo courtesy of Smithsonian Office of Anthropology, Bureau of American Ethnology Collection.)

of stone which, at night, was used as a shelter for the women and children, or most of them.

Our stockade made by digging a trench three feet deep entirely around the buildings and setting fir logs close together, then a log over each crack. These timbers being very solid and 11 and 12 feet long, also 10 to 14 inches in diameter, we felt quite safe behind them at that time as there were no high power rifles…in those days.

In the stockade were some 40 women and children. To defend them and do the work on the defences there were 23 men, poorly armed. Five of them having breach loaders. The writer had one of these besides an old muzzle loader. For the breech loader he had five cartridges.—H. W. Cone (Slate Creek resident)[68]

105

Although the feared attack never materialized, the little fort did serve as sanctuary for some of the women and children who were victims of the second raid.

After the Battle of White Bird, the Nez Perce camped just north of Slate Creek.

> *Exulting over their victory fought with the troops on the 17th, the Indians came the next day in force to Slate Creek. They moved their camp to Horse Shoe Bend...and were in sight of our stockade continuously, coming twice to talk to us under truce.... Some of these Indians had contracted small accounts for groceries they bought at the little store run by Wood and Fockler. The little bills were all paid, the Indians sending the different sums to settle them by the warriors who came to talk to us. They said they might not come back as there were too many soldiers, but they that would never give up until forced to do so.—H. W. Cone (Slate Creek resident)[69]*

Proceed 0.5 mile back to US 95. Then travel north on US 95 for 1.3 miles to the first of two bridges over the Salmon River, at mile marker 216.

Horseshoe Bend

East of the southern bridge over the Salmon River, the trio returning from the first raid on June 14 met Charles Cone, a resident of Slate Creek.

> *They told him the Indians were on the Warpath, killing lots of people, and naming most of the residents of Slate Creek, said for them to stay home.... With this warning they rode away. Mr. Cone, after the Indians were out of sight, returned home, and gave the alarm, which was carried to all the white settlers above on the Salmon River and as far down as...the Mason store.—H. W. Cone (Slate Creek resident)[70]*

Continue north for 0.2 mile, crossing the next bridge over the Salmon River.

106

Crossing the Salmon River

Just north of the bridges is where the three nontreaty bands of Joseph, White Bird, and Toohoolhoolzote crossed the river after the Battle of White Bird.

You have asked me how we crossed the Salmon and other deep, swift streams with our families and goods. I will tell you all, how done. Owning that country, the Nez Perces knew all such streams. Crossed them often without difficulty. They understood to manage.

At this crossing was only one canoe. But we had plenty of buffalo skins. With them we made hide boats. In making such boat, the hide, hair side up, was spread flat on the ground. Across the hide were laid green willow or other limber poles about the thickness of your thumb. The hide and poles were bent up and lashed to other bent poles forming a long circled rim. This rim was on the outside. That was all. Such boats carried big loads, and children and old people rode on top of the packs. Everything—tepee covers, cooking pots, pans, blankets—all were ferried in these boats. No paddles used. Boats were hauled by ponies guided by men. Two, maybe three or four, ponies to a boat. Two men swam at the sides to steady it.—Yellow Wolf[71]

After burying the dead at White Bird, General Howard's troops took up the chase and arrived on the east side of Horseshoe Bend on June 29.

The women could not sleep when soldiers were so near, so we moved camp high into the mountains.

But the warriors remained behind, hiding among ridges, waiting for soldiers to cross. Waited until the sun went down, and the darkness came. Then we all went home, to the camp.

Came the morning, and when some of us scouted back we saw the soldiers still on north side of the Salmon. They were making to cross.... We waited half a sun for the soldiers, but none crossed. Then the chiefs said, "We will move out of their way."

Scouts remained to watch, and the families packed up and moved about twenty miles down the Salmon and camped.—Yellow Wolf[72]

When Gen. Howard raised the American flag in his camp on Salmon river, the Indians on the opposite side raised a red blanket and invited the troops across.... Many of the Indians were in sight on the opposite side,...he counted 87 in one circle, that they were tantalizing the troops, shaking their blankets at them and daring them to cross and fight with them.—Lewiston Teller, July 7, 1877

107

Camp on Salmon River, Idaho. Have just crossed the swift and dangerous Salmon River in a skiff with four men and four oarsmen. The stream at this point is about 200 yards wide, with a plunging current. By a good deal of labor and loss of time, a large rope has been stretched across.... This morning a number of horses and mules were made to swim the river and a famous swim they made of it. Some of them were turned over and over, and others carried away down the stream, but I think all got over.—Lt. Harry L. Bailey, June 30, 1877[73]

We have been two days in making a difficult crossing of the Salmon River. Joseph was on the opposite bank when the troops reached the stream and paraded his warriors to our view with much pomp. He disappeared as we prepared to cross.—Capt. Stephen Jocelyn, July 1, 1877[74]

Quite a contrast to the Nez Perce account of their crossing! One scouting party must have been among the first to cross the river.

We pushed on up the mountain.... We found the mountain very steep and hard to climb. On reaching the summit, we soon struck Joseph's trail, which was broad and easily followed, as Joseph had hundreds of horses with him. These trails we followed some distance; then swung around, and returned by way of Pittsburg Landing. Arriving at the summit of the mountain, we tried for some time to attract the attention of those at headquarters on Salmon river, twelve or fifteen miles away, but we failed to "catch their eye."—George Hunter, captain of Dayton volunteers

While the troops had struggled to get across the Salmon River, the Nez Perce were delighted to have them there on the southwest side of the river.

Next morning scouts brought word the soldiers were on our side of the Salmon. This was good. We immediately crossed back to the north side.—Yellow Wolf[75]

It rained all day and all night. Several pack-mules were lost—overboard!—in the steep climb; the animals would slip and flounder in the mud, under heavy loads, and in the struggle to get foothold in some particularly steep places several lost their balance and went rolling down the mountain side, nearly two thousand feet, with frightful velocity. Of course, there was not much pack and very little serviceable mule left when the bottom was reached.—Lt. William R. Parnell[76]

108

From Horseshoe Bend, proceed north on US 95 for 2.6 miles to Skookumchuck Creek. Then 0.4 mile north of the creek, turn west into a large pullout that leads onto a paved road that runs right alongside the river. In 1.5 miles, this frontage road reconnects with US 95. At the junction, look straight ahead to the flat land on the east side of the highway called Cooper Bar.

Cooper Bar

In a cabin on this bar lived Harry Mason and his sister, Helen Walsh, and her two children. Mason's former brother-in-law, William Osborne, lived three-quarters of a mile away, right on the river.

> *Harry Mason whipped two Indians early in the spring. A council of arbitration met to decide who was in fault, Mr. Elfers, a white man…being a member of that council. That decision of the council, as one might have predicted, was unfavorable to the Indians.* —Gen. O. O. Howard[77]

Osborne Cabin

As you continue to sit at the junction of the frontage road with US 95, you have already passed the location of the Osborne cabin, about half a mile back. On June 15, realizing that a raiding party of seventeen warriors was nearby, Helen Mason Walsh, her two children, her brother Harry Mason, his brother-in-law William Osborne, Mrs. Osborne, and the four Osborne children ran from Mason's house down to Osborne's cabin on the river. By this time, the warriors had already killed James Baker, Samuel Benedict, and August Bacon in White Bird.

> *We made a dash for the Osborne cabin, and all got in. One Frenchman, named Louis [Francois Chodoze], was with us….*
>
> *Three men, two women, and six children, all crowded into that two roomed cabin. Waiting for the next move of the Indians; and we did not have long to wait.*
>
> *While Mr. Osborne and the Frenchman were working at the door, Harry was peering intently through the space between the logs…. The Indians were there dismounting. Suddenly my brother stooped lower and thrust the muzzle of his new Winchester rifle between the logs. Mrs. Osborne cried, "Don't shoot! They are friends of ours. Perhaps we can pacify them…"…*
>
> *At Mrs. Osborne's cry, he [Harry Mason] hesitated, and looked around at her, then turned again and prepared to shoot. Then Mr. Osborne turning from the door cried, "For God's sake, don't shoot Harry!" Again my brother*

109

hesitated, but as I could see, reluctantly. Then a volley was fired from the other side; and the bullets came crashing through the window.

Harry sprang off the bed; and they all raised their rifles to fire; but before they could do so, a second volley struck every man.

The Frenchman never moved but once after he fell. Mr. Osborne sprang up again and tried to raise his rifle, shouting, "You devils you!" and then fell back dead.

Harry was not dead, his right arm was shattered and bleeding fearful.

My brother, weak from loss of blood had become delerious.... Then he seemed to rouse himself. The Indians were now breaking in the bedroom door, and he seemed to be conscious of it.

They [the Indians] told us to come out [from underneath the bed]. Mrs. Osborne replied, "No. We will not come out. You will kill our papooses." "No!" one of them answered. "No kill papoose. No kill Kluchmen [wives]. No kill white haired man." This was the command that Chief Joseph had given them, as we learned later.

We still hesitated to come out, until one of them got on the bed; and jumped up and down on it over us. Then we came out, Mrs. Osborne first.

The sight of her husband, lying dead at her feet, seemed to madden her; and fill her with a fierce courage. She commenced to berate the Indians....

As I was endeavoring to come from under the bed with my baby on my arm, one of the Indians took her from me. Another reached down and took my hand to help me up. As he did so, he caught sight of the revolver in my pocket. He...gave me a peculiar look, pushed me back; and reaching down, took it from my pocket. He looked at it closely; and then looked at me; and I thought for a moment, that he was going to turn it on me; but he reached back and stuck it in his belt; and then helped me to my feet.

Then the Indian, who held my baby, placed her back in my arms.... I took my baby, and sat down on the edge of the bed.... The Indians began to drag out the bodies.

They dragged Harry out by his shattered arm. In his distress, he cried out, "Oh shoot me!" And they did—they shot him.

In the meantime we sat together on the bed, our children around us, waiting for whatever our fate might be.

110

Mrs. Osborne, whom I think, had also become distraught in her mind, began to question the Indians concerning the fate of some the settlers with whom we were acquainted.... My mind was in a dazed condition, and seemed benumbed....

We had no idea what they intended doing with us, our mother fears, being mostly for our children. Imagine our relief when they came to the door and said to us, "You go now. You go Lewiston. You go Slate Creek. You go where you like."

Then we heard them getting on their horses; and they rode away down the river, leaving us with our dead.

Slate Creek was nine or ten miles up the river.

The children trudged the weary miles without complaint, though my little boy became completely exhausted; and could walk only while Mrs. Osborne and I held his hands, he walking between us. —Helen Mason Walsh[78]

Mrs. Osborne, whose husband was killed on the bar when Mason was killed, appeared at the residence of Mr. Cone, on Slate creek, three days afterwards, with her little children. The only garments she had on were her stockings and chemise. She was covered with blood, and in every way gave evidence of having received the most inhuman treatment.—George Hunter (captain of Dayton volunteers)

After the battle of White Bird the Indians returned to Mason's store and spent a night in carousing and general debauchery, ending their merry making by burning the buildings.—An Illustrated History of Northern Idaho

As noted in the section on the **Cemetery**, just north of the mouth of White Bird Creek (see page 91), the bodies of Mason, Osborne, and Francois Chodoze were burned along with the buildings. The men's remains were buried twelve days later by the volunteers accompanying General Howard's command.

Turn north on US 95 for 1.0 mile to the junction of old and new US 95.

Continue with the Mainstream Traveler for the return to Grangeville. Or join the Adventurous Traveler for a trip to Cottonwood via Pilgrim Ridge Road. Or join the Adventurous Traveler for a sidetrip to Pittsburg Landing.

For the Mainstream Traveler

Junction of old and new US 95 to Grangeville

Continue driving north on US 95 for 17.6 miles to the junction with Idaho 13 at Grangeville.

Join the Mainstream Traveler at Grangeville at the beginning of the next chapter.

For the Adventurous Traveler

Sidetrip

Junction of old and new US 95 to Pittsburg Landing

Miles: 36.6, round-trip
Map: Nez Perce National Forest

From the junction of old and new US 95, near mile marker 222, turn west on old US 95 and proceed along the river for 0.9 mile. Turn west over the bridge across the Salmon River for 0.1 mile. Then turn south on Deer Creek Road as soon as you have crossed the bridge. This sidetrip will take you to Pittsburg Landing, an area where Chief Toohoolhoolzote's band wintered from 1840 to 1870. The drive is quite scenic, affording spectacular views of both the Salmon River country and Hells Canyon of the Snake River. The steep switchbacks demand first gear.

6.1 miles from the bridge over the Salmon, Deer Creek runs alongside its namesake.

Deer Creek

The 29th [of June] we marched down on to Deer Creek to Ben Browns and camped. it was here that the Indians had been camped while General Howard was crossing the [Salmon] here we was successful in finding a great many caches and distroyed such things as we could not use or carry away, which consisted in.

10,000	lbs of flour	50	Grass bags
2,000	Roots Camas & Co	20	Brass Kettles
250	sugar	2	Do pans
100	tea	4	saddles
75	Camas hooks	6	over coats
25	Axes	6	Robes buffalo
3	drawing Knives		

and a great many articles that I did not make a memorandum of[.] we drove over 147 head of horses.—Luther P. Wilmot (Mount Idaho volunteer)[79]

Continue 10.3 miles on NF 493 down to your choice of Pittsburg Landing or Upper Pittsburg Landing.

Pittsburg Landing

The trip down to Pittsburg Landing has led through the home territory of Chief Toohoolhoolzote's nontreaty band. Sparsely settled even now, the band who lived here originally was not as pressured by white encroachment onto their traditional lands as the nontreaty bands of White Bird and Joseph.

Chief Toohoolhoolzote was the primary speaker for the Nez Perce case during the final council at Lapwai in May 1877. An assertive traditional chief, Toohoolhoolzote eloquently stated the beliefs of his people. Although an old man, he was still powerful and vigorous and led the young warriors in battle. Due to his adherence to his beliefs, General Howard called Toohoolhoolzote a "cross-grained growler" and ordered him jailed during the negotiations.

Return to the junction of old and new US 95 and join the Adventurous Traveler there for the trip to Cottonwood. Or join the Mainstream Traveler for the trip to Grangeville.

113

For the Adventurous Traveler

Junction of old and new US 95 to Cottonwood

Miles: 56.4
Map: Nez Perce National Forest

This two-hour trip gives you a flavor of the country that the Joseph, White Bird, and Toohoolhoolzote bands traveled through in their successful efforts to elude General Howard.

From the junction of old and new US 95, near mile marker 222, proceed west on old US 95 for 0.9 mile to the bridge over the Salmon River. Turn west across the bridge for 1.3 miles to Hammer Creek Recreation Area. Then the road goes up, up, up. The aerial-looking views are picture-postcard perfect. 8.1 miles past Hammer Creek, you have arrived on the Doumecq Plains, and the road Ys.

Turn south and follow Pilgrim Ridge Road, which then skirts around several other look-alike ridges for 13.2 miles to the junction with the Camp Howard Road, two tracks leading off through a gate.

Camp Howard Ridge

Camp Howard, referred to in the following quotes, is about six miles southeast of this junction.

> Two days of hard climbing brought us to the summit of Brown's Mountain [Camp Howard Ridge] on the evening of July 2. A severe storm of snow and rain contributed to our discomfort. We were minus several pack horses which had lost their footing and unceremoniously rolled down the steep mountain sides en route. We remained in camp July 3 to recuperate. Our supply of bacon running short, we feasted upon the juicy steaks of some of the innumerable horses running wild in the mountains.—Eugene T. Wilson (Lewiston volunteer)[80]

> It was storming, about half and half snow and rain. About eight miles from the river we came to where a house had been burned; the logs were yet on fire, making a good place to stop and warm.—George Hunter (captain of Dayton volunteers)

We started at eight o'clock in the morning [of the 3rd] with our clothing soaking wet from the night's unpleasant experience in the rain, but after a while the sun came out and our garments began to steam and smoke, so that we were completely dry by the time we returned to camp late in the afternoon. We had a sweat bath in the saddle.—Lt. William R. Parnell

Continue for 8.1 miles across the Joseph Plains.

Joseph Plains

Dug Bar, where the Joseph band crossed the Snake River on May 31, is about ten miles west of this road. The Wallowa band then came through here, heading east on their way to Tolo Lake the first of June. A month later, the nontreaty bands traveled north through this same country, perhaps gathering some stock, while General Howard's troops were figuring out how to cross the Salmon River.

The trail was very broad and plain, having been traversed by the whole band of Indians, with innumerable horses.—Frank Parker (scout and war correspondent)

Found that after travelling a distance of (5) miles that the Indians had separated into two (2) parties, one going in the direction of the Salmon River and the other toward the Snake, we continued our march and struck their Camp, which appeared to be about three (3) days old, after leaving this Camp we found that the trails again come together.—Ed McConville (colonel of Lewiston volunteers), July 3, 1877

Cattle were rounded up and herded south of Salmon River. Water was too high and swift for their crossing. All the young calves—there were many— would be drowned. So would the old cows.—Yellow Wolf[81]

The T in the road marks the point where the east-west trail taken by the Joseph band in early June intersects the north-south route taken by the three bands in early July. At the T, turn east and follow this road for 8.0 miles by Fall Point and down the switchbacks of Box Flats. This is the general route that Joseph's band took when headed toward Tolo Lake in early June.

From the junction of Rice Creek and Center Creek Roads, proceed 2.6 miles to the Rice Creek bridge.

Crossing the Salmon River

*Toward night we camped on a small rivulet, nearly opposite the mouth of
Rocky canyon. Just after forming our camp we received word by courier that
Joseph had...swung around back to Camas Prairie; that he then had Perry's
and Whipple's commands surrounded near the Cottonwood House.*

*This news resulted in my company of forty-five men and Captain
McConville's company of fifteen Lewiston volunteers being sent on a forced
march across the country by the way of Rocky canyon to the Cottonwood
House, to the relief of Colonels Whipple and Perry.*

*The next morning the boats reached us about daylight, when we ferried
our men and supplies over, swimming our horses, and pushed on over the
mountain for Camas prairie.*—George Hunter (captain of Dayton
volunteers)

The three nontreaty Nez Perce bands actually crossed the Salmon about fifteen
miles northwest of the Rice Creek bridge. Today that route is a jeep trail on
private land.

*We were again on the trail and nearing the river. Dodging and crawling
between rocks and hollows we all at once reached an eminence in sight of
the river again. Here was a sight worth all our previous night's experience!
Hundreds of horses had already been crossed from a point fully a mile above,
where they had landed on the opposite side and been carried down that
distance by the mighty river, then at its highest mark. Still crossing, with yells
from the Indians on both banks, were scores of other horses, some with
squaws and papooses hanging to them, with only their heads above water.
Hundreds of warriors, hanging to the manes of their war-steeds and holding
rifles high in the air, were swimming and drifting down-stream in very
picturesque bodies.*

*Soon the advance came in sight and, upon signaling them, they came
down the mountain with General Howard, to whom we gave details of our
experience. He marched to the river and camped. It was an old ferry station,
formerly owned by, and named after,...Colonel Craig.... An old log cabin
was all that remained on the place.*—Frank Parker (scout and war
correspondent)

The Nez Perce crossed the Salmon River on July 2. General Howard reached
the crossing three days later.

We want to cross to the north side of the Salmon again. Some of the command have been working all night to build a raft for the purpose of ferrying us over.... I know Joseph had crossed this God feared boiling caldron five times.... We can't cross it once....

Our duty is to see that no Indians steal on us or surprise the camp or command in a scalping bee while in the act of preparing our crossing of the river.

My writing desk is a folded rubber blanket. I am lying on my belly at an angle of 30 degrees, trying to write, stopping every few moments and taking my glasses to look at all the hills and approaches. I have a blanket on a stick for a shade under which I am doing the writing.—Capt. Robert Pollock, July 6, 1877

Ineffectually General Howard endeavored to cross, making a raft out of the only house at the ferry, which was lost in launching by the violence of the stream.—Thomas Sutherland (war correspondent)[82]

These Indians excited our admiration by their despatch in crossing rivers. James Reuben, (an Indian,) who brought me a message at Craig's ferry, told me how it was done: "Make skin rafts, and load them; tie four horses, abreast to the rafts with small ropes; put four Indians, naked, on the horses, and then boldly swim across." He gave us a practical demonstration by swimming his half-breed [horse] over to us and back across the fearful torrent. Brave Scout Parker attempted the same, but failed to get many yards from shore.—Gen. O. O. Howard[83]

Having failed the attempt to cross the river at Craig's ferry, Howard's command began backtracking to White Bird, where they did manage to reach the other side of the river.

General Howard recrossed the Salmon river early in the second week of July, (after great difficulty, losing several horses by drowning).—Thomas Sutherland (war correspondent)[84]

From Rice Creek Bridge, follow the road alongside the Salmon River for 1.2 miles. Then turn north on Rocky Canyon Road for the next 3.5 miles. At the break in the basalt cliffs, Rock Creek comes in from the east, while Graves Creek continues from the north.

Rocky Canyon

On their way to Tolo Lake, which is at the head of Rock Creek, Joseph's Wallowa band traveled east up Rocky Canyon during the first few days of June.

Continue north on Graves Creek Road for 8.5 miles into Cottonwood. Turn south onto Business 95 (Main Street), then immediately turn back northeast on King Street for 1.0 miles to the north junction of US 95 and Business 95.

Join the Mainstream Traveler for the sidetrip to William Foster's grave at the beginning of this chapter or continue with the Adventurous Traveler at Cottonwood.

For the Adventurous Traveler

Cottonwood to Grangeville

Miles: 18.9
Maps: BLM—Orofino

At the north junction of Business 95 with US 95, turn south on US 95. 1.0 miles later, at the south junction of Business 95 and US 95, look up to the hill on the west side of the road. Perhaps it was from here that a detachment of cavalry watched helplessly as Nez Perce warriors and citizen volunteers from Mount Idaho fought each other on Camas Prairie two days after the Rains Massacre.

Cottonwood Skirmishes

After this the Indians moved their camp with about 1,500 head of stock across the Prairie between Cottonwood and Rocky cañon and in the direction of Clearwater. They had crossed the Mt. Idaho road. No move was made by Col. Perry to intercept them during this time. Soon a small squad of men was seen coming from the direction of Mt. Idaho and were recognized to be volunteers.—Lewiston Teller, July 14, 1877

From the southern junction of US 95 and Business 95 into Cottonwood, drive south on US 95 for 1.4 miles to a Historic Site pullout.

The Brave Seventeen

The Indians opened fire at day-break and kept it up until noon. At that time we could see a small party approaching from Mount Idaho to our aid.—Pvt. Frederick Mayer, July 5, 1877[85]

The seventeen volunteers in that small party from Mount Idaho have their names engraved on the Idaho-shaped stone you see in front of you.

Capt. Randall called for 25 volunteers to go to the assistance of the soldiers at Cottonwood. Seventeen was all that could go.... There was seven men in that bunch that had no business in such an expedition. While they were good and brave men but they had never been under fire and were not good marksmen.—Luther P. Wilmot (Mount Idaho volunteer)[86]

I said, "Boys, if our Captain [Randall] should be killed he might serve as a breastwork—he is so big [236 pounds and six feet tall]. But this poor fellow," indicating Houser, "is so thin that a prairie dog could not hide behind him." Thus, laughing and joking, we rode along at a brisk canter. —E. J. Bunker (Mount Idaho volunteer)[87]

When we got a little over half way across, to the Cottonwood house, we could see large bodies of stock coming down the mountain from Grave creek, and for a while we could not tell what they were, but it was stock being driven, for they were moving fast.... Soon, we could see small bunches of what looked like men horseback, and a mile before we got to Shebang creek we could tell they were Indians.—Luther P. Wilmot (Mount Idaho volunteer)[88]

The next sun the families moved to a spring, Piswah Ilppilp Pah [Place of Red Rock]. While this was doing, a small bunch of young warriors went separately.... Coming to the wagon road,...we saw them—about twenty armed horsemen. Not uniformed soldiers, but more like citizens. Not riding a close company, but strung out along the road. When they saw us, they bunched and came a little faster. Came straight towards us! Seemed to me they cared not for us.... We now knew there was to be a fight.—Yellow Wolf[89]

119

I took the liberty of taking the first shot that was fired by our party. I had to dismount to do it, and when I fired, my horse frightened and nearly broke away from me. When I mounted the horse and started to overtake my company they had gotten quite a distance ahead of me, and as it seemed lonesome where I was I let my horse move a lively gait. I had not gone far when I reached Frank Vansise whose horse was shot. I took him up behind me and we lumbered along at a lively gait until we reached the command....

Captain Randall must have been shot where he ordered the halt as it was a poor place to make a defense. Then, Indians were in our rear and to our right, which left the way open for the volunteers to retreat to Cottonwood, a distance of one and a half miles.

Our force at that time was reduced by three wounded, two killed, and one sent to guard D.H. Howser, one of the wounded. Four others went to the soldiers to solicit assistance for the dead and wounded.—Henry C. Johnson (Mount Idaho volunteer)[90]

Frank Fenn had both lips burned, and a tooth loosened by a bullet as well as four holes shot through one trousers leg.

I think we had nine horses killed in the fight.—Luther P. Wilmot (Mount Idaho volunteer)[91]

One young white man among those fighting us was brave.... Some said he had been raised right among the Indians.... His father was a friend to us. Had always been our friend.

When we were mixing close, this boy killed the horse of Weesculatat. Then this same young man shot Weesculatat in the leg below the knee. He then shot him through the breast and again a little lower down. But the bullets did not go through his body.

With two bad wounds, he could not hold his life. Not old, about middle-aged, he was the first warrior killed. We lost a good fighter.—Yellow Wolf[92]

The loss of Lieutenant Rains and twelve other men two days previously and the sniping of that evening and the preceding day made Colonel Perry, at Cottonwood, extremely cautious about committing any of his 113 men to a conflict.

On the morning of the 5th about 11 o'clock, was discovered coming from the direction of Mt. Idaho, two mounted men, some three or four miles distant from our position at Cottonwood, at the same time seeing some distance in their rear, objects which we were unable at the time to determine to be mounted men or loose stock. Coincident with seeing the two men and the objects in their rear, we saw the Indians leaving their position on our

right, for the purpose, as we supposed of intercepting and cutting off the two men advancing on the Mt. Idaho road three or four miles from the position occupied by the Indians. In this movement the Indians passed directly across our front about one and a half miles from us. The distance from the Indians to the two men, when first discovered was, as nearly as I can judge about the same as that of the two men from Col. Perry's position at Cottonwood. Upon seeing the approach of these two men, and the efforts of the Indians to cut them off, Col. Perry ordered some of the command to be mounted, but before the order could be executed the two men came in closely followed by the Indians. This exciting chase diverted the attention of all parties from the objects which were at first observed in the rear of the two men and who were at first supposed to be loose stock. I, on the safe arrival of the two within our lines, left the bluff which overlooked the whole scene, and went down to the [Cottonwood] house to learn from whence the two men came and what news they brought. After being a very few minutes off the bluff, I heard a few shots, to which I paid little attention as we had, during the morning been firing at intervals at an Indian who came within range of our guns: the firing however, in a few moments rapidly increased when I again mounted my horse and started for the hill, in ascending which I met Col. Perry coming down: he said to me, that those men we saw are some of your people from Mt. Idaho, if I had had my command mounted I might have saved them, but it is now too late, as they are already surrounded. He further said, I can no longer look at it, it makes my heart sick—and went off the hill; while I went on to the top of the bluff, where I at once saw that they were indeed surrounded about one mile and a half from the position we occupied. I remained with many others looking at the bloody work for some time, (probably fifteen or twenty minutes) when the firing gradually decreased, when I remarked that the poor fellows were all killed. We soon however, discovered some two or three were approaching us, who proved to be white men and part of Capt. Randalls party. Again a lively firing was resumed, which convinced me that some of our men were still alive and defending themselves. I remarked that it was a shame and an outrage to allow those men to there and perish without an effort being made to save them. I then mounted my horse and dashed toward them as fast as he would carry me, reaching them I think in less than five minutes, having my horse shot entirely through the body just as I reached their assistance also.—
George Shearer (Mount Idaho volunteer), July 26, 1877[93]

121

Shearer dashed down to their assistance, exclaiming as he went: "The man who goes down there is a d——d fool, but he's a d——d coward if he don't."—Eugene T. Wilson (Lewiston volunteer)[94]

After remaining about fifteen or twenty minutes with Randalls men, the firing again almost wholly ceased, growing impatient at the tardiness of the line under Capt. Whipple reaching us, I remounted my horse and returned to him who was still some five or six hundred yards in our rear and halted—on reaching them I saw Lieutenant Shelton who had joined Capt. Whipple with some mounted men, and asked him why they did not move on to our relief and enable us to get our wounded from the field. He became a little furious and asked why I talked to him, as he was not in command of the line. Whereupon Capt. Whipple inquired why we did not bring off the wounded, when I reported to him what I had said to Lt. Shelton. He replied that he could not move any further as his right was threatened; where upon one of the men in the ranks said loudly and distinctly, "Shearer, you need not come to the 1st Cavalry for assistance, as you will not get any." This remark was made as a rebuke to his officer, as I understand it, for some of the men actually advanced from their line to come to our relief and were preemtorially ordered back. I then asked for some one to be at once sent for a wagon and returned to the men, who were still keeping up a desultory fire upon the fast retreating Indians. Matters remained in this position until we had taken our wounded from the field, and the Indians after having secured considerable time for their stock to get out of reach had all gone, when Capt. Whipple advanced his line over the ground on which the fighting had occured.—George M. Shearer (Mount Idaho volunteer), July 26, 1877[95]

The Indians cut them off, and a hot skirmish took place, until one of our Troops [Shearer] was mounted and charged in among the Indians and saved the remainder of the party. The party were 17 men from Mount Idaho, who voluntiered to come to our aid thinking we were in danger, but 5 of them were killed and two wounded[96] before we rescued them from the Savages. After this the entire command of 3 troops mounted and charged on the Indians and drove them towards the Clearwater River.—Pvt. Frederick Mayer, July 5, 1877[97]

We did not know why the soldiers in their dugout rifle pits did not come to the fighting.—Yellow Wolf[98]

A court of inquiry convened in September to investigate Colonel Perry's inaction. Members of the Brave Seventeen minced no words and called Perry a coward. Less than a week after the skirmish here, Lew Wilmot became so incensed at seeing Perry that he refused to give Howard intelligence regarding the Nez Perce location on the South Fork of the Clearwater. (Read **Walls** on page 144 of Chapter 4.)

The skirmish on July 5 with the Brave Seventeen was the last time the nontreaty bands of Nez Perce set foot on Camas Prairie. Nevertheless, the settlers who lived there were still very skittish.

McConville's Command remained on the Prairie to protect the scattered settlers, some of them now returning to their ruined homes.... The settlers began to breath more freely, despite the many wild and groundless rumors that arose. The people's imagination was excited to a point where they could see an Indian in every shrub and fence corner, when there was no Indian near.... McConville, with about twenty men and myself, went to Cottonwood house for supplies. Reaching that point, the Colonel threw out his pickets to guard against surprise. I was given a position on the Lewiston side of Cottonwood. When on the hill, I saw two persons up Cottonwood creek some distance. They went into the low bushes that fringed that stream. I at once communicated the same to the Colonel. He detailed six men to go with me to see what it meant and who it was. We cautiously approached the spot where I had seen them enter the low bushes, and found a white woman. I called to her to come out. She refused. I told her that we were friends. She had fled from the Indians, and had looked for nothing else but Indians until she could see only redskins. Dismounting, I approached, and found her to be the wife of H.C. Brown, of Salmon river. She was slow to recognize us as of her own race and color. She had been wandering in the mountains for fourteen days, subsisting upon roots and berries. She was accompanied by a small dog, the companion of all her wanderings. We asked her where H.C. was. She said he had gone into the bushes just above.

I put her on a horse behind one of the men, and sent her to Cottonwood House, and went in quest of H.C., proceeding cautiously, for we knew he was well armed and desperate, judging by the condition of the wife, and the fact of his leaving her. We realized that it would be more than our lives were worth to approach him while in hiding. After following up the creek about a mile and a half from where I had seen them enter the bushes, we discovered H.C., armed to the teeth. He had a double-barreled shot gun and a breech-loading rifle. We kept out of gun shot and called his name, telling him we

123

were his friends, and recalling circumstances familiar to him in other days. At length, after we had exhausted our ingenuity in trying to make him know us, addressing him with the old familiar names by which we had known him, and assuring him of our good intentions, he threw down his guns, and, approaching us, muttered, as though to himself, "Yes, they are my friends— my old friend Eph, too." We shook him by the hand, too full for words. Although possessed, under ordinary circumstances, of the strength of two men, the reaction left him as helpless as a child.—E. J. Bunker (Mount Idaho volunteer)[99]

Proceed south on US 95 for 0.3 mile and turn east on Twin House Road. Although this is the long way to get to Grangeville, the road parallels the route across the prairie taken by the 500 or so Nez Perce. Continue along this road for 4.5 miles. At the T, turn north on McDonald Road for 1.8 miles. Then turn southeast on Kube Road and stick to it as it winds around for the next 2.7 miles.

The Nez Perce continued on east across Camas Prairie, but this guide makes a sidetrip to Grangeville here by turning south on the road named Highway 7 for 5.3 miles. At the junction with US 95, turn east for 1.9 miles to Grangeville.

Join the Mainstream Traveler at Grangeville in the next chapter.

For Further Reading

Forlorn Hope, by John Dishon McDermott, gives a detailed account of the events surrounding the White Bird Battle. The variety of and reliance on original source material makes interesting reading out of what would otherwise be too many facts to fathom.

Every year a commemoration ceremony of the White Bird Battle is held on or around June 17. Contact the Nez Perce National Historical Park for more information, 208-843-2261.

Terry C. Johnston wrote a novel about the Battle of White Bird, titled *Cries from the Earth*.

CHAPTER 4

The Battle of the Clearwater

Attack on the Reservation

Grangeville to Kamiah, Idaho

I tried to surrender in Idaho but my offer was rejected. The soldiers came upon my camp and the first thing I knew the bullets were flying around my head. The soldiers lie so that I have no more confidence in them.—Chief Looking Glass

It is a well known fact that when Joseph, White Bird and Looking Glass joined forces, they had, all told, just 220 warriors, 25 percent of whom were armed with only bows and arrows.—Duncan McDonald (Nez Perce reporter)

The Indian way of fighting is not to get killed. Killed today, there can be no fighting tomorrow.—Roaring Eagle[1]

The Story

After the murders on the Salmon River, the Looking Glass band and the Palouse band distanced themselves from the hostilities by returning to the Looking Glass camp near Kooskia on the reservation. Two weeks later, on July 1, their village was attacked by a detachment of cavalry accompanied by volunteers. During the raid, a mother and child were shot; the pair drowned while attempting to escape across the Clearwater River. The soldiers plundered the village and took 725 head of horses. This unprovoked attack shifted Looking Glass out of a neutral position and aligned his band and the Palouse band with the nontreaty bands of Joseph, White Bird, and Toohoolhoolzote.

My relations and friends. I had no idea of fighting the white man…. My father's warriors fought many battles as allies of the United States soldiers west of the Rocky Mountains…. Two days ago my camp was attacked by the soldiers. I tried to surrender in every way I could. My horses, lodges, and everything I had was taken away from me by soldiers we had done so much for. Now, my people, as long as I live I will never make peace with the

125

treacherous Americans. I did everything I knew to preserve their friendships and be friends with the Americans. What more could I have done?—Chief Looking Glass[2]

The Looking Glass band and the Palouse band sought sanctuary in Red Owl's traditional camp on the South Fork of the Clearwater near present-day Stites. They were still on the reservation. A few days later, they were joined by the other nontreaty bands.

On July 7, a scouting party of seventy-five volunteers left Mount Idaho and discovered the camp of the nontreaty Nez Perce the next day. Shortly afterward, the Nez Perce detected the volunteers' camp on a plateau west of the Clearwater. A siege ensued in which the Nez Perce harried the volunteers and, around midnight, drove off forty-three horses—some of the same horses that the soldiers had taken from the Looking Glass band the preceding week. The volunteers named the place of their embarrassment Misery Hill because they had no access to water for the twenty-four hours they were marooned there. Failing in their efforts to coordinate with General Howard and squeeze the Nez Perce camp, the volunteers finally trudged back to Mount Idaho.

Meanwhile, General Howard and his troops were traveling on the ridge east of the Clearwater. On July 11, they happened onto the Nez Perce camp purely by luck: a lieutenant rode to the edge of the ridge to see the view and saw the Nez Perce village. A cannon was fired, the Nez Perce were surprised, and the Battle of the Clearwater began. Within minutes, the cavalry was pinned in place by Nez Perce sharpshooters. For the remainder of the day, the accuracy of the Nez Perce warriors was telling on the embattled soldiers—eight were killed and twenty-five were wounded, three mortally. The Nez Perce losses were four warriors killed and another four wounded.

The next day, more and more warriors dropped out of the fighting and hung out in the smoking lodge. Although the best warriors were ready to make a stand, their strategy did not gain the support of all the other fighting men. As a result of this disagreement, all the warriors left the battlefield.

With no resistance facing them, Howard's infantry pushed forward. The Nez Perce camp, in disarray, hurriedly retreated north to cross the Clearwater at Kamiah. The army declared a victory and plundered yet another Nez Perce camp.

The next day, General Howard's command followed the Nez Perce to Kamiah. Unable to cross the river, the troops stalled for a day, after which the Nez Perce took off for the Lolo Trail.

Chronology of Events

1877

1 July   Captain Whipple's troops attack and plunder Looking Glass's village near Kooskia. The Looking Glass band repairs to Red Owl's camp on the South Fork of the Clearwater, accompanied by the Palouse band of Husishusis Kute.

6 July[3]   Looking Glass is joined by the bands of Joseph, White Bird, and Toohoolhoolzote.

8 July   Seventy-five volunteers leave Mount Idaho to look for the Nez Perce. They encamp on a hill west of the South Fork of the Clearwater.

9 July   General Howard camps at Walls, east of the South Fork of the Clearwater.

               Nez Perce warriors harry the volunteers at Misery Hill, west of the South Fork of the Clearwater.

11 July   Howard surprises the Nez Perce, and the Battle of the Clearwater begins.

               The volunteers at Misery Hill return to Mount Idaho.

12 July   The Nez Perce withdraw from the Battle of the Clearwater and camp that evening near Kamiah.

               Troops occupy and plunder the former Nez Perce camp on the South Fork of the Clearwater.

13 July   The Nez Perce cross the Clearwater at Kamiah.

               Howard stalls on the south side of the river.

15 July   The Nez Perce move to Weippe.

16 July   Returning from Montana, Red Heart's band of thirty-five people is arrested at Kamiah.

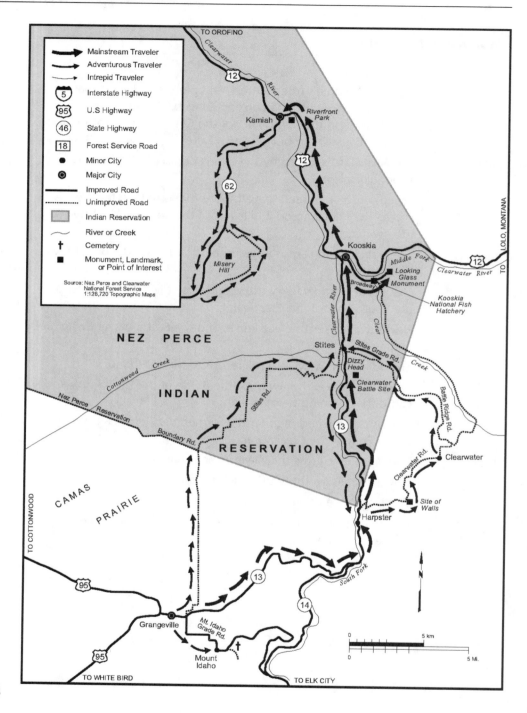

Travel Plan

Grangeville to Kamiah, Idaho

Mainstream Traveler	Adventurous Traveler	Intrepid Traveler
Grangeville	follow Mainstream	follow Mainstream
	Sidetrip Grangeville to Mount Idaho	follow Adventurous
Grangeville to Stites	Grangeville to Stites	follow Mainstream or Adventurous
	Sidetrip Battle Ridge loop	follow Adventurous
Stites to Kooskia	follow Mainstream	follow Mainstream
Sidetrip Kooskia to Kamiah	follow Mainstream	follow Mainstream
	Sidetrip Kamiah to Misery Hill	follow Adventurous

For the Mainstream Traveler

Grangeville

> From the junction of US 95 and Idaho 13, turn east into town for 0.5 mile to the corner of Main and Hall Streets.

Grangeville Grange Hall

In 1877, a Grange Hall was the only building in Grangeville. Settlers in the area built a stockade around the Grange Hall for their protection. The rescue party for the Norton and Chamberlin families set out from here. (See **Norton-Chamberlin Party**, on page 69 in Chapter 3.) The Grange Hall stood on the northeast corner of Main and Hall Streets, where the brick Schmadeka Building constructed in 1910 now stands.

129

> From the center of Grangeville, drive east on Idaho 13, Main Street, for 0.5 mile to Mt. Idaho Grade Road.

> Join the Adventurous Traveler for a sidetrip to Mount Idaho. Or continue with the Mainstream Traveler or join the Adventurous Traveler for the trip from Grangeville to Stites.

For the Adventurous Traveler

Sidetrip
Grangeville to Mount Idaho

Miles: 6.0, round-trip
Map: Nez Perce National Forest

This sidetrip affords a look at Mount Idaho, which was, in 1877, the main settlement in these parts. On the east edge of Grangeville, turn south onto the Mt. Idaho Grade Road for 2.9 miles.

Mount Idaho

This collection of houses on the hillside was the site of bustling activity in 1877. At that time, Mount Idaho had two stores, a post office, a hotel, and a saloon. None of these buildings remain today. At the outbreak of the hostilities, Mount Idaho became the communication center for events happening elsewhere on Camas Prairie. Settlers from miles around fled here for protection.

> *Some of the young Indians were very friendly with John and the other boys—used to race horses with them and on June 13, some of these young bucks came to John and told him there was going to be trouble and that they had better move. There wasn't any Grangeville then, just a Grange hall. They stood logs up around the hall later. Your father [John Adkison] took me to Mt. Idaho where my aunt and uncle were. The town was crowded as soon as we heard of the murders along Slate creek and White Bird creek. The hotel was turned into a hospital, taking care of people....*
>
> *I can't understand, when I think of it, why there were so few rifles in town—more shotguns and pistols. Guards would pass their rifles on to the next guards and they would make sure that they were loaded....*
>
> *We were afraid that the Indians would ride through the town at night and shoot into the crowded houses and tents, so wagons and logs were tied across the lanes into Mt. Idaho at night. We felt they could sneak in through*

the trees any time and kill us in our beds. A sort of fort was built on the hill at the north end of the town where the Masonic hall was built later. Trenches were dug, logs stacked up and Uncle Loyal who ran the mills gave many sacks of flour to make it safer.... The women and children were put there, some in tents, some out in the open. There was no water up there and they had to go down the hill to the creek. Kind of scary at night!

One night I was up on the hill helping John cast bullets, by cutting off the little end of the bullets after casting. We could hear the Indians running their horses close to town and firing their guns. They ran off all the horses from the pastures close to town, one woman lost one hundred.—Harriet Brown (nineteen years old, Mount Idaho resident)[4]

In Mount Idaho, bear east on Mt. Idaho C E Road and follow it for 0.1 mile to the cemetery.

Mount Idaho Cemetery

Half of the settlers killed by the second Nez Perce raiding party on June 15 are buried here in the Mount Idaho cemetery. Ben Norton, Johnathan Chamberlin and his daughter Hattie, Joe Moore, and Lew Day were all killed or mortally wounded while crossing Camas Prairie on the night of June 14. (Read **Norton-Chamberlin Party**, on page 69.)

James Baker, a White Bird settler, lies alone in the southwest corner of the cemetery. (See **White Bird**, on page 91.) A headstone memorializes Jeanette Manuel, also of White Bird, although her body was never actually found. (Read **White Bird Creek** on page 79.)

Also buried here is D. B. Randall, who was captain of The Brave Seventeen, the volunteers from Mount Idaho who were going to the rescue of the soldiers at Cottonwood on July 5th. The graves of Ben Evans and D.H. Houser, both of the Brave Seventeen, are here as well, but Houser has no headstone. (Read **The Brave Seventeen** on page 119.)

D. H. Howser, chairman of Board of Commisioners of this County, died last night at 8 P.M., from his wound received in the desperate fight at Cottonwood on the 5th.—Lewiston Teller, July 18, 1877

Return to Idaho 13 and join the Mainstream Traveler or the Adventurous Traveler at Grangeville.

For the Adventurous Traveler

Grangeville to Stites

Miles: 18.7
Map: Nez Perce National Forest

At the junction of Idaho 13 and the Mt. Idaho Grade Road, proceed north on the Grangeville Truck Route for 0.1 mile. At the T, turn east on Vrieling Road. After 1.4 miles, it joins Lukes Gulch Road, which later becomes Stites Road. After crossing Reservation Boundary Road in 5.8 miles, this route parallels the Nez Perce Trail, which lies in Cottonwood Canyon, about a mile to the northwest. So once again, you are following the course of the Nez Perce camp as it ventured across the open prairie after leaving the protection of the rough Salmon River country. Continue following the main trunk of the pavement for 7.0 miles as it jogs east and north.

Just as the switchbacks begin, look across the canyon to Battle Ridge. There's an excellent view of the Clearwater battlefield from here, if you can figure out where to look. Find the rimrock of exposed basalt about one-third of the way up the hillside from the river. This formation is called Dizzy Head. The battle took place above and on the next point north of Dizzy Head. The Stites Grade Road is in the cleft north of that next point. The ravines on either side of Dizzy Head are the paths taken by the Nez Perce warriors to get up to the battlefield. The Nez Perce camp site, which cannot be seen from this location, is just on this side of the South Fork of the Clearwater River.

Switchback the 2.8 miles down to the river, and turn north at the T to parallel the Clearwater. In 0.5 mile, you will be across from Dizzy Head. Between here and Cottonwood Creek, 0.3 mile north, the Nez Perce were camped on the flat on the west side of the road.

Cottonwood Creek

The land between the confluence of Cottonwood Creek and the South Fork of the Clearwater was the traditional home of Red Owl, a sub-chieftain of the Looking Glass band. Thus caches of food and supplies were stocked here. The entire Looking Glass band had retreated to Red Owl's camp after the attack on the main village on July 1. The three fleeing bands of Joseph, White Bird, and Toohoolhoolzote joined Looking Glass here at the end of the first week in July.

> From the bridge over Cottonwood Creek, proceed north along the river for 0.7 mile. Follow the road as it turns east for 0.1 mile and crosses the South Fork of the Clearwater River at Stites.
>
> Continue with the Adventurous Traveler on the Stites loop or join the Mainstream Traveler at Stites.

For the Mainstream Traveler

Grangeville to Stites

> From the Mt. Idaho Grade Road, proceed east on Idaho 13. Leaving Camas Prairie behind, you descend to the valley created by the South Fork of the Clearwater. 9.7 miles from Grangeville, Idaho 14 junctions with Idaho 13. Idaho 14 leads to the route of the Southern Nez Perce Trail.

Southern Nez Perce Trail

The Nez Perce traditionally used two routes to cross the Bitterroot Mountains into Montana—the Lolo Trail and the Southern Nez Perce Trail. The Southern Nez Perce Trail begins here and ends at Conner, Montana, where the West Fork and East Fork of the Bitterroot River converge. If you tell people around here that you are following the Nez Perce Trail, they will understand that phrase to refer to the Southern Nez Perce Trail rather than the Nez Perce (Nee-Me-Poo) National Historic Trail.

> Continue north on Idaho 13 for 10.1 miles through Harpster to the area of the Clearwater Battle site of the Nez Perce National Historic Park.

Clearwater Battle

After being attacked at their home on the reservation, near present-day Kooskia, the Looking Glass band and the Palouse band moved to the mouth of Cottonwood Creek, which is just across the river from the historic sign. By July 7, the other three nontreaty bands had converged here: Joseph's Wallowa band, **133** White Bird's Salmon River band, and Toohoolhoolzote's band from the country between the Snake and Salmon rivers. Whether the bands thought they were safe is not clear. In point of fact, they had arrived on the reservation. Technically they had followed through on their promise to General Howard to move onto

Two well-equipped warriors stand in front of their horses. (Photo courtesy of Idaho State Historical Society.)

the reservation. Warriors harried the seventy-five volunteers at Misery Hill on July 9, but they were not prepared for what happened next.

On July 11, General Howard's command was riding from south to north along Battle Ridge, on the east side of the river, above the road here. Because of the steepness of the bluffs, no one saw the Nez Perce camp directly below them until one of Howard's aides, Lieutenant Fletcher, just happened to ride away from the main column in order to survey the view. From about a mile and a half north of here, he discovered the large encampment of the nontreaty Nez Perce on Cottonwood Creek. A cannon was brought into position and aimed at the village. While some of the Nez Perce men were racing their horses on the bench above the river, the cannon was fired at them.

> *I do not doubt that they were as much surprised at our attack as we were to find them in their very comfortable old home ground by the gurgling stream, all evidences...showing that the camp had long been occupied, and had wonderful stores of supplies.*—Lt. Harry L. Bailey[5]

Surprised the Nez Perce were. But within minutes the warriors took action. The soldiers were up on the ridge east and somewhat north of the historical information sign here.

> *I saw soldiers strung out a long way off; far up along the mountain's brow.... The chiefs called an order, "Split up! Make three bodies!"*
>
> *About twenty of us young warriors joined together. Chief Toohoolhoolzote was our leader. The other two companies must stay at camp. We hastened upriver a short ways. We crossed and rode into the timber. We hurried up the wooded slope of a canyon, leading to south side of this battlefield.*—Yellow Wolf[6]

134

The warriors in this picture did not have time to put war paint on their horses. (Photo courtesy of Idaho State Historical Society.)

I saw the warriors stripping for the battle. I saw a bunch of them, mounted and led by Chief Toohoolhoolzote, run their horses a ways up the river, where they crossed and climbed the mountain to meet the soldiers. Soon there was fighting up there and the guns were heard plainly. It was then that other warriors left the camp, hurrying to join in the battle. They were led by Wahchumyus [Rainbow], followed on a swift gallop. They had waited to protect the families, had Toohoolhoolzote and his warriors failed to hold General Howard's army on the mountain flat. Less than one hundred warriors in all went up against the enemies. Many of the tribe were not fighters.—Wetatonmi[7]

From near the mouth of this [Cottonwood] canyon where our camp was on the banks of the Clearwater, we went up the steep, rock-bluff of the hill. I was one of the mounted orderly boys carrying water to the warriors fighting on a big flat at top of the hill. The soldiers and Indians were not far apart, perhaps a quarter of a mile. They were that close when I got there before noon.—Eelahweemah (About Asleep, fourteen years old)[8]

Amazingly, the warriors quickly traveled up to the top of the ridge where the battle happened. For a view from the Battle Ridge Road, Adventurous Travelers can take the Stites loop sidetrip.

Our commanders were not scared of bullets, not afraid of death.... Many fewer than one hundred warriors met the hard fighting here, as throughout the war.—Yellow Wolf[9]

135

Fewer than a hundred warriors took part in the battle, but they fought fiercely. So intense was the shooting that soldiers exaggerated the actual size of the Nez Perce fighting force by 300 percent.

Yellow Wolf, in 1909, was about fifty-three years old. (Photo courtesy of MASC.)

Our command numbered 400, and Joseph had 300 brave and determined warriors. The fighting was carried on very carefully on both sides. The Indians fought in a recumbent position and kept up a steady fire from behind rocks, trees, and every advantageous rise in the ground, like skirmishers and sharp shooters. Our men were forced to approach through open table land and received a galling fire.—Helena Herald, July 16, 1877

Our chief looked around. It was early afternoon.... He saw we were hemmed in on three sides and gave orders that we go. He was last to leave. We crawled a ways, then ran. We hurried, for bullets were singing like bees. My heart beat fast. Thinking only for escape, I ran away from my waiting horse....

Then I came to myself. I missed my horse, and I grew hot with mad! I made myself brave! I turned and ran for my horse—many soldiers shooting at me. Why, I did not care what I ran into! I got my horse and led him away.

With soldiers still shooting, I jumped on my horse and galloped down the hill.... I whipped my horse for all in him....

While making that ride, I thought it my last day.—Yellow Wolf[10]

136

The enemy manifest extraordinary boldness, planting sharp-shooters at available points, making charges on foot and on horseback.—Gen. O. O. Howard, August 27, 1877

At one point of the line, one man, raising his head too high, was shot through the brain; another soldier, lying on his back and trying to get the last few drops of warm water from his canteen, was robbed of the water by a bullet taking off the canteen's neck while it was at his lips. An officer, holding up his arm, was shot through the wrist; another, jumping to his feet for an instant, fell with a bullet through the breast. So all day long under the hot July sun, without water and without food, our men crawled about in the parched grass, shooting and being shot.—Lt. C. E. S. Wood

As for the marksmanship of the frontier troops,

At this era of our army we had had almost no target practice.—Lt. Harry L. Bailey[11]

This photo of Peopeo Tholekt was taken in the early 1900s. (Photo courtesy of Idaho State Historical Society.)

137

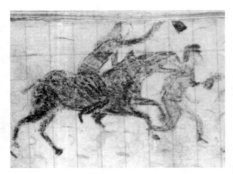

A Nez Perce warrior chases a civilian packer. (Photo courtesy of Idaho State Historical Society.)

So although it sounds like braggadocio, it was probably simply a statement of fact when one of the warriors said,

Standing before General Howard's soldiers was not too dangerous. Nothing hard!—Yellow Wolf[12]

Gen. Howard he no come over river to fight Joseph. Me think canyon too deep, he scared. All us Indians we make much laugh at Gen. Howard and his white soldier. They all time scared. They no want to die.
—Peopeo Tholekt (Bird Alighting)[13]

Not only were the Nez Perce excellent marksmen, they shot strategically.

Otstotpoo [Fire Body] had come back to me....
He said to me, "Dear son, we are going to die right here! Do not shoot the common soldier. Shoot the commander!"—Yellow Wolf[14]

One bullet went through the top of my hat and removed a handful of hair.—Lt. E. S. Farrow, July 16, 1877[15]

Private Winters...was wounded severely in the hip during our Clearwater battle of July 11th and 12th. He was near me and had his hat shot off three times, and his cartridge belt cut entirely off by a bullet, the leather being cut as by a knife, as I saw it the moment it occurred. Rather a hot place, wasn't it? He kept saying that some of our own men had shot him (and it did seem so to me....)—Lt. Harry Bailey, September 14, 1877[16]

One man was shot within ten feet of me in our second engagement and the bullet whistled dangerously near my own head. I can tell you sister it is as peculair sometimes to have the shot strike within a foot of your head, and bounce the sand and ground in Your face not knowing what minute you may get shot. and every moment witness the fatal misal strike some poor man on your right or left, to see them raise their hand to the fatal wound and their last dieing words would be that of some loved one at home.—Pvt. Bernard A. Brooks, July 21, 1877[17]

138

When night fell there was almost complete cessation of shooting, and the Indians could be distinctly heard in various forms of expression, sometimes in earnest talk, sometimes in harangue; the chief exhorting the hardy to

greater bravery on the morrow and anon reproving the delinquent. Now and then the female voice could be detected in a plaintive wail of mourning, sometimes in low and tremulous unison, then breaking into a piercing cry.— Capt. Joel G. Trimble

*During the first day's fighting, there were four Indians killed and four wounded.—*Duncan McDonald (Nez Perce reporter)

*Still at night our position was not a very good one as the enemy lay contiguous to my communications and I was short of rations. This morning we began operations by regaining our spring of water from several sharp shooters.—*Gen. O. O. Howard, July 12, 1877

The greatest torture for the soldiers on the first day of fighting was being cut off from water. The draw where the spring is located is 0.6 mile north of here.

*Just as were ready to recommence offensive work, Capt. Jackson with a pack train appeared in sight beyond the Indians position [to the south]. Miller pushed out in skirmish order, met the train and escort successfully. They had hardly formed junction with us when the Artillery Battallion already beyond the enemy's flank made a rapid movement with gattling gun and howitzer along. The Indians made one desperate effort to flank Miller but failed and then gave way.—*Gen. O. O. Howard, July 12, 1877

The Indians captured the smaller pack train and killed two packers, while the larger pack train got through. But that was the last offense undertaken by the warriors. Dissension was brewing among the Nez Perce.

*For a sun and a half we held the soldiers, then gave way because many of the warriors hung back from fighting. They argued, "No use fighting when soldiers are not attacking our camp."—*Roaring Eagle[18]

The fight was quit for a reason!
   Wahchumyus [Rainbow], Pahkatos [Five Wounds], Teeweeyownah [Over the Point], Sarpsis Ilpilp [Red Moccasin Tops], Wahlitits [Shore Crossing], and Tipyahlanah Kapskaps [Strong Eagle] were in one place. Teeweeyownah said to us older men, "Get ready! Let the young men mount their horses! We will go mix the soldiers! We will make a desperate fight!"
   But there were cowards who refused....
   Teeweeyownah then said to the brave men, "Let us quit the fight!" Then he turned to the other men and spoke to them, "You cowards! I will die

139

soon! You will see hardships in bondage. You will have a hard time. Your freedom will be gone. Your liberty robbed from you. You will be slaves!"

The leaders then left the fighting, the cowards then following after. I did not know this and was left behind. I could hear shots from but one gun and I hurried to see what was wrong. I found only Yellow Wolf, all others gone. It was his rifle I heard. I called him, then thought to save myself.—Wottolen (Hair Combed Over Eyes)[19]

The battle continued some hours. It must have been about ten o'clock, and soldier bullets still rained. Of course there was some cannon shooting. The soldiers began leaving their shelters, coming towards us.

Suddenly I heard my partner, Wottolen [Hair Combed Over Eyes], call to me: "Nobody here! We will quit!"

I raised partly up. No Indians could be seen fighting. All had left the battle! Wottolen and myself were holding back the troops.

I now understood why soldiers crowded so. No warriors opposing them!

All yesterday fighting; all this morning they did not crowd us. But now, meeting no Indian bullets, they came charging bravely.

Then I ran, again forgetting my horse. I ran back where he was tied in the timber edge. Mounting, I started down the mountainside.... My horse never missed footing.—Yellow Wolf[20]

Dizzy Head is the name of the peninsula of exposed basalt just east of the turnout. A local story tells of a warrior racing down the hillside toward Dizzy Head, chased by troops who were sure he was cornered. At the last minute he veered, rode down the side of Dizzy Head, and escaped. Supposedly, the long dark streaks on the hill above the road were made by warriors sliding down the talus slop to join the fleeing tribe.

Not until the last of us leaped away did soldiers make their charge. Some tepees, robes, clothing, and food were left. The women, not knowing the warriors were disagreeing, quitting the fight, had no time to pack the camp.[21]

Crossing the river and reaching where the now empty camp stood, I heard a woman's voice. That voice was one of crying. I saw her on a horse she could not well manage. The animal was leaping, pawing, wanting to go. Everybody else had gone.

I hurried toward her, and she called, "Heinmot! I am troubled about my baby!"

I saw the baby wrapped in its tekash [cradleboard] lying on the ground. I reached down, picked up the tekash, and handed it to the woman. That mother laughed as she took her baby.... Riding fast, we soon overtook some rear Indians entering the canyon [of Cottonwood Creek]....

This woman with the little baby was Toma Alwawinmi [possibly meaning Spring of Year, or Springtime], wife of Chief Joseph. Her baby girl was born at Tepahlewam [Tolo Lake] camp a few days before the White Bird Canyon battle.—Yellow Wolf[22]

The Indians were now running their horses for the mouth of the canyon [of Cottonwood Creek], leaving most of the tepees and other material. No time to save only a part of the camp. It was wild hurrying for shelter of the canyon hills.—Eelahweemah (About Asleep, fourteen years old)[23]

For a few minutes there is stubborn resistance at the enemy's barricades. Then the whole line gives way. Immediately the pursuit is taken up by the infantry and artillery...and the remaining cavalry as soon as they can saddle and mount....

They are closely pursued through the ravines into the deep cañon, thence to the river, over rocks, down precipices, and along trails almost too steep and craggy to traverse. The footmen pursued them to the river opposite the Indian camp. The river being too deep and rapid for the men to ford, they here awaited the cavalry....

The cavalry worked its way as rapidly as it could from its position on the left down the rugged mountain steeps to the deep ford, and crossed slowly into the Indian camp...while...the Indians...were fleeing in every direction up the heights to the left of Cottonwood Creek and beyond the Clearwater.—Gen. O. O. Howard, August 27, 1877

Everything was then pushed to the pursuit. We shelled them rapidly from the high bluffs as they escaped from the left bank of the river and followed them escaping in every direction as far as the river and are now across and going into camp at 7:30 P.M.... Their camps were abandoned in great haste leaving much plunder.—Gen. O .O. Howard, July 12, 1877

141

The only living objects that were abandoned by them [the Nez Perce] were about half a dozen crippled horses and one poor aged squaw.—Capt. Joel G. Trimble

The Indian camp, abandoned in haste, had the lodges still standing, filled with their effects,—blankets, buffalo robes, cooking utensils, food cooking on the fires, flour, jerked beef, and plunder of all descriptions.—Gen. O. O. Howard

The Indian camp appeared to have been their home for a long long time. The order was, "Burn everything!" The packers and citizens (for it was marvelous how many citizens seemed to arrive), showed us how to find the caches or underground storages, by prodding with our ramrods. It was a wonder to see tons and tons of flour and other goods, and fine Indian goods, mostly burned. There was gold dust jewelry, and fine silver tableware, some of which I judged dated from an early Hudson's Bay period. All this being brought to light, the packers and citizens helped themselves.—Lt. Harry L. Bailey[24]

You should see some of the Indian garments that were taken from the camp the day of the battle when the Indians left in such a hurry. They are made of beautifully tanned skin, soft as chamois skin, and cut something like we used to cut our paper dollie dresses. The bottom is fringed, and the body part down to the waist is heavy beaded. You never saw such bead work, and the beds make them so heavy. These, of course, are their costumes for grand occasions. One of them I could not lift. Then they have leggings to match, and if it is a chief or big man, they have an outfit for his horse of the same style. Doctor Sternberg is an enthusiast on the subject of collecting curiosities, and he purchased from men who had gotten them, four or five of these garments. For one, he gave ten dollars in coin, and for another with a horse fixing, 25 dollars. So you see, they must be handsome.—Emily FitzGerald (Army doctor's wife), August 5, 1877[25]

The Nez Perce had been driven from the battlefield and had fled their camp. However, the price of the military victory was quadruple the number of Nez Perce dead and wounded.

On the evening of the 12th I was left on the battlefield to gather the dead lost by our side. We found eight bodies and buried them near about.

...There were twenty-five wounded to take charge of and guard to Grangeville, Idaho Territory. While en route, three of the wounded died.—Capt. Robert Pollock, July 17, 1877

142

It is not agreeable sight to see wagon loads of men brought in after the battle, and to hear the wounded groan and cry with pain.—Pvt. Bernard A. Brooks, July 21, 1877[26]

The soldiers stayed at the Nez Perce camp that night, continuing their plunder. The next morning, they again picked up the trail of the Nez Perce and headed to Kamiah.

The next morning most of the troops were engaged in destroying the "caches" and burning the tepees. About 7 o'clock James Reuben, a friendly Nez Perce, rode into camp and informed General Howard that the hostiles were crossing the river at the ford near Kamiah.... General Howard hurried ahead with the cavalry.—Thomas Sutherland (war correspondent)[27]

Continue north on Idaho 13 for 1.1 miles to Stites. At mile marker 22, look across the river to the site of the Nez Perce camp and look up to see the site of the battle.

Continue with the Mainstream Traveler at Stites. Or join the Adventurous Traveler for the Stites loop.

For the Adventurous Traveler

Sidetrip
Stites Loop via Battle Ridge

Miles: 23.5
Maps: Nez Perce National Forest

This sidetrip follows the course taken by General Howard's troops just prior to their discovery of the Nez Perce camp. From the center of Stites, head south on Idaho 13 for 0.5 mile. The spring that the soldiers sought to gain on the first day is up the draw to the east. 0.6 mile farther south is the sign commemorating the Clearwater Battle. If you took the Adventurous Traveler route from Grangeville to Stites, you will recognize the road you were just on across the river. For a description of the battle, see the section titled **Clearwater Battle** on page 133.

> From the historical sign at Nez Perce National Historic Park site 14, proceed south for 7.8 miles to Harpster. Just after leaving the reservation, turn east for 1 block. At the T, turn north on Wall Creek Road and continue winding up the hill in a generally easterly direction. At the Y in 1.5 miles, bear north. Continue for 1.5 miles. The place where the road crosses a small bridge and the road Ys is the location of the former way station of Walls.

Walls

After leaving Grangeville, General Howard's troops camped here on July 10, the night before the battle of the Clearwater. Why the troops were headed up the east side of the river is unknown, especially since the reconnaissance party of seventy-five volunteers was four miles west of the river. Lew Wilmot arrived bearing a dispatch from Colonel McConville, who was commanding the volunteers at Misery Hill.

Just as the sun was rising we rode into General Howard's camp.

General Howard shook hands with me and introduced me to Colonel Perry and added, "this is the man you charged with cowardice."

Colonel Perry said that I had lied to the general.......

I cursed Colonel Perry and I used language that is not fit to use here. And then General Howard said to his guard, "Arrest that man." I jumped on my horse and started to run for the timber, but the guard was too near and he caught my horse by the bridle and I dismounted.

They took my rifle and revolver, and took the cartridges out.

Then General Howard said it made his blood boil to hear a man blaspheme an officer.

I said: General Howard...you told me to make out the charges in writing and to have all the survivors of the company sign them, and you would have Colonel Perry courtmartialed. I told you that we [the Brave Seventeen] had met the Indians before noon [on July 5] and it was nearly 4 in the afternoon when Captain Winters came down to within about 200 yards of where Captain Randall was killed, and that it was less than one mile and a half from where we could plainly see Colonel Perry with his command [at Cottonwood]....

General Howard said he was very sorry the way it had turned out, and he said: "Feed your horse and get some breakfast, and we want you to go with us and show the way to where Joseph is camped tomorrow."

144

I asked for my rifle and cartridges, and told him I would do nothing of the kind; that I was going home.... I told him I would rather take my chances with Joseph than with his officers, and I rode off, against the advice of my friends.—Luther P. Wilmot (Mount Idaho volunteer)[28]

Lew Wilmot was understandably upset. Three of his neighbors in the Brave Seventeen had been killed or mortally wounded while going to relieve Colonel Perry at Cottonwood. Yet Colonel Perry had kept his men safely in their trenches, watching the skirmish, rather than joining the fight in support of the seventeen citizen volunteers. Colonel Perry requested a Court of Inquiry, which convened two months later and cleared his name.

As a result of Wilmot's sense of integrity, General Howard left camp here on July 11 without knowing the location of the Nez Perce camp.

> Turn north on the Elk City Wagon Road for 2.2 miles. At the T, turn east onto the paved Clearwater Road for 1.0 mile. At the T in the small community of Clearwater, turn north on Jericho Road for 0.4 mile. At the next Y, turn east for 0.3 mile, and then turn north on Battle Ridge Road for 5.0 miles.

Battle Ridge Road

The citizen scouts and so-called guides took us far around and onto the wrong side of the Clearwater River and almost gave us a defeat.—Lt. Harry L. Bailey[29]

The battleground is on the west side of Battle Ridge Road. The area of the battle itself is on private property and is not open to public access. The column was actually about a mile and a half past this point when,

About 12 o'clock my aide-de-camp, Lieutenant Fletcher, discovers the enemy in a deep ravine near mouth of Cottonwood Creek.—Gen. O. O. Howard, August 27, 1877

The distance in a direct line from where we discovered the enemy to the new position was not more than half a mile, but by the detour we had to make to our left, around a deep and impassable ravine [Stites Grade], the distance was fully a mile and a half.—Thomas Sutherland (war correspondent)[30]

145

> Continue north on Battle Ridge Road for 0.4 mile. At the Y, turn west down the Stites Grade for 2.1 miles.

Stites Grade Road

While engineers were surveying for the Stites Grade Road in the early 1900s, they found a dead soldier with several canteens in this ravine.[31]

> *A spring in a ravine was secured, but one man sent to fill canteens never returned, and it was found that the enemy were in possession of it. Next day, however, the spring was retaken.*—Lt. C. E. S. Wood

At Idaho Route 13, turn north for 0.2 mile to the center of Stites.
  Join the Mainstream Traveler at Stites.

For the Mainstream Traveler

Stites to Kooskia

From the center of Stites, continue north on Idaho 13 for 3.7 miles to the north side of Kooskia. Just past milepost 26, turn east on Broadway Avenue for 2.0 miles, staying on the south side of the Clearwater. The Kooskia National Fish Hatchery is located on Clear Creek, about where the Looking Glass band's home camp on the reservation was. Proceed about 200 yards past the gate to the Fish Hatchery and pull off on the north side of the road. A short interpretive trail leads to a monument commemorating Looking Glass.

Clear Creek

Looking Glass had selected this area on the reservation as his home camp at the Lapwai Council in May of 1877. His band normally came here every year for root gathering. After the killings on the Salmon River in mid-June, Looking Glass returned here to establish his neutrality. He knew that in a conflict between his people and the U.S. Army, his people would surely be the loser.

> *The evening of the 29th [of June] positive information is obtained that Looking Glass, who, with his people, had stood aloof from the hostiles, had been furnishing re-enforcements to them of at least twenty warriors, and that he proposed to join them in person, with all of his people, the first favorable opportunity....*
>
> *With a view of preventing the completion of this treachery, I sent Captain Whipple, commanding his own and Winter's companies, and the Gatling*

Kooskia as it appeared in the 1880s. Here the South Fork of the Clearwater converges with the Middle Fork of Clearwater River. (Photo courtesy of Idaho State Historical Society.)

guns, with instructions to make a forced march, surprise and capture this chief and all that belonged to him.—Gen. O. O. Howard, August 27, 1877

Although Howard's intelligence may have told him that Looking Glass was going to join the nontreaty bands, Looking Glass himself denied this allegation.

It was Sapalwit [Sunday] and some Indians had gone down to the Kamiah Dreamer church for worship…when soldiers were seen coming down the mountain to the south and across Clear Creek. Immediately there was excitement throughout the village. I was in the tepee of Looking Glass where breakfast was being served with usual Sapalwit ceremony, conducted by the Chief…. My Chief said to me, "You better go meet the soldiers and say to them, 'Leave us alone. We are living here peacefully and want no trouble.'"

With this message on my mind, I mounted my horse, crossing the Creek and met the soldiers on the first flat of the hillside…. One man greeted me friendly in Nez Perce, and I gave him my Chief's message that we want no trouble and therefore had I come from my people.

But those soldiers would not listen. They seemed drinking. They came near killing me. I understood little English. One said to me, "You Looking Glass?" He jabbed me in the ribs with his gun muzzle. He did not hit easy! The first man told him, "Hold on! This not Looking Glass! Only one of his boys."

I went back and entered Looking Glass's tepee. I told him what the soldier said, and that maybe they want to have council. The Indians had seen the soldier strike me with his gun, and they said the soldiers wanted to kill their chief. This made Looking Glass afraid to trust the soldiers, and he did not go, but sent me again. Kalowet, an old man, could speak little English. He was selected to go with me….

147

He then raised a white cloth on a pole between Looking Glass's tepee and the creek, plainly facing the soldiers....

With Kalowet, I again rode up to the meeting place and said to the interpreter, "I am Peopeo Tholekt [Bird Alighting]. Looking Glass is my Chief. I bring you his words. He does not want war! He came here to escape war. Do not cross to our side of the little river. We do not want trouble with you whatever!"

Kawan Kalowet also spoke for peace.... But those soldiers would not listen. The same one again struck his gun against me and said to the interpreter, "I know this Injun is Looking Glass! I shall now kill him!"

Of course I thought I was to be killed.... But the interpreter told him that I was too young for Looking Glass, and the soldier was made to draw back his gun. Then the commander with two or three others and the interpreter rode back with Kawan and me across the stream. We stopped near the white flag and the commander said, "I want to see Chief Looking Glass."

Looking Glass was still in his tepee, and while we were having this little talk, there came the sound of a gun from the other side of the creek. Red Heart was sitting on the bank and a soldier fired across, wounding him in the right thigh, but not fatally wounded. At this, the white men whirled their horses and hurried to their own side of the stream, and the soldiers opened fire from the hillside.

Of course that settled it. We had to have a war.—Peopeo Tholekt (Bird Alighting)[32]

Immediately a parley was arranged, and Captain Whipple and his escort went forth to meet Lookingglass. While this parley was progressing Washington Holmes, who had a half-breed wife, took it upon himself to commence the engagement by firing into the camp.... The Indians soon fled eastward into the mountains, leaving their tepees, nearly all their camp equipage and over seven hundred ponies. Some of the horses were captured by the troops and the tepees and equipage were burned. One Indian child was killed in the exchange of shots, but the whites escaped unscathed.—*An Illustrated History of Northern Idaho*

148

A woman...with her baby wrapped to her back, tried to escape across the Clearwater north of the village. She never reached shore. Her horse was drawn under by the strong current and all drowned.—Peopeo Tholekt (Bird Alighting)[33]

Capt. Winters and Lieut. Rains and a large majority of the soldiers were eager for the fight, but were held in check by the Col. Our boys finally became indignant and opened fire. They killed a few Indians, burnt their lodges, and drove off about a thousand ponies.—Idaho Tri-Weekly Statesman, July 14, 1877

After the soldiers left, we returned to our ruined homes. Several tepees had been burned or otherwise ruined. Much had been carried away and many objects destroyed or badly damaged.... Growing gardens trampled and destroyed.

This was the regular home of our band. Some kept cows and had milk for their children, their own foods. These cows and their calves and a great many horses were driven off by the robber enemy.

We had a plow and raised good gardens. Potatoes, corn, beans, squash, melons, cucumbers, everything we wanted.—Peopeo Tholekt (Bird Alighting)[34]

When the Paloos and Wawawai [bands of Palouse] reached Kamiah and learned that all their stock, both horses and cattle, had been appropriated by the whites, they decided there was nothing left for them but to join the war party.—White Hawk (twelve years old)[35]

The loss of the ponies and the attack unfortunately had the effect to give prompt re-enforcement to those who were fighting, and caused me some disappointment.—Gen. O. O. Howard, August 27, 1877

Thus, through the precipitate and uncalled-for attack by the soldiers, the Looking Glass band was radicalized and joined the other nontreaty bands. Strategically, Looking Glass was a very important addition because, as a buffalo hunter, he knew the route to buffalo country. For the succeeding month, Looking Glass was the chief who guided the five nontreaty bands.

Return to Idaho 13 and turn north for 0.3 mile to the junction with US 12.
Continue with the Mainstream Traveler in Kooskia for sidetrips to Kamiah and Weippe. An Adventurous Traveler sidetrip from Kamiah to Misery Hill highlights the events preceding the Battle of the Clearwater. Or join the Mainstream Traveler in Kooskia for the trip to Montana in the next chapter.

For the Mainstream Traveler

Sidetrip

Kooskia to Kamiah

This sidetrip to Kamiah completes the story of the aftermath of the Battle of the Clearwater. For Intrepid Travelers desiring to drive the Lolo Trail, this is not a sidetrip, but the next leg of the journey. Turn west on US 12 for 7.1 miles to Kamiah. As soon as you cross the bridge over the Clearwater, turn east into Riverfront Park.

Kamiah Riverfront Park

Fleeing from the Battle of the Clearwater, the Nez Perce reached Kamiah and forded the Clearwater on July 13.

> *Only about half the camp was across the river when they saw Howard's troops approaching. There was quick work done then. It only took a few minutes to cross the balance of the camp.*—Duncan McDonald (Nez Perce reporter)

> *Crossing the families to north side of the river was easy. While this was doing, we saw soldiers riding down the distant hill toward us. We found hiding and waited for soldiers. When they reached the riverbank, we fired across at them. Many soldiers jumped from their horses and ran to any shelter they saw. Others galloped fast back toward the hills. We laughed at those soldiers.*—Yellow Wolf[36]

> *The river road taken by Whipple wound around in one place very close to the bank on the Indian [north] side, and as he arrived at this point he was met with a very brisk fire (say fifty shots in two minutes) from some hostiles in ambuscade. The men jumped from their horses and took to the grain fields on their left, and joined us on foot at the ford.... Some of our best shots were stationed in good positions to pick off every Indian who might show himself. The firing was kept up until dark, on both sides, although of a very desultory character.*—Thomas Sutherland (war correspondent)[37]

The exchange of shots resulted in only one wound—an artilleryman had his scalp creased by a bullet. Both camps settled where they were.

> *Here we were camped on the south of the Clearwater and all the Indians were camped in plain sight on the north.*—Luther P. Wilmot (Mount Idaho volunteer)[38]

And so it remained all during the day of July 14. Negotiations seemed about to begin.

> *Dispatches from the front have just come in. They say Joseph wants a talk with General Howard. He says he is tired of fighting. He was drawn into it by White Bird and other chiefs, and he wants to stop. We hear there is great dissatisfaction among the hostiles themselves. The squaws are wanting to know who it was among their men that took the responsibility upon themselves of getting into this war with the Whites. They have lost their homes, their food, their stock, etc.*—Emily FitzGerald (Army doctor's wife), July 16, 1877[39]

The following morning, July 15,

> *Howard conceived the plan of sending the volunteers and cavalry via the ferry to the intersection of the road and trail, thereby getting a strong force beyond the Indians cutting off their escape into Montana, while he would attack them from the rear with his remaining force, both detachments closing upon the enemy as rapidly as possible....*
>
> *Orders were given for reveille to sound at 3 o'clock next morning and for the volunteers and cavalry to proceed with all possible haste to Dunwell's Ferry, cross over the river and follow the road to its intersection with the [Weippe] trail, returning upon the trail in the direction of Kamia until the enemy was struck. At 3 o'clock the bugle was sounded and by half past four we were on the march, but the inevitable bugle continued to sound first "Forward!" then a "Halt!" and again "Forward!" Its notes plainly heard in the camp of Chief Joseph, just across the river.*—Eugene T. Wilson (Lewiston volunteer)[40]

> *The soldiers were afraid to cross and have a battle. Next morning we saw General Howard dividing his soldiers. Some left, riding down the river....*
>
> *The chiefs called the command, "We will move camp! No use staying here. They do not want to cross and fight us!"*—Yellow Wolf[41]

151

As soon as it was light he started his squaws and non-combatants to gather up his hundreds of horses, tepees were taken down and loaded upon pack animals, while Joseph himself sauntered down to the river's bank upon a mission of diplomacy. —Eugene T. Wilson (Lewiston volunteer)[42]

Actually, the man who rode down to the river was not Chief Joseph.

It was Zya Timenna [No Heart] who did the calling across the river, pretending we would surrender. —Yellow Wolf [43]

Calling to General Howard, he signified his intention of surrendering and asked for a cessation of hostilities. Howard immediately caused the good news to be signaled to our detachment, and we were ordered to halt for further orders. Hour after hour passed without the hoped-for signal to proceed, the hot sun pouring down upon our heads.... This diplomatic exchange of courtesies was continued between Joseph [actually, No Heart] and General Howard until after the sun had reached the meridian, when, believing that his people had now got a sufficient start to reach the crossing of the trail before we could do so via Dunwell's [at Greer], he fired a shot from his rifle in Howard's direction, slapped that portion of his anatomy which his leggins did not reach, and rode off. —Eugene T. Wilson (Lewiston volunteer)[44]

With their quarry escaped and the opportunity for squeezing them between two forces gone, General Howard and his troops crossed the Clearwater the succeeding day, July 16.

As soon as it was positively discovered that the Indians had begun to cross Lolo Trail towards the mountains, General Howard crossed the Clearwater with his command as speedily as possible; it taking a day, as considerable time was lost in repairing the wire ferry. —Thomas Sutherland (war correspondent)[45]

Once across the river, a scouting party was sent out to follow the Nez Perce. For that story, follow the Adventurous Traveler route from Kamiah to Weippe. Then on July 18,

The entire day was spent in recrossing. Ten men were taken over at a time in a boat (the one I had built six weeks before). I saw several mules drowned in swimming the river that day. —Frank Redfield (sub-agent of Nez Perce Reservation)[46]

Red Heart's Band

Just as the fleeing Nez Perce arrived at Weippe, twenty miles north of Kamiah, they met a small band led by Chief Red Heart returning from the Montana buffalo country.

> Here [at Weippe] we found Indians who had not been in the war. They were Chief Temme Ilppilp's [Red Heart] band. Friendly to both sides. Next morning, coming daylight, one of General Howard's Nez Perce scouts came riding in....
>
> But he came and said to these Indians, "It will be best to come on your own reservation. There you will be safe."
>
> "We will go," answered most of those Indians. There were about twenty of them, men, women, and a few children. They had not joined us. Never had been in any of the war. Coming from Montana, they had only met us there. Those Indians not joining with us in the war now bade us all good-by—a farewell, that we would never return to our homes again!—Yellow Wolf[47]

> Red Heart and sixteen of his warriors and 23 women and children came and gave themselves up as prisoners and are under guard.—Lewiston Teller, July 17, 1877

> The Indian prisoners arrived at Lapwai on Friday and their hair cut short (it should have been under the scalp) and then they were placed in irons.—Lewiston Teller, July 19, 1877

Totally innocent of the war, the people of Red Heart's band were nonetheless taken as prisoners of war when they arrived in Kamiah. After nine months in prison at Fort Vancouver, Washington, the innocent Nez Perce were finally returned to Lapwai in April, 1878.

Kamiah

Settlers everywhere panicked and did not want to be left without protection. Rumors were flying that all the tribes in the Northwest would join the Nez Perce. General Howard waited at Kamiah for additional troops to join him. These companies came from Fort Yuma in Arizona, San Francisco, and Fort Klamath in southern Oregon. By July 29, there were 360 foot soldiers and 200 cavalry, 25 Indian scouts and 150 armed citizens, and 350 mules with 75 packers.

153

General Howard gathered a pack train of supplies before setting out on the Lolo Trail. Here more supplies wait at Cottonwood. (Photo courtesy of Idaho State Historical Society.)

Though I did not understand it at the time, I have in later years understood that the reason for not following up the advantage and pressing the Indians was that General Howard felt that there might be a better way of gaining entrance to the Lo Lo trail.—Pvt. William Connolly[48]

Eleven companies are on their way here from California, will be here this week, and will go into camp until things are settled. A whole regiment of infantry is also on the way.—Emily FitzGerald (Army doctor's wife), July 18, 1877[49]

The Infantry (15 companies including the artillery) numbers about 600 now, and the command altogether will be 800 or thereabouts.

...But honestly, I don't think we shall see an Indian hostile.... The impression is general that we will have some hard marching only, with no fighting of any kind.—Dr. John FitzGerald, July 29, 1877[50]

The fifteen companies of infantry and four companies of cavalry pulled out of Kamiah on July 30.

Join the Adventurous Traveler for a sidetrip to Misery Hill. Or join with the Mainstream Traveler or Adventurous Traveler at Kamiah for a trip to Weippe in the next chapter. Or return to Kooskia and join the Mainstream Traveler there in the next chapter.

For the Adventurous Traveler

Sidetrip
Kamiah to Misery Hill

Miles: 20.6
Map: BLM—Orofino

This sidetrip goes to Misery Hill, where 75 Mount Idaho volunteers were besieged by the Nez Perce off and on for over a day. From Riverfront Park in Kamiah, proceed west on US 12 for 0.4 mile. At the junction with Idaho 162, turn south and follow Idaho 162 for 8.8 miles. Just after climbing out of the canyon and onto the prairie, turn east on Tram Road. In about 2 miles the hill north of the road is Misery Hill.

Misery Hill

On July 8th, volunteers left Mount Idaho to scout for the Nez Perce. General Howard was returning from his unsuccessful attempt to catch the Nez Perce on the Joseph Plains between the Snake and Salmon rivers.

> There was some bad blood brewing between Eugene Wilson and Capt. Hunter. It was claimed that Col. Hunter had obtained some whiskey and was under its influence. In returning from a scouting they got into a heated argument. Eugene thought the Col. was going to shoot him. Eugene jerked out his revolver and fired at the Col. The bullet took effect in the Col.'s shoulder. The boys come on to Mount Idaho where the Col. was put in the hospital and Eugene was arrested by civil authorities and put in jail.... It was decided that the best way to quiet the boys down would be to take them out from town. I was selected to take them on a scouting trip if they would go....
> We left Mount Idaho and went northwest. I knew the Indians had followed the main trails from Salmon River to the Clearwater. Quite a while before we reached the main trails we could see where the ground was cut up by large bands of stock. We followed on the main trails until we had reached the last range of hills on the south [fork] of the Clearwater. Here we stopped in order to determine what we should do. I told the boys we were less than a mile and a half of Looking Glass camp, and I was certain that was where Joseph

155

would go. There was quite a number of the Mount Idaho volunteers along, so we were about 75 all told. It was decided we would camp where we were.—Luther P. Wilmot (Mount Idaho volunteer)[51]

The volunteers originally camped about half a mile away from Misery Hill, four miles away from the Nez Perce camp on the South Fork of the Clearwater. The next day,

Capt Cearly and Lieut Wilmot (both brave and gallant Officers) went out scouting alone to ascertain the exact position of the Indians, and after being out about four (4) hours, returned to Camp with the information that the Indians were encamped at the mouth of the Cottonwood on the opposite side of the River, shortly after their return one of the men accidentally fired his rifle, and in a few minutes there were several Indians in sight.—Ed McConville (colonel of volunteers), July 9, 1877[52]

Everything was going fine until about 10 a.m. Johny Atkinson while monkeying with a 50 Cal. Springfield let it go off accidentally. Never did I hear or think I had heard a rifle make such a report. We did not have very long to wait until we saw a couple of Indians come out onto a piece of high ground from where they could see our horses and some of us. They went back in a hurry. Our camp was thrown into quite a commotion. About 1/2 mile from where we were there was quite a high hill. It was flat on top and one of the finest places any one could wish to make a stand. We filled what kettles and cantines with water and moved up to the top of what was afterwards known as Misery Hill.

We had not long to wait after we got moved. Before we had callers. First 19 Indians come up onto a mountain overlooking us. They staid for quite awhile and dared us to come over and fight. It was not long before more than 100 come up. We did not try to shoot any. They were over 1/2 mile from our position. —Luther P. Wilmot (Mount Idaho volunteer)[53]

After being harried all day, the volunteers had a brief respite until shortly after midnight.

Indians attacked us this morning about one o'clock and kept up a strong fire on us till daylight and succeeded in stampeding our horses, we loosing (43)[54] but had no men hurt, about 7 o'clock A.M. the following morning the Indians came up in strong force and formed line to attack us but after holding council among themselves they came to the conclusion not to try it

*and took up their march toward the Clearwater.... I immediately had a
dispatch written to General Howard informing him of the attack of my
command and of the loss of my horses, Lieut Wilmot went with the dispatch
to Genl Howard.*—Ed McConville (colonel of volunteers), July 10, 1877[55]

Adventurous Travelers who took the Stites loop route have read Wilmot's
account of what happened when he arrived at Howard's camp at **Walls**.
(See page 144.)

*Lou Wilmot was sent to Howard with the information and the suggestion
that he might send his cavalry to our assistance and close in upon the
enemy from the north side with his artillery and infantry, thus practically
surrounding them. This General Howard declined to do. When Wilmot
received his answer he was about to mount his horse for a return to the
volunteer camp, but perceiving Perry standing near, his temper overcame his
prudence and he proceeded to pay his respects to that worthy in language
more forcible than polite. Howard ordered him under arrest.... By this action
no reply was received from the General and the volunteers were left in
ignorance as to whether or not the regulars would be send to their
assistance. In fact, no word having been received from Wilmot, it was
generally believed by his comrades that he had been murdered by the
Indians before reaching Howard.*—Eugene T. Wilson (Lewiston volunteer)[56]

*Not hearing anything of Genl. Howards movements, I waited until 12
o'clock when being short of provision and more than half of my command
dismounted I came to the conclusion (after consulting with my Officers) that
it was better for me to move towards Mt. Idaho and procure provisions, and
horses to remount my men I reached Cearly's Ranche about 7 o'clock P.M.
having marched forty three of my men on foot twenty five (25) miles.*—Ed
McConville (colonel of volunteers), July 11, 1877[57]

The volunteers left Misery Hill just as Howard's troops discovered the Nez
Perce camp on the Clearwater.

*It was a procession of disgusted men that trudged into Mount Idaho that
evening.*—Eugene T. Wilson (Lewiston volunteer)[58]

Continue traveling northeast on Tram Road for 0.8 mile. At the crossroads, turn north on Fort Misery Road. In 0.8 mile continue straight ahead, downhill, for 2.1 miles to Idaho 162. Turn north on Idaho 162 and return to US 12 in Kamiah in 5.3 miles. Return to Riverfront Park by turning east on US 12 for 0.4 mile.

Join either the Mainstream or Adventurous Traveler at Kamiah in the next chapter.

CHAPTER 5

Lolo Trail

The Road to Buffalo Country

Kamiah, Idaho, to Lolo, Montana

The trail ahead being obstructed by fallen trees of all sizes and descriptions, uprooted by the winds and matted together in every possible troublesome way, a company of forty "pioneers," with axes, was organized and sent ahead to open the trail, wherever possible. It is true that the Indians had gone over this trail ahead of the troops; but they had jammed their ponies through, over and under the rocks, around, over and under logs and fallen trees and through the densest undergrowth, and left blood to mark their path, with abandoned animals with broken legs or stretched dead on the trail.—Lt. E. S. Farrow

The Indians ride with a hair-rope knotted around the under jaw for a bridle. The men use a stuffed pad, with wooden stirrups. The women sit astride, in a saddle made with a very high pommel and cantle, and in travelling carry their infants either dangling by the cradle-strap to the former, or slung in a blanket over their shoulders; while children of a little larger growth sit perched upon the pack-animals, and hold on as best they may.—George Gibbs (surveyor and ethnologist, 1855)[1]

For ten days we toiled along this pathway. The marching hour was sunrise, the camping hour sunset. Often the hillsides were so steep that we could not sleep comfortably without digging out a bed. Each cavalryman had been required to start with ten pounds of grain for his horse, but several times horses and patient pack-mules were tied up at night without a mouthful of any kind of fodder.—Lt. C. E. S. Wood

159

The Story

After the Battle of the Clearwater, the Nez Perce fled north and crossed the Clearwater at Kamiah. They camped on the north side of the river while General Howard's command stalled on the south side. Once again, as had happened twice on the Salmon, crossing a river stymied the soldiers. The two camps had totally different views of the stalemate. Howard spent an entire day awaiting the beginning of negotiations. When the Nez Perce saw that the soldiers were not going to cross the river and fight, they simply packed up and headed north to Weippe. On July 16, they began their trek eastward over the Lolo Trail.

Except for a couple of sites, the Nez Perce camps along the Lolo Trail may only be guessed at. What their trip across the mountains was like is left to the imagination: healthy people leading the horses ridden by those wounded in the Clearwater battle, old women yelling at pack animals to get them to move through the downed and criss-crossed timber, boys herding their family's share of the two thousand horses, arguments about who was supposed to be riding in front of whom if the pecking order somehow became disordered.

General Howard did not immediately follow up his advantage. Instead of pressing the Nez Perce, he awaited the arrival of troops from Arizona, California, and Georgia. While he was organizing his command, Howard telegraphed a message to the post commander of the three-week-old Fort Missoula, Captain Charles Rawn. He asked Rawn to hold the Nez Perce back on the trail. With 25 enlisted men and 150 volunteers, Rawn marched to the eastern end of the Lolo Trail, about five miles west of present-day Lolo, Montana. There his men constructed a log barricade, which, a few days later, was named Fort Fizzle. Howard's plan was to squeeze the Nez Perce between the barricade and his pursuing forces. However, his two-week delay in getting started meant that the threat of a squeeze was negligible.

The Nez Perce arrived at Fort Fizzle on July 26 and proceeded to negotiate. Captain Rawn demanded unconditional surrender, but the Nez Perce refused to give up their rifles. They did, however, promise to pass peacefully through the Bitterroot Valley. After one day of parleying, the Nez Perce avoided further confrontation by simply traveling up on a ridge and bypassing Fort Fizzle.

Two days later, on July 30, Howard and his six hundred troops left Kamiah and headed east over the Lolo Trail. A crew of fifty woodsmen joined them a few days afterward. This gang, under the command of Captain William Spurgin, cleared the Lolo Trail to permit easier passage for the troops.

While they were camped at Lolo Hot Springs on August 6, a courier arrived from Colonel John Gibbon informing General Howard that Gibbon was close on the heels of the Nez Perce and expected to give battle soon. Leaving his infantry behind to make the best time they could, Howard dashed ahead with the cavalry and entered the Bitterroot Valley on August 8. He was ten days behind the Nez Perce.

Chronology of Events

1877

15 July	The Nez Perce camp at Weippe.
16 July	The nontreaty bands head east on the Lolo Trail to buffalo country.
17 July	A military scouting party is ambushed south of Weippe by the Nez Perce rearguard.
25 July	Fort Fizzle is constructed five miles west of Lolo, Montana.
26 July	The Nez Perce council with Captain Rawn at Fort Fizzle.
28 July	The Nez Perce detour around Fort Fizzle.
30 July	General Howard leaves Kamiah and camps at Weippe.
31 July	Howard camps at Musselshell Meadows.
2 August	Captain Spurgin's fifty axemen join Howard.
6 August	Howard camps at Lolo Hot Springs with his cavalry and infantry.

Travel Plan

Mainstream Traveler	Adventurous Traveler	Intrepid Traveler
Sidetrip Kamiah to Weippe loop	follow Mainstream	Kamiah to Weippe
Kooskia to Shotgun Creek Road	follow Mainstream	Weippe to junction of Shotgun Creek Road with US 12 with connections between the Lolo Motorway and US 12
Shotgun Creek Road to Lolo Pass	follow Mainstream	follow Mainstream
	Sidetrip Packer Meadows	follow Adventurous
Lolo Pass to Graves Creek Road	follow Mainstream	follow Mainstream
	Sidetrip Graves Creek Road	follow Adventurous
Graves Creek Road to Lolo	follow Mainstream	follow Mainstream

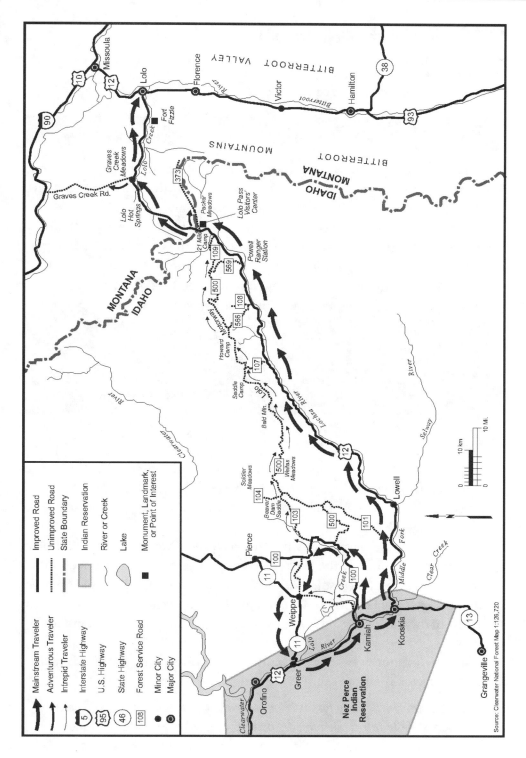

Source: Clearwater National Forest Map 1:126,720

163

For the Mainstream Traveler

Sidetrip
Kamiah to Weippe Loop

> **Special considerations:** This route includes six miles of a wide gravel road.

This sidetrip takes you to the traditional camas-gathering ground at Weippe, where the Nez Perce saw their first white men when the starving Lewis and Clark emerged from the Lolo Trail. Ironically, five bands of Nez Perce were now fleeing their homeland to escape the pressure brought to bear on them by white men. A footnote to history tells that one of the elder Nez Perce on the flight was the son of William Clark. This seventy-two-year-old man, Halahtookit (Daytime Smoke) was accompanied by his daughter, Iltolkt and her baby.

> From Riverfront Park in Kamiah, turn north on US 12 for 0.2 mile. As soon as you cross the bridge, turn northwest on the road along the north side of the river. In 0.4 mile, turn northeast on Tom Taha/Glenwood Road, NF 100 for 32.3 miles. Just after crossing little Brown's Creek Bridge, drive straight ahead, west, onto the gravel Musselshell Road for 8.1 miles into Weippe.

Weippe

Weippe was a traditional camas-gathering ground where the Nez Perce congregated in the early summer to dig the bulbs of the blue camas flower. These sweet and nutritious bulbs were as important as meat in the Nez Perce diet.

By 1877, a couple of ranchers had homesteaded here and a trading post marked the beginnings of the town of Weippe. The Nez Perce burned all the ranch buildings and killed some of the cattle. The dried meat would be used for the trek over the Lolo Trail, since much of the food supply had been lost at the Battle of the Clearwater and since game could be scarce in the high mountain country.

While the women were busy preparing the food supply, the chiefs held a council to decide their next move.

> *What are we fighting for? Is it for our lives? No. It is for this land where the bones of our fathers lie buried. I do not want to take my women among strangers. I do not want to die in a strange land. Some of you tried to say*

The son of William Clark, Tzi-kal-tza, was an old man of seventy-two when he participated in the flight of the Nez Perce from Idaho. (Photo courtesy of Montana Historical Society.)

once that I was afraid of the whites. Stay here with me now and you will have plenty of fighting. We will put our women behind us in these mountains and die on our own land fighting for them. I would rather do that than run I know not where.—Chief Joseph

Joseph, however, was in the minority. Chief Looking Glass became the acknowledged leader of the bands, and he opted for going to the buffalo country of Montana. The decision to leave forced a split in several families. Some people stayed in Idaho with their relatives in the treaty bands; others decided to flee with the nontreaty bands. Leaving a rearguard behind, the Nez Perce launched their journey eastward.

Before leaving the Weippe Valley, the Chiefs asked for five young men volunteers to remain at the camping grounds for three suns, watching for enemy scouts and troops. If none were seen during that time, they were to come on and overtake the camp. But should enemies be sighted, two were to ride ahead with news of the danger, so that the warriors could prepare to

165

hold the troops back on the trail until the families could escape to a place of safety. —Sewattis Hihhih (White Cloud)[2]

The Nez Perce warriors did ambush some of Howard's advance scouts, and that story is told under **Incendiary Creek** on page 168.

General Howard's command arrived at Weippe on July 30, two weeks behind the Nez Perce.

> *At the "We-ipe,"…there was quite a lengthy opening in the forest, and plenty of water and grass. The hostile Indians had pastured this plat pretty well, and had dug over much of the land for the camas roots.* —Gen. O. O. Howard

The Weippe Prairie of that era was about a thousand acres, much smaller than the amount of cleared land you see here today.

> You may join the Intrepid Traveler at Weippe for a trip on the Lolo Motorway.
>
> Otherwise, continue straight ahead, west, on Idaho 11. In 17.7 miles, after descending a ridge via a series of switchbacks, you reach Greer. Turn east on US 12 for 0.7 mile.

Greer

In 1877, Dunwell's Ferry was located at the place now called Greer. General Howard had originally planned to have a detachment cross here to go to Weippe and then squeeze the Nez Perce between the force from Weippe and his force from Kamiah. Those plans were foiled when the Nez Perce up and left Kamiah before a squad of volunteers could reach Weippe. And the volunteers had other problems with getting to Weippe.

> *The object of the expedition being to get in rear of Joseph on the Lo Lo. trail and to keep him back. On arriving at the river I sent three (3) men down…to see if the Ferry boat was in sight, after being gone about two (2) hours, he returned reporting the boat down the river about two (2) miles camped for the night, distance marched twenty (20) miles.* —Ed McConville (colonel of volunteers), July 15, 1877[3]

The ferry house had been burned and the boat cut adrift from its wire. With no way to cross the river, the volunteers returned to Kamiah to rejoin Howard.

Continue on US 12 for 14.4 miles to Kamiah Riverfront Park.

Continue on US 12 for 7.0 miles to Kooskia.

Join the Mainstream Traveler at Kooskia.

For the Intrepid Traveler

Sidetrip

Kamiah to Weippe

Miles: 20.0

Map: Clearwater National Forest

Special considerations: Intrepid Travelers who are planning to take the Lolo Motorway should fill up on gas.

The Lolo Creek portion of this route is closed by winter snow and may be impassable because of early spring mud.

This trip follows the approximate route of the Nez Perce camp and Howard's command on their journey from Kamiah to Weippe.

From Riverfront Park in Kamiah, turn north on US 12 for 0.2 mile. As soon as you come off the bridge, turn northwest on the road along the north side of the river. In 0.4 mile turn northeast on the Tom Taha/Glenwood Road, NF 100, for 1.3 miles. Turn north for 4.0 miles on Adams Grade, which gives spectacular views of the surrounding ridges. As soon as you break out of the trees into farmland, turn north on Carabel Road for 3.5 miles. At the Y, turn north onto the very narrow Lolo Creek Road, which switchbacks down steeply to cross Lolo Creek in 2.3 miles.

Lolo Creek

The ascent of the heights beyond Kamiah was tedious in the extreme. It was raining hard, and the muddy, slippery trail was almost impassable, filled with rugged rocks and fallen timber. The descent to the Lo-lo Fork was made by slipping, crawling and scrambling over rocks and through thick underbrush. At the "We-ipe" was an opening in the forest with water and grass. Here was a camp made for the weary, footsore animals and exhausted men, after a sixteen mile march of the greatest severity.—Lt. E. S. Farrow

167

This photo of Lolo Creek gives a sense of the downed and criss-crossed timber which had to be negotiated by 800 Nez Perce, their 2,000 horses, and the 800-man army following them. (Photo courtesy of Montana Historical Society.)

Climbing up from Lolo Creek is as rough as climbing down was. In 3.8 miles, turn north at the T and follow 3 Mile Road as it jogs north and east for the next 1.9 miles.

Incendiary Creek

On July 17, a scouting party following the Nez Perce was ambushed near here.

Left Kamiah at 4 o'clock A.M. and took the Lo Lo trail for the Camas ground or Weipe after marching some twenty (20) miles. (The Indian scouts accompanying the column) ran into an ambush of hostile Indians, who wounded two (2) and killed one (1) of the Scouts.... Immediately after the firing began I dismounted my men... Myself and Capt Winters marched through the dense underbrush and fallen timbers, until we found one (1) of the wounded Indian Scouts. We then with our own command skirmished through the woods until we found the body of "Levy" (also one of the Scouts) We then returned to the edge of the timber.... We reached Lo Lo Creek about 11 o'clock P.M. and camped for the night. —Ed McConville (colonel of volunteers), July 17, 1877[4]

Turn north on Cemetery Road for 2.5 miles to Weippe. At the T, turn west on Pierce Street for four blocks to reach Main Street.

Mainstream Travelers can return to Kooskia by following the Mainstream Traveler, Kamiah to Weippe Loop. Or join the Intrepid Traveler at Weippe for a trip on the Lolo Motorway.

For the Mainstream Traveler

Kooskia to Shotgun Creek Road

In this section, Mainstream and Adventurous Travelers will drive east along US 12, which follows the drainage of the Lochsa River up to Lolo Pass.

From the junction with Idaho 13 at Kooskia, follow US 12 east. In 1.9 miles, a "Historic Site Ahead" sign gives very brief warning of a turnout. For a fuller description of story told by the historical information sign, read **Clear Creek** on page 146. Across the river from the sign, Clear Creek, along which the Looking Glass camp was located, flows into the Clearwater.

Proceed east for 93.1 miles to Shotgun Creek Road at mile marker 169.

For a taste of the Lolo Motorway, Intrepid Travelers can connect to NF 500 after milepost 139, on NF 107, Saddle Camp Road for 8.6 miles; or, before milepost 154, take NF 108, Squaw Creek Road, for 0.5 mile to NF 566, which junctions with NF 500 in 10.0 miles; or, at mile marker 162, turn north on the easy NF 569, Parachute Hill Road, for 5.8 miles.

US 12

US 12 was not completed until 1962. Although this modern paved road is five to ten miles south of the original Lolo Trail, it still retains an air of wildness. Even today there are stretches of sixty-four and forty miles with no services and next to no signs of human habitation.

169

Continue with the Mainstream Traveler at Shotgun Creek Road.

For the Intrepid Traveler

Weippe to Junction of Shotgun Creek Road with US 12

Miles: 104.0

Maps: Clearwater National Forest

Special considerations: A full tank of gas is a must. Although it's only 97 miles to a gas station at Powell, on US 12, or 135 miles to the first gas station in Montana, almost all those miles will be done in gas-eating first or second gear.

There are several primitive campgrounds along the way, but the only lodging between here and Montana is at Powell.

Plan to spend at least two days driving the route. The trip can be done in one day, but that results in some very weary travelers. Driving time between Weippe and Lolo on the Lolo Motorway, with minimal breaks, is ten hours of intense concentration.

The Lolo Motorway is a one-lane dirt road. Snow does not generally melt from the road until late June or early July

During July, August, and September, there is an average of fewer than five cars a day on this road. During hunting season in October, there can be fifty vehicles a day on the road. The road is closed by snow in November.

The Lolo Motorway acquired its quaint name when it was constructed in the 1930s, and it has not materially improved since then. People who do not feel comfortable driving in the mountains should not drive on this road.

This road is not for the faint-hearted. In fact, at times it requires some real stoutness of nerve. One of the road's idiosyncracies is this: To prevent the road from washing out, curves are frequently banked to the outside. It can be very disconcerting to feel your vehicle angled out toward a dropoff rather than banked into the inside of the mountain.

On the other hand, the beauty of the Lolo Motorway is that it offers a unique opportunity to see some very wild country from your car or truck. (The road is not suitable for trailer or motor home traffic.) Once past the logging operations around the eastern and western entrances, the hand of man is infrequently apparent.

From the crossroads where Idaho 11 turns north in Weippe, follow Pierce Street, which becomes Musselshell Road and which remains paved for a while, east for 8.1 miles. At Peterson Corners, the junction with NF 100, continue east across Brown's Creek Bridge for 3.8 miles to Musselshell Creek.

Musselshell Meadows

Musselshell Meadows, north of the road, extends for half a mile beyond Musselshell Creek. This was site of the first Nez Perce camp after leaving Weippe. Two weeks later, on July 31, General Howard's troops also camped here.

> Last night we had rather an unpleasant time…for we went to bed without our tents, and it began to rain about midnight. So I had to get up and make a shelter with a tent fly which I had laid on the ground as a sort of mattress. Doctor Newlands and I were bunking together. However, we finally made it comfortable and rain proof, and then slept on till morning.—Dr. John FitzGerald, August 1, 1877[5]

In the 1890s, after Weippe Prairie was settled, Musselshell Meadows became a prime camas gathering ground. Traditional women still come here to dig camas with their special camas-digging sticks.

Continue on NF 100 for 1.2 miles. Turn north on NF 103. In 5.5 miles, just across Yoosa Creek, is a Nee-Me-Poo Trail marker. This trail leads to Soldier Meadows and thence to Beaver Dam Saddle. Continue driving for 9.4 miles to Beaver Dam Saddle where you will see another Nee-Me-Poo Trail marker.

Soldier Meadows, where Howard camped on August 1, is 3.6 miles northwest of Beaver Dam Saddle.

Turn east on NF 104 for 0.8 mile to the junction with NF 500. Turn north on NF 500 for 5.7 miles to Weitas Meadows.

Weitas Meadows

Apparently the Nez Perce camped on this lovely meadow. What a relief to see some open space! General Howard arrived here with his troops on August 2.

> Got up at 5 A.M. but did not march until 11 A.M., and then only went 8 miles and made the nicest camp we have yet had in among partially wooded hills, or rather mountains. We had some fine mountain views yesterday and today. We were so high up that the whole extent of mountainous country was spread around us.
>
> Captain Spurgin, 21st Infantry, caught up with our army last night, and today some beef cattle arrived to serve as food for us all, poor things. We find for the last 3 nights hardly any grass for our horses and pack mules.— Dr. John FitzGerald, August 1, 1877[6]

171

Continue east from Weitas Meadows for 16.6 miles to Bald Mountain.

Bald Mountain

On August 3, Howard's command camped here at Bald Mountain.

The command left Camp Winters at seven, A.M. Artillery at head of column. Day clear and pleasantly cool.... The trail led through woods of the same general character as before; rather a "slow trail," owing to mountainous country and fallen timber. The summit of the hills was covered with rough granite boulders, making the path quite difficult. There was a plenty of excellent springs on trail; our men travel it well, and are in good order. We march sixteen miles and encamp on a slope of the mountain. Poor grazing, indeed, here. The only feed consists of wild dwarf lupine, and wire-grass. Several mules were exhausted, and some packs of bacon were abandoned by the way.... Loose Indian horses, broken-down always, were seen along the trail.—Gen. O. O. Howard, August 2, 1877

This Friday morning...it is almost cold enough to make ice. We are making a late start this morning, for our mules are almost played out.... We start at 6 a.m. and work hard all day and make about sixteen miles by 6 p.m.

Our train and troops string out about five miles in length. ...No one can travel a foot off the trail.... The scenery is very grand from the tops of the mounts we cross, while all day long it has been very pleasant to travel through the dense woods, with the sunlight glinting through the trees.

4:30 p.m.... We marched for eight miles through the mist, or rather clouds....

We would like to travel faster than we do, but it is useless to make more than we do.... It is always from two to three hours after we get in before the rear guard arrives. We have about six hundred animals. They string out over these rough trails at a great rate. It is a fortunate thing I did not bring my horses. They would have been ruined by these rough trips....

...My fingers are cold so I will stop.—Major Edwin Mason, August 3, 1877[7]

172   The sites of several of Howard's camps have been identified because of artifacts found on location. One of the cannon balls discovered here is on display at the Clearwater Historical Society Museum in Orofino.

Continue northeast on NF 500 for 5.8 miles to the historical sign for Smoking Place. Here a Nee-Me-Poo hiking trail, #40, is an easy 45-minute walk to the historical sign for Sinque Hole. One person can drive the 3.2 miles while the other stretches her or his legs for 2.2 miles and makes the gradual 630-foot descent. Great views too.

From Sinque Hole, it is 2.3 miles to Saddle Camp. NF 107, Saddle Camp Road, connects back to US 12 in 8.6 miles, for those who are tired of driving on this road. Otherwise, Howard Camp is 3.6 miles farther east on NF 500.

Howard Camp

This scrubby knoll is where Howard's command camped on the night of August 4.

> Our American horses were not used to the fodder of the native cayuse. We carried no forage. If we should chance upon one of the little mountain valleys where there should be grass, we found it either trampled down by Joseph's ponies or destroyed in some other way. Many is the time we have cut bark from the trees for our horses. Colonel Sanford, in charge of the cavalry arm of the service reported that there were not more than 20 or 25 horses in the entire command fit for a run of 70 or 80 miles.—Pvt. William Connolly[8]

> [D]ispatches from Capt. Rawn…says he talked with White Bird and Looking Glass, that the Indians are very short of ammunition and are offering as high as a dollar for cartridges…. The citizens are selling them goods and buying their horses. That they are going into the Sioux country. That they are only travelling about 5 or 6 miles per day in order to rest their stock…. We are camped again on a mountain side, which slopes as steep as the roof of our house. I have been obliged to dig out a place for my bed to lay level…. I am well, comfortable and dirty.—Major Edwin Mason, August 4, 1877[9]

Continue traveling east on NF 500. It is 6.6 miles to NF 566. To connect back to US 12, take NF 566 for 10.0 miles, then turn south on NF 108, Squaw Creek Road, for 0.5 mile.

Junction of NF 566 and NF 500

> Diehards and travelers recently arrived from US 12 via NF 566 can proceed east on NF 500. Another 18.5 miles brings you to Papoose Saddle.

The Lolo Trail

The Lolo Trail began to be used extensively when Native Americans of the region acquired the horse sometime between 1710 and 1730. The added mobility provided by horses made it worthwhile for the Nez Perce to go spend time in the buffalo country of central Montana. Thus, the Nez Perce called this route the Buffalo Trail.

The use of the horse defined the location of the trail. In order to feed the horses on the trek, which usually took at least six days, the trail went from meadow to meadow. Unlike some other trails, which hug riverbanks and stay at the bottom of drainages, the Lolo Trail was a ridgetop trail. Since south-facing ridges are dry and have fewer trees, it's much easier for horses to travel through scattered trees than through forests choked with downed timber.

In 1866, the Lolo Trail had been improved in an effort to connect Lewiston in Idaho Territory with gold-prosperous Virginia City in Montana Territory. But even with improvements, the trail was nothing more than a pack trail and thus never became a viable commercial route. Even though every winter downed more trees and branches along the way, the Nez Perce continued to use the trail regularly. By 1877, when the Nez Perce fled eastwards, the "improved" Lolo Trail was again choked with timber.

> About twelve years ago several thousand dollars were appropriated by Congress to have the Lolo Trail surveyed, and, judging from the great distances between the mile posts, the engineers were in league with some one who wanted to get a further appropriation for a wagon road. In connection with the extraordinary length of these miles, they are nearly all straight up and down mountains.—Thomas Sutherland (war correspondent)[10]

The great buffalo hunters of the various Nez Perce bands knew the Lolo Trail well. Rainbow and Five Wounds had returned to Idaho from buffalo country the day after the Battle of White Bird. Looking Glass, who was the leader of the five fleeing bands during July, was a great warrior and buffalo hunter and presumably had been over the Trail to the Buffalo Country many times. He had just returned in May from an extended stay in buffalo country.

At Papoose Saddle, you have two choices for attaining US 12. NF 569, Parachute Hill Road, a relatively easy and short drive on a one-and-a-half lane road arrives at US 12 in 5.8 miles.

To more closely follow the route of the Nez Perce, turn north on NF 109, which has steep drop-offs to Shotgun Creek, for the next 9.3 miles. At the junction with US 12, turn northeast.

Join the Mainstream Traveler at Shotgun Creek Road, NF 109.

For the Mainstream Traveler

Shotgun Creek Road, NF 109 to Lolo Pass

From Shotgun Creek Road, at mile marker 169, the Lolo Trail closely parallels US 12 over to Lolo, Montana. About 2 miles later, around mile marker 171, look off to the west to see Crooked Fork and the approximate location of 21 Mile Camp of August 5.

21 Mile Camp

We had passed the last tine of the Clearwater, where at night, after twenty-one miles of the roughest country, with Spurgin's pioneers ahead, cutting out the trail, we came into camp in the twilight, where we had heard loud echoes of firing by the advanced scouts, and thought they had come upon Joseph's rear-guard. Then we spurred up the weary animals into a tired trot, and, along this narrow trail descended for miles through the almost impenetrable forest, till we came to the narrowest of valleys, to find not a mouthful of food for horse or mule, but the nicest of salmon for the men, in water about knee-deep,—water clear as crystal, rushing and plashing over the rocks. The echoes which deceived us into thinking the enemy near, were from the scouts' carbines, shooting the bigger fish, as they were swimming up the Clearwater [Crooked Fork].—Gen. O. O. Howard

Proceed north on US 12 for 3.3 miles, to Lolo Pass.

Chief Looking Glass became the leader of the five non-treaty bands because of his experience in the buffalo country. This photo was taken in 1871 by W.H. Jackson when the Looking Glass band was camped on the Yellowstone River. (Photo courtesy of Smithsonian Institution National Anthropological Archives, Bureau of American Ethnology Collection.)

Lolo Pass Visitors' Center

The Lolo Pass Visitors' Center has exhibits on the Lolo Trail. During the winter season, it is open only on weekends.

Join the Adventurous Traveler for a sidetrip to Packer Meadows. Or continue with the Mainstream Traveler at Lolo Pass.

For the Adventurous Traveler

Sidetrip
Packer Meadows

Miles: 2.2, round-trip
Map: Clearwater National Forest
Special considerations: This road is closed by snow from November to May.

At the north side of the Lolo Pass Visitor's Center, turn east on NF 373 for 1.1 miles to Packer Meadows.

Packer Meadows

In these beautiful meadows, General Howard made a five-hour breakfast camp with his cavalry and infantry on August 6. Because of the amount of grass available, the Nez Perce may have camped here a couple of weeks earlier.

> Here was the place where mule and man enjoyed a rest and a breakfast far more satisfying than in inhabited regions which are replete with abundance.—Gen. O. O. Howard

From Packer Meadows, return to US 12 and rejoin the Mainstream Traveler at Lolo Pass.

For the Mainstream Traveler
Lolo Pass to Graves Creek Road

Lolo Pass

Having finally reached the top of the Bitterroot Mountains, you have also reached the traditional eastern limit of Nez Perce territory. Although you crossed the boundary of the Nez Perce reservation over ninety miles ago, the crest of the mountains was the original border between the two nations of the Nez Perce and the United States, according to the Treaty of 1855. East of here lies aboriginal Salish land.

177

> Proceed north on US 12 and cross the border into Montana and the Mountain Time Zone. It's all downhill for the 7.2 miles to Lolo Hot Springs.

Lolo Hot Springs

Two young men from Stevensville were at Lolo Hot Springs on a summer outing when the Nez Perce appeared here on July 25. Escaping on stolen horses, they hurried home to the Bitterroot Valley and spread the news that the Nez Perce had arrived. Other visitors appeared in the Nez Perce camp that night as well.

> *When the Nez Perces camp reached the Hot Springs on the Lo Lo trail…three Indians met them in their camp. One of these Indians was Nez Perces, but his home was in the Bitter Root valley. He told Looking Glass there were some soldiers on the trail watching for them to come.*—Duncan McDonald (Nez Perce reporter)

The soldiers waiting in front of the Nez Perce had barricaded the trail. Although General Howard wanted to squeeze the Nez Perce, his troops did not reach this spot for eleven more days. On August 6, their pleasure at reaching such a beautiful spot was evident.

> *The last two days we have been in rather a handsome country, i.e., since we struck the eastern Lolo River [Lolo Creek], which is a tributary of the Bitter Root River. Last night we had the most picturesque camp I have ever seen— a very remarkable spot where there are 4 hot springs.… I bathed my feet in one of them last night and found it as hot as I could bear comfortably. There was good trout fishing in the Lolo nearby, and Colonel Sanford and I got quite a fine string and had them for breakfast.*—Dr. John FitzGerald, August 7, 1877[11]

> *Yesterday we camped at "Hot springs," a wonderful place, great basins of boiling hot water, flowing over the rocks in cascades–a grand sight and a fine place to wash clothes.*—Major Edwin Mason, August 7, 1877[12]

A courier from Colonel Gibbon arrived at this camp. His dispatch informed General Howard that Gibbon's command was following the Nez Perce, and expected to overtake them shortly and give battle. Howard rushed out of camp next morning with the cavalry, leaving the infantry behind to make the best time it could. The foot soldiers would not catch up with the cavalry again for two weeks.

178

At half-past five, A.M., Spurgin, with his axemen, was already out on the trail, working hard, to get well ahead of the command, so that it might make, to-day, the utmost distance over this terribly rough and obstructed pathway. He cleared away the fallen trees, made bridges across chasms, and, when there was time, by side-digging or walling with fragments of the rock, he improved portions of the break-neck trail.

At half-past six, A.M., with some reluctance leaving these hot springs and this charming camp, we set out, and made twenty-two miles.—Gen. O. O. Howard

From Lolo Hot Springs, continue northeast on US 12 for 6.6 miles.

Just before milepost 14, turn north for 0.1 mile to take a walk on the Lolo Trail at Howard Creek.

Return to US 12 and continue east for 2.1 miles to Graves Creek Road.

Join the Adventurous Traveler or continue with the Mainstream Traveler at Graves Creek Road.

For the Adventurous Traveler

Sidetrip
Graves Creek Road

Miles: 1.8, round-trip
Map: Lolo National Forest

To see the site of one of the Nez Perce camps, turn north on Graves Creek Road, just past milepost 16. In about 0.6 mile, Graves Creek Meadows can be seen.

Graves Creek Meadows

In the narrow valley created by Graves Creek, the main party of Nez Perce women, children, and old people camped on the nights of July 26 and 27. They stayed a safe distance away while the chiefs negotiated with Captain Rawn at Fort Fizzle.

Proceed another 0.3 mile to a Y and turn around. Return to US 12 and rejoin the Mainstream Traveler at Graves Creek Road.

For the Mainstream Traveler

Graves Creek Road to Lolo

Proceed east on US 12 for 6.8 miles.

Woodman Creek

While the women and children camped safely at Graves Creek, the warriors bivouaced on Woodman Flats during the Fort Fizzle negotiations.

Riding through here, where the valley widens just a bit, ten days later, General Howard noted that "so fine a wagon trail here began, on hard, level ground...." After traveling through the forest for nine days, the cavalry was probably quite happy to see a real road.

Continue east on US 12 for 4.8 miles, and pull off at the Fort Fizzle Historic Site to read the historical information signs.

Fort Fizzle

Only three weeks earlier, Fort Missoula had been established. For its first assignment, the fledgling post was called upon to halt the progress of about seven hundred Nez Perce and their two thousand horses.

> *Commanding Officer, Post of Missoula Montana:*
> *Sir: —All reports seem to indicate that what are left of the hostile Indians, with their stock and plunder, have escaped by the Lolo Trail, and may reach you before this dispatch.... If you simply bother them and keep them back until I can close in, their destruction or surrender will be sure.—Gen. O. O. Howard, July 25, 1877*

180   The commanding officer of Fort Missoula, Captain Charles C. Rawn, responded as best he could with five officers, thirty enlisted men, and one hundred fifty volunteers.

The people of Missoula also formed volunteer associations for the purpose of protecting themselves. The excitement increasing, I on the 25th of July with every available man that could be spared, proceeded to Lo-Lo, entrenched my command in what I considered the most defensible and least easily flanked part of the cañon.—Capt. Charles C. Rawn, September 30, 1877

We commenced a barricade by felling trees across the stream and the canyon. We were here only one night; in a sort of drizzling rain.—Sgt. Charles Loynes[13]

Fifteen Salish warriors had accompanied Rawn to act as intermediaries. To emphasize their neutrality, they were without arms or ammunition. But the Nez Perce were dismayed to see their friends on the side of the soldiers.

I saw Salish Indians at the soldiers' fort. They seemed quite a bunch. All had white cloths tied on arm and head. This, so as not to shoot each other. So the soldiers would know they were not Nez Perces. They were helping the soldiers. Always friends before, we now got no help from them, the Flatheads. No help any time.—Yellow Wolf[14]

On the 27th of July, I had a talk with Chiefs Joseph, White Bird and Looking Glass, who proposed if allowed to pass unmolested, to march peaceably thru the Bitter-root valley, but I refused to allow them to pass unless they complied with my stipulations as to the surrender of their arms.... We separated without agreement.—Capt. Charles C. Rawn, September 30, 1877

The Nez Perce were absolutely insistent in their position: they would not lay down their arms.

Rainbow called out loudly from where he sat his bay war horse, "Do not tell me to lay down the gun! We did not want this war!... General Howard kindled war when he spoke the rifle in the peace council! We answered with the rifle and that answer stands to this sun! Some of my people have been killed, and I will kill some of the enemies and then I shall die in the battle!"—Two Moon[15]

181

We must go to buffalo country. If we are not allowed to go peaceably we shall do the best we can. If the officer wishes to build corrals for the Nez Perces he may, but they will not hold us back. We are not horses. The country is large. I think we are smart as he is and know the mountains and road as well.—Chief Looking Glass

Looking Glass promised the volunteers that if they would let his followers pass unmolested he would see to it that the Indians should shed no blood in the Bitter Root Valley. This disgraceful proposition was accepted by the volunteers.—Thomas Sutherland (war correspondent)[16]

Although accepting the proposal of peace was considered disgraceful by the troops who were two weeks behind the Nez Perce, the offer sounded pretty good to the people who lived in the Bitterroot Valley.

Exspected an atack from the Indians. They like sane cible falows found a way around us and let us alone.—John P. Martens (Bitterroot volunteer), July 28, 1877[17]

While a few warriors climbed among rocks and fired down on the soldier fort the rest of the Indians with our horse herd struck to the left of main trail. I could see the soldiers from the mountainside where we traveled. It was no trouble, not dangerous, to pass those soldiers.—Yellow Wolf[18]

Nobody was hurt, but the truth was, some of our citizens were pretty badly scared.—Henry Buck (Stevensville merchant)[19]

> From Fort Fizzle, continue east on US 12 for 3.4 miles to Sleeman Creek.

Sleeman Creek

After detouring along the ridge north of the road and bypassing Fort Fizzle, the Nez Perce caravan returned to the main trail at Sleeman Creek.

> Continue driving east on US 12 to the junction with US 93 at Lolo, Montana, in 0.9 mile.

Lolo

In the meantime that portion of the volunteers, some 100 or more, representing Bitter-root valley, hearing that the Nez-Perces promised to pass peaceably through it, determined that no act of hostility on their part should provoke the Indians to a contrary measure, and with leave, left in squads of from one to a dozen. On the 28th the Indians moved from the cañon to the hills, ascending the sides one half mile in my front, passed my flank and went into the Bitter Root valley. As soon as I found that they were passing around me, and hearing that they had attacked a rear guard I had established to prevent desertions, I abandoned this breastworks, formed a skirmish line across the cañon with my regulars and such of the volunteers as I could control and advanced in the direction the Indians had gone. They did not accept a fight but retreated up the Bitter-root. At the mouth of the Lo-Lo and before reaching it, all the volunteers had left me, but a dozen to twenty Missoula men, and I was obliged to return to this post [at Missoula].—Capt. Charles C. Rawn, September 30, 1877

Howard camped near here on August 7.

Saturday, Sunday and Monday we spent in working our way over this difficult mountain trail, climbing up one mountain for miles, only to plunge again into a deep gorge and do the same thing over again. Most tiresome work, and as we have had little else for the horses to feed on than leaves from the brush, they are in wretched condition, hardly able to move a leg.— Major Edwin Mason, August 7, 1877[20]

Continue with the Mainstream Traveler at Lolo, Montana, in the next chapter.

For Further Reading

The Lolo Trail: A History and a Guide to the Trail of Lewis and Clark, by Ralph Space, is an interesting, fact-packed booklet about the history of the trail. Space, formerly the supervisor of the Clearwater National Forest, traveled the Lolo Trail for forty-six years before writing this book in 1970. Thus, he had an opportunity to see many historical sites, including the grave of Lolo, before logging disturbed the area. His quite plausible deductions are based on a combination of historical research and personal experience.

Clearwater Country!: The Traveler's Historical & Recreational Guide: Lewiston, Idaho–Missoula, Montana covers a lot more historical territory than 1877, but is an interesting companion for Mainstream Travelers on US 12. Written by two local residents, Borg Hendrickson and Linwood Laughy.

In Nez Perce Country: Accounts of the Bitterroots and the Clearwater after Lewis and Clark is a collection of accounts by travelers on the Lolo Trail, compiled by Lynn and Dennis Baird. This book also covers a lot more history than 1877 and is an interesting companion for Intrepid Travelers on the Lolo Motorway.

Hike Lewis and Clark's Idaho and the Nee-Me-Poo Trail that runs near the Lolo Motorway. This guidebook by Mary Aegerter and Steve F. Russell has detailed instructions for eleven segments of Trail #40, plus many other hikes along the way.

CHAPTER 6

Bitterroot Valley

A Peace Proposal is Accepted

Lolo to Big Hole Battlefield, Montana

Indian troubles were always considered hair-raising events and people generally on the frontiers were suspicious that something awful might happen when there was a raising of bad blood amongst the natives.—Henry Buck (Stevensville merchant)[1]

I fight when I cannot avoid it, but not otherwise.—Chief Looking Glass

The Indians were allowed to pass through this valley by the scalawag population that bought their stolen horses. And it is said some of them traded ammunition, powder, etc., to the redskins for their stolen property, gold dust, etc.—Dr. John FitzGerald, August 30, 1877[2]

We traveled through the Bitterroot Valley slowly. The white people were friendly. We did much buying and trading with them.

No more fighting! We had left General Howard and his war in Idaho.
—Yellow Wolf[3]

Our people in the Bitter Root, and in Montana generally, felt very sore at General Howard and severely censured him for chasing his Indians out of Idaho and onto us while in peaceful pursuits of our daily avocations.—Henry Buck (Stevensville merchant)[4]

It is a monstrous outrage that the Nez Perces shall be allowed to pass through our territory.—J. H. Mills (Editor, *New North-west*)

As was always customary with Indians traveling on horseback, they jogged their ponies along on a little dog trot. Being curious enough to gain some idea of their number, took out my watch and timed their passing a given point. It took just one hour and a quarter for all to move by and there were no gaps in the continuous train. —Henry Buck (Stevensville merchant)[5]

The Story

Excitement rolled through the Bitterroot Valley in successive waves during the summer of 1877. News of the Indian uprising in Idaho swept into the valley in late June. As early as July 10, people in the Bitterroot were building two sod forts—one in Corvallis and one near present-day Hamilton. Residents of Stevensville busily renovated Fort Owen, which had been abandoned in 1871 and was by this time beginning to crumble.

On July 26, two young men rushed into Stevensville with their news. They had been camping at Lolo Hot Springs when hundreds of Nez Perce arrived. Taken captive so the news of the Nez Perce arrival would not be spread, the boys had stolen two horses and escaped under cover of darkness. Upon hearing that the Nez Perce were close by, over a hundred men volunteered to go stand the Indians off at what later became known as Fort Fizzle.

The Nez Perce themselves arrived in the valley on July 28. By detouring around Fort Fizzle on the Lolo Trail, the Nez Perce reached the Bitterroot Valley ahead of the citizen volunteers. Fifty or sixty of the volunteers blundered into the first camp the Nez Perce made south of Lolo. At this camp, the Nez Perce reaffirmed to the settlers the promise they had made at Fort Fizzle: they would not harm anyone or anything, and they would pass peacefully through the valley. They had always traveled peacefully through the valley in prior years on their way to buffalo country; this passage would be no exception. Nevertheless, the Nez Perce caravan created high levels of anxiety among the settlers.

The Nez Perce were no strangers to the Bitterroot Valley. Bands going to and from the buffalo country of central Montana frequently traded with the merchants of the Bitterroot Valley. In fact, one band of about thirty lodges of Nez Perce lived permanently in the Bitterroot Valley.

Unique in the annals of Indian wars, this pledge of peace was honored by the Nez Perce as they leisurely traveled south along the Bitterroot River. Anxious settlers forted themselves up. Meanwhile, outside the confines of the valley, the governor called for volunteers to fight the public enemies, newspaper editors were outraged, and military men were infuriated that the settlers would accept such a promise of peace.

186 The next episode of this thrilling summer began on August 4 when Colonel John Gibbon left Fort Missoula with 149 men. Traveling twenty-five to thirty miles a day, with his infantry in wagons, he was soon on the heels of the unsuspecting Nez Perce. Seventy volunteers rushed to join up with his command. Although the Nez Perce had left them in peace, the citizens would not return the favor. Only half of the volunteers actually went all the way to the Big Hole; the other half sensibly returned home.

General Howard finally made it across the Lolo Trail with his cavalry on August 8 and rushed down the valley to the aid of Gibbon. But he was too late.

The tide seemed to have turned when news of the Big Hole Battle came rolling in from the south. Neighbors and relatives of Bitterroot settlers who had volunteered to go with Gibbon to surprise and fight the Indians had been surprised themselves. Of the thirty-four citizen volunteers, five were dead and four were wounded.

The final ripple of excitement was caused by Howard's infantry. Lagging far behind the action, the foot soldiers trudged through the Bitterroot Valley from August 10 to 13. They would not catch up with the cavalry again for two weeks.

Chronology of Events

1877

28 July	The Nez Perce camp in the Bitterroot Valley.
29 July	The Nez Perce camp with Chief Charlo near Stevensville.
30 and 31 July	The Nez Perce go shopping in Stevensville.
1 August	The Nez Perce leave Stevensville.
4 August	Colonel Gibbon arrives in Stevensville with 131 men.
5 August	The Nez Perce raid Lockwood's ranch on Rye Creek and camp above Ross Hole.
	Gibbon camps at Sleeping Child Creek.
6 August	Gibbon camps below Ross Hole.
	The Nez Perce camp on Trail Creek.
7 August	The Nez Perce camp at Big Hole.
	Gibbon camps at the foot of the Continental Divide.
8 August	General Howard and his cavalry camp at Stevensville.
	Gibbon camps on Trail Creek.
9 August	Howard camps at Rye Creek.
10 August	Howard camps on Trail Creek.
	Howard's infantry camps at Stevensville.

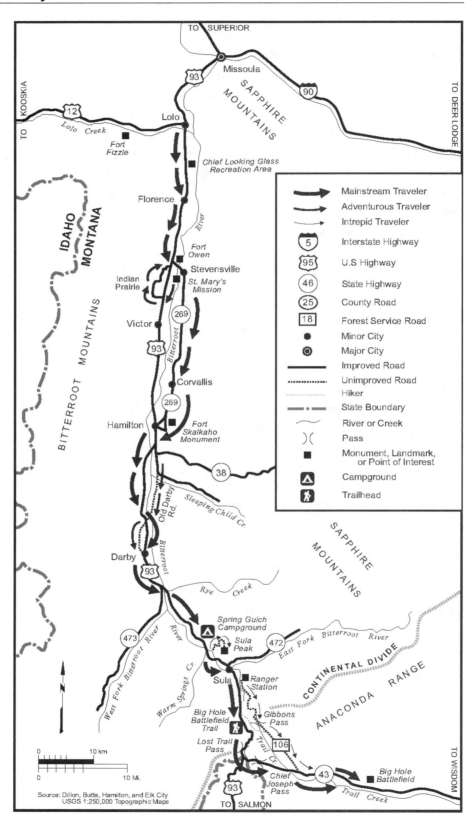

Travel Plan

Mainstream Traveler	Adventurous Traveler	Intrepid Traveler
Lolo to Stevensville	follow Mainstream	follow Mainstream
	Sidetrip Indian Prairie Loop	follow Adventurous
Stevensville to Hamilton	follow Mainstream	follow Mainstream
Hamilton to Darby	Hamilton to Darby	follow Mainstream or Adventurous
Darby to Spring Gulch Campground	follow Mainstream	follow Mainstream
		Sidetrip Sula Peak Lookout
Spring Gulch Campground to Sula	follow Mainstream	follow Mainstream
Sula to Big Hole Battlefield	follow Mainstream	Sula to Big Hole Battlefield

For the Mainstream Traveler

Lolo To Stevensville

In Lolo, at the junction of US 12 and US 93, proceed south on US 93 for 6.6 miles to the turnoff for the Chief Looking Glass Recreation Area.

Sidetrip
Looking Glass Recreation Area

Turn east on the paved Chief Looking Glass Road for 0.9 mile, then turn north on Ellison Lane into the Chief Looking Glass Recreation Area.

With so many mountain streams feeding into the Bitterroot River, it's no wonder that the river itself retains a refreshing, clear quality. The Chief Looking Glass Recreation Area affords an opportunity to spend some time close to this beautiful, rocky river.

Named for the man who led the Nez Perce out of Idaho and down the Bitterroot Valley, the recreation area has a historical information sign that commemorates the first camp the Nez Perce caravan made in the Bitterroot Valley after skirting around Fort Fizzle on the Lolo Trail. Because of the marshiness caused by so many creeks flowing into the river, the camp was probably on higher ground a bit west of the river.

About fifty or sixty of the Bitterroot volunteers returning home from Fort Fizzle found the camp situated between them and their families who lived farther up (south) in the valley. The prospect of being separated from their wives and children encouraged the men to accept the Nez Perce peace proposal.

> *When we overtook the Indians, Looking Glass told us he would not hurt any persons or property in the valley if allowed to pass in peace, and we could pass through his camp to our homes. We decided it would be silly to uselessly incite the Indians to devastating our valley, and I do not think our critics would have done otherwise had they and their families and homes been situated as ours. If they want Indians for breakfast they are still within reach, and have been ever since the fiasco at Fort Fizzle on the Lolo.* —W. B. Harlan (Bitterroot volunteer), August 4, 1877[6]

At this camp, the chiefs made the final decision regarding which route to take: north via the Flathead reservation, or south to their friends the Crows and buffalo country.

> *Looking Glass then called a council.... White Bird and Red Owl agreed; they wanted to go by the [Flathead or Salish] reserve. Joseph did not say a word. Looking Glass wanted to go by Big Hole and down the Yellowstone to join the Crows, according to agreement, because the Crows promised them that whenever the Nez Perces fought the whites, they would join them. There was a disagreement, but quarrelling among themselves they concluded it was best to let Looking Glass have his way.* —Duncan McDonald (Nez Perce reporter)

190

Although this brand of consensus decision-making sounds strange to our own majority-rules way of thinking, Chief Looking Glass had other factors operating in his favor. He had been in buffalo country several times while the leaders of the other bands had seldom or never traveled to central Montana.

Chief Charlo of the Flatheads in a photo taken around 1910. The Bitterroot Valley was the aboriginal home of the Flathead Nation. (Photo courtesy of Montana Historical Society.)

Thus he had been the acknowledged leader of the five nontreaty bands since the chiefs decided to leave Idaho.

The strategy behind this plan was to spend the winter with their friends, the Crows. Then, the following spring, when all the excitement had died down, they would return home to Idaho. They had no quarrel with the people of Montana and expected their peace pledge to be honored. The Nez Perce truly believed they had left the war behind them.

> Return to US 93. Continue south on US 93 from Chief Looking Glass Road for 10.0 miles to the junction with Montana 269.
>
> Join the Adventurous Traveler for the Indian Prairie loop sidetrip, or continue with the Mainstream Traveler at Stevensville.

For the Adventurous Traveler

Sidetrip
Indian Prairie Loop

Miles: 9.4
Map: Bitterroot National Forest

This tour circles around the land claimed by Charlo, chief of the Salish (Flathead) band living in the Bitterroot. From the junction of US 93 and Montana 269, proceed south on US 93 for 3.6 miles to Indian Prairie Loop. Turn west on Indian Prairie Loop for 1.2 miles, then turn north on St. Mary's Road for 1.8 miles. Turn north on Salish Trail for 2.0 miles. At the T, turn east on South Kootenai Creek Road for 0.3 mile to the junction with US 93. Turn north on US 93 for 0.5 mile to return to the junction with Montana 269.

Indian Prairie

The story of the Salish (Flatheads) and their homeland in the Bitterroot Valley parallels that of the Nez Perce. In 1855, the same Governor Stevens who had negotiated the Nez Perce treaty also negotiated a treaty with the Salish guaranteeing them the Bitterroot Valley. But in 1872 a new treaty was made and signed. This treaty shrank Salish land to the size of the current Flathead reservation in northwestern Montana. The primary chief of the Salish, Chief Charlo, claimed he did not sign the treaty of 1872. James Garfield, the treaty negotiator and future president of the United States, claimed he had obtained Charlo's signature. Thus the Salish land of the Bitterroot Valley was lost to its original owners.

The Salish had been converted to Catholicism, and St. Mary's Mission was located close to them in nearby Stevensville. The band numbered around five hundred fifty, including about twenty-five Nez Perce.

The Salish and Nez Perce had a long history of friendship and intermarriage. It was natural that the Nez Perce would expect to camp with their old friends.

On reaching the place of Charlos, the Salish chief, Looking Glass summoned a number of his warriors to accompany him to visit Charlos and inquire of him where the best place to camp was to find good grass. On approaching Charlos' house Looking Glass thought it would be honorable to extend his hand to Charlos before making his inquiry. But Charlos refused to accept the extended hand saying, "Why should I shake hands with men whose hands are bloody? My hands are clean of blood." Looking Glass replied: "Your hands are as red with the blood of your enemies as mine are. Why should my hands be clean when I have been forced to fight the white man? Your hands are as bloody as ours. I did not come to talk about blood. I came to ask you the best place to camp." Charlos answered: "Above my house is the best spot to camp." And there they accordingly pitched their tents.— Duncan McDonald (Nez Perce reporter)

While camped with Chief Charlo near here for two nights, the Nez Perce did some trading in Stevensville.

It was my father's boast that his hand had never in seventy years been bloodied with the white man's blood, and I am the son of my father.

*We could not fight against the Nez Perces because they helped me several years ago, against my enemy the Blackfeet, but we will not fight with them against the whites.—*Chief Charlo (Salish)[7]

Both Nez Perce and whites were angry at Charlo because he walked the tightrope of neutrality. Twenty Salish warriors, wearing white handkerchiefs around their heads, had stood with the Bitterroot citizen volunteers at Fort Fizzle. Now the Nez Perce were camping with Charlo. Although several settlers realized Charlo's beneficial role, he received no thanks for his role as mediator. In 1891, Charlo was ordered off the parcel of land that had been surveyed for him and which this tour circumscribes. The Salish were forced to leave their Bitterroot home forever and move onto the Flathead reservation.

> Join the Mainstream Traveler at Stevensville.

For the Mainstream Traveler

Stevensville to Hamilton

> Turn east on Montana 269 for 0.9 mile to reach the Fort Owen State Monument. Turn north into the quarter-mile-long driveway. Fort Owen is a one-acre state monument located on a working ranch.

Fort Owen as it appeared in 1887. Here 240 Bitterroot citizens lived during much of the month of July, 1877. (Photo courtesy of Montana Historical Society.)

Fort Owen State Monument

The east barracks is all that remains of the original Fort Owen. Adobe bricks forming the other three sides of the enclosure have melted back into the earth.

Built in 1841 as the Catholic mission of St. Mary's, the buildings were sold in 1850 to John Owen, who enlarged his fort to the size you see outlined today. Never an actual military post, the fort served as a trading post and as protection from marauding Blackfeet. Owen acted as a Flathead agent for six years and then suffered a mental breakdown in 1871. Fort Owen was auctioned at a sheriff's sale and began to deteriorate. With more people settling in the valley, the need for a fort had passed. Or almost passed.

By the time the Nez Perce camped with the Salish near here on July 29, 1877, some of the families of Stevensville and vicinity had already been cooped up inside Fort Owen for almost three weeks. Its walls protected 243 women and children and the 15 men guarding them. Imagine that many people, the majority of them active children, confined in such a small space!

> *Think of us people of Stevensville and vicinity falling heir to the use of such valuable property when in dire need for protection. The fort at this time was in good repair, except a portion of the front or north end, which had crumbled down. We cut green sods and built it up again.*—Henry Buck (Stevensville merchant)[8]

194

From Fort Owen, continue east on Montana 269 for 0.4 mile into Stevensville.

Stevensville

The Buck Brothers store was located on the northeast corner of Main and Third Streets in Stevensville.

> *Buck Brothers (Fred, Amos and myself) were at that time conducting a general store business in Stevensville.... We had, during these trying times, moved all our goods to the Fort for safety, but that morning, July 31st, decided to move back into the store again. We had one wagon load brought in and were busy arranging the goods on the shelves, when low and behold a band of squaws from the Nez Perce camp, accompanied by a few armed warriors, appeared. They soon made known their wants to us, saying they needed supplies and had money to pay for them, but if we refused to sell, would take them anyway. Our stock comprised but a handful of such articles as they wanted. However, we held a consultation over the matter and decided that "Prudence was the better part of valor", so decided to trade with them. Flour was their main desire and we had none; but near Fort Owen was located the flour mill to where they repaired for a supply....*
>
> *All passed quietly that day but not trusting too much to the honor of an Indian, especially when on the war path, we again returned to the Fort for the night.*
>
> *Peace and quiet reigned supreme and when morning came, August 1st, we felt sure that no more would be seen of the intruders, yet with a grain of caution concluded not to remove the balance of our stock or merchandise to the store for a day or two, but rather take our time in watching maneuvers.*
>
> *Brothers Fred and Amos and myself went up town to the store that morning, August 1st, and about ten A.M. were surprised by the appearance of one hundred and fifteen warriors, well armed with Henry rifles, riding into our little village under the leadership of White Bird. We were lost to know what this day would bring forth. Never shall I forget their formidable appearance, their stern looks, their aggressiveness and their actions, which in themselves placed us immediately on the defensive. This added another stimulus to our present fear, which made a life-long impression.*
>
> *They were all well dressed with apparently new showy blankets, well armed and rode the finest of horses.... The Nez Perces were by far the finest looking tribe of Indians I have ever seen.... We had always considered the Nez Perces as a wealthy tribe and on this visit they seemed to have plenty of money, all in gold coin, but they did not come to trade this day, nor did they buy anything to my knowledge except some whisky sold them by unscrupulous individuals who had no care of the well-being of our community.*

195

During their stay in town many of them came into the store, some of whom I knew personally. They told me that they held no animosity against the white people of the Bitter Root, as they had always treated them kindly. They also told me of their troubles at home, causes leading up to the outbreak, depredations they had committed, and in short were free to talk to me— speaking good English—of their oppressions in Idaho; how the white settlers wished to crowd them onto a reservation and the resulting conflict which crystalized their determination to seek a new home rather than submit to the will of their oppressors.

As a safeguard and caution against trouble, Chief White Bird took his stand about quartering across the street from our store where he sat on his horse all the time the Indians were in town and talked to them constantly in the Nez Perce tongue.

A goodly number of our friendly Flathead Indians, armed with rifles such as they had, gathered in to protect us, seeing there were but a handful of us white people to defend ourselves.

Finally, it was noticed that some of the Nez Perces were getting drunk and on investigation found that a white man by the name of Dave Spooner, who tended bar in the Reeves saloon was selling the whisky. The liquor was seized by a party of us and transported on a wagon to the Fort. Strong talk of lynching the dispenser of the firewater was indulged in, yet at the same time we were afraid that if we enforced the vigilante act, it would incite the Indians to violence. The next move was to enter the general store of Jerry Fahy, the only other place in town where liquor was sold.

I might explain that in those days it was customary for storekeepers to have a barrel of whisky, not especially for sale, but to treat customers, thereby retaining their trade and good-will; but Fahy, like Spooner in his eagerness for the almighty dollar, forgot the graveness of the situation and it developed upon a part of our citizens to demand that "his barrel be given up". Fahy at first resented and wished to know, "By what authority we had for making such a demand". ....A South Methodist minister by the name of Reverend T.W. Flowers stepped forward with his pistol in hand, leveled it and said, "By this authority". Jerry, realizing the situation, remarked, "That's pretty good authority all right; there is the barrel, take it". The whisky was then loaded onto a wagon and also taken to the Fort.

196

I had a Henry rifle and plenty of ammunition lying on a shelf under a closed counter and took special care to keep close to it all the time that the Nez Perces were in town, as well I knew, from maneuvers and the number of drunken Indians in sight, that it only wanted one shot to be fired and all would be off and the crisis at hand. I thoroughly determined to sell my life as dearly as possible. I had no thought of ever going through the day alive, yet I was as cool and deliberate as one could be under such circumstances.

The older people of the Nez Perce tribe were well disposed, and tried in every way, to keep the peace and deal squarely with us; but the younger warriors knew no bounds and were hard to control, especially while under the influence of liquor....

While in town the tribe as a rule meant peace, but the drunken Indians sought trouble.... One of them, going to the home of our village blacksmith, Jacob Herman...was boisterous and insulting. He drew up his gun to shoot Mrs. Herman, when a Flathead Indian standing near by grabbed the fire arm and thus saved her life, which really meant saving the lives of us all....

About two P.M., a little squad of half a dozen Nez Perces sat on the ground directly across the street in front of our store, in company with three Flathead Indians who were on the guard. One of the Nez Perces drew up his gun, saying, "See me kill that man in the store". But by a quick move of one of the Flatheads, his gun was wrenched from him before he could pull the trigger. At this juncture White Bird, sitting on his horse some fifty feet away and seeing the fracas, alighted from his pony and sprang to the Indian, gave him a whipping with his quirt and then sent him and his little band up the road to camp.

From this time on, the Nez Perces followed in little squads, until about three o'clock P.M., when all had left town....

As soon as the Indians had gone and the town was quiet again, I turned the key on the store door and made good my "getaway' to Fort Owen. Upon arriving, my nerves gave way to the awful strain and I collapsed, trembling like a leaf, when I looked back over the scene which we had just passed through, and realizing how near we came to the close of our earthly careers. —Henry Buck (Stevensville merchant)[9]

During their two days of trading in Stevensville, the Nez Perce spent over $1,000.

From the corner of Main and Third Streets, proceed south on Main Street for one block to Fourth Street. Turn west on Fourth Street for three blocks to St. Mary's Mission.

St. Mary's Mission

The Nez Perce left Stevensville on August 1. On the evening of August 4, Colonel John Gibbon and his troops marched into town.

> *As we rode into Stevensville the loud barking of the dogs brought out all the inhabitants still remaining in the place.... On reaching the Mission, surrounded by the teepees of Charlo's band of Flatheads, I was hospitably received by the priest in charge.... The head priest of the mission, Father R. [Ravalli], had been confined for a long time previous to his bed by illness, from which he was not yet recovered.... I was glad to receive an invitation to visit him in his chamber....*
>
> *He gave me a great deal of information in regard to the Nez Perces, who had remained in this vicinity for some days, frequently visiting the town and freely trading with the inhabitants. In the course of conversation he asked me "how many troops I had."... I answered in a general way, "About two hundred."[10]*
>
> *"Ah," said the old man, "you must not attack them, you have not enough. They are bad Indians, they are splendid shots, are well armed, have plenty of ammunition, and have at least two hundred and sixty warriors."*—Col. John Gibbon

In 1877, St. Mary's Mission did not yet have the addition visible in this picture. (Photo courtesy of Montana Historical Society.)

Father Ravalli's advice would prove to be very sound. Although 260 was an overestimate of the number of Nez Perce warriors, they were in fact "splendid shots," and that accuracy worked to their advantage five days later during the Battle of the Big Hole.

The log house just north of the church was the living quarters and pharmacy of Father Ravalli where Colonel Gibbon visited him. At that time, St. Mary's Church was about two-thirds its present size.

> From St. Mary's Mission, return to Main Street.

The Nez Perce traveled down the west side of the Bitterroot Valley because it was less settled. Their route was the same as that taken by US 93 today. This guide, however, will advance down the east side of the valley to Hamilton because there are more historical points of interest to note.

> Proceed south on Montana 269. About 13 miles south of Stevensville was the approximate location of Fort Corvallis. No traces of it remain today. Another 0.6 mile will bring you to a monument commemorating Fort Corvallis located in front of the Ravalli Valley Electric Coop, across from mile marker 6.

Fort Corvallis

Green sod stacked 12 feet tall and 2 feet wide was used for the outer, protecting walls of this home-made fort. Inside, families lived in tents while anticipating the arrival of the Nez Perce. Since Corvallis had a population of less than a hundred, the 100-foot-square fort here was not nearly as crowded as Fort Owen.

Poker Joe

Somewhere a mile or two south of Corvallis lived a band of Nez Perce. Eagle From the Light, who had signed the 1855 Treaty, had formerly been chief of this band. Originally from the Salmon River country, he had become so disgusted with conditions in Idaho he had moved his band here to the Bitterroot Valley. Although he and several others chose not to go with the five nontreaty bands, some families were swept along in the Nez Perce tide.

199

> *The Nez Perces started from Idaho with 77 lodges. They got 12 more lodges in Bitter Root valley, taking them by force, making 89 lodges in all.*—Duncan McDonald (Nez Perce reporter)

Duncan McDonald, son of a Scottish trader and a Nez Perce woman, wrote a series of articles in 1878 for the newspaper The New North-west *telling the Nez Perce side of the story. (Photo courtesy of Montana Historical Society.)*

The most notable of these Bitterroot Nez Perce was Poker Joe, sometimes called Lean Elk or Chief Hototo, a sub-chief of mixed blood. After the Battle of the Big Hole, leadership of the Nez Perce flight was transferred from Looking Glass to Poker Joe, who kept his people ahead of the army for the next seven weeks, over the course of seven hundred miles.

The addition of Looking Glass to the nontreaty bands in early July had been fortuitous. He had the experience to guide his people to buffalo country. The unexpected addition of Poker Joe, who turned out to be an excellent strategist, was a similarly fortunate occurrence.

Between seven hundred fifty and eight hundred Nez Perce were now on the move. Since a lodge or tepee usually housed an extended family of between eight and twelve persons, estimates of the total number of Nez Perce on the flight range from seven hundred fifty to nine hundred.

Continue south on Montana 269 for 5.3 miles to Kurtz Lane. Turn south on Kurtz Lane. 0.5 mile south of the junction is a monument to Fort Skalkaho. No trace remains of the original embankment.

Fort Skalkaho

Nicknamed Fort Run for the speed of the local citizenry in getting inside its walls, the five-foot-high earth embankment called Fort Skalkaho provided minimal protection for the small settlement of Skalkaho. The sloping walls could easily have been ridden over in case of attack.

From fewer than eighty residents in 1877, the town, now called Hamilton, has grown into the largest town in the Bitterroot Valley.

> Continue south on Kurtz Lane for another 0.2 mile to the T with Golf Course Road. Turn west on Golf Course Road, which in 0.4 mile junctions with US 93 or First Street, as it is known in Hamilton. Turn south on First Street.
>
> Join either the Mainstream or Adventurous Traveler in Hamilton.

For the Mainstream Traveler

Hamilton to Darby

> Proceed south on US 93 for 15.9 miles from Hamilton to downtown Darby.

Bitterroot Valley

After struggling for days across the Bitterroot Mountains on the Lolo Trail, traveling in the Bitterroot Valley was a breeze.

> *It is wonderful how much distance can be made in a day by a steady pace. Walk your horses as fast as you can, keeping them together, the men chat with one another, and rest themselves occasionally by a puff or two from short clay pipes. At the end of fifty minutes, call the halt, dismount, and if there should happen to be short intervals, do not close them. Rest just ten minutes. Then mount and go on again, for another fifty minutes. After just ten minutes' halt, proceed as before.*—Gen. O. O. Howard

> Continue with the Mainstream Traveler at Darby.

201

For the Adventurous Traveler

Hamilton to Darby

Miles: 15.5
Map: Bitterroot National Forest

From the junction of Golf Course Road with US 93 (.7 mile south of Main Street in Hamilton), proceed 2.0 miles south to Montana 38. Turn east onto the Sleeping Child/Skalkaho Pass Road. After 0.6 mile, turn south onto county highway 501, Sleeping Child Road. Another 2.3 miles brings you to the turnoff for the Old Darby Road. Turn south on Old Darby Road, which becomes a dirt road. This road, being older than US 93, is probably closer to the actual route taken by both the Nez Perce and the army.

Sleeping Child Creek

Leaving Stevensville in the morning, Colonel Gibbon camped near the junction of Sleeping Child and Old Darby Roads on August 5.

> *We had up to this time been passing regularly Indian camping grounds, which showed that they were moving at the rate of about 12 or 14 miles a day; so that if we could continue to double the distance, the question of overtaking the enemy was simply one of time.... It was observed, also, that the teepee-poles, always left standing in their camps, were collected each night for temporary purposes, and no signs of teepee-poles nor travois for wounded were seen on the trail.*—Col. John Gibbon, September 30, 1877

General Howard's cavalry camped here the night of August 9. The next day, in an effort to reach Gibbon, Howard made fifty-three miles. Compared to the leisurely trot of the Nez Perce, who had made twelve to fourteen miles a day, and the pressing pace of Gibbon, who made twenty-five to thirty miles a day, Howard's fifty-three miles required tremendous exertion. Today, however, that distance can be covered in a little over an hour.

From the junction of Old Darby Road and Sleeping Child Road, drive south on Old Darby Road for 5.8 miles, which will bring you to the junction with US 93. Continue south, straight ahead, on Old Darby Road for 3.9 miles, which will again junction with US 93. Turn south on US 93, which reaches downtown Darby in 0.9 mile.

Rejoin the Mainstream Traveler at Darby.

For the Mainstream Traveler

Darby to Spring Gulch Campground

Drive south on US 93 from Darby for 4.7 miles. After crossing back to the east side of the Bitterroot River, just at milepost 26, Rye Creek flows in from the east.

Rye Creek

The Bitterroot Valley is steadily narrowing, and here along Rye Creek, on one of the last wide flats of the valley, Myron Lockwood had settled.

> *A certain band of the Nez Perces were under the command of T-whool-we-tzoot.... This was...a very unruly lot. While passing Lockwood's ranch, some of this band went into the cabin and helped themselves to about 200 pounds of flour, 30 or 40 pounds of coffee, one file, two or three shirts, and some other small articles. On reaching camp they went to Looking Glass and told him what they had done. Looking Glass was very angry and told T-whool-we-tzoot that unless they obeyed his order they should be put out of the camp. He said he would not permit plundering, and demanded seven head of horses from those Indians as payment for the articles they had stolen. The thieves consented to give up seven head of horses and leave them at the ranch, but Looking Glass would not be satisfied unless they branded the horses with Lockwood's brand and left them at his ranch. I understand that Lockwood, not satisfied with the seven horses left him, went on the war path, joined Gibbon's command, got shot at the Big Hole battle and lost his brother at the same place.*—Duncan McDonald (Nez Perce reporter)

Closing the gap between his command and the unsuspecting Nez Perce, Colonel Gibbon came by Rye Creek on August 6, just two days after the Nez Perce.

> *Our road continued good, although we crossed several large tributary streams coming in from the west, and forded the main stream three times, and it was one o'clock before we reached Lockwood's ranch, the last house up the Bitter Root Valley. Here we stopped to noon, get dinner, and rest and graze our animals. Mr. Lockwood, the owner of the ranche, was with us, having with his family left his home, and sought safety in one of the forts*

203

lower down the valley. On now returning to it he had occasion to recognize the futility of the truce between the Indians the inhabitants of the Bitter Root valley. His house inside was a perfect wreck. Trunks were broken open and their contents scattered about, whilst furniture, crockery, and everything perishable was broken up and strewed over the place in every direction.— Col. John Gibbon

Here at Rye Creek, seventy Bitterroot volunteers caught up with Gibbon's command.

*We overtook the soldiers the first day out, and there we were informed that the General did not care to be encumbered with citizens. But we stuck.—*J. B. Catlin (captain of Bitterroot volunteers)[11]

Thirty-four of these citizen volunteers from the Bitterroot stayed with Gibbon's command, while the other thirty-six had second thoughts and returned to their homes.

*Now some have accused us of going out just to steal the horses; that gives the wrong impression, as we did not think of that until the general [Gibbon] made us the offer. He told us that we could have all the horses except enough to mount his command, if we could whip the Indians. (But we never got to ride many of that bunch of ponies, you bet.)—*Tom Sherrill (Bitterroot volunteer)[12]

From here, Gibbon's command followed the road east along Rye Creek and down into Ross Hole, where they again picked up the trail of the Nez Perce. The Nez Perce had continued south along the Bitterroot River, as does US 93.

Proceed south of Rye Creek 10.1 miles to Spring Gulch campground.

Join the Intrepid Traveler at Spring Gulch campground for a sidetrip to Sula Lookout, or continue with the Mainstream Traveler at Spring Gulch campground.

For the Intrepid Traveler
Sula Peak Lookout

Miles: 7.6 miles, round-trip
Map: Bitterroot National Forest
Special conditions: The road is kept open by hunters after the snow falls but becomes treacherous. Driving downhill on packed snow (i.e., ice) is terrifying.

Not for the timid or even the slightly anxious, this one-lane dirt road with first-gear switchbacks leads up to a lookout with a 360-degree view. Just 0.2 mile south of Spring Gulch Campground on US 93, right after crossing the Bitterroot River, turn east onto NF 5727, a narrow dirt road that leads up to Sula Peak Lookout. For the first 0.2 mile, the road stays on the river bank, but at the Y, choose the east or uphill fork.

At Low Saddle, 2.6 miles farther up, the Nez Perce went on east and over into Ross Hole. The road, however, continues another 0.8 mile up to the Lookout for a beautiful view of Ross Hole to the east, the Bitterroot Valley to the northwest, and the Continental Divide to the south and southeast.

Return to US 93 and rejoin the Mainstream Traveler at Spring Gulch Campground.

For the Mainstream Traveler
Spring Gulch Campground to Sula Ranger Station

The original trail between Spring Gulch and Ross Hole led over the ridge east of Spring Gulch because the head of the Bitterroot Valley is so narrow and brushy. Today's route, US 93, continues south for 2.8 miles to Sula, the southwestern edge of Ross Hole.

Ross Hole

At one of the camps near the head of the Bitterroot Valley, some of the Nez Perce began to sense that something was wrong.

But there was something—a feeling some of us could not understand. One morning a young man who had medicine power rode about camp, calling loudly to the people, "My brothers, my sisters, I am telling you! In a dream last night I saw myself killed. I will be killed soon! I do not care. I am willing to die. But first, I will kill some soldiers. I shall not turn back from the death. We are all going to die!"

This young man was Wahlitits [Shore Crossing].... He was killed only a few days later in our next battle, the Big Hole....

Lone Bird, a brave fighter, also rode about one camp wanting more hurry. His voice reached all the people as he warned, "My shaking heart tells me trouble and death will overtake us if we make no hurry through this land! I can not smother, I can not hide that which I see. I must speak what is revealed to me. Let us be gone to the buffalo country!"—Yellow Wolf[13]

Proceed south from Sula for 1.7 miles to the Sula Ranger Station. Stop here to see a historic information sign about the Bitterroot–Big Hole Road.

Join the Intrepid Traveler or continue with the Mainstream Traveler at Sula Ranger Station.

For the Intrepid Traveler
Sula Ranger Station to Big Hole Battlefield

Miles: 26.3
Maps: Bitterroot and Beaverhead National Forests
Special considerations: The Bitterroot–Big Hole Road over Gibbons pass is closed by snow from October to May.

From the Sula Ranger Station, proceed south on US 93 for 0.1 mile. Turn east on Edwards Road for 0.2 mile. At the T, follow the sign and turn south on Forest Service 106. This 15 mph, one-lane road with grass growing in the middle of it climbs steadily uphill for 8.6 miles to Gibbons Pass on the Continental Divide, where you can read historical information signs.

Gibbons Pass

While today's road is narrow and switchbacks up to the Continental Divide, climbing this mountain presented a real challenge to the army marching over it in 1877. Their route was that of the Nee-Me-Poo Trail, which comes in from the west and junctions with the road here at Gibbons Pass.

Two days after Gibbon's command passed by here, General Howard's small detachment of cavalry reached this point. Ever so slowly, Howard was gaining on Gibbon.

> When in a dense forest beyond Ross' Hole, they [General Howard and his 37 men] were met by six citizens coming from Gibbon, who were the first to give information that a fight had taken place. As these men were sadly demoralized they told very exaggerated stories of Gibbon's defeat.—Thomas Sutherland (war correspondent)[14]

Howard was too late to reinforce Gibbon, since the Battle of the Big Hole had taken place the preceding day. He did have something, though, that Gibbon's men desperately needed—doctors!

From Gibbons Pass, continue southeast. At the Y in 0.7 mile, bear east. Road 106 immediately bridges Trail Creek, which continues alongside the road for the next 7.8 miles to the junction with Montana 43, where there are historical information signs.

In surprising contrast to the steep climb up, the east side of the Continental Divide is a surprisingly flat, gentle descent. Turn east on Montana 43 for 8.9 miles to the Big Hole Battlefield.

Join the Mainstream Traveler at the Big Hole Battlefield in the next chapter.

For the Mainstream Traveler

Sula Ranger Station to Big Hole Battlefield

Proceed south from the Sula ranger station. For the next 4.4 miles, US 93 coincides with the Nez Perce Trail.

To see the Nee-Me-Poo Trail, turn east on a little dirt road about halfway between mileposts 7 and 6. It is 0.2 mile to the trailhead.

Nee-Me-Poo Trail

The Nee-Me-Poo Trail is the route taken by the Nez Perce and the army to cross the Continental Divide at what today is called Gibbons Pass, which is 3.8 miles from here.

> *The command started up the main divide of the Rocky Mountains. Three miles of hard climbing was before them—three miles of steep mountain trail, filled with rocks and fallen trees. Teams were doubled and dragropes manned and at 11 o'clock, after 6 hours of hard unremitting toil the summit was reached.*—Lt. C. A. Woodruff[15]

The trailhead has a large parking area and a horse loading ramp.

Return to US 93 and continue south for 6.3 miles to Lost Trail Pass. Turn east on Montana 43 for 16.4 miles to the Big Hole Battlefield.
    Join the Mainstream Traveler there in the next chapter.

CHAPTER 7

Big Hole

A Massacre and its Consequences

Big Hole Battlefield, Montana, to Spencer, Idaho

We understood that there was to be no war. We intended to go peaceably to the buffalo country, and leave the question of returning to our country to be settled afterward.—Chief Joseph

One-fourth of his munitions were not adjusted to his weapons. The efficacy of some of his weapons had long ago gone out of date and some were utterly worthless, only carried for impression or as a club of last resort.... Gibbon fired twice the quantity the Indians fired.... The Indian was under every disadvantage save one, which in all ages and wars is the greatest, to conquer or die, and he resolved to die rather than give up his camp to the assailants. Here is the cause of Gibbon's defeat.—Angus McDonald (Flathead reservation trader)

It is the business of the squaws in traveling to pack the animals, the men contenting themselves with catching them up; and they pile on the most heterogeneous assortment of luggage with a skill that would immortalize a professional packer.—George Gibbs (Surveyor and ethnologist), 1855[1]

The Story

In this part of the country, the prairies lying between mountain ranges are called holes rather than valleys. The Nez Perce arrived in the Big Hole on August 7 after leaving the Bitterroot Valley behind them and crossing the Continental Divide. They intended to stay here a few days and prepare for the journey east. Women cut trees and peeled them for tepee poles; in the brief sojourn here the poles would begin to dry and could be then be taken to the plains. Men hunted for game to feed the hundreds of mouths. Children played.

General Day-After-Tomorrow Howard, as the Nez Perce later came to call him, and his cavalry were just beginning their ride through the Bitterroot Valley. On the night of August 8, they were camped at Stevensville. The Nez Perce felt secure. What they did not realize was that they were, in fact, being pursued.

Colonel John Gibbon, who left Fort Missoula on August 4, had marched through the Bitterroot Valley, traveling in one day the same distance the Nez Perce had taken two days to cover. By the morning of August 8, Gibbon's advance scouting party had discovered the Nez Perce camp.

Gibbon's command of 132 enlisted men, 17 officers, and 34 volunteers charged the sleeping village just before dawn on August 9 and killed about 90 Nez Perce—mostly women and children.

Despite their initial disadvantage, the warriors rallied and drove the attackers back across the river, up onto the hillside, and into the trees. Just as the sun was rising, the soldiers and volunteers dug themselves into shallow rifle pits and holed up for the rest of the day. Colonel Gibbon had miscalculated badly. "There was no place to retreat to," he admitted later.

While sniping warriors kept the soldiers pinned down, the dead Nez Perce were hurriedly buried by placing the bodies beside the river and then caving a bank down on top of them. The women packed up the camp and the wounded and started off to the south.

Twenty-four hours later, the last few warriors left the battleground, just after they heard the cheering that greeted the news brought by a courier. Without knowing English, the warriors understood that General Howard would soon be arriving.

Howard reached the battlefield the next morning, August 11. With him were two doctors, who attended to the forty wounded troopers, since Gibbon had brought no doctors with him. On the 12th, Gibbon's entourage headed toward the hospital at Deer Lodge. General Howard resumed the chase.

After the Big Hole, the Nez Perce took all the stock in their path and trusted no white person. Angry, grieving, and sad, they finally declared war against the people who were warring against them. General Howard had "spoken the rifle" during the May peace council. The Bitterroot settlers with whom they had made a compact of peace were the very ones who had volunteered to attack them in the night. Every family had lost someone at Big Hole, and the losses continued as several wounded people died at each camp now.

> *A white man must have no respect for himself. It makes no difference how well he is treated by the Indians, he will take the advantage.*—Chief White Bird

210

The leadership of the Nez Perce entourage changed. Chief Looking Glass, who had counseled going slow and who had refused to do any back scouting at the Big Hole, was replaced by Poker Joe, a sub-chief of the Bitterroot band. For the next seven weeks, over the course of seven hundred miles, Poker Joe kept the camp of seven hundred people moving at a rapid rate.

Leaving the battlefield, Howard's command rode to Bannack, the former capital of Montana Territory. There he received word that the Nez Perce had killed five men and stolen over a hundred horses on Horse Prairie, the next valley south of the Big Hole.

After traversing Horse Prairie, the Nez Perce continued due south, over the mountains. The first settlement they came to in Idaho was Junction, near the present-day town of Leadore. The settlers there were stockaded, and the Nez Perce camped nearby for a mid-day break, then headed southeast. Two days later, they met some freight wagons bound for Salmon. Although the warriors originally said they would let the freighters go, discovery of some whiskey among the cargo changed the tenor of the encounter. Five of the whites were killed; one escaped, as did two Chinese who were with the group.

The Nez Perce continued riding southeast and crossed the Corinne Road near present-day Spencer, Idaho.

General Howard, in an effort to intercept the Nez Perce, had ridden southeast from Horse Prairie and then south on the Corinne Road (approximately where interstate 15 now is). His shortcut worked. The Nez Perce had lost their three-day lead. General Howard was now only one day behind them.

Chronology of Events

1877

7 August	The Nez Perce arrive at Big Hole.
8 August	The Nez Perce remain at Big Hole.
9 August	Battle of the Big Hole.
11 August	General Howard reaches Big Hole.
	The Nez Perce camp on Horse Prairie. Montague, Flynn, Smith, Farnsworth, and Cooper are killed.
13 August	Gibbon heads to hospital at Deer Lodge.
	Howard leaves Big Hole.
	The Nez Perce cross Bannock Pass and make a mid-day stop near Leadore, Idaho.
15 August	Howard passes Bannack and camps on Horse Prairie.
	The Nez Perce kill freighters on Birch Creek.
16 August	Howard camps at Red Rock.
17 August	Howard camps at Snowline. He sends a detachment due east to Henrys Lake.

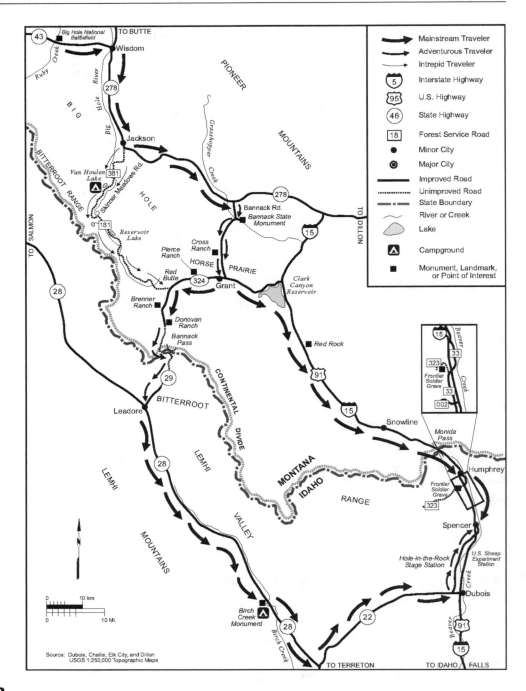

Legend:

- Mainstream Traveler
- Adventurous Traveler
- Intrepid Traveler
- 5 Interstate Highway
- 95 U.S. Highway
- 46 State Highway
- 18 Forest Service Road
- ● Minor City
- ◎ Major City
- Improved Road
- Unimproved Road
- State Boundary
- River or Creek
- Lake
- ▲ Campground
- ■ Monument, Landmark, or Point of Interest

Source: Dubois, Challis, Elk City, and Dillon
USGS 1:250,000 Topographic Maps

Travel Plan

Mainstream Traveler I	Mainstream Traveler II	Adventurous Traveler	Intrepid Traveler
Big Hole Battlefield to Jackson		follow Mainstream	follow Mainstream
Jackson to Bannack Road		follow Mainstream	Jackson to Red Butte
follow Adventurous		Bannack Road to Grant	
Sidetrip Grant to Red Butte		follow Mainstream	
Sidetrip (cont'd) Red Butte to Donovan Ranch		follow Mainstream	follow Mainstream
Grant, Montana to Humphrey, Idaho		Donovan Ranch, Montana to Leadore, Idaho	follow Adventurous
	Leadore to Dubois	follow Mainstream II	follow Mainstream II
Humphrey to Spencer		Dubois to Spencer	follow Adventurous

For the Mainstream Traveler

Big Hole Battlefield to Jackson

Visitor Center, Big Hole Battlefield National Battlefield

In Montana, two national battlefields commemorate battles between Native Americans and the frontier army—the Big Hole Battlefield and the Little Big Horn Battlefield National Monument. Indians won both encounters, yet the battlefields are tributes to the final glory and waning power of the original owners of this land.

Inside the Visitor Center, you can browse through the small exhibit room and watch the slide show. Then view the battlefield from either the theater or the deck of the Visitor Center. Map plaques along the windows and railings describe the routes of action. Also from here you can see the tepee poles of the Nez Perce camp.

The Nez Perce arrived here at the area they called Izhkumzizlakik, the place of ground squirrels, on August 7.

> Stopping at Big Hole, Chief Looking Glass announced that the band would not travel the next day, but remain over and rest. A part would go to the timber and cut poles and put up tepees. Some of us could go to the mountains and hunt for game, so our wants would be supplied. We were going to visit the Crows, and would need the tepee poles.—Husis Owyeen (Wounded Head)[2]

Tepee poles doubled as travois while traveling. In their own country, the Nez Perce seldom used travois. But now that they had crossed the mountains and were headed toward the plains, this was a good place to stock up on lodge poles.

While traveling through the Bitterroot Valley, Lone Bird and Wahlitits (Shore Crossing) had had dreams warning them that death was on their trail. Now yet another warrior had a distinct premonition.

> One man, Wottolen [Hair Combed Over Eyes], had strong powers. That first night he dreamed of soldiers. Ten, maybe twelve, of us wanted to scout back over the trail.... After our first night at Big Hole,...two young warriors said to an old man, "Loan us your horses."
>
> "No," said old man Burning Coals. "I will not loan you my horses."
>
> Not getting the horses, nothing could be done. It proved bad....
>
> Had the scout been made, many Indian lives would have been saved....
>
> Sarpsis Ilppilp [Red Moccasin Tops] and Seeyakoon Ilppilp [Red Spy] had no

good horses. Best race horses must be for the scouting. Old man Burning Coals had such horses. But he liked his horses and refused to let them go.

Chiefs Looking Glass and White Bull also opposed our going. Looking Glass was against everything not first thought of by himself. White Bull always sided with him. They said, "No more fighting! War is quit."

They would not mind Wottolen. The scout was not made!—Yellow Wolf[3]

Most people felt they had left danger far behind them.

Below the camp toward the creek the boys played the "stick" or "bone game." They were noisy, having lots of fun. I was with them.... It finally grew dark, and we had a fire for warmth and light.

Two men came there wrapped in gray blankets. They stood close, and we saw they were white men. Foolishly we said nothing to our older people about it. We ran away, then came back again to our playing. The strangers were gone. We resumed our game, having lots of fun. —White Bird (nine years old)[4]

Even the adults were relaxed and playful.

That night the warriors paraded about camp, singing, all making a good time. It was first since war started. Everybody with good feeling. Going to the buffalo country! No more fighting after Lolo Pass. War was quit. All Montana citizens, our friends....

It was past midnight when we went to bed.—Yellow Wolf[5]

Meanwhile, Colonel Gibbon's command was only three miles away, on the west side of Battle Mountain which you see in front of you.

Two days rations and 100 rounds of ammunition per man were issued, and orders given to move forward at 11 o'clock that night. The wagon train,

215

"The warriors paraded about camp…" to the tune of beating drums. (Photo courtesy of Idaho State Historical Society.)

Women dressed up, perhaps for a parade or dance. (Photo courtesy of Idaho Historical Society.)

under Hugh Kirkendall was parked and left with a guard and the howitzer with one pack mule and 2,000 rounds of ammunition left with it but ordered to move up at daybreak.—The New North-West, August 17, 1877

Leaving the squeaky, clanky wagon-train and other rattling accouterments behind, 17 officers, 132 troopers, and 34 citizen volunteers advanced quietly in the dark on the Nez Perce encampment. Refer to the map plaque to see the route taken by the soldiers.

We tripped over the fallen timber, and now and then crossed streams and marshy places where we sunk over shoetops in mud. Once or twice a break occurred in the column, and the rear part got lost, so that the front had to halt, and finally to march at a snail's pace to enable the rear to keep up. The night, although bright starlight, was still so dark that objects could not be seen more than a few feet off.

The trail led us along the bluffs overlooking the brush-covered valley of Ruby Creek, and as we moved stealthily forward I could hear a cautious whisper, "There they are—look!" On the opposite side of the little narrow valley lying at our feet a single light appeared, glimmering in the darkness, and then another, and Bostwick [a scout] whispered, "A couple of straggling tepees." Soon getting abreast of these, we caught sight of numerous lights lower down the valley, and the main camp of our enemies was as plainly in sight as the dim starlight permitted. Our trail now led us through a point of timber, composed of small pines, jutting down from the hills, and emerging from that we were startled by moving bodies directly in our path on the sidehill, and realized the fact that we were almost amongst a herd of several hundred horses, many of which as they moved away commenced to neigh and whinny. The startled dogs in camp took the alarm and commenced to bark, and for a few anxious moments it seemed as if discovery was inevitable; but the startled horses moved away up the hill, and we glided along between them and the camp, and halting directly opposite the lights, sat down on the trail to observe and await events.

Everything now died into perfect quietness in the camp, and even the dogs seemed to have been lulled into silence, and Bostwick said, "If we are not discovered, you will see the fires in the tepees start up just before daylight, as the squaws pile on the wood.—Col. John Gibbon

The main herd of horses were on the bald hillside on the southeast face of Battle Mountain. As was customary, the war ponies were tethered in camp.

My Company remained on the hill-side in line of battle, for probably two hours, waiting for daylight. A little before daylight I received an Order from Lieut. C. A. Woodruff ...to move my Company down to the river bottom and form line in the willows connecting with Company "K" (Capt. Sanno's) on the left. About 20 minutes afterwards, as day was clearing, I received another order from Lieut. Woodruff to the effect that the General desired my Company to move forward to the attack at once, and to approach as near the Hostile camp as possible before commencing to fire, and that after firing had commenced, I should take possession of the Enimies Camp, if I could, and that "K" Company (Capt. Sanno) would support the movement. I proceeded to execute this order at once. My Company moved forward, slowly in skirmish line, through the willows, to within forty or fifty yards of the Camp.—Capt. Richard Comba, September 11, 1877[6]

On the west side of the creek, the troopers were screened by willows.

While we were lying in wait, hardly breathing, one Indian herder, who could not see a group of us that had crouched down in a hollow, came straight toward us, not knowing of our location, and walked up to within six yards of us. We knew that he would be right on us in a few seconds and thus give his tribe the signal, so the only thing for us to do was to shoot him down at

*once, and three of us fired on him all at once. This, of course, was a signal
for our men to attack, and the whole line pushed rapidly forward through
the brush.*—Tom Sherrill (Bitterroot volunteer)

*I noticed that as soon as the rifles commenced to crack, all the different
herds of horses ran right together, bunched up like a flock of frightened
sheep, and then moved off. The small herds in the valley were soon under
control of the Indians, and immediately after we got possession of the village
mounted men could be seen moving at full speed over the hills, some giving
orders and others collecting the horses.*—Col. John Gibbon

Leaving the Visitor Center, drive the 0.7 mile down to the Battle Area
parking lot and walk the 1.2 mile round-trip trail to the Nez Perce Camp.

Nez Perce Camp

You know how you feel when you're awakened after two or three hours of
sleep. Imagine yourself in the position of the warriors.

*It must have been about three o'clock in morning, just before daylight, when
I heard it—a gun—two guns! I knew not what was the trouble! The sound
was like a small gun, not close. I was half sleeping. I lay with eyes closed.
Maybe I was dreaming? I did not think what to do! Then I was awake. I
heard rapidly about four gunshots across there to the west. We did not know
then, but it was those first shots that killed Natalekin, who was going to look
for his horse. This gunfire made me wide awake. Then came three volleys
from many rifles, followed by shouting of soldiers.*—Yellow Wolf[7]

The volleys fired at close range at twilight killed many women and children.
The official rationale was this:

*The killing of women and children was, under the circumstances,
unavoidable. The action commenced before it was fully light, and after
daylight, when attempts were made to break open the tepees, squaws and
boys from within fired on the men, and were of course fired on in turn; but
the poor terrified and inoffensive women and children crouching in the brush
were in no way disturbed.*—Col. John Gibbon

A volunteer told the story somewhat differently. Before the battle,

*We got to talking about what we would do with the prisoners we were about
to take, and Major Catlan went over and spoke to Gibbon concerning it.*

Gibbon said that we did not want any prisoners. He came back to us, made his report and said, "Boys, you know what to do now."—Tom Sherrill (Bitterroot volunteer)[8]

In one lodge there were five children. One soldier went into it and killed every one of them.—Duncan McDonald (Nez Perce reporter)

A rapid advance [was] made to the river bank, on the opposite side of which the Hostile camp was located. Seeing that the stream was fordable, I gave the order to Charge. The men obeying promptly, and with a loud cheer we were in an instant fighting in the enimies Camp. "K" Company on the left took up the charge. Both Companies entering the Camp, almost at the same time. The surprise was complete. The Indians being terribly punished in the first attack. Large numbers being killed in their lodges etc. The Indians who escaped, however, soon rallied and as our line was insufficient to cover the whole front of the camp, the Indians were enabled to pass around our Flanks, and take position in the willows and wooded hills in our rear, from which points they kept up a destructive fire on our men, who were exposed in the open field. Every possible effort was made to clear the willows along the river banks of Indians. But as fast as they were driven out in front, others would appear in our rear.—Capt. Richard Comba, September 11, 1877[9]

At the tepee between Chief Looking Glass and Na-tal-le-kin, the following incident occurred:

Here by his tepee sat smoking Wahnistas Aswetestk, a very old man. He was shot many times! As he sat on his buffalo robe, one soldier shot him. He did not get up. Others shot him. Still he sat there. Others shot him. He did not move. Just sat there smoking as if only raindrops struck him! Must have been twenty bullets entered his body. He did not feel the shots! After the battle, he rode horseback out from there. He grew well.... The wounds did not seem to grow. It was just as you see mist, see fog coming out from rain. We saw it like smoke from boiling water [steam], coming out of his wounded body. He was not shot in the head. —Yellow Wolf[10]

This old man was not the only Nez Perce who had the ability to repel or be unaffected by bullets. A shot in the head, however, would be fatal even to one who had these strong powers.

219

> As you come to the top of the loop, look to the north. One of the tepees on the farthest edge served as a maternity ward.

In this tepee during the night before the attack the wife of Wyeatanatoo Latpat [Sun Tied] gave birth to a baby. Wetahlatpat's sister, Tissaikpee [Granite (Crystal)], an oldlike woman, was with her as nurse....

Inside we found the two women lying in their blankets dead. Both had been shot. The mother had her newborn baby in her arms. Its head was smashed, as by a gun breech or boot heel. The mother had two other children, both killed, in another tepee. Some soldiers acted with crazy minds.—Yellow Wolf[11]

Chief White Bird was the leader of the Salmon River band.

White Bird was the first to rally his warriors to a charge upon the soldiers. "Why are we retreating?" he shouted in Nez Perces. "Since the world was made, brave men fight for their women and children. Are we going to run to the mountains and let the whites kill our women and children before our eyes? It is better that we should be killed fighting. Now is our time; fight! These soldiers cannot fight harder than the ones we defeated on Salmon river and in White Bird Canyon. Fight! Shoot them down. We can shoot as well as any of these soldiers." At these words the warriors wheeled around and started back to fight the soldiers in their camp.—Duncan McDonald (Nez Perce reporter)

Stop at the tepee of Wahlitits.

When the attack came, just before daylight, Wahlitits [Shore Crossing] and his wife ran to a shallow depression fronting their tepee. Wahlitits placed a very slim and short piece of log on the edge of the depression, facing the river brush. Very poor fort protection. A small bunch of willows was there. This was about fifteen, maybe twenty, steps from the heavy willow thickets through which the soldiers were charging. Wahlitits said to his wife: "Go with people to hiding!"

She started; Wahlitits did not know she immediately returned. He did not see her drop down back of him. Shooting was not going on, and he heard his wife speaking, "I am shot!"

Wahlitits turned and saw her lying there. He called out before the people, before the warriors, "My wife is shot to die! I will not leave her! I will go nowhere! I am staying here until killed!"

Those were the last words spoken by Wahlitits....

Eloosykasit was seventeen in 1877. After the Big Hole, he returned to Idaho where he was arrested. (Photo courtesy of MASC.)

Right away a soldier broke through the willows fronting Wahlitits, who dropped him with a single shot. Then Wahlitits was killed by a soldier, the bullet entering at his chin. I did not see what I now tell, but others told me this about his wife.

Though bad wounded, she reached her husband's rifle and killed the soldier who had shot him. She was quickly killed by other soldiers.... A good-looking woman, she was soon to be a mother.—Eloosykasit (Standing on a Point)[12]

Thus died Wahlitits (Shore Crossing), one of the original trio who had murdered the first white men in Idaho and thereby instigated this war. His wife was the only woman at Big Hole who shot at a soldier, according to Nez Perce accounts.

221

Walk on a few yards. On the inside of the loop, across from the sign "Toohoolhoolzote" stood the tepee of Two Moon.

There was quite a mix-up; but I, Two Moons, could not get into the fighting very quickly. My gun was tied to the tepee pole up over my bed. My wife started up but I told her to lie down close the ground. Bullets were singing through the tepee, splintering the poles. They came thick—like summer hail—for a time, and I did not dare raise up. Shouts and war-whoops mingled with the firing and children and women were crying.

At last I sprang up, got my rifle from the pole and rushed out to meet the soldiers. They were about fifteen yards from me. I could not hear anything! I could not see which way I was going! I was out of my senses from the sound of the guns, until I came to a little knoll and lay down behind it.

Then did the soldiers fire at me, bullets falling as the oak-acorns in the autumn winds. I felt the dirt showered on me from my low shelter, as the raining lead came fast. I could not lift my head to return the shots until the cease of the firing. Then I sprang up and ran to the creek...and jumped into a narrow wash-out.

I crouched there waiting till the soldiers should appear in sight. Waiting—that very moment—one came out in a view, and I shot and killed him. I was where the enemies could not well see me. Tall grass, and a willow bush hanging close over me. A horse stepped near me, nearly stepping on me, but I was not discovered by the rider. I did no more shooting, for the soldiers were now too many and too close to me. They could have seen my powder smoke.

I lay still until all the soldiers passed across to our camp. It was then that I rose up and ran up the creek for better shooting, when I met Chief Joseph. He spoke to me: "Remember I have no gun for defending myself!" He was holding a little baby in his arms, so I said to him: "Skip for your life! Without the gun you can do nothing! Save the child!"—Two Moon[13]

> Look across the water. Just behind some willows is the death site of Rainbow.

I was told that Rainbow, the great warrior had been killed down in the lower part of the willows, where hard fighting took place....

I jumped on my horse, and rode away to find where Rainbow lay dead. Going, I did see my old-time warmate and friend lying dead. I saw the wound where the bullet had entered his breast, to pass through the side of his heart. Stripped as for battle, he lay, his face uncovered to the sky. He had often said to me, "I have the promise given that in any battle I engaged in

Thomas Lindsay was Rainbow's grandson. (Photo courtesy of MASC.)

after the sunrise, I shall not be killed. I can there walk among my enemies. I can face the point of the gun. My body no thicker than a hair, the enemies can never hit me, but if I have any battle or fighting before the sunrise, I shall be killed."

Rainbow, my warmate, was certainly killed before sunrise at the Big Hole.

Soon after this, Pahkatos [Five Wounds] came to see the dead body of Rainbow. When he saw him lying there by the willows, he began weeping, crying. He lamented, "My brother has passed away. I too will now go, as did his father and my father die in war. They lay side by side where the battle was strongest; and now I shall lay down beside my brother warmate. He is no more, and I shall see that I follow him."

We all followed Pahkatos out from the main thicket of willows.... Pahkatos stood apart, his gun resting on the ground, as if meditating. The order came that the warriors there go to the lower side of the soldiers' trenches, and guard that part of the field. Only a few of us remained with Pahkatos, who stood in deep silence.

223

Soon he again took up his march, and I, Two Moon, following closely. Drawing nearer to the danger line, I skipped from willow branch to willow branch, keeping hid from the soldiers. I reached a place from which I could fire, where I took position and fired from there.

Pahkatos kept going; Thomas Lindsay with him. Lindsay tried to stop him; tried to head him off from climbing the bluff to where the soldiers were entrenched, but could not do so. Reaching the brow of the bluff, Pahkatos was fired on by the soldiers and killed....

Another great warrior was gone. His mind no longer on the battle, his Wyakin[14] power had left him. There was nothing to protect him from enemy bullets.—Two Moon[15]

Ollokot's wife remembered:

It was not yet full daylight. I saw a young boy lying dead under the riverbank, near the water. Nearly half-grown, a fine-looking boy.... I have never forgotten seeing that boy dead on the rocks by the clear water. Everybody liked that boy.—Wetatonmi[16]

As you complete the loop, look toward a tepee to the southwest.

An Indian with a white King George blanket about him was standing farthest up the river, alone. Of the Paloos Waiwaiwai band, his name was Pahka Pahtahank [Five Fogs]. Aged about thirty snows, he was of an old-time mind. He did not understand the gun. He was good with the bow, but had only a hunting bow....

He was just in front of his own tepee. Soldiers were this side, not far from him. He stood there shooting arrows at the enemies. The soldiers saw, and fired at him. That Indian stepped about a little, but continued sending his arrows. Three times those soldiers fired and missed him. The fourth round killed him.

Looks wonderful to me, three volleys—not exactly volleys together—should miss him not more than ten steps away.—Yellow Wolf[17]

With seven hundred people fleeing, things became very confusing, as the following series of accounts indicate.

224

During the scrimmage, a soldier met me at close range. I shot and missed him, he missing me. Next shot I killed him.

Just then another soldier shot me through the hair. My hair in front was all tied up in a bunch, and the shot going through that, the strong bullet

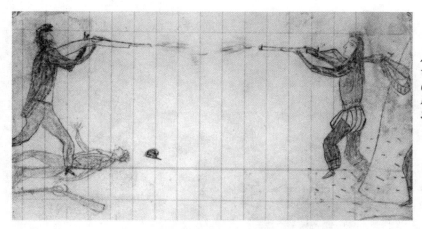

A soldier and a warrior trade shots. (Photo courtesy of Idaho State Historical Society.)

just chipped my head. It knocked me out of sense, but in a few moments I got my senses back, knowing that I had been shot in the head.

I still have a strip of wolf's hide with which I tied my hair at the time I was shot in this fight. The hide I have had ever since I was a boy old enough to know anything. I have kept it all my life time, kept it for purpose of going to war and engaging in battle. Up to the present day, this hide is in my possession. The reason I keep this hide in my possession, this animal, hemene [wolf], once upon a time gave me by the spirit its strength and power to face battle and go through it without danger, which I have done time and time in all my battles. At this fight it occurred. The spirit has always helped me to keep it safe.—Husis Owyeen (Wounded Head)[18]

Under a buffalo-skin robe, I was sleeping soundly in our tepee beside Chee-Nah my grandmother.... Suddenly a rifle shot, then neighing of startled horses roused us. Chee-Nah rose to peer out and a bullet pierced her left shoulder...blood streamed from the wound as she pushed me from the tepee crying, "Suhm-Keen [Shirt On], run to the trees and hide." I raced up the slope as fast as I could...bullets kept whizzing past clipping off leaves and branches all around me. I was very afraid...soon some other boys joined me there and we watched trembling at the awful sight below. Our tepees were set afire and our people shot as they tried to run for cover in the timber.—Suhm-Keen (Shirt On, ten years old)

I hid under some willow brush.... A little girl lay close, my arm over her. Bullets cut twigs down on us like rain. The little girl was killed. Killed under my arm.—Penahwenonmi (Helping Another)[19]

225

These three men were children in 1877, young White Bird on the right. (Photo courtesy of University of Washington Libraries.)

We were awakened by shots and neighing of our horses. My two brothers ran from our tepee to take cover in the willows. My mother gathering up little sister and taking me by the right hand, she started to run after them. A single shot passed through the baby and her. She dropped down without saying a word.... My father bent over her and although I did not realize it, she was dead.... He tried to take my hand and pull me with him, but I would not leave my mother.... Seeing that I was determined to stay there, he covered me with our big buffalo robe and cautioned me to stay perfectly still.... I was very frightened as sound of guns and screams of wounded increased...but I never moved. I tried not to cry, I must be brave.—Josiah Redwolf (five years old)

My father showed us where to go and told us not to go anywhere else. He made several shots at the soldiers. Seven of us, five women, my little brother and myself were in the shallow place. It was not deep, and when the soldiers saw us they began shooting at us. I saw one woman killed. It was my mother, the first to be killed.... I looked around, and saw all four of the other women had been killed. I now said to my little brother...: "We got to get out from this place!"

226

We jumped from there, and soldiers fired at us. I do not know how many shots, but seemed as many as they could while we were in sight. There was a creek, and we got under its bank. I saw one Indian lying there dead. — Eelahweemah (About Asleep, fourteen years old)[20]

*Horses hitched over night, ready to go for the other horses, were all killed.—
White Bird (nine years old)[21]*

*Mother picked me up, saying: "Come son! Let us get away somewhere!" She
took my right hand in her left and we ran. A bullet took off her middle finger,
end of her thumb and shot off my thumb as you see. The same bullet did it
all. Mother pointed to the creek and said: "Get down to the water. There, we
may escape away!"*

*I started and she told me to go up the creek to some bushes out in the
stream. I noticed one woman digging in the bank so she could hide. One
soldier was shooting at every body. We reached the bushes, and mother sat
down, her head only out of the water. I stood up, the water to my neck.
While there was some brush, we could be seen. Five of us were there, and
two more came. One little girl was shot through the under part of her upper
arm. She held the arm up from the cold water, it hurt so. It was a big bullet
hole. I could see through it.*

*It was not full light when we ran to the creek, but it grew light and the
sun came up…. The woman I saw digging was shot in the left breast. She
pitched into the water and I saw her struggling. She floated by us and
mother caught and drew the body to her. She placed the dying woman's
head on a sand bar just out of the water. She was soon dead. A fine looking
woman, and I remember the blood coloring the water….*

*All at once a soldier saw us. He pointed and others saw us. The soldiers in
skirmish formation turned, bringing their guns bearing on us. Mother ducked
my head under water. When I raised out, I saw her hand up. She called out:
"Women! Only women!"*

*When mother called those words, the order must have been given those
soldiers to quit. They brought their guns back, and turned the other way. I
was the only boy among those hiding in the water. Some of the soldiers
waded in the water and shook hands with the women.*

*We remained there in the water. It was very cold.—White Bird (nine
years old)[22]*

*I left and went down the creek for a short distance where I saw two squaws,
one of them holding a papoose, near a bunch of willows that had become
uprooted and had fallen into the water. I pulled my pistol and took aim at
the old squaw who was holding the child. I was a good shot and aimed right
at her head, but she did not waver a particle. She looked me in the eye, and
say, I began to think. Why should I shoot an Indian woman, one who had
never injured me a bit in the world.*

227

Tom Sherrill, a twenty-year-old Bitterroot volunteer with Gibbon's command, later became the overseer of the Big Hole battlefield before it became a National Battlefield. (Photo courtesy of Montana Historical Society.)

I put up my gun and left. A little later in the day I hear a fellow bragging that he had killed those two women.—Tom Sherrill (Bitterroot volunteer)[23]

Early morning came news that Wahchumyus [Rainbow] and Pahkatos [Five Wounds], Sarpsis Ilppilp [Red Moccasin Tops] and Wahlitits [Shore Crossing] had been killed. Four best fighters of the Nez Perce tribe. This touched my feelings. Laid me low, and downhearted. I did not want to attend the battle further.—Husis Owyeen (Wounded Head)[24]

The Indians were taken entirely by surprise, and without waiting for arms or clothing, they fled to the willows, and the squaws in several instances were seen running after them with gun and belt. We waded the creek through water waist deep, and then we lost a lot of valuable time trying to burn the Lodges. —J. B. Catlin (captain of Bitterroot volunteers)[25]

228 After the initial surprise, the soldiers were unable to hold their position in the village as the warriors began to repulse the attack.

Only about ten brave warriors made here a desperate stand after...the tepees were afire. Some had already mounted horses and were fighting, scattered. Others were in the willows fighting. I joined to save the tepees.

I came against the soldiers on side opposite the other warriors. Those warriors—not more than ten—were scattered, shooting from sheltered places.

From all sides we mixed them up. I made an advance against some soldiers. Got close enough to take good aimed shots....

*Those soldiers did not last long. Only about thirty at that place were left standing. Scared, they ran back across the river. We could not well count how many dead soldiers, but we killed a good few. They acted as if drinking. We thought some got killed by being drunk. —*Yellow Wolf[26]

The soldiers were about to begin to retreat.

*Spurring my horse across the stream and up the steep bank on the other side, I realized the fact that horseback was not the healthiest position to be maintained. Four horses only were taken into the fight; three of them had already been shot—the rider of one being killed, the rider of another wounded. Hastily dismounting and holding my horse's rein, I stood looking at the scene around me, when an officer close by called my attention to the fact that my horse was wounded, and glancing around, I discovered that the poor beast had his foreleg broken near the knee. I had, in a dim way, realized the fact that I had received a shock of some kind, but it took me a second or two to discover that the same bullet which broke my horse's leg had passed through mine.—*Col. John Gibbon

*At that time I noticed one man on an irongray horse. He was driving his men. I saw the horse whirl around. It had been shot, crippled. This man had on a yellow coat, looked like a slicker. He was soon out of sight.... As soon as the horse was shot the soldiers retreated, going to the upper land.—*White Bird (nine years old)[27]

Gibbon noticed that the Indians had us almost surrounded, and he gave the order for us to retreat....

By this time the Indians began to rally and drove the whites back through the camp and across the creek.

After we got across that blamed creek we did not know what to do. We seemed to be waiting for orders, and as we were bunched together an Indian behind the big tree was simply giving us hell. The fact is we were so close

together that he couldn't miss us and several were killed right there. I heard Gibbon give the command to scatter, then came the order to take the timbered point away from them and intrench. "Charge the point and rake the brush with your rifles," was the command.

That was no easy place to take. It was a steep hill and the Indians were on top shooting down at us. I saw fellows fall over backward and fall to the bottom.

We managed to force them away from their position and hold it.—Tom Sherrill (Bitterroot volunteer)[28]

It soon became evident that the enemy's sharp-shooters, hidden behind trees, rocks, &c., possessed an immense advantage over us, in so much that we could not compete with them. At almost every crack of a rifle from the distant hills some member of the command was sure to fall.—Col. John Gibbon, September 30, 1877

> Return to the parking lot and take the 0.8 mile round-trip trail to the Siege Area to experience first-hand the scene where the next action took place.

Siege Trail

> Continue past the trail to the howitzer into the Siege Area and save the howitzer for the end of your visit.

The surprised Nez Perce camp was a place of much confusion. As warriors sprang to the defense of their families, women and children ran to the bare sheltering safety of the willows. The early death of Lieutenant Bradley, whose company had charged the northern end of the camp, left that force without a leader. As his troops drifted toward the center to join other companies, the advantage of surprise was lost. The Nez Perce were indeed the "splendid shots" that Father Ravalli had warned Colonel Gibbon about, and their accuracy told on the soldiers. The attack blunted, the soldiers sought shelter of their own here on this wooded hillside. Captain Comba, whose company had charged the middle of the camp, reported the retreat dispassionately, despite the fact that he had only four men of his own command still with him.

230

The fighting in camp had been in progress for more than hour, When I recieved an order from General Gibbon, (who remained on the field in active command, though wounded, early in the fight.) to fall back slowly toward a wooded Point, on the hill-side, in the direction of our train and to bring all our wounded with us. I communicated this order to Capt. Rawn, and other officers, and proceeded to execute it myself. All the wounded of my Company were brought along. Most of them being able to walk. Upon reaching the wooded point, refered to, and where the command had taken position as they arrived, I found myself in command of eight or nine men. Lieut. Van Orsdale and four enlisted men of my own Company. The rest belonging to other companies. I took position immediately upon entering the woods in continuance of the line already formed by the Troops first arriving. Here the fighting was kept up all day with slight interruption.—Capt. Richard Comba, September 11, 1877[29]

Take the sidetrip to the Overlook for a view the Nez Perce camp. From the Overlook, imagine the soldiers scrambling up the hillside for cover.

The soldiers were now running to the hill. Desperate fighting in the brush, among the willows, and in open places. Close pressed, the soldiers hurried up the bluff. On the flat they stopped to barricade themselves....

Up to this time not twenty Indians had rifles. Every gun taken was quickly used. When they could, soldiers spoiled those of partners who were killed. They broke a few Indian guns as well.—Yellow Wolf[30]

It was about sunrise when the soldiers gathered on the flat and dug hiding places. The fighting then stopped for a while, and the Indians returned to the partly ruined camp. They all cried when they saw what had been done. Boys, girls, women, and children, and men who had no guns, no arms, lay scattered among dead soldiers, burned tepees, and bedding.—Red Elk[31]

The troops hurriedly dug rifle pits, while the Nez Perce returned to their camp to find out who was dead, who was wounded, and who was still alive.

> **Return to the Siege Area.**

Several of us young fellows had taken from home, a butcher knife. We had them ground sharp and on the road over to the Big Hole, we would take our knives out of the scabard and run a thumb over the edge to see if they were in good shape to raise a scalp with. Well the first work I had for my scalping-knife, was to dig a hole to get into. It looked like a saw blade next morning.—Bunch Sherrill (Bitterroot volunteer)[32]

231

I had picked up a trowel bayonet on the battlefield thinking that it would come handy before I got from among those Indians. It proved to be the most valuable thing I ever had in my possession. I did not get a very deep hole dug but it proved to be all right. While I was busy (say and busy is the right word) digging that hole I was in plain sight of the Indians from the creek and brush in the valley below, which made it rather dangerous for a fellow who didn't know whether he was right with his Maker and didn't want to get a closer acquaintance with the keeper of the "pit."

I did not get a scratch but the bullets struck all around. The only way I was safe was by lying full length on my back.—Tom Sherrill (Bitterroot volunteer)[33]

But lying flat in a shallow rifle pit for an hour or two proved to be dull, especially for a young man, twenty years old. So Tom Sherrill went to check out the situation and talk to a friend.

Finally I crawled up the little hill on my stomach, shoving my gun ahead of me, to George's hole. I looked but did not see anything very alarming, and could not see an Indian any place. "Well, George," I said, "I don't see any Indians anywhere in sight." "Oh, they are there all right," he replied.... I told him there was no danger. His parting shot was "You'll see."

When I got down to my pit my gun was filled with dirt and gravel to the muzzle. I sat up to clean it out and while doing so the Indians down in the bottom in the brush got funny and tried to pick us off by shooting up the gulch at us. I fell back into my hole....

I heard a noise like some one running and just had time to look when a soldier plunked himself down in my hole with me, and just as far as he could possibly get in. "Say", I said, "don't you see that there is hardly room for one here, if he is to use his gun?" "Can't help it," he said, "don't try to shoot." "What did you come here for?" I asked. No answer. "Say," I said, "what did you come here for? Didn't you come to fight Indians?" "Yes, but let the other fellows fight. Lay still," he said. We had another volley about this time, and I got up fired a few shots at the smoke down in the willows, which did no good, as there was no one in sight. When I stretched out again my mate said: "You are a d—n fool to sit up there in plain sight. Some of these Indians will get you yet, if you don't lie down and stay there."

While I was busy noticing...things...I had not taken any trouble to see what my partner was doing. When I did have time to look at him he was sound asleep, lying on his back with his mouth wide open. When I made my pit I found a flat rock about a foot square and three inches thick which I put at one end and threw a little gravel and leaf mould on top of it, about two inches deep. I was looking at him and wondering how he could take things so easy, when a bullet struck the rock and filled his mouth full of dirt and gravel. ...That was the only time he raised up during his stay in that hole. Say, of all the coughing and snorting you ever heard, that fellow did it right then and I was sure he was hit. ...I think he slept in that hole all the rest of the day....

Every once in a while a fellow on the bench would say, "Another Custer massacre."

Darned talk like that did not make a fellow feel very happy you can well believe. And especially in such a close place where his prophesy might come true any minute.

About ten or eleven o'clock I took a survey of the coulee and found that about everyone had left, so I thought that I would do so myself.

I got on my feet and my soldier friend said, "What are you going to do." I replied that I was going to go on the hill with the rest of the boys and asked him if he didn't want to go too. He looked at me again and said, "No, you damn fool, no, lie down." I gripped my gun and ran up onto the bench to the east. There was a large tree, the biggest that stood on the ground where we were making our last stand. This tree was on the break of the hill. From it I could look all over the valley, the Indian camp and the mountains. I threw myself down by and to the left of a dead man.... I only took one glance at the corpse, raised my gun to my shoulder with my left elbow resting on the ground. My left hand was holding the barrel and facing the creek bottom. Still looking for Indians down there over the sights of my gun. I had just got in this position when an Indian saw me from behind upon the mountain side, and blazed away. The bullet passed through my hat, from the back, cutting a trail through my hair and just missing the piece of ivory in which I had been trying to carry my brains around with me for the past twenty years, instead of leaving them at home where they would have been much safer than in a fight with fellows such as Joseph had at the battle of the Big Hole. —Tom Sherrill (Bitterroot volunteer)[34]

We lay there all day in the hot sun, with not a drop of water, nor a mouthful of food, with the exception of Lieut. Woodruth's dead horse, with the Indians pelting us from about every side, until eleven o'clock that night.—J. B. Catlin (captain of Bitterroot volunteers)[35]

233

I noticed from my position the camp of Joseph; the squaws and papooses were busy gathering up the camp outfit, buffalo robes, blankets and saddles and saddling the horses and packing them. They were tying wounded Indians to them, and other wounded they were putting on travels [travois]. As fast as they could get an Indian strapped on a pony they would turn it loose.... I could see that they were badly crippled up from the number of wounded they had tied to the horses. The squaws were very busy.—Tom Sherrill (Bitterroot volunteer)[36]

When the soldiers were driven from our village, women took down the tepees, and packed the camp while others with some men buried the dead. Lots of women killed, lots of children killed. What a shame was this! I saw little babies lying dead. Many bad wounded all around. While this was being done we boys helped bring in the horses. By mid-day the camp was moving; a few of the worse wounded hauled on the travose.—Eelahweemah (About Asleep, fourteen years old)[37]

In each family, the nearest relations did the burying. If a warrior lost a child or his wife, he quit the fight to bury his dead. If any of his family were bad wounded, he quit fighting to take care of them. Because of this, some of our bravest warriors were not in the fighting after driving the soldiers to the timbered flat. —Yellow Wolf[38]

Battle Gulch is where Sarpsis Ilpilp (Red Moccasin Tops) was killed. He and Wahlitits had killed the first four white men in Idaho in this conflict. Now, both of the perpetrators were dead.

It was about ten o'clock.... Someone hallooed, making announcement to quit fighting. The order was called, "All the brave warriors have been killed, with Sarpsis Ilppilp [Red Moccasin Tops], our last best man. We must stop now until later on. We will then fight again."

We all stopped and left the trenches. Going back to our camp across the creek, we counted how many were killed.—Peopeo Tholekt (Bird Alighting)[39]

Only twelve real fighting men were lost in that battle. But our best were left there.—Yellow Wolf[40]

Not many warriors stayed at the fighting. A very few could hold the soldiers.... Where the soldiers buried themselves, one warrior, going from tree to tree while shooting, could be as three, maybe as five or seven, rifles. —Yellow Wolf[41]

In the early morning, while the troops were digging in, they heard two shots from the howitzer.

We in the breastworks were very anxious for the men with the cannon to get to us, as they were to bring the extra ammunition, which was badly needed, as we only had what was in our belts. We never got any more than what we had, as the Indians captured all of it. From that time on we had to be very careful and make all the shots count.—Tom Sherrill (Bitterroot volunteer)[42]

One trench was occupied by Colonel Gibbon during the siege.

There was no place to retreat to.—Col. John Gibbon

After completing the trail around the Siege Area, follow the trail up to the howitzer.

I will tell you how we got this gun. Six of us were mounted....

We were scouts on the lookout.... From across the valley...I heard a voice—a Nez Perce voice— call a warning, "Look this way!"

Looking, we saw three scouts riding fast toward us. Drawing near, one of them yelled, "Two white men riding on trail towards you!"

We ran our horses in that direction. Soon we saw them! We chased those two white men back the way they came. We fired at them. Up there we found the cannon.... While we charged this cannon, the men having it in keeping fired it twice. But some distance away, we scattered, and nobody hurt. I saw a warrior off his horse running afoot towards this cannon from the opposite side. This was Seeyakoon Ilppilp [Red Spy].... That soldier did not see him. Then Seeyakoon, still at a good distance, shot him in the back, killing him. At the same time Tenahtahkah dropped the right-hand lead mule. The cannon was completely stopped. Some other soldiers with it skipped to the brush, escaping with their lives....

This little fight over, we again heard one scout across the creek calling, "Coming down this way leading one pack horse, about ten soldiers!"

235

We mounted in a hurry and went to meet these new enemies.... Those ten or eleven soldiers ran their horses fast back up the trail. When we got to that pack horse, we cut the rope holding the packs, dropping them to the ground. With rocks, the boxes were broken open. It was ammunition, more than two thousand cartridges....

We all piled after that ammunition. Some got only few cartridges, some got more. Later it was divided evenly by the chiefs. Just one kind of rifles it fit—those we took from the soldiers.—Yellow Wolf[43]

The howitzer disabled, their ammunition captured, the soldiers and volunteers settled into their shallow rifle pits to wait out the siege.

> Begin walking back to the Parking Area.

So, in the evening all the warriors, all but thirty, left to join the camp, to be there before darkness came, to watch for soldiers through the night. We remaining would fight as we could, and bring news if other soldiers came.

Peopeo Tholekt drew these pictures of capturing the howitzer. (Photos courtesy of Washington State University Libraries, MASC.)

Night drew on.... We crawled close to those trenches. We heard soldiers talking, swearing, crying.—Yellow Wolf[44]

The discomforts of that night cannot well be exaggerated. We were all soaked to the waist; we had no covering except pine boughs, and the night was cold enough to freeze the water in the ponds near us. We had nothing to eat, and the extra rations furnished by Lieutenant Woodruff's horse were, from the lack of fire, not available till daylight.—Col. John Gibbon

We did not charge. If we killed one soldier, a thousand would take his place. If we lost one warrior, there was none to take his place.—Yellow Wolf[45]

The stalemate of the long night was penetrated by a courier.

It was almost dawn when we heard the sound of a running horse. Soon a white man came loping through the timber. He was heading for the trenches. We did not try to kill him.... Some warriors...said, "Let him go in! We will then know what news he brings the soldiers!"

When that rider reached the trenches, the soldiers made loud cheering. We understood! Ammunition had arrived or more soldiers were coming.—Yellow Wolf[46]

The courier was from General Howard, whose troops would not arrive for another twenty-four hours. After hearing the cheers that greeted the courier's arrival,

We gave those trenched soldiers two volleys as a "Good-by!". Then we mounted and rode swiftly away. No use staying. Those soldiers buried, hiding from further war. We quit the fight.—Yellow Wolf[47]

And on the morning of the 10th [of August] we formed ourselves behind formedable Breastworks, ready to repel any attack. But soon learned that the main body of the Indians had disappeared, leaving us in quiet posession of the Battlefield.—Capt. Richard Comba, September 11, 1877[48]

The burning horseflesh still smouldering in the Indian campfires where the animals had fallen when shot, gave out such an awful odor that it is easy to imagine that I can scent it yet.—John W. Redington (scout)[49]

237

After the battle, I walked up the coulee, to see what had happened there, and I found that the Indians had dragged their dead all out of the gulch.

*The rocks and trees were literally covered with blood, where they had
dragged them....*

*There were quite a number of citizens and soldiers down on the battle
field ahead of us engaged in burying the dead, that they could find. You see
some of the men were killed in the brush, and it took a great deal of hunting
around, to find them....*

*The Indian Camp was a curiosity to look at. There were riding saddles,
pack saddles, frying pans, bake ovens, coffee pots, tin pans, buffalo robes,
dead horses, crippled horses, and dead dogs scattered all over the ground. It
was rather a sad and exciting day.*—Tom Sherrill (Bitterroot volunteer)[50]

*On the evening of the tenth, Hugh Kirkendall, who had charge of the
transportation for General Gibbons, came down with the teams and
provisions. This was the first mouthful of food we had had since Wednesday
night [August 8], when we left camp for the battle.*—J. B. Catlin (captain of
Bitterroot volunteers)[51]

On the morning of August 11,

*The advanced Indian Scouts that General Howard had with him, came down
in the Valley with a good sweeping gallop. I was well out on the open
ground when I first saw them. I took them to be some of the other warriors
coming back. I had a very fleet saddle horse. I whirled him around, headed
for the brush, and gave him the spur. I was soon at the edge of the willows,
and pulled him up to take another look and saw that those Indians all had
white plumes in their head dress, then I turned and rode back. Those Indians
ran all over the battle field.*

*The first Indian that was killed, was never buried by the tribe, and those
fellows found him, took his scalp, kicked him in the face, and jumped on his
body and stamped him. In fact they did everything mean to him that they
could.* —Tom Sherrill (Bitterroot volunteer)[52]

One of the two doctors who came with Howard reported:

*We found a horrible state of affairs. There were 39 wounded men without
Surgeons or dressing, and many of them suffering intensely. General Gibbon
had not taken any medical officer with him....*

*The savages sustained greater losses, however, than the soldiers, for we
found over 30 dead bodies (mostly women and children). I saw them
myself.... I was told by one of General Gibbon's officers that the squaws
were not shot at until two officers were wounded by them, and a soldier or*

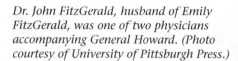

Dr. John FitzGerald, husband of Emily FitzGerald, was one of two physicians accompanying General Howard. (Photo courtesy of University of Pittsburgh Press.)

two killed. Then the men shot every Indian they caught sight of—men, women, and children. I saw five or six children from 8 to 12 years old, as near as I could determine. I also saw six or seven braves, and the remainder of those I saw were squaws—eleven or twelve of them. I was informed that there were some eight or ten more bodies of men further down the stream.— Dr. John FitzGerald, August 14, 1877[53]

According to the Nez Perce count, eighty-seven of their people were killed at Big Hole, of which thirty-three were warriors. This coincides closely with the military reports of eighty-nine bodies found. Gibbon's losses for the day were twenty-nine killed and forty wounded, two of them mortally. Of the command's seventeen officers, fourteen were either killed or wounded. The column of wounded headed toward Deer Lodge, Montana, and the hospital there.

*With the exception of Lieutenant English and Sergeant Watson, who were the two carried on "travoirs" constructed in our camp, and both of whom afterwards died in Deer Lodge, all the wounded were carried in common baggage wagons without springs. For some distance there was no road, and our way lay over a rolling prairie, covered with bunch and buffalo grass and sage brush. As our wagons bounced over these, the effect on the wounded may be imagined, but cannot be described.—*Col. John Gibbon

239

The Nez Perce headed south from the battlefield, staying along the western edge of the Big Hole. As you drive out of this National Battlefield, imagine the broad swath of a path left by the Nez Perce caravan.

There was no stuttering about picking up trails along there, for the main big trail of the hostiles led right off to the south.—John W. Redington (scout)[54]

From the Big Hole National Battlefield, follow Montana 43 east for 9.5 miles to Wisdom, thereby crossing nearly the width of the big valley known as Big Hole. Then turn south on Montana 278 for 17.8 miles to Jackson. The Bitterroot Mountains form the western edge of the Big Hole, and the Pioneer Mountains bound the valley on the east.

Big Hole

Chief Looking Glass, who had insisted on traveling slowly through the Bitterroot Valley and who had decided not to send scouts back over the trail, was now relieved of the responsibility for guiding the camp.

From the Big Hole, Chief Hototo [Lean Elk or Poker Joe] was the guide and leader of the Nez Perces. He had been all over that country, east and north, and he knew the land and the trails. He understood, and would have the people up early in the morning, and travel till about ten o'clock. Then he ordered a stop and cooking was done while the horses filled upon grass. About two o'clock he would travel again. Kept going till about ten o'clock at night.... In this way the people covered many miles each sun. They were outdistancing the soldiers, gaining on them all the time. Everybody was glad.—Wottolen (Hair Combed Over Eyes)[55]

Join the Intrepid Traveler or continue with the Mainstream Traveler at Jackson.

For the Intrepid Traveler

Jackson to Red Butte

Miles: 43.5

Map: Beaverhead National Forest

Special considerations: The Skinner Meadows Road is closed by snow from November through May.

This route roughly follows the path of the Nez Perce out of Big Hole and into Horse Prairie. South of Jackson 0.8 mile, turn west on Skinner Meadows Road, which leads to Van Houten Lake. Follow this packed dirt and gravel road, which becomes NF 381, for 10.6 miles. Having traversed the width of the Big Hole to its southwestern corner, at the Y take the southern fork, which leads past South Van Houten Lake campground in another 0.3 mile.

Nez Perce Camp

Traveling was hard on the wounded. So bad that when we reached more safe places, several of them stopped. Remained scattered and hidden away. A few of these were never afterwards heard of.—Yellow Wolf[56]

At the next Indian camp I came to, the still warm ashes showed that the Indians were not far ahead.

The saddest sight at this camp was an old, helpless Indian lying on a few old buffalo robes, with only a bottle of water alongside. He looked as though the snows of a hundred winters had fallen on his head, but still there was no trace of baldness. He volunteered a wan smile at the sight of a human being, and made a feeble motion with one arm, pointing to his forehead, making a mumble with his poor toothless mouth.... I could understand that he was inviting me to shoot him in the forehead and end his misery. Instead of accommodating him I fed him half the piece of bread I had found, which he ate ravenously. He seemed quite disappointed when I made a motion of flapping my wings to indicate that I must skiddoo and be on my way.—John W. Redington (scout)[57]

241

Several people died each night at camp. Every morning, healthy people leading horses ridden by the wounded would leave camp early, ahead of the main caravan, and would travel slowly throughout the day.

Continue past the turnoff to South Van Houten Lake campground for 6.4 miles. Pine woods give way to willow thickets growing along the Big Hole River. At the Y, turn east, past Skinner Lake, for 1.5 miles. At the next Y, turn east on Road 181.

Bloody Dick Creek

Beginning at the junction with 181, after crossing the Big Hole Divide, Bloody Dick Creek runs alongside the road. This creek is the namesake of Dick Greene, an Englishman who had a ranch on the stream. He was known to his neighbors as Bloody Dick because he freely used the epithet "bloody" to describe almost everything.

Proceed east on NF 181, which runs by Reservoir Lake campground in 4.3 miles and then continues down willow-lined Bloody Dick Creek. In 12.8 miles, continue east on NF 181 for 6.8 miles to highway 324.

The attention-getting rock formation half a mile before the junction with highway 324 is Red Butte.

Take a sidetrip to Bannack by proceeding east on county highway 324 for 6.9 miles to Grant and then following the Adventurous Traveler, **Bannack Road to Grant**, in reverse. Or join the Mainstream Traveler at Red Butte.

For the Mainstream Traveler

Jackson to the Bannack Road

Special considerations: This route connects to an Adventurous Traveler route; the gravel Bannack Road is wide and relatively flat.

Continue on Montana 278 past Jackson for 25.6 miles. The highway climbs out of the Big Hole and crosses the divide into the basin of Grasshopper Creek.

Howard's Route

Montana 278 follows General Howard's route, as his command took an easier path into Horse Prairie than the Nez Perce had taken.

I am too tired tonight to write much.... We have traveled uninterruptedly for eighteen days, averaging nearly 20 miles a day and the men are greatly worn.—Capt. Stephen Jocelyn, August 16, 1877[58]

The soldiers were three days behind the Nez Perce. The Nez Perce had left Horse Prairie the same morning General Howard left the Big Hole and thus had about a sixty-mile lead.

> Join the Adventurous Traveler at the junction of Montana 278 and the Bannack Road to Grant. No Mainstream Traveler route connects Montana 278 directly to Grant.

For the Adventurous Traveler

Junction of Montana 278 and Bannack Road to Grant

> **Miles:** 16.2
> **Map:** Beaverhead National Forest
> **Special considerations:** This road is not snowplowed in the winter but is kept open by local traffic.
>
> Turn south on this paved road to Bannack for 3.0 miles. Turn east on the gravel road for 0.7 mile toward Bannack.

Bannack State Park

Today, Bannack is a state park with several restored buildings that give a flavor of bygone days. After gold was discovered in Grasshopper Creek, Bannack became the capital of Montana Territory for one year, in 1864. The next year, the territorial capital was moved to Virginia City. Bannack then became the county seat of Beaverhead County until 1881.

> *We passed in sight of Bannock city, the entire town turning out in holiday attire to welcome General Howard and his brave soldiers.—Thomas Sutherland (war correspondent)*[59]

Walk down Main Street to the Hotel Meade. In 1877, this big brick building was the brand-new courthouse.

> *All the women on Horse Prairie and Red Rock moved into Bannack: we were there about two weeks; the men had the court-house barricaded and two*

243

Bannack, Montana. The courthouse is in the center of the photo. (Photo courtesy of Montana Historical Society.)

barrels of water taken there, and the windows had feather beds piled against them, so the shot wouldn't reach us: the men also had a small fort in the middle of the street near the well.... We had two or three runs for the court-house; once a woman fainted in the street because she couldn't find her little girl; another woman's sachel flew open, and instead of pearls, she dropped her silver spoons; almost as valuable and scarce at that time.—
Alice Barrett (Horse Prairie settler)[60]

Although the Nez Perce caravan didn't come any closer than fifteen miles to Bannack, their proximity generated tremendous excitement and anxiety.

Turn north up Hangman's Gulch, the street just past the Hotel Meade, and walk about fifty yards to a historic sign commemorating the Nez Perce War.

Continue walking up Hangman's Gulch to the gallows and turn right (east) up the old freight road. Climb uphill to see Bannack's old cemetery. Apparently four of the men murdered on Horse Prairie are buried here, although tombstones are not to be found for Montague, Flynn, Farnsworth, or Smith. (See page **Brenner Ranch** on page 247.)

From Bannack, return to the junction with Bannack Road and turn south at the T. Proceed south on the gravel road for 10.1 miles to the Cross Ranch. This road approximates Howard's route into Horse Prairie.

Horse Prairie

Less than four miles south of Bannack, you crest a small ridge and cross the divide out of the Grasshopper into Horse Prairie. Since the advent of the horse, Lemhi, Blackfeet, and Nez Perce had frequented this high prairie with its nutritious native hay. Bison probably lived here until they were hunted out in the 1820s. Horse Prairie was so named because it was here that Lewis and Clark bought horses from Cameahwait, Sacajawea's brother.

The Cross Ranch

Martin and Alice Barrett's ranch was originally located where the Cross ranch is today. On August 12, 1877,

> *Mr. R. H. Hamilton...from Horse Prairie...told us that the Indians were on his place, and he had cut the traces of his team and rode for his life:... he stopped at our place, and woke up the "boys," who had gone to bed without a horse in the stable; so one of them slipped out and took Mr. Hamilton's horse to correl theirs; he was indignant.* —Alice E. Barrett (Horse Prairie settler)[61]

Alice and Martin Barrett owned a ranch, now called the Cross Ranch, on Horse Prairie. Howard's troops camped there the night of August 15, 1877. (Photos courtesy of Montana Historical Society.)

The men at the Barrett ranch escaped to Bannack. Then, three days later, on August 15, Howard's command camped here.

> *My husband...buried account books, etc. and came home, and cached household goods in the willows and when Gen. Howard came through with his soldiers, he put a guard with the goods, but "others" came by and took various things besides food, which we did not begrudge them, only what was wasted; one brave fellow took a Confederate bill out of my cabinet, also a switch of hair! was his wife in need of it, or did he think it would serve as a scalp-lock?* —Alice E. Barrett (Horse Prairie settler)[62]

Continue traveling south for 1.8 miles. At the T just prior to the junction with county highway 324, turn west for 0.4 mile to drive up onto the pavement. Then, turn west for 0.2 mile to Grant, a small assemblage of buildings and corrals.

Join the Mainstream Traveler at Grant.

For the Mainstream Traveler

Sidetrip
Grant to Red Butte

Proceed west on highway 324, a road of patchwork pavement and some rollercoaster dips. About 4.5 miles west of Grant on the north side of the road, where mile marker 17 should be, is the Pierce ranch.

Pierce Ranch

The retreating Nez Perce stayed along the western end of Horse Prairie. No longer following a policy of non-violence, they took eighty-seven head of horses from the Pierce ranch.

Continue west on county road 324. 2.4 miles west of Pierce Ranch is the junction with NF 181 near Red Butte.

Continue with the Mainstream Traveler at Red Butte.

For the Mainstream Traveler

Sidetrip (cont'd)
Red Butte to Donovan Ranch

Proceed south on county highway 324 for 2.7 miles from the junction with NF 181.

Brenner Ranch

What is now the Brenner ranch, to the southeast, was in the 1870s the ranch of W.L. Montague and Daniel Winters. The house on the west side of the highway, which comes into view in about a quarter of a mile, is located about where the former house then stood. The men had heard of the Big Hole Battle and had sent the women and children to Bannack. Not believing there was really any danger, the men stayed behind to put up hay with their hired hands Flynn, Smith, Farnsworth, Herr, and Norris.

> *Montague and Flynn were cooking dinner when the Indians surrounded the house. They put up a terrific fight, but the Indians over-awed them. Montague being shot entirely through, laid down on the bed where he died. Flynn was found dead lying on the floor. The house was pretty well shot up. Farnsworth and Winters were coming into the barnyard with a load of hay. Farnsworth was shot and killed, but Winters managed to escape into the brush. Mike Herr, Nobeles [Norris] and Smith, being in the hayfield, and seeing what was going on at the house, made for the willows along the creek, but Smith was killed before reaching the brush, while the others made their get-away.—Alexander Cruikshank (Horse Prairie resident)*[63]

> *They [Winters, Herr, and Norris] had to cross the creek and in doing so jumped into some quicksand. They all wore loose cowhide boots in those days. The boots stayed in the mud and they ran on in their sock feet.—*Anonymous Horse Prairie resident[64]

Mrs. Winters, who must have been a strong woman, drove out from Bannack the next day with a group of men, to see what had happened. The rescue party found the house in disarray, with feathers all over the place. The feather bed tickings had been emptied of their contents and taken as bandages. But they found each body covered with a blanket, and Montague still had $200 in his pocket. Daniel Winters was not among the dead.

247

Mr. Winters...later...got to Bannack, hatless and shoeless but alive with some others, who had kept hid, and followed the creek and foothills.—Martin Barrett (Horse Prairie settler)[65]

The four dead men—Montague, Flynn, Smith, and Farnsworth—were taken to Bannack for burial.

> Continue south on county road 324 for 5.5 miles to the end of the pavement.

Donovan Ranch

The Donovan ranch in 1877 was owned by Thomas Hamilton, the "Ham" of the following account. In the gulch behind the ranch, several men were placer mining.

> *Cooper was standing in the front of the corrall watching the Indians.... All at once, he said, "Andy, let me take your gun and I will try and shoot one of those fellows." I gave him my gun, he took aim, but did not fire. In the meantime, the two brothers had taken the brush, and so had old Jack and Mr. Howard, two old men that lived just down the gulch. The last I saw of "Ham" was the dust that his horse made, about a mile up the gulch. He went that way to tell the Chinamen, that were engaged in mining two miles above his house, that the Indians had come. I started to go up the Gulch and told "Coop" to come with me. He was quite reluctant but pretty soon followed me until we were at the big hole near the spring, over there. We stopped under the tree and watched the red fiends, two or three had said, "Come back, you fools, what are you afraid of? We won't hurt you." Cooper said that he would go back. "Here take your gun Andy, and belt, if they get me they shan't have your gun." He was bound to go. Nothing that I could say would stop him. I watched until he got to them, and then I started into the bushes. Before getting far in, I tied the pony to a sapling, thinking perhaps to save one horse, if no more.*
>
> *When I got to the thickest part of the willows, I found Old Mr. Howard, a man sixty-five years old. He says, "Where is Cooper?" I told him that Cooper had gone back to the Indians. Not long after we heard two shots. "Sporty", the Shepherd dog was with "Coop". When we left, Mr. Howard said, "There's one for Coop and one for Sporty." Poor Coop! That was just at sundown....*

We had made our minds to go as soon as possible after the day broke and see if we could find Cooper. We had searched the cabins at "Ham's" and knew that he was not in any of them. That was one of the longest nights that I ever put in in my life. Cooper and I had been friends for years and worked as partners many summers in the placer mines. He was as nice a man as I ever knew.

We waited for day to break and when it did we went once more to "Ham's" and looking in the stable.... We found one of the mules dead in there.... We had taken a look from the hill above the spring and could see the Indian camp two or three miles away near the foot of the range. We could see them in motion and did not know what they were doing at first but soon saw that they were getting ready to move. We went down and walked up the road to see if we could find Cooper. We had left Slim the Chinaman on the hill to watch the Indian camp and to call our attention if he should see any of them coming our way. Old man Howard was with me on the hunt for Cooper. We had only gone about one fourth of a mile up the road toward Junction when we found him. We had to go up the gulch and get a sluice box in order to make a coffin. This we soon got and leaving Slim to watch we took the body into the sage brush and proceeded to give it as good a burrial as possible.—Andrew Meyers (Horse Prairie prospector)[66]

Mainstream Travelers return to Grant to pick up Howard's route to Humphrey, Idaho. Adventurous Travelers can continue on highway 324 by following the Donovan Ranch to Leadore section.

For the Adventurous Traveler

Donovan Ranch, Montana, to Leadore, Idaho

Miles: 20.0
Maps: Beaverhead National Forest and Salmon National Forest

If the Nez Perce camped at the edge of Horse Prairie, as the preceding account indicates, they made this trip during their morning march of August 13.

249

Although the pavement ends at the Donovan ranch, a wide, well-maintained gravel road leads over Bannock Pass to Leadore, Idaho. It is 6.7 miles up to Bannock Pass and the Continental Divide, where county road

324 changes its number to Idaho 29. After entering Idaho, it is 5.3 miles to Cruikshank Road, which is named after the Alexander Cruikshank quoted in the following passage.

4.0 miles past Cruikshank Road the pavement begins. About 3 miles beyond the beginning of the pavement, around milepost 1, look over to the northwest to see approximately where the town of Junction was located. The only trace of Junction that remains today is a cemetery.

Junction

The town of Junction preceded the present-day town of Leadore.

> *The people of this vicinity had erected a stockade and a dozen families were within its walls for protection. It was made of timbers set on end in the ground and stationed in two rows, the space between being filled with earth to break the force of bullets. Port-holes were made at intervals through which to shoot Indians, if attacked by them.*
>
> *[The Nez Perce] camped where Leadore now stands for part of a day, but in the evening broke camp and moved.—Alexander Cruikshank (scout)[67]*
>
> *The Nez Perce Indians came in here at 10 A.M., about 60 in number with Looking Glass and White Bird. We have had a talk with them. They seem to be friendly disposed toward citizens.—Anonymous[68]*

Making their mid-day camp at Leadore, the Nez Perce confiscated some local cattle for lunch and future provisions. They also took some horses, which the local populace seemed not to begrudge them, and then the caravan moved on.

Continue south on Idaho 29 for 1 more mile to the junction with Idaho 28 at Leadore.

Join the Mainstream Traveler at Leadore.

For the Mainstream Traveler
Leadore to Dubois

At Leadore, named for the lead ore mined near here, turn south on Idaho 28 for 45.7 miles. The broad Lemhi Valley runs between the Bitterroot Mountains to the north and the taller peaks of the Lemhi Range to the south. The Nez Perce raced east along this valley. Meanwhile, General Howard risked taking a shortcut. He stayed on the Montana side of the Bitterroots and headed east-southeast toward Spencer, Idaho.

Just before milepost 44 turn west into the Birch Creek Campground to see the Birch Creek Monument.

Birch Creek Monument

On August 15, a convoy of three freight outfits was traveling north along Birch Creek. One wagon was loaded with merchandise for George L. Shoup of Salmon, and the other two were for merchants in Leesburg, a mining camp west of Salmon. The four freighters and two men helping them were accompanied by two Chinese. The freight wagons bound for Salmon were waylaid at this middle crossing of Birch Creek.

> *Mr. Lyons, the only survivor of the massacre, says while they were on the road they noticed a heavy dust rising in the distance. In a short time one hundred Indians approached, headed by a half-breed. They told the teamsters not to be alarmed, that they would not be injured, that they intended to fight nobody but troops, and asked for whiskey. The chiefs did not arrive with the warriors, but came up a short time afterwards, when the half-breed introduced them to the white men. After getting drunk the Indians took the men a short distance from the wagons, where they were killed. Lyons made several attempts to escape before he succeeded.... Mr. Lyons thinks the Indians, before getting drunk, did not intend to kill them.— The Semi-Weekly Idahoan, September 28, 1877*

> *A train of eight wagons was captured.... Loaded with different kinds of goods, and lots of whisky.... Some Indians got bottles and rode away; but many began getting drunk there at the wagons. In the meantime three of the white men were killed in a fight. Two Chinamen with the wagons were not hurt. They cried, and were left to go see their grandmother. —Yellow Wolf[69]*

251

This Nez Perce joke about going to see grandmother may be lost on us, but it apparently saved the lives of the two Chinese. Later that day, just at nightfall, the two Chinese ran into Colonel George L. Shoup on Ten Mile Creek, about eleven miles southeast of Leadore. Shoup was out scouting with forty men, about half of whom were Lemhi Indians. Two of the white men went ahead and followed the Nez Perce trail with the Lemhi led by Chief Tendoy, while Shoup returned to Junction with the rest of the scouts.

> We went to their camp and found the remains of Colonel Shoup's wagons, which had been burned. We found all sorts of merchandise scattered around.
>
> Soon I found two of the murdered freighters, who evidently had put up a hard fight before they died. Later Colonel Shoup, Dave Woods, and Billy Price came along with a pack horse, some grub and a pick and shovel. The two men I found were Jim Hayden and Dan Combs. Dave Woods found the body of Al Green, another freighter, in the creek, where he evidently fell when shot. Colonel Shoup saw magpies flying around up the creek and found a fourth freighter's body beside that of a dead mule. We never discovered his identity.
>
> Hayden's gun was broken and bent, the barrel still gripped in his hands. Dan Combs had his mule whip lash wrapped around his hand, and the shot-loaded butt was covered with blood and hair, which showed that he had done some work with it.
>
> The only freighter unaccounted for was Al Lyons. We judged that he had escaped, and this later proved to be the case. We were just on the point of leaving when we found a fifth body of a white man in the brush about 10 feet from where Green lay. He had died fighting with an ax, which still was gripped in his hands and showed that he had accounted for at least one Indian. He was a stranger; evidently a man working his way through with the outfit. He had $50 in his watchfob pocket.—Alexander Cruikshank (scout)[70]

From the Birch Creek campground, continue southeast on Idaho 28. 13.4 miles later, as the ridges on both sides of the valley peter out and a vista of the broad flat plains of the Snake River basin opens up, turn east on Idaho 22 for 29.6 miles to milepost 68.

The Nez Perce had had a three-day lead on General Howard when they left Horse Prairie. Now, having taken the outside track, so to speak, they headed for the Corinne Road. General Howard was already on the Corinne Road.

Join the Adventurous Traveler at Dubois in this chapter. Or continue with the Mainstream Traveler at Dubois in the next chapter.

For the Adventurous Traveler

Dubois to Spencer

Miles: 13.9

Map: Caribou-Targhee National Forest: Dubois and Island Park Ranger Districts

Just past milepost 68 on Idaho 22, turn northwest on a county paved road, part of the Lost Gold Scenic Trails loop. At the Y in 0.6 mile, follow the pavement and bear north. In 4.5 miles, the paved road junctions with the gravel road to the U.S. Sheep Experimental Station. Southeast of this T is where the Hole-in-the-Rock stage station was located.

Hole-in-the-Rock Station

Although you'd never guess it from looking out across the flat sagebrush plain, Beaver Creek has cut a very narrow, deep canyon half a mile east of here. The importance of the Hole-in-the-Rock stage station was that the canyon walls subside on both sides of the creek, enabling horses and wagons to ford the stream. The next feasible crossing of Beaver Creek is in Spencer, nine miles north of here.

> *They crossed the stage road yesterday afternoon and are going up Camas Creek towards 'Henrys Lake.' It is a very large outfit and took them five hours to cross. They did not do any damage that I heard of. They crossed between Hole-in-the-Rock station and Camas Creek station and went along straight. I was the man that was along the road.... There were five or six bucks came to Hole-in-the-Rock, but they found five of us there; we run them off and brought away all the stock and what we could.... No stage this morning.*
> *The soldiers camped last night at Red Rock station 40 miles north of here.*—E. M. Pollinger (road agent), August 17, 1877

From the Sheep Experimental Station Road, continue north on the pavement for 5.1 miles. Just past the junction with NF 323, the road bridges Dry Creek.

Dry Creek

All through traffic on the Corinne Road had come to a halt when word came that the Nez Perce were nearby. But a few days later, when the road was safe and open to traffic again, the first travelers found sign of the Nez Perce.

> *The night we camped at the Camas Creek stage station, I was night herding and ran across two dead Indians lying in the dry bed of Dry Creek a few hundred yards below where the stage road crosses, and was scared out of a years growth in consequence. Daylight investigation showed them to be two squaws who had been abandoned by the rest of the tribe, as they were sick, and they had crawled off into the brush and died from exposure.*—Frank T. Conway (twelve years old)

From Dry Creek, continue north for 3.7 miles to the Spencer-Kilgore Road. Join the Adventurous Traveler at Spencer in the next chapter.

For the Mainstream Traveler

Grant, Montana, to Humphrey, Idaho

From Grant, continue east on county highway 324 for 12.2 miles to Clark Canyon Reservoir and turn south on Interstate 15. 7.0 miles south of the reservoir, at exit 37, is Red Rock.

Red Rock

Interstate 15 approximates the route of the Corinne Road, which went from Virginia City, Montana, to Corinne, Utah. As the terminus of the Union Pacific railroad in 1877, Corinne supplied points north. General Howard followed this well-traveled stagecoach and wagon route from Red Rock, Montana, down to Spencer, Idaho. He knew that the Nez Perce had turned east, and he hoped to intercept them along the stage road.

On August 16, Red Rock stage station was Howard's first camp after leaving Horse Prairie.

Proceed south on I-15 for 27.6 miles to exit 9 for Snowline.

Snowline

Although there is absolutely nothing to see at Snowline, the interstate has an exit here just as the railroad and stagelines had stations here in prior years. Back then, Snowline was called Williams Junction, because a road from Virginia City junctioned here with the Corinne Road.

> *The evening of 17th August brought us as far as Junction Station. Firewood three miles off; poor grazing, owing to the superabundance of alkali. Here fifty-five [Virginia City] Montana volunteers, under Captain Calloway, came up.*—Gen. O. O. Howard

Howard had been hurrying to catch the Nez Perce. Now he heard that they were just twenty-five or thirty miles in front of him on the Corinne Road. That day, he didn't order camp broken until three p.m., thereby allowing the men to rest and the animals to graze. His rationale is creditable: he was trying to decide whether to send his troops south along the road or east to Henrys Lake. Finally he did both.

From Junction, or Snowline, as it is called today, General Howard sent a small detachment under Lieutenant Bacon farther east to head off the Nez Perce at a pass near Henrys Lake. The main column continued south on the Corinne Road.

9.0 miles south of Snowline is Monida Pass, on the Montana-Idaho border. Proceed another 5.8 miles south to Humphrey, exit 190.

Join the Mainstream Traveler or the Adventurous Traveler at Humphrey.

For the Adventurous Traveler

Humphrey to Spencer

Miles: 10.8
Map: Caribou-Targhee National Forest: Dubois and Island Park Ranger Districts

At the Humphrey exit, turn east under the underpass for 0.1 mile. At the T, turn south toward Pleasant Valley and follow the old highway for 2.8 miles as it runs alongside the interstate. Just after going through the underpass under the interstate, turn north on NF 323, Pleasant Valley Road, a gravel road. 0.6 mile brings you to a sign indicating a Frontier Soldier Grave.

Howard left his infantry behind at Lolo Hot Springs. They did not catch up with him again until Camas Meadows. This artist's sketch appeared in Harper's Weekly. (Photo courtesy of Smithsonian Office of Anthropology.)

Frontier Soldier Grave

The Pleasant Valley stage station was just one establishment in a small collection of stores, saloons, and shops located here in 1877. General Howard drove here on the morning of August 18; his cavalry followed him later in the day. He knew he was hot on the trail of the Nez Perce camp.

Three days later, after the Battle of Camas Meadows, the casualties were sent back this way to Virginia City. Not all of the wounded survived the trip, however. Samuel Glass, a blacksmith with the 2nd Cavalry, was in great pain as a result of being shot through the bladder during the Camas Meadows engagement. After suffering for two days, he died and was buried here.

Samuel Glass's grave in Pleasant Valley. (Photo courtesy of Eileen Bennett.)

Return the 0.6 mile to the paved road. Proceed south for 2.7 miles to the Stoddard Creek exit. Enter onto I-15 and continue south for 4.0 miles to Spencer, exit 180.

Join the Adventurous Traveler or the Mainstream Traveler at Spencer in the next chapter.

For the Mainstream Traveler

Humphrey to Spencer

From Humphrey, travel south on I-15 for 9.5 miles to the Spencer exit.

Generations of roadways run side by side here—the railroad of the last century, the old US highway from the early twentieth century, and this youngster of an interstate highway. Only the great-grandparent—the stageroad—and its ancestor, the Indian trail, are obliterated from view.

Join the Mainstream Traveler or the Adventurous Traveler at Spencer in the next chapter.

For Further Reading

Aubrey Haines, for many years Park Historian of Yellowstone, turned his attention to the Battle of the Big Hole in *Elusive Victory*.

The results of an archeological dig at the Big Hole Battlefield in 1991 is catalogued in *A Sharp Little Affair*, by Douglas Scott.

A commemoration ceremony is held at the Big Hole National Battlefield on the weekend nearest to August 9. Contact the Battlefield for more information: 406-689-3155.

CHAPTER 8

Camas Meadows

The Nez Perce Take the Offensive

Spencer, Idaho, to West Yellowstone, Montana

The whole command is weary and tired of marching. This game of hide and seek is getting mighty monotonous.... My men are in excellent health. They do their duty without much grousing. The lack of women and whiskey are of more concern than the Indians.—Capt. Robert Pollock, August 25, 1877

The soldiers did not hurry to follow us. They slowed after losing their pack mules.—Yellow Wolf[1]

The Story

The race was close. The Nez Perce were in the outside lane and were ahead by the length of only one day now. They crossed the Corinne stageline near Spencer on August 18. Finishing second, having taken the inside track, Howard's cavalry crossed the Continental Divide and turned east at Spencer the next day. Howard's shortcut lopped two days off the lead held by the Nez Perce and put the cavalry within reach of the fleeing camp.

> *The next day, Sunday, the 19th, we leave the stage-line and take the road to our left, soon coming into the large Indian trail.*—Gen. O. O. Howard, August 27,1877

General Howard had not been this close to the Nez Perce since Kamiah, the day after the Battle of the Clearwater, five weeks before.

On the night of August 18, the Nez Perce camped at Camas Meadows, east of Spencer. Here the warrior Black Hair had a vision: He dreamed that the Nez Perce captured Howard's horses. The next day, as the camp continued its easterly course, the war chiefs decided to act on the vision. Halfway through their fifteen-hundred-mile flight, the Nez Perce took the offensive for the first and last time. A raiding party returned to their camp of the preceding night, at Camas Meadows, where General Howard's cavalry was now encamped.

The strategy worked. Surprising the sleeping soldiers' camp, the Nez Perce made off with one hundred fifty animals. However, as the day dawned, the warriors were dismayed to find that they were driving mules instead of horses.

Despite the chaos created by the surprise attack, three companies of cavalry were soon chasing after the mules and the Nez Perce. During the pursuit, these three companies became widely separated. The Nez Perce pinned down one company, that of Lieutenant Norwood, while the other two companies retreated toward camp. Ensconced in a defensible position, Norwood's company withstood the attack for three hours before the Nez Perce decided to leave. Not long afterward, General Howard arrived with reinforcements.

The damage had been done. The loss of the mule pack-train to carry supplies crippled Howard's command. The troops spent a last burst of energy pursuing the Nez Perce as far as Henrys Lake, and then collapsed. With only five days of rations left, no blankets, no underwear, and worn-out shoes, they paused to relax and refit. General Howard rode seventy miles to Virginia City and nearly bought out the town. He also communicated by telegram with General McDowell, who was his immediate superior, and with General Sherman, the General of the entire U.S. Army, who happened to be in Helena at this time. Although Howard and his men were tired and ready to give up the unsuccessful chase, Sherman chastised Howard. With the threat of being replaced by a younger man ringing in his ears, Howard renewed his efforts and continued to trail after the Nez Perce.

By the time the decision was made and the supplies and the new pack animals were bought, however, the troops had spent four days resting at Henrys Lake. The Nez Perce thus gained a respectable lead as they entered Yellowstone Park.

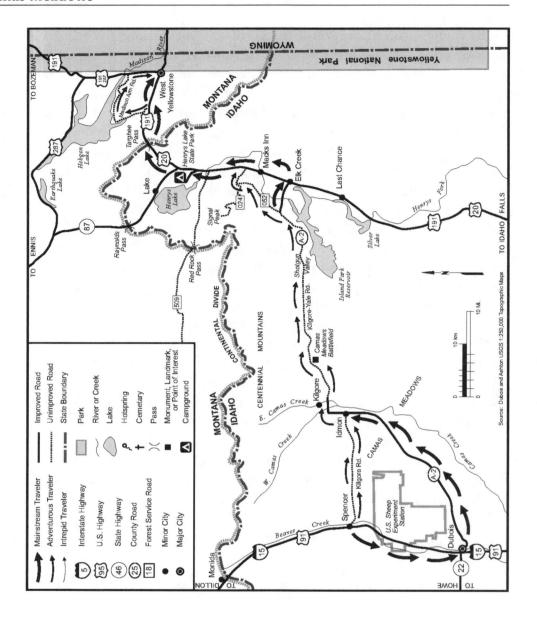

Chronology of Events

1877

10 August	Radersburg tourists camp at Henrys Lake.
18 August	General Howard camps near Spencer.
	The Nez Perce camp on Camas Creek.
19 August	Howard camps on Camas Creek.
20 August	The Nez Perce raid the soldiers' camp and make off with the mules. The Battle of Camas Meadows follows.
	Howard's infantry catches up with the cavalry, which remains at Camas Creek for the night.
21 August	The Nez Perce camp at Henrys Lake.
22 August	S. G. Fisher and fifty Bannock scouts join Howard.
24 August	Howard's command camps at Henrys Lake. Howard rides to Virginia City to buy supplies. He telegraphs generals Sherman and McDowell.
25 and 26 August	
	Howard's troops remain at Henrys Lake.
27 August	Howard returns from Virginia City to his command at Henrys Lake.
28 August	Howard leaves Henrys Lake.

Travel Plan

Mainstream Traveler	Adventurous Traveler	Intrepid Traveler
Spencer to Dubois	Spencer to Idmon	follow Adventurous
Dubois to Idmon		
follow Adventurous	Idmon to Stamp Meadows Road	follow Adventurous
Stamp Meadows Road to Henrys Lake	Stamp Meadows Road to Henrys Lake	follow Mainstream or Adventurous
Henrys Lake to Targhee Pass	follow Mainstream	follow Mainstream
Targhee Pass to West Yellowstone	Targhee Pass to West Yellowstone	follow Mainstream or Adventurous

261

For the Mainstream Traveler
Spencer to Dubois

Proceed south on I-15 from Spencer for 13 miles to Dubois, exit 167. Continue with the Mainstream Traveler in Dubois.

For the Adventurous Traveler
Spencer to Idmon

Miles: 14.2
Maps: Caribou-Targhee National Forest: Dubois and Island Park Districts
Special conditions: This road is closed by snow during the winter.

In Spencer, proceed east 0.1 mile from Interstate 15. At the T, turn south for 0.1 mile. Then turn east on the Kilgore Road and cross the railroad tracks.

Here, finally, a break in the canyon walls of Beaver Creek enables people, stock, and vehicles to cross from one side of the stream to the other. For miles, both north and south, the twenty- to forty-foot-deep canyon presents an obstacle to crossing. The Nez Perce headed east here on August 18; Howard crossed the creek the next day.

Proceed east for 14.0 miles to the stop sign at Idmon.

Kilgore-Spencer Road

Perhaps somewhere along this road, closer to Idmon, the following incident took place.

> *Gosawyiennight [Bull Bait] and I were traveling behind the camp. The tribe was ahead, and not that anyone ordered us to scout, but we were following slowly. Another young man fell back with us named Lakochets Kunnin [Rattle Blanket]. We three traveled on slowly, following the rest of the people. I said to the two boys, "Let's go on the hill here."*
>
> *So we did and reaching the summit, we got down from our horses.... We then sat on the hill, where we could see all. We had a glass, and watching*

through it, we finally saw soldiers coming, following on the trail of the band. They were not far, and the dust showed there was a big bunch of them trailing us....

Gosawyien jumped on his horse and rode swiftly to take the news to the tribe ahead. But Gosawyien had scarce reached the band when we saw the soldiers were approaching very near us, and I said to Rattle Blanket, "Go hurry! Get your horse and notify the people the soldiers are now right up with us. In a few minutes there will be an engagement."

Rattle Blanket left and I remained alone. It was about middle of day, and soon I saw soldiers appearing below me.... The soldiers were looking at me....

Mounting my horse, I passed from sight of the soldiers, hurrying fast as I could go to my tribe. I overtook them. The families were going on with the packhorses, the warriors had stopped. They were smoking their pipes, preparing for battle. They were silent, keeping quiet. They were not singing their war songs, but were remaining rather still and quiet. They only asked me, "Tell us the news, what the next news?"

"Let's meet the soldiers and have a fight," I said to them.

"No, we will wait for them here," said the leading man. "If it is the case, we can fight overnight. We will be all right."—Peopeo Tholekt (Bird Alighting)[2]

By smoking a pipe, the warriors were centering themselves, bringing themselves into tune with the universe. From this psychospiritual state, they quietly considered the vision Black Hair had had when the Nez Perce were camped at Camas Meadows on Camas Creek.

It was the night before that to Black Hair, who was wounded and could not sleep, there came a good vision. He saw the warriors go back over the trail in the darkness to where we were then camped and bring away the soldiers' horses. So, when one of our scouts brought word that General Howard had stopped at Camas Meadows, our old camp, Black Hair's vision was considered. We knew all the country, and in council it was determined to make an attack and try capturing all the horses and pack mules of the enemies just as Black Hair had seen and foretold.—Wottolen (Hair Combed Over Eyes)[3]

263

Continue with the Adventurous Traveler at Idmon.

For the Mainstream Traveler
Dubois to Idmon

Special considerations: This portion of the Mainstream Traveler route connects with an Adventurous Traveler route, which includes fifteen miles of flat, wide, gravel road.

From the I-15 overpass at Dubois, proceed east on Main Street for 0.6 mile and follow the signs for Clark County A-2. Bear south with the pavement at the end of Main Street onto Reynolds Street for 0.2 mile. Turn east, across the railroad tracks, onto Clark County A-2, Kilgore Road. 22.4 miles on the paved road brings you to Idmon, a town of two boarded-up houses and a quonset hut, all of which are easy to drive by without noticing them.

Join the Adventurous Traveler at Idmon.

For the Adventurous Traveler
Idmon to Stamp Meadows Road

Miles: 29.1
Maps: Caribou-Targhee National Forest: Dubois and Island Park Districts.
Special considerations: East of Kilgore, the road is closed by snow from December through April.

Camas Meadows

Sagebrush and lava rock have given way to green pastures. The native camas that grew here abundantly has given its name to a creek and to the meadows near here. This flowering, edible bulb was a staple in the diet of northwestern Native Americans.

The Nez Perce camped on Camas Creek, about a mile east of Idmon on August 18; Howard's cavalry stayed there the succeeding night. The site of this camp is on private land and is not accessible to the public.

264

The command makes camp 18 miles distant, just across the Camas Meadows, quite early in the afternoon, and takes up a very strong natural position on the first elevated ground which overlooks the meadows toward the west and some lava-beds toward the north and east.—Gen. O. O. Howard, August 27, 1877

Colonel Mason was more particular than ever in the placing of pickets, our little camp being completely surrounded by them, out beyond the grazing herd. This night the entire command went to sleep with a confidence that everything was safe, it being the first time many of us had taken off all our clothes, on retiring, since the Clearwater battle.—Thomas Sutherland (war correspondent)[4]

Before night every animal was brought within, the horses tied to the picket-ropes, the animals with the few wagons to their wagons, and the bell-mares of the packtrains were hobbled. Captain Callaway's volunteers [from Virginia City] came up and encamped about one hundred yards from me, across a creek. They are between two streams of water [Camas Creek and Spring Creek] whose banks were fringed by thickets of willows. Two or three Indians were seen by one of our scouts just before night, but as this was an ordinary occurrence, it excited little notice. An unusual feeling of security pervaded the camp.—Gen. O. O. Howard, September 1, 1877

Night descended and quiet reigned. The soldiers' camp had taken the utmost in security precautions. Being this close to the Nez Perce engendered a sense of confidence among these not-yet-successful campaigners. Meanwhile, not far away, last-minute plans were being made in the darkness.

Chiefs Ollokot and Toohoolhoolzote were the outstanding leaders of my company. These men were always in lead of every fight.... Brave men with swiftest horses were always at the front in war movements.

We rode on through the night darkness. Before reaching the soldier camp, all stopped, and the leaders held council. How make attack? The older men did this planning. Some wanted to leave the horses and enter the soldier camp afoot. Chief Looking Glass and others thought the horses must not be left out. This last plan was chosen—to go mounted.

Chief Joseph was not along.

Then we went. It was not yet daylight when we ran into soldiers. They must have been guard soldiers. I heard a white man's voice call, "Who are you there?"

Then a gun sounded back of us....

The soldier camp was alarmed.—Yellow Wolf[5]

Too soon the alarm is sprung! Not many cavalry horses are yet cut loose when a gun gives off a report. It is back of the front riders, back toward the rear.

"Who in hell do shooting?"

Our plans are now spoiled. The signal shot was not to come from that direction. When that gun sounded, fired by Otskai [Going Out], as we learned later, the Indians gallop close, and shooting into the soldiers' camp.—Wottolen (Hair Combed Over Eyes)[6]

Otskai was known for his inappropriate actions.

Everybody knows it was Otskai [Going Out] who done the first shot. He did not obey orders of the leaders. We wanted to get close mixed with the soldiers. Everybody knew he did the carelessness.... Always Otskai was doing something like that. Crazy actions. Nervous, he broke our plans for getting all the horses.—Wottolen (Hair Combed Over Eyes)[7]

And the result of that single shot?

We were awakened by a disconcerting concert of demoniacal yells and a cracking of rifles, while the whizzing of bullets could be heard well overhead. Everyone was out in a minute, and all we could see as a magnified imitation of a swarm of fireflies flitting in the alders, as the rifles spoke; while the tramping of hundreds of hoofs added to the din.—Sgt. H. J. Davis

As the [Virginia City] volunteers had camped across the creek from the main command, in the immediate vicinity of the firing and war-whoops, our guns were almost useless.... Sweeping around our camp could be distinguished a herd of stampeded horses and mules, galloping at their highest possible speed, with a considerable band of Indians behind them goading them on with loud cries, and discharge of rifles.—Thomas Sutherland (war correspondent)[8]

Calloway and his [Virginia City] volunteers, not so used to sudden alarms, find it hard to get in order. One takes another's gun, some get the wrong belts, others drop their percussion caps; their horses get into a regular stampede, and rush in the darkness toward the herd of mules, and all the animals scamper off together, while the citizens plunge into the water above their knees, and cross to the regular troops at a double-quick.—Gen. O. O. Howard

266

I heard them cry like babies. They were bad scared.—Yellow Wolf[9]

And then, all of a sudden, the raid was over.

The stampeded horses gone, we do not stay to fight soldiers. We leave them firing like crazy people in the darkness. Nothing they can hit.—Wottolen (Hair Combed Over Eyes)[10]

Except the noise we were making ourselves, nothing could be heard but receding hoofbeats and faint yells, as the enemy returned from whence they came, taking with them, as a souvenir, about one hundred and fifty mules, our pack-train. Our company horses had pulled one picket-pin, and had then milled 'round and 'round and twisted themselves into a grotesque puzzle.— Sgt. H. J. Davis

The dazed soldiers' camp began to bustle.

I ordered Major Sanford to have the cavalry saddle up at once and to move out just as soon as it was light enough to see, and to attempt to recover the lost animals. Carr's, Norwood's, and Jackson's companies galloped out a few minutes later, accompanied by Major Sanford in command. The moving column of Indians and animals could then just be discovered four or five miles away.—Gen. O. O. Howard, August 27, 1877

We try driving the herd fast, but the speed is slow. Daylight soon coming, we have only mules! Just a few horses in the herd. Then we know why the slow traveling.—Wottolen (Hair Combed Over Eyes)[11]

After traveling a little way, driving our captured horses, sun broke. We could begin to see our prize. Getting more light, we looked. Eeh! Nothing but mules— all mules!... I did not know, did not understand why the Indians could not know mules. Why they did not get the cavalry horses. That was the object the chiefs had in mind—why the raid was made.—Yellow Wolf[12]

The warriors may not have been too happy about stealing a bunch of mules. But the animals were valued at about $10,000—no small loss to an army for which Congress had appropriated no funds this year.

The succeeding battle took place six miles farther northeast, during the morning and afternoon. The cavalry then returned to Camas Meadows and camped there again the night of August 20.

267

Col. Miller with two hundred and thirty Infantry overtakes us to-night. Pursuit continues to-morrow. Lost one hundred and ten mules and several scouts horses.—Gen. O. O. Howard, August 21, 1877

Bugler Bernard Brooks was the only casualty on the day of the Camas Meadows fight. He is buried at the site of the Camas Meadows camp. (Photo courtesy of Eileen Bennett.)

The infantry under Colonel Miller had made a tremendous push to catch up with the cavalry. Just that day they had come forty-eight miles. For the first time since August 7, at Lolo Hot Springs, the cavalry and infantry were together. In the intervening two weeks, the infantry had lagged days behind the cavalry.

Located near the Camas Creek campsite, on private property, is the grave of 21-year-old Bugler Bernard Brooks, the only fatality on the day of the Camas Meadows battle.[13]

> From Idmon, proceed north on Clark County A-2. In 1.9 miles, the road jogs east and remains paved for 2.3 more miles. After the end of the pavement, continue driving east for another 4.2 miles.

Clark County A-2

In the twilight preceding dawn, quite a horse race was being run through the sagebrush and lava knolls on either side of what is now the Kilgore-Yale Road, Clark County A-2.

Three companies of cavalry dashed out of the camp at Camas Creek: Company B, 1st Cavalry under Captain Jackson; Company L, 2nd Cavalry under Lieutenant Norwood; and Company I, 1st Cavalry under Captain Carr. Jackson and Carr were flanking Norwood's company, which rode in the center.

We looked back. Soldiers were coming!... Then we divided our company. Some went ahead with the mules; others of us waited for the soldiers. Then we fought, shooting from anywhere we found hiding.—Yellow Wolf[14]

The cavalry succeeded in striking the escaping herd, and at first recovered at least half; but many, made wild by the charge and the firing, ran to the enemy.—Gen. O. O. Howard, August 27, 1877

I did not know how many mules we got. All were kept for packing and riding, but the warriors did not ride them.—Yellow Wolf[15]

After mile marker 31, a historical sign made by a local Scout troop marks the entrance to the Camas Meadows Battleground. A gate on the south side of the road leads onto BLM land. Mainstream and Adventurous Travelers will want to park alongside the road, while Intrepid Travelers may drive back to the battlefield.

To strong-arm the gate closed (or open), use the rusty metal bar hanging beside the gate on the fencepost. Wrap the bar around the gatepost and pull the bar so that the attached chain gives the gatepost a bearhug. This leveraged pressure will allow you to slip the wire wreath "latch" on or off the gatepost.

Leaving the gate as you found it (closed or open), proceed south along the two-track ranch road for 0.4 mile to a copse of aspen on a mound of lava rocks.

Camas Meadows Battleground

You'll know you've arrived at the Camas Meadows Battleground when you see a plaque that was placed here in 1985 by the Appaloosa Horse Club.

Somehow the three companies lost touch with each other. Lieutenant Norwood's company retreated to this small basin of lava rock and held it for three hours on the morning of August 20.

The soldiers follow and we stop to have a fight. Back of a ridge we dismount to await their coming. We do not stop too close to that ridge. Soon some soldiers appear on that ridge top, but do not stay. Immediately they drop back from sight. We do not charge or follow them. Waiting where lined with our horses shots soon come from hiding places on that ridge. Long range shooting, nobody is hurt. It is only to hold the enemy that we return the fire. —Wottolen (Hair Combed Over Eyes)[16]

269

The morning air was extremely chilly and crisp and the horses rank, so that what was an orderly gallop, at first, soon developed into a race. After half an hour of this we approached a ridge, which was the first roll of the foot-hills. The first ones to make the summit of the ridge suddenly stopped and then quickly returned to the foot; as the rest of us came up we soon learned that the Indians had made a stand just over the ridge. We dismounted, and the Number Fours, each holding four horses, being unable to fight, left about thirty-five of us to meet the Indians. Brawling to the top we saw a line of dismounted skirmishers, standing behind their ponies, on open ground and about a thousand yards away. We deployed along the ridge, and for twenty minutes or so exchanged shots with them with but little damage on either side, as the range was long for our Springfields and longer for their Winchesters. Lieutenant Benson of the 7th Infantry, who was attached to our company for the day, standing up for an instant, just at my side, received a bullet which entered at the hip-pocket and went out at the other, having passed entirely through both buttocks; this, while we were facing the enemy, caused us to realize that we had no ordinary Indians to deal with, for while we had been frolicking with the skirmishers in front, Chief Joseph had engineered as neat a double flank movement as could be imagined, and we were exposed to a raking fire coming from right and left. The horses had been withdrawn, more than five hundred yards, to a clump of cottonwoods; and when we turned around there was no sight nor sign of them. For a brief period there was a panic, and then we heard the notes of a bugle blowing "Recall" from the cottonwood thicket. The race to that thicket was something never to be forgotten, for a cavalryman is not trained for a five hundred yard sprint; luck was with us, however, and no man was hit in that mad race for safety. I had a horse's nose-bag slung over my shoulder containing extra cartridges, and a bullet cut the strap and let it fall to the ground. A hero would have stopped, gone back and recovered that bag, but not I. We all reached the horses and found the place an admirable one for defence; it was a sort of basin, an acre or so in extent, with a rim high enough to protect our horses, and filled with young cottonwoods in full leaf. It was oval in shape, and we deployed in all directions around the rim.—Sgt. H. J. Davis

270

One of the warriors described the decoying action at the ridge that resulted in Lieutenant Benson's ungracious wound.

While exchanging with the hidden enemies, drawing their minds to us, a few good-shot warriors are crawling on them from another part of the hill. Now shots are heard from that direction. Those soldiers become scared. A bugle sounds down in the cottonwoods. These soldiers run like deer for the shelter brush.—Wottolen (Hair Combed Over Eyes)[17]

The song recalling the cavalrymen may have been the last breath of Bugler Bernard Brooks, who was shot out of his saddle near here.

Once Norwood's company arrived in this one-acre bowl, they went to work piling up rocks to use as breastworks. As you look around and walk through the sagebrush, you can easily discover most of the twenty-three rifle pits used by the soldiers that day.

> *For two hours it was a sniping game and our casualties were eight. The Indians crawled very close, one shooting Harry Trevor in the back at about fifteen feet, as we knew by the moccasin tracks and empty shells found behind a rock after the engagement. Poor Trevor's wound was mortal as was that of Sam Glass, who was shot through the bladder; a bullet hit Sergeant Garland's cartridge-belt and drove two cartridges from it clean through his body; his wound never healed and he blew his brains out a few years later.... This was the amount of damage done to us, and what we did to the Indians we never knew, as they retreated in good order taking their dead or injured with them, after they found they could not dislodge us. Three dead ponies and some pools of blood were all the records we found of their casualties.*— Sgt. H. J. Davis

The soldiers had found a very defensible spot, as the Nez Perce realized.

> *Then we crept close and shot whenever we saw a soldier.... It was a sharp fight for some time. After a while I heard the warriors calling to each other, "Chiefs say do no more fighting!"*—Yellow Wolf[18]

> *Soon all shooting stopped. The soldiers could not be driven from the woods and the captured herd now out of danger, we left for camp.*—Wottolen (Hair Combed Over Eyes)[19]

General Howard's version of events was somewhat different. According to him, his arrival with reinforcements made the Nez Perce fall back. And the soldiers found no dead Nez Perce because there were none. Three hours of shooting had resulted in only two injured warriors.

271

> *No Indians killed. A bullet hurt Wottolen's side only slightly.*
>   *A bullet clipped me here; making a bad feeling through my head. My senses were killed. When I returned to life I was at bottom of the bluff, and*

some rock bruises on me.... Not feeling to do more fighting, I recovered my gun and went to where I had left my horse. The fighting did not last long.—Peopeo Tholekt (Bird Alighting)[20]

No shirt where the bullet struck me, a black spot came as large as a good-sized apple. Maybe the ball glanced from a rock. It must have been weak not to enter my body.—Wottolen (Hair Combed Over Eyes)[21]

Later, one of the sergeants asked the nagging question:

I could never understand how those two companies of the 1st Cavalry could have missed the Indians and gotten entirely out of touch with us, when we started together and we were fighting within half an hour and kept it up for nearly three hours.—Sgt. H. J. Davis.

According to the records, "Retreat" was sounded and the other two companies did retreat. Lieutenant Norwood found his company in the center of the action and decided to defend his position rather than retreat. Apparently Norwood's company was not missed until the captains of the other two companies met up with General Howard while returning to camp. Howard promptly extended his reinforcements into a skirmish line and moved eastward to find Norwood.

After the Nez Perce had retired, the soldiers returned to camp at Camas Meadows, taking with them the dead bugler, Brooks, along with five wounded and two mortally wounded soldiers.

> Return to Clark County A-2 and proceed east for 20.7 miles to the junction with Stamp Meadows Road, NF 052.

Kilgore-Yale Road, Fremont County A-2

Somewhere along the Kilgore-Yale Road, Howard's command was joined by S. G. Fisher two days after the battle at Camas Meadows.

On the way to Henry Lake we were joined by fifty Bannock Indians, under a very daring scout from Fort Hall [near Pocatello], named Fisher.—Thomas Sutherland (war correspondent)[22]

272

The leader of these scouts, or the "chief scout," as he was called, deserves special notice. He was a tall, pale man, of fair proportions, being slightly deaf. A stranger would see little that was remarkable in him. Yet of all the scouts in our Indian campaign, none equalled this chief, Fisher. Night and day, with guides and without, with force and without, Fisher fearlessly hung

S. G. Fisher joined Howard's command with fifty Bannock scouts from the Fort Hall reservation. His interesting diary contains very detailed entries. (Photo courtesy of Idaho State Historical Society.)

upon the skirts of the enemy. The accuracy, carefulness, and fullness of his reports, to one attempting to chase Indians across a vast wilderness, were a delight.—Gen. O. O. Howard

Fisher's consummate skill as a scout would be put to good use in Yellowstone Park. Meanwhile, the Bannock scouts showed real enthusiasm for their job and were ready to get to work the day they arrived.

About midnight, after the war-dance and its council had subsided, Buffalo Horn and a thick-set...half-breed, who was called Rain, came to head-quarters, and asked for authority to kill our Nez Perce herders, "Captain John," "Old George," and one other Indian of the tribe.—Gen. O. O. Howard

Permission was not granted. Captain John and Old George, both of whom had daughters with the fleeing bands, did some interpreting during the negotiations of the final battle.

273

Join the Mainstream or the Adventurous Traveler at Stamp Meadows Road.

For the Adventurous Traveler
Stamp Meadows Road to Henrys Lake

Miles: 16.3
Map: Caribou-Targhee National Forest: Dubois and Island Park districts
Special conditions: Stamp Meadows Road is closed by snow from November to May.

Turn north on Stamp Meadows Road, NF 052, for 7.9 miles. This narrow dirt road follows the route of the Nez Perce as they left the marshy lowlands of the Shotgun Valley and headed toward Henrys Lake. At the T with Sawtelle Peak Road, NF 024, turn east for 1.8 miles to the junction with US 20. Turn north on US 20 for 6.6 miles to Henrys Lake State Park.
   Join the Mainstream Traveler at Henrys Lake State Park.

For the Mainstream Traveler
Stamp Meadows Road to Henrys Lake State Park

Continue driving east on Fremont County A-2 for 3.6 miles to the junction with US 20 at Elk Creek. Turn north on US 20 for 11.6 miles to Henrys Lake State Park. North of Mack's Inn, the trees give way to an open valley, and the Henrys Lake Mountains come into view.
   Continue with the Mainstream Traveler at Henrys Lake State Park.

For the Mainstream Traveler
Henrys Lake State Park to Targhee Pass

Henrys Lake State Park

The two-mile entrance into this state park leads to a jewel set in the mountains, as the Continental Divide cradles Henrys Lake on three sides. Today's recreational opportunities at the lake include camping, boating, fishing, and bird-watching—the same activities that the first tourists to this area enjoyed.

A party of nine people from Radersburg, Montana, stopped at Henrys Lake on their way into Yellowstone National Park. Unbeknownst to them, they would,

This photo of Sawtell's ranch was taken in 1871 by W.H. Jackson. The Radersburg tourists stayed here in early August on their way into Yellowstone Park. Howard's troops rested here in late August. (Photo courtesy of National Archives.)

two weeks later, be captured by the Nez Perce. One of these sightseers described their stopover at the lake.

> We see below us, glistening in the bright sunlight like a mirror, a beautiful sheet of water, dotted here and there with little islands of green. Pelicans, swans, sea gulls and geese floated upon its surface....
>
> We found a good camping ground near the ranch of Mr. Sawtell, which was then unoccupied. We found boats moored near us, and...started to visit an island about a mile from shore. As we rowed out we saw some fine trout below us that were distinctly visible through the clear water, and swimming near us, we saw a number of swans with their young....
>
> Our camp is delightfully situated about three hundred yards from the lake on the mountain side, and we have a beautiful view of it as it lies calmly sleeping in the moonlight....
>
> During the night the wild birds on the lake kept up a continual chorus of discordant sounds, swans, pelicans, cranes and geese vying with each other in their efforts to make the night hideous.—Frank Carpenter (tourist, Radersburg party)[23]

275

The "little islands of green" are no longer to be seen. These islands were actually floating accumulations of logs and debris, with plants and small trees growing on them. Visitors might camp on the shore only to wake up in the morning surprised to find themselves adrift. The islands were dynamited in 1924 to prevent clogging the dam that was then being built.

The dam increased the average depth of Henrys Lake from five feet to twelve feet. The size was increased as well, making today's lake almost twice as large as the lake of 1877. Thus the actual camping sites of the Radersburg tourists, the Nez Perce, and the army are probably now all under water.

Prior to the arrival of the Nez Perce, a squad of forty men under Lieutenant Bacon arrived in this area. General Howard had detached the company and sent it due east from Snowline.

> *I send this picked force, increased by the Indian scouts...with instruction to set out at midnight, and proceed by Red Rock Lake to Mynhold's [Raynold's] Pass, near Henry Lake, with a view of intercepting and hindering the Indians should they come in that direction, or of procuring and transmitting to me early information of value.*—Gen. O. O. Howard, August 27, 1877

> *I was made one of a special detail to make a detour and get ahead of the Indians and fortify at Henry Lake. This detachment consisted of Lieuts. Bacon and Hoyle, myself, Guide Poindexter and 15 men. We started out at 3 a.m., and nearly all the camp saw us off, never expecting to see us again. We travelled hard for two days. At the lake we found some cattle men, grazing their herds along the lake. We warned them that Joseph was likely to pass that way, and they thanked us for the warning and moved their animals off. I never knew what Lieut. Bacon's orders were. They were evidently to wait at the lake for two days and if the main column did not reach us by the expiration of that time to return as best we could. Whatever his orders may have been, that is exactly what we did, rejoining Howard's main column four or five miles from the lake, near the trail we had previously passed over. But on our return we made a wide detour in order to avoid the Indians.* —Pvt. William Connolly[24]

276

Although General Howard later rationalized that he had expected the men to hold the Nez Perce back, such were not their orders nor did a detachment of forty men stand much of a chance against the Nez Perce.

The Nez Perce camped at Henrys Lake on the night of August 22. General Howard's troops arrived two days later and rested at Sawtelle's cabin. Gilman Sawtelle had been the first settler on the lake, in 1868, and built his home about where Staley Springs is now located, diagonally opposite to the state park. After having marched an average of over nineteen miles a day for the past twenty-six days, the soldiers presumably enjoyed themselves as fully as the Radersburg tourists had when they camped there.

> *The General intended to follow right after the hostiles but this was impossible because it was found that the command has but five days rations.*—Capt. Robert Pollock, August 25, 1877

> *The command is very deficient in overcoats, blankets, socks, and shoes. Some of the men already complain of rheumatic pains.*—Major C. T. Alexander (surgeon)

> *General Howard inquired how many days would be needed to bring the necessary clothing to the camp from Virginia City, and was informed that it could not be done in less than five. The General was positive it could be done in less time, and without more ado, started for Virginia City, traveling night and day until he returned with all the stock of blankets, shoes, etc., in the town. Besides communicating with General Sherman and McDowell, through the telegraph office, while at Virginia City, Howard also directed further clothing supplies.... A herd of cayuse horses was also brought to serve as pack-animals.*—Thomas Sutherland (war correspondent)[25]

> *We nearly bought them out.*—Gen. O. O. Howard

Recently retired after ten years of being the capital of Montana Territory, Virginia City was still an important center of commerce and communication in 1877. Virginia City is seventy miles from Henrys Lake.

> *Another cause of embarrassment has been the absolute want of money by every department, and the necessity of giving vouchers that do not even pledge the credit of the government.*—Gen. O. O. Howard, August 27, 1877

Congress had appropriated no money for the Army before adjourning the preceding March. While campaigning, the soldiers received no regular pay and were, in fact, broke as well as ragged.

277

> *My personal energy is not great as you know and it is completely exhausted by the time I have ridden 25 miles horseback, waited two or three hours in the sunshine for the pack train to come up and then opened my desk and pitched into orders and telegrams for the day. My work is never foreseen*

never dawns upon me but bursts forth with the most startling unexpectedness. A ragged courier or a naked Indian dashing madly into camp at any hour of the day or night may bring to me work enough to last a month.

In fact I wish to impress you with the idea that I am an overworked much abused individual and so enough of Self. The command is pretty well—I might insert "tired" there—but rather homesick I imagine….

We are all equally penniless, naked and careless as becomes banditti of the frontier. I am probably more artistically and picturesquely ragged than any other officer…. I stand clothed in dignity and a pair buckskin patched pants out at the knees and fringed at the bottoms, with the wreck of a white slouch wilted on my head and a tattered blouse fluttering on my back.—Lt. E. S. Farrow, August 24, 1877[26]

Many of the enlisted men are unable to march, and they are all leg-weary.—Asst. Surgeon W. R. Hall

Everyone, believe me, is sick and tired of a fruitless pursuit of these Indians…. General Howard seems determined to follow them up in the (vain) hope I suppose, of overtaking them…. Not many officers are in sympathy with him, and a great many think he is guilty of folly of the gravest kind to follow on at the expense of loss in men and animals in a hopeless pursuit.—Dr. John FitzGerald, August 23, 1877[27]

Howard actually was ready to give up the pursuit. When he crossed the Bitterroot Mountains into Montana, he had also crossed the border of the Department of the Columbia, for which he was responsible. His immediate superior was General McDowell, whose Division of the Pacific was headquartered in San Francisco. Howard's troops were now in the bailiwick of the Division of the Missouri, under the jurisdiction of General Phil Sheridan in Chicago. Howard had complained to McDowell via telegram that his troops were tired and ill-supplied, and that he was beyond his jurisdictional boundary. McDowell replied that he was to pay no attention to department and divisional boundaries and was to follow the Nez Perce until they were defeated or driven out of the country.

William Tecumseh Sherman, General of the entire U.S. Army, had just **278** completed a tour of Yellowstone Park and was in Helena. Howard wired him that he was ready to wind up the campaign, to which Sherman replied:

That force of yours should pursue the Nez Perces to the death, lead where they may…. If you are tired give the command to some energetic officer and let him follow them, go where they may, holding his men well in hand, subsisting them on beef gathered in the country, with coffee, sugar and salt, on packs. For such a stern chase, infantry are as good as cavalry.—Gen. William T. Sherman (general of the U.S. Army)

As the general who had marched from Atlanta to the sea, Sherman doubtless believed he knew what he was talking about. He and his troops had lived off the land during the waning days of the Civil War, and he now ordered Howard to follow the same tactic. Of course Sherman hadn't had the Nez Perce in front of him, driving off all the stock in the swath of his path. By the time Howard's troops arrived, fresh horses and cattle had either been slaughtered or driven off. Some of the men complained that the only critters the Nez Perce hadn't been able to scare off were the wormy fish in the rivers of Yellowstone Park.

A chastised Howard got the message. He replied to Sherman:

> *Yours of the 24th received. You misunderstood me. I never flag. It was the command, including the most energetic young officers, that were worn out and weary by a most extraordinary march. You need not fear for the campaign. Neither you nor General McDowell can doubt my pluck and energy. My Indian scouts are on the heels of the enemy.—Gen. O. O. Howard[28]*

And so General Howard's command rolled out of Henrys Lake on August 28.

> From Henrys Lake State Park, continue northeast on US 20 for 5.2 miles to Targhee Pass.

Rescue of a Radersburg Tourist

The Radersburg tourists had been captured by the Nez Perce on August 24. One by one they escaped, and one by one they were picked up by Howard's scouts and by the main command. As the troops left Henrys Lake on August 28, they happened onto one of the tourists, a man named Henry Meyers.

> *The first man we encountered, breathless, hatless, almost starved, with his feet wrapped in rags, was so wild that he could give no intelligible account of himself. It was: "Three Indians fired on me, and I got away. They are all killed. The rest all killed!"—Gen. O. O. Howard*

279

Targhee Pass

The Nez Perce Trail crosses the Continental Divide for the third and final time at Targhee Pass. For the past three or four weeks, the Nez Perce and their pursuers had been traveling close to the Continental Divide, through high mountain prairies where no month of the year is guaranteed to be frost-free.

> *The weather has usually been warm by day, but of late the nights exceedingly cold, water freezing in the basin overnight an inch thick at Henry Lake, and also at other camps.*—Gen. O. O. Howard, August 27, 1877

Join the Adventurous Traveler or continue with the Mainstream Traveler at Targhee Pass.

For the Mainstream Traveler

Targhee Pass to West Yellowstone

From Targhee Pass, proceed on US 20 for 9.2 miles to the town of West Yellowstone.
   Join the Mainstream Traveler in West Yellowstone in the next chapter.

For the Adventurous Traveler

Targhee Pass to West Yellowstone

Miles: 19.7
Map: Gallatin National Forest

Because the lodgepole pines grew so thickly, the Nez Perce hugged the Madison River and made a circular entrance into Yellowstone Park.

East of Targhee Pass 4.9 miles, turn north on Madison Arm Road, a wide, gravel road.

Madison River

> Joseph's trail led us over the main range of the Rockies through a very low
> pass called 'Tachers Pass', and thence down a gradual descent, over bunch
> grass lands and through thickets of lodge pole pines, to the Madison river,
> where we camped for the night, quietly and peacefully, knowing that Joseph
> was fully a week's march in our advance.
>
> The next morning, the 29th, we rolled out as usual in hot pursuit.—
> Henry Buck (wagon-train driver)[29]

Proceed on the Madison Arm Road for 11.4 miles to the junction with US
287 and US 191. Turn south for 3.4 miles into West Yellowstone.

Join the Mainstream Traveler at West Yellowstone in the next chapter.

For Further Reading

Snake River Echoes (volume 12, number 2, 1984) is devoted to the
Camas Meadows Battle. Because this issue is out of print, it may be
difficult to obtain a copy except by writing to the Upper Snake
River Valley Historical Society, P.O. Box 244, Rexburg, Idaho 83440.

CHAPTER 9

Yellowstone National Park

A Different Group of Tourists

West Yellowstone to Cooke City, Montana

The marvelous sights of the National Park were worth the toil and fatigue of the entire march.—Capt. Stephen Jocelyn, September 13, 1877[1]

We then marched on to the Yellowstone Basin.
  On the way we captured one white man and two white women. We released them at the end of three days. They were treated kindly. The women were not insulted. Can the white soldiers tell me of one time when Indian women were taken prisoners, and held three days and then released without being insulted?—Chief Joseph

The Story

The first national park in the world was created in 1872 when Congress dedicated Yellowstone as a "public park or pleasureing-ground for the benefit and enjoyment of the people." Five years later, the fleeing Nez Perce caravan of seven hundred people and two thousand horses traveled through the park in late August. Then, as now, summer sightseers were marveling at Yellowstone's geothermal wonders. Altogether, the Nez Perce came into direct contact with twenty-two of these tourists. The lives of several others, who never saw the Nez Perce, were also affected.

A sightseer who just missed the Nez Perce was the General of the U.S. Army. Second only to the Secretary of War, General William T. Sherman was the chief commander of the U.S. Army. He and his small entourage had left the park the preceding week. While the Nez Perce were journeying through Yellowstone, General Sherman was in Helena, upbraiding General Howard by telegraph.

282   During their second day in Yellowstone, the Nez Perce swept the lone prospector, John Shively, and the Radersburg tourist party along with them. By sunset of that day, seven of the ten tourists had either escaped or been shot, so that the prospector and the siblings, Emma Cowan and Frank and Ida Carpenter, were the only white people remaining with the Nez Perce camp. The following day, Emma, Ida, and Frank were released.

Just before the brother and two sisters were set free, the Nez Perce captured another solitary tourist. J.C. Irwin, who had recently been discharged from the army at Fort Ellis, near Bozeman, was seeing the sights in the park. He stayed with the Nez Perce for a week before he escaped. John Shively finally escaped two days after Irwin.

As a result of the accounts by Shively and Irwin, several books state that the Nez Perce got lost in the Yellowstone. This allegation was hotly denied by the Nez Perce themselves.

> *We knew that Park country, no difference what white people say!*—Yellow Wolf[2]

Howard's Chief Scout, S. G. Fisher, dogged the Nez Perce trail for two weeks, but he then became cynical about the military ever catching up. Indeed, the soldiers had reason to dally: they were enjoying the sights of the park and waiting for more supplies to catch up with them.

While the main entourage headed east, a Nez Perce scouting party raided the camp of ten tourists from Helena. One man was killed and the others fled to safety. Five days later, another Nez Perce scouting party followed the Yellowstone River out of the north entrance of the park, but they turned back when they met a detachment of cavalry coming toward the park on a

Yellow Wolf was the twenty-one-year-old warrior leading the scouting party that captured John Shively and the Radersburg tourist party. (Photo courtesy of Montana Historical Society.)

283

reconnaissance expedition of their own. As they retreated through Mammoth Hot Springs, the warriors killed Richard Dietrich, one of the Helena tourists. Standing in the doorway of the hotel, Dietrich had been awaiting word about the fate of his friends. He, however, made a good target.

Just how the Nez Perce left the park is still a matter of contention. Historians have proposed at least four different possible routes. Where, exactly, the Nez Perce did go in eastern Yellowstone remains a mystery even today.

Chronology of Events

1877

23 August	Nez Perce scouts capture John Shively in Yellowstone National Park.
24 August	Nez Perce scouts capture the ten Radersburg tourists. By the end of the day, seven have escaped or been shot.
25 August	The Nez Perce release Radersburg tourists Emma Cowan, Ida Carpenter, and Frank Carpenter.
	J. C. Irwin is captured by the Nez Perce.
	The Nez Perce camp at Indian Pond.
26 August	Nez Perce scouts raid the camp of the ten Helena tourists and kill Kenck.
	Emma, Ida, and Frank find Lieutenant Schofield and are escorted out of the Park, along with Pfister of the Helena party.
28 August	General Howard's commands picks up tourists Meyers and Oldham along the Madison River.
30 August	George Cowan is picked up by Howard's entourage.
31 August	Howard goes over Mary Mountain Trail and camps near Mary Lake.
	A Nez Perce reconnaissance party encounters Lieutenant Doane's detachment at Henderson's ranch north of Mammoth. While retreating to the main Nez Perce camp, the scouts kill Helena tourist Dietrich at Mammoth Hot Springs.
1 September	Howard camps on the Yellowstone River.
	Scout Fisher meets Irwin, who has escaped from the Nez Perce camp.
3 September	Howard camps near Yellowstone Falls.
4 September	Howard travels over Mount Washburn.
5 September	Howard crosses Baronett's Bridge.

Travel Plan

Mainstream Traveler	Adventurous Traveler	Intrepid Traveler
West Yellowstone to Fishing Bridge	follow Mainstream	follow Mainstream
	Sidetrip Fishing Bridge to Indian Pond	follow Adventurous
Fishing Bridge to Tower Junction	follow Mainstream	follow Mainstream
Sidetrip Tower Junction, Wyoming, to Corwin Springs, Montana	follow Mainstream	follow Mainstream
Tower Junction, Wyoming, to Cooke City, Montana	follow Mainstream	follow Mainstream

For the Mainstream Traveler

West Yellowstone, Montana, to Fishing Bridge, Wyoming

> From West Yellowstone, follow US 20 east, through the West Entrance, for 8 miles. Immediately after crossing the Madison River, pull into the history exhibit turnout, on the south side of the road, to read a bit about the Nez Perce retreat.

Madison River

Just nine days before the Nez Perce traveled along the Madison River, some tourists from Radersburg, Montana, had driven their wagons through here.

> *We come to vast quantities of fallen timber and we find our progress impeded to such an extent that we are compelled to call our axes into requisition, and cut our way for more than a mile, when we again find open timber.* —Frank Carpenter (tourist, Radersburg party)[3]

Later, Frank Carpenter joked that the Army should pay him and his friends for improving the road for General Howard. On the other hand, he also noted that the road clearing had probably eased the flight of the Nez Perce.

285

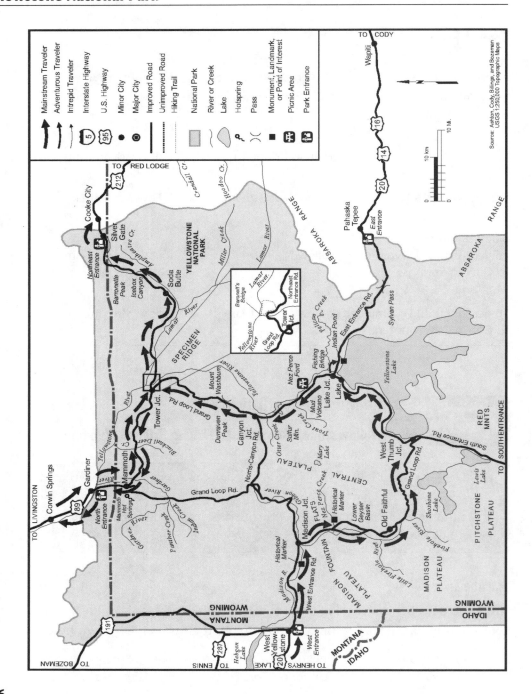

> Continue driving east on the West Entrance Road for 6.0 miles to Madison Junction.

Madison Junction

One of the major campgrounds in the park is located at Madison Junction. A natural setting for a campsite, the Nez Perce probably camped in this vicinity on August 23. Two days later, while camped near here, the scouts in advance of Howard's command discovered two of the Radersburg tourists who had escaped from the Nez Perce.

> *Camped in canyon. After I had camped Madison John told me he had seen a white man on oposite side river going down. Tried to get Madison John to go back and find him. Finaly had to give him $10 to go and show me where he saw him.... We rode down about six miles when we overtook him. He proved to be an escape prisoner from the enemy. His name was Harrison [Harmon]. Took him back to camp.... Just after getting back to camp Paguite and the desperado came in with another escape prisoner (Chas Mann) who they had found above the camp. Man had a ball hole through his hat.*—S. G. Fisher (scout), August 25, 1877[4]

> At Madison Junction, turn south for 5.9 miles to a turnout with the Chief Joseph historical sign. The Firehole River alongside the road is rushing to meet the Gibbon River to form the Madison River at Madison Junction.

Fountain Flats

Leaving the Firehole Canyon, you enter onto Fountain Flats, which appears to be a steaming meadow. On the afternoon of August 30, 1877,

> *While working our way up Firehole canyon, we picked up a poor unfortunate young man by the name of Al Oldham. He had been shot through both cheeks and was all covered with blood and withal was a sad looking spectacle.*—Henry Buck (wagon-train driver)[5]

Contrary to the nearly hysterical tourist, Henry Meyers, who had already been rescued by Howard's command near Henrys Lake a couple of days earlier, Oldham furnished reliable information. But maybe Oldham was less hysterical because his injury prevented him from talking much. He had to communicate by writing notes because,

The ball had penetrated the left cheek, and, passing downwards, had cut the tongue and come out beneath the jaw on the right side. The wound was very painful....

I then dropped down in the bushes and laid there until Saturday night, thirty-six hours from the time of the shooting. My sufferings during the time were intense....

On Sunday...I killed a grouse...but I could eat none of it, as my tongue was swollen so badly it protruded from my mouth. It was with the greatest difficulty that I could breathe.

On Monday night I crossed the Madison and hid among some willows on a little island, and on the following morning I saw some Indians on Gibbon's Fork. I watched them closely, intending, if they came near me, to try and kill one of them and get his pony. The ford was close by, and presently I saw two coming across. As they came closer I got up onto my knees so as to make a sure shot, when I saw they were white men. I stood up then, but I could not speak, and could only make a grunting noise. They heard me, and, riding up to where I was, I motioned for a pencil, which they gave me, and I wrote what I wanted them to know. They camped near by and began doctoring me up. After they got some sugar in my mouth, and about the roots of my tongue, the swelling began to go down, and I soon got so I could talk a little and swallow some food they had prepared for me. They then moved on to Howard's command, where I found [my fellow travelers] Arnold and Mann.—Albert Oldham (tourist, Radersburg party)[6]

Continue south another 0.1 mile to the bridge over Nez Perce Creek.

Nez Perce Creek

The ten tourists from Radersburg camped in the Lower Geyser Basin, about a mile south of here. Prospector John Shively set up his tent half a mile away from the Radersburg group. He had talked with them on August 23 and was getting ready to leave with them the following day.

He [John Shively] was the most wretched looking specimen of humanity I had ever seen....

He says he has lost his horses; had traced them this far, and inquires if we have seen them. Being answered in the negative, he asks if we will carry his "traps" to the settlement, in case he does not find his horses, and we consent.—Frank Carpenter (tourist, Radersburg party)[7]

Shively did leave with the Radersburg tourists, but not in the manner or direction he had planned.

> On the evening of the second day, after leaving the Radersburg party, I was camped in the Lower Geyser Basin. I was eating my supper, and, on hearing a slight noise, looked up, and, to my astonishment, four Indians, in war paint, were standing within ten feet of me, and twenty or thirty more had surrounded me not more than forty feet off. I sprang for my gun, but was rudely pushed back.—John Shively (prospector)[8]

Although Shively emphasized their malevolent appearance, the Nez Perce believed they were being reasonable and even friendly, considering the circumstances.

> We heard chopping.... We went there where we heard the chopping. It was a white man doing cooking. We went up to him, one on each side, in back of him. We grabbed him! He was armed but did not offer fight. Otskai [Going Out] understood a little English and talked with him. We stayed there quite a while, and then a lot of Indians came—just to be friendly with him.
>
> We did not want to do him harm. Only if he had horses or things needed, we might take them for ourselves....
>
> This white man was asked if he knew the way to the head of Yellowstone Park, toward the Crow Indian lands.... He said he did and would go with us. Said his horses were lost, and he was on hunt for them. The warrior told him he would give him a horse to ride, and that it would be a gift for him to return on....
>
> The Indians were partly lost for a short time. Not sure of their way. This man who was oldlike, this white prisoner, was all the guiding they had. Showed them for half of one sun. He was kept a few suns, but we did not try holding him longer.—Yellow Wolf[9]

While Shively was entertaining his unexpected visitors, the tourists from Radersburg were in camp half a mile away, amusing themselves.

> Thursday, the 23rd of August, found us all at the home camp, as we termed it, ready to retrace our steps towards civilization.... We also received the impression that we might meet the Indians before we reached home....
>
> Home seemed a very desirable place just at this particular time, and we decided with one accord to break camp in the morning.... Naturally we felt somewhat depressed and worried over the news received. My brother Frank and Al Oldham, in order to enliven us somewhat, sang songs, told jokes, and

289

finally dressed up as brigands.... They made the woods ring with their nonsense and merriment for some time.—Emma Cowan (tourist, Radersburg party)[10]

The campfire around which the diversion was happening was seen by the Nez Perce scouts who were at Shively's camp.

I saw a light at some distance, a small light. I called the others to come. Pointing, I said, "Look that way!"

Nosnakuhet Moxmox said, "That is fire burning!"

"Yes," I answered. "It may be soldiers or other white people. We will go see why it is."

But one boy thought different. He warned, "We better not go there. It is a swampy place. Our horses might mire down, for we cannot see good."

I replied, "We will lie right here till morning. Then we are going to have a fight with them."

All agreeing, we took our blankets, but built no fire. No fire when scouting....

Early, at breaking light, I awoke the boys. All got ready. We saddled horses and rode on a swift gallop along a draw....

When we got there, we saw four persons lying close to the fire. Then we saw two more not so close, and a little apart was a small tent. These people were not soldiers, but all white people seemed our enemies. We talked what to do with them. I said we would kill them. But the half-blood, Heinmot Tosinlikt [Bunched Lighting or Henry Tababour], said, "No! We will capture them. Take them to the chiefs. Whatever they say will go."

Then some of us, not all, went close to the fire. Two boys stayed back. The white men were getting up.—Yellow Wolf[11]

The Nez Perce scouts surprised the tourists from Radersburg as completely as they had surprised John Shively.

Before morning [on August 24] the entire Indian encampment was within a mile of us, and we had not heard an unusual sound, though I for one slept lightly.

I was already awake when the men began building the camp fire, and I heard the first guttural tones of the two or three Indians who suddenly stood by the fire.—Emma Cowan (tourist, Radersburg party)[12]

Henry, our interpreter, told them we would not hurt them. The leader [A.J. Arnold] was a fine looking man. He shook hands with us....

290

Because I shook hands with him put me in mind not to kill him. He looked at me and said, "I am going to ask you. Why you come here? I hear a little about you."

I answered by the interpreter, "Yes, I am one of the warriors."

Then these white men got afraid. The leader asked, "Would you kill us?"

"They [the other warriors] are double-minded," I told him.

It was hard work, this talking to the white man. Not understanding many words of his language made hard work....

While we were there, the leading white man gave us sugar, flour, and two good pieces of bacon. The food made our hearts friendly.

But the white man from the tent [Cowan] showed mad. He said something to the leader, who then stopped giving the food.—Yellow Wolf[13]

Yellow Wolf assumed that the man who gave them food was the leader and treated him as such. A. J. Arnold was not the leader of the party, however. George Cowan was the one who ordered people around.

The Indians came into camp in small parties all on foot and well armed until they probably numbered at least fifty. About this time I noticed that one of the party had opened the sugar and the flour that was in the baggage wagon and was preparing to issue it out to the redmen who in turn were holding their blankets preparatory to receiving their share. I ran to the baggage wagon and thrusting the Indians aside with my rifle I ordered the man to tie up the sacks and to get down from the wagon stating that we had just about enough rations to last until we reached our homes and I did not care to be starved by a bunch of Indians.—George Cowan (tourist, Radersburg party)[14]

His wife believed that Cowan's action resulted in bad feeling which was later vented back onto him. Interestingly enough, George Cowan would soon be exactly where he did not care to be—in a starving condition.

After some consultation the men decided to break camp at once and attempt to move out as though nothing unusual was at hand. No one cared for breakfast save the Indians, who quickly devoured everything that was prepared. By this time twenty or thirty Indians were about to [the] camp, and more coming. The woods seemed full of them.... While Mr. Cowan was engaged elsewhere one of the men—Mr. Arnold, I think—began dealing out sugar and flour to the Indians on their demand. My husband soon observed this and peremptorily ordered the Indians away, not very mildly, either. Naturally they resented it, and I think this materially lessened his chances of escape. —Emma Cowan (tourist, Radersburg party)[15]

291

Frank Carpenter recorded the story of the Radersburg tourist party's encounter with the Nez Perce in Adventures in Wonderland. He and his two sisters were released by the Nez Perce the day after everyone else in their party had escaped. (Photo courtesy of Montana Historical Society.)

At first the Radersburg tourists were free to go. But then they ran into a larger group of warriors who were not as amicable as the scouts who discovered them had been.

> *Becoming alarmed as to the safety of our horses I ordered one of the men to bring them into camp, harness up and prepare for the homeward journey.... As I gave the command to start a band of about seventy-five mounted Indians rode out of the brush and formed in line in front of the baggage wagon, each with his horse facing in the direction of the wagon and with the but of his rifle resting upon his leg and held in his right hand. I turned to the Indian who had been doing the talking and told him that if he had any authority over these mounted Indians to tell them to get away and let the wagons pass. If not no doubt some of them would be hurt because I was becoming disgusted with the way that they were acting.* —George Cowan (tourist, Radersburg party)[16]

Although George Cowan bossed his friends around, asking a Nez Perce warrior **292** to treat his compatriots in the same manner hit a cross-cultural snag. The warrior who had been doing the talking did not have any authority over the other scouts; that is not the Native American way. In their tradition, each person is his or her own authority. The leader of the scouting party that discovered the tourists told the story from his point of view.

After we traveled part of that sun, I heard a great noise ahead of us. The other Indians had seen us. Not the chiefs, only the warriors. Quickly they made for us. The warriors mixed us up. They did not listen to anybody. Mad, those warriors took the white people from us. Going on, I saw them no more for a time. —Yellow Wolf[17]

As the tourists came toward Nez Perce Creek, they saw the extent of the throng that was engulfing them.

We could see about three miles of Indians, with one thousand or fifteen hundred ponies, and looking off to the left we could see more Indians looking at the geysers in Fire Hole Basin. —Frank Carpenter (tourist, Radersburg party)[18]

South of Nez Perce Creek 0.2 mile is the trailhead for the Mary Mountain Trail. Because the Mary Mountain Trail goes through bear habitat, this guide does not recommend hiking here.

Mary Mountain Trail

The tourists were now no longer free to go their own way. They were forced to travel along with the Nez Perce camp up the Mary Mountain Trail.

We continue in this manner for three or four miles, when we come to fallen timber lying across the trail and we see that we are compelled to abandon our wagons, as we cannot travel further with them. The party halts and we proceed to unhitch the horses and saddle them for Mrs. Cowan and Ida to ride. The Indians are all around us watching every movement and constantly telling us to hurry. —Frank Carpenter (tourist, Radersburg party)[19]

It gave us no pleasure to see our wagons overhauled, ransacked and destroyed. Spokes were cut from the buggy wheels and used as whip handles. We did not appreciate the fact that the Indians seemed to enjoy the confiscated property. One young chap dashed past us with several yards of pink mosquito bar tied to his horse's tail. A fine strip of swansdown, a trophy from Henry Lake, which an ugly old Indian had wrapped around his head turban fashion, did not please me either. —Emma Cowan (tourist, Radersburg party)[20]

293

Exhibiting typical American naïveté and bravado, Frank Carpenter looked for the authority in charge to see if something could be done about this situation.

Emma Carpenter Cowan was twenty-four years old when she was captured by the Nez Perce on the day of her second wedding anniversary. (Photo courtesy of Montana Historical Society.)

> *While the boys are busy saddling up, I propose that I ride ahead and see if I cannot see Looking Glass and White Bird, and get the party out of this scrape.*—Frank Carpenter (tourist, Radersburg party)[21]

The naïve aspect of the seemingly logical request to see the chiefs was this: Joseph would probably be open to negotiation, but White Bird, for example, might not stop his warriors from killing the tourists.

> *Whatever now happened to their lives, I could not help. I did not tell them go see the chiefs. It was their own mind—their own work—that they were going. They heard me say the Indians were double-minded in what they can do.*—Yellow Wolf[22]

Luck, however, was with him. Frank Carpenter was taken to see Chief Looking Glass, who turned him over to Poker Joe. Poker Joe, a Nez Perce-French mixed-blood who spoke English, would prove to be a good friend to the tourists. When Frank and Poker Joe rejoined the rest of the tourists, some trading was begun.

> *After quite a lot of talking we were informed that if we would give up everything that we had including my gun and our fresh horses that the Indians would give us an equal number of their worn out horses and would set us at liberty.... I talked it over with the rest of my party telling them that*

George Cowan lived through his encounter with the Nez Perce despite wounds in his head, hip, and leg. He crawled fourteen miles in five days, during which time he had only a few cups of coffee for sustenance. (Photo courtesy of Montana Historical Society.)

I was satisfied that I would be able to get only one shot but felt sure that I would kill at least five Indians as they were sitting so close together. Mrs. Cowan begged me not to do it, saying that it would be very little satisfaction and that if I did so the entire party would be killed immediately. Poker Joe, stated that many of the young men had lost friends and relatives in the fight at the Big Hole, a short time before and were very angry and wanted to kill us and in case we refused to give up all that we possessed the young men would no doubt kill us. I told the Chiefs that we would accept their proposition.—George Cowan (tourist, Radersburg party)[23]

While George Cowan was flexing his banty-rooster muscles by proposing to shoot himself some Indians, Emma Cowan saw quite plainly what the outcome would be.

Every Indian carried splendid guns, with belts full of cartridges.—Emma Cowan (tourist, Radersburg party)[24]

No wonder Albert Oldham remarked that his friends were "the easiest crowd to trade with" that he ever saw. The bartering conditions had been effactually spelled out: swap or be killed. On these terms the tourists accepted worn-out Nez Perce horses for their own healthy mounts.

While all eyes were on the horse-trading, two of the tourists now made good their escape with a little help from a friend.

295

I looked around and found that Arnold and Dingee were gone.—Frank Carpenter (tourist, Radersburg party)[25]

During the "swapping" that was carried on by the Indians, Poker Joe...pointed out a large grey horse standing near the woods, and told me to go and get him. I started to do so, and he went with me. Reaching the horse, he placed his hand on the saddle to see if it was on well, and then turned to me, and, putting his hand on my shoulder, said:

"You get'm in woods. Stay in woods. No get'm in trail again. Go quick;" and gave me a shove into the timber. He shook me by the hand as he did so, and I got into the bushes as quickly as I could, then stopped and looked back to see what was going on.

Down below me I saw Dingee walking backwards and leading a horse around a marshy place, while an Indian followed him.... The rest of the party began to move, and the Indian stopped and looked around. I then spoke to Dingee and told him to leave the horse and come with me. The Indian then turned again, but Dingee was gone....

We started ahead, and by nightfall had made Gibbon's Fork.... As we had neither coats nor blankets, we amused ourselves that night by crawling over fallen trees to keep warm....

We reached the canyon of the Madison on the evening of the second day....

By the time we had made the summit of the mountain it was night, and the air being extremely cold we were compelled to travel all night to keep warm....

We traveled all that day, but very slowly.... That night we suffered severely as it was extremely cold and so dark that we could not see which way to go. During the night I ascended a mountain to see which way to go, and left Dingee to wait my return. In returning I got lost, and wandered about a long time before I returned to him. On my return I found that he had built a fire, but as it was in a ravine I did not see it until I got close to him.

I was very weak and tired on my return, and sat down by the fire and dropped asleep. I awoke suddenly and found my clothing on fire. This would not do, so we began traveling again over fallen timber and through ravines until daylight....

That night we reached the main [Targhee] pass of the Rocky Mountains on the Madison Road....

We could see Henry's Lake below us....

At daylight we began the descent, and as we left the mountains, we could see the campfires lighting up in different places. I then thought we had struck another Indian camp, and was discouraged. We pushed on to reconnoiter, however, and as we approached, we heard a strain of the most beautiful music that I ever heard. It was a bugle call. We had found the soldiers.—A. J. Arnold (tourist, Radersburg party)[26]

After nearly four days, these two tourists had eventually found safety. Returning now to the events on the Mary Mountain Trail, the story of the rest of the Radersburg tourists continues.

When we camped for noon, I saw those prisoners. They were all alive.— Yellow Wolf[27]

Poker Joe, mounted on my husband's horse, made the circle of the camp, shouting in a sonorous voice some commands relative to the march apparently, as the squaws soon began moving.—Emma Cowan (tourist, Radersburg party)[28]

Those nine [there were ten] prisoners the warriors bothered. The chiefs took the two women away from them. One was full grown, the other young and small. Both good looking. I saw everybody making to travel.... Then, soon, I heard some gun reports.

It was the bad boys killing some of the white men.—Yellow Wolf[29]

I was riding beside Albert Oldham a little ways behind George and Emma. The Indians were all around us. I saw two Indians on horses coming down in front of us at a full gallop. They stopped suddenly and fired, and George jumped or fell from his horse. At the same moment Albert Oldham dropped from his horse, being shot by an Indian a little ways above and behind us. Emma jumped from her horse and ran to Cowan, and the Indians made a rush and surrounded her and George. I sprang from my horse and started to run to where George was lying, with Emma kneeling by his side, but I was so terrified I could scarcely walk. I was benumbed all over, and the froth from my mouth was like paste. I thought certainly that I was soon going to be killed. I spoke to George and asked him where he was hurt, and he replied that his leg was all shattered.

Emma was kneeling with her arms around Cowan's neck, when an Indian came up, and, catching her by the hand, tried to pull her away. He pulled one of her arms from his neck, and then another Indian, seeing that

Ida Carpenter, sister of Frank Carpenter and Emma Cowan, was thirteen years old in the summer of 1877. (Photo courtesy of Montana Historical Society.)

Cowan's head was exposed, put a pistol to his face and shot him in the forehead. Emma fainted, then, and I jumped and screamed, and ran in and out among the Indians and horses. The Indians ran after me, and one caught me by the throat and choked me. I bore the prints of his fingers on my neck for two weeks. As he loosened his hold I had the satisfaction of biting his fingers.—Ida Carpenter (thirteen years old, tourist, Radersburg party)[30]

Emma believed she had witnessed the death of her husband. As fate had it, August 24 was the Cowans' second wedding anniversary.

After my husband was shot in my arms, I was long in recovering consciousness.—Emma Cowan (tourist, Radersburg party)[31]

I had not the heart to see those women abused. I thought we had done them enough wrong in killing their relations against the wishes of the chief, and knew we were in the wrong. While I was endeavoring to stop the bloody work, Poker Joe came up, having been sent by Looking Glass. He did not arrive in time to save those already shot, but he and I prevented other injuries being done the party.—Red Scout [32]

In the confusion created by the shooting of Cowan and Oldham, three other tourists escaped into the brush—Meyers, Mann, and Harmon.[33] Now Frank Carpenter and his two sisters, Ida Carpenter and Emma Cowan, and the prospector, John Shively, were the only four captives remaining with the Nez Perce. As they traveled on, the daily routine of the camp continued around them.

The pack animals also caused trouble, often getting wedged in between trees. An old squaw would pound them on the head until they backed out. And such yelling! Their lungs seemed in excellent condition.—Emma Cowan (tourist, Radersburg party)[34]

Arriving at the main camp, a council of the chiefs was formed, and I was told to take a seat inside the circle. They asked me who I was, and what I was doing there. I told them. They asked me if I would show them the best trail leading out of the park to Wind River, where they were going. I told them I would, as I knew all about the country. This seemed to be satisfactory, and the council broke up, and the camp was moved up a mile or two, where an encampment for the night was formed. A robe was given me, and an Indian named Joe was detailed to sleep with me. He spoke very good English; said that I must not attempt to escape; that he would be my friend; that they had come that way to get away from Howard; that the trail by that route to Wind River was not known to them, but other Indians had told them about it, and that if I told them the truth they would not harm me.—John Shively (prospector)[35]

The squaws soon had supper, and gave me some bread, and tea made of willow-bark. The tea was so bitter I could not drink it. I could not eat, although they insisted on my doing so. They were very kind to me.

They made my bed on some buffalo robes, and the squaws laid down all around me, and thus watched me until morning.—Ida Carpenter (thirteen years old, tourist, Radersburg party)[36]

The Nez Perce proceeded east on the Mary Mountain Trail to the other side of the Central Plateau, emerging near Mud Volcano.

Meanwhile, General Howard's forces were arriving on the scene. First, the advance scouts came through two days after the Nez Perce. Two days later the infantry and cavalry followed. In order for the supply wagons to get through on the Mary Mountain Trail, a road had to be built.

Here...our wagon-road ended....

From this point to the banks of the Yellowstone, and down that river we cut and constructed our own road, the work being done by civilian employes under charge of Capt. W.F. Spurgin, Twenty-first Infantry. It was a most tedious and laborious task, and may be appreciated in the fact that a wagon-road through that section has been always considered...an impossibility.—Gen. O. O. Howard

Building a road delayed the wagon train carrying the supplies for the army.

Arriving at the foot of the mountain that lies between the Yellowstone and the Lower Basin, the wagons stopped, but the cavalry and infantry went on to the Mud Wells. We, who were left behind, were well protected that night, as there was not a gun in the whole outfit.

299

The next morning the teamsters got out early to get up their horses, as they were afraid the Indians would get them....

Here we learned that our horses had been stolen by the Indians of Howard's command.—A. J. Arnold (tourist, Radersburg party)[37]

The Bannock scouts were tiring of an unsuccessful pursuit; they had stolen none of the Nez Perce horses. To make up for their losses, they confiscated some more accessible horses—those belonging to the supply wagons. Howard held several of the Bannocks prisoner until the horses were returned.

> Howard's command followed the Nez Perce across the Central Plateau. Circling around the south side of the Plateau, this guide will pick up the trail again, just north of Yellowstone Lake.
>
> From the Mary Mountain trailhead, proceed south for 0.8 mile to Lower Geyser Basin.

Lower Geyser Basin

The Radersburg tourists were camped near here when the Nez Perce discovered them. And from the amount of steaming geyser activity around here, you can see why the scouts agreed among themselves to wait until daylight to raid the camp of the tourists.

By the time the military scouts arrived at Nez Perce Creek, six of the tourists had been rescued. Arnold and Dingee had made their way to Howard's camp at Henrys Lake. Harmon, Mann, and Meyers, who had escaped during the horse-trading, became separated from each other but were discovered by Chief Scout S.G. Fisher near Madison Junction. Albert Oldham, wounded by a shot through the cheeks, had straggled out to where Nez Perce Creek enters the Firehole River, where he was also discovered by scouts. Now only George Cowan remained missing. After being left for dead along the trail, Cowan revived. He had already been shot in the leg, then shot in the head.

> *In about two hours I began to come back to life, as I did so my head felt benumbed.... My head felt very large, seemingly as large as a mountain, and I mechanically raised my hand and began feeling my face and head. I found my face covered with blood and my hair clotted with blood that had cooled there.... Feeling my leg, I found it completely benumbed, but there were no bones broken....*
>
> *As I raised up I saw an Indian close by me sitting on his pony quietly watching me. I turned to run into the willows close at hand. The Indian*

300

observed the movement and started down toward me. As I was hobbling away, I glanced backward and saw him on one knee aiming his gun at me. Then followed a twinging sensation in my left side, and the report of the gun and I dropped forward on my face. The ball had struck me on the side above the hip and come out in front of the abdomen....

I now took another inventory of my wounds, and in trying to rise found that I could not use either of my lower limbs. They were both paralyzed. I then turned upon my face and began crawling by pulling myself with my elbows....

I kept on down the trail, or rather by the side of it, and Indians kept passing by me every little while, driving ponies as they went. I could hear them approaching and then I would lie down and wait till they passed.

I kept this up until Monday morning, having crossed the East Fork [Nez Perce Creek] Sunday night, and reached the wagons that we had abandoned on Friday. I had crawled about nine miles in sixty hours....

As I reached the wagon I found my faithful dog, Dido, laying beneath it. I called to her, and she came bounding to me, and covered my face and wounds with caresses. The pleasure of the meeting was mutual....

I could find nothing to eat.

It occurred to me that I had spilled some coffee when in camp, on Thursday in Lower Geyser Basin, and calling my dog we started for it, I crawling as before, and the dog walking by my side. The coffee was four miles distant, but I thought not of that. The only idea was to possess the coffee. I was starving.

While crawling along close to the trail, my dog stopped suddenly and began to growl. I grasped her by the neck, and placed my hand over her nose to keep her from making a noise. Peering through the brush, I saw two Indians sitting beneath a tree but a few feet from me. I began moving back cautiously and made a circuit around them, keeping the dog close by me. I thus avoided them, and reached the Lower Geyser Basin on Tuesday night.

Here, as I anticipated, I found some coffee, and a few matches. I found about a handful of coffee, and placing it in an empty can that I had found, I pounded it up fine. I then got some water in another empty can, that had contained molasses, and building a fire, I soon had some excellent hot coffee that refreshed me greatly. This was the first refreshment that I had taken for five days and nights....

I remained where I was Tuesday night....

I made some more coffee, and drank it, which seemed to give me renewed strength, but as my strength returned I felt more keenly the horrors of my

301

position. I thought now I would crawl to where the East Fork [Nez Perce Creek] empties into the Fire Hole River, so calling my dog I began my journey. I found that I was gradually growing weaker, as I could now crawl but a little ways when I would be compelled to stop and rest. At about a mile and a half distant I...had to cross the river, but as the water was not deep, I made it without mishap.... I was now exhausted and could go no farther. It was an expiring effort, and having accomplished it I gave myself up for dead.

In about two hours, I heard the sound of horses coming, but so completely tired out was I that I did not care whether they were Indians or not. My dog began to growl, but I did not try to stop her. The horses drew nearer, and approached and stopped. The riders had seen me. I looked up and saw that they were white men. They alighted and came to me....

One of them kept talking to me, and asking questions that I cared not to answer, while the other built a fire and made some coffee for me. They told me that they were scouts from Howard's command, and that the troops would reach me some time during the next day. They left me some "hardtack" and a blanket.... After they were gone and I had eaten, my desire for life returned, and it seems the spirit of revenge took complete possession of me. I knew that I would live, and I took a solemn vow that I would devote the rest of my days killing Indians, especially Nez Perces.

I laid here until Thursday afternoon, when I heard the sound of approaching cavalry, and shortly afterward General Howard and some of his officers rode up to me. In a few minutes I saw Arnold coming. He came up, recognized me, and knelt beside me. We grasped hands, but neither spoke for some minutes. I could only gasp:

"My wife!"

"No news yet, George," he replied. He added that Oldham was with the command, and that Mann, Harmon, Dingee and Myers had gone to Virginia City.—George Cowan (tourist, Radersburg party)[38]

Cowan, of course, was imagining the worst and was extremely worried about his wife.

Cowan was a most pitiful looking object. He was covered with blood, which had dried on him.... His clothing was caked with dry mud....

The ambulance soon came up, and we placed him in it with Oldham.... When we encamped the soldiers gave us blankets to make Cowan a bed.... The surgeon did not come, as he promised, and I went in quest of one, but could find none. At sundown I went again and saw Dr. Fitzgerald, who said that Dr. Hall was the one that should look after Cowan. However, Fitzgerald said he would go, and soon came over. He seemed to be angry and did his probing, I thought, in a manner not in keeping with the wounded man's condition. During the operation of probing and extracting the ball from his forehead, some of them held a blanket up to secure Cowan from the wind, and to keep the candles from blowing out.

After the probing the surgeon left us, saying that it was not his place to dress the wounds. I then, with the assistance of the boys, washed and dressed the wounds as best I could, and some of the boys gave him some underclothing. The officers of the command offered us nothing, although they were supplied with everything. Neither Cowan, Oldham, or myself were in any way indebted to the surgeons or the officers for anything.

Cowan wanted to be forwarded home by way of Henry's Lake, but Howard said that in his condition he needed the best of medical attendance, (which was true), and that he would see to it that he received it, and that he would send him to Fort Ellis [Bozeman], (which was untrue). The treatment that he received and the attention shown him was to be placed in an old wagon and jolted over the worst road that ever was passed over by a wagon. The officers and surgeons would have let him rot alive. Some of the teamsters gave him underclothing, that was of great service to him, as his wounds discharged a great deal.

During our encampment near the basin, there would not have been an officer or a surgeon captured by the Indians, in case of an attack, as they were all off visiting the geysers.—A. J. Arnold (tourist, Radersburg party)[39]

Arnold, who had taken the initiative in doling out food to the Nez Perce scouts when they first arrived at camp, now showed more leadership. While all the other rescued tourists were sent back home via Virginia City, Arnold remained with Cowan, bouncing along in a supply wagon for the next three weeks.

Continue south to Geyser Basin. It is 8.3 miles to the Old Faithful exit, another 17.6 miles to West Thumb junction, and 18.8 more miles to the Lake area junction. From Lake, proceed north for 1.6 miles to the junction at Fishing Bridge.

Join the Adventurous Traveler for a sidetrip to Pelican Creek Trailhead. Or continue with the Mainstream Traveler at Fishing Bridge.

303

For the Adventurous Traveler

Sidetrip

Fishing Bridge to Pelican Creek Trailhead

Miles: 7.2, round-trip
Map: Yellowstone National Park

This would normally be a sidetrip for Mainstream Travelers because the road to Indian Pond is paved. But there's no really good place for RVs and trailers to turn around. At the Fishing Bridge junction, turn east, across Fishing Bridge, for 3.2 miles to Indian Pond, keeping the north shore of Yellowstone Lake in sight most of the way.

Indian Pond

Indian Pond, formerly called Squaw Lake, derives its name from the fact that the Nez Perce camped here the night of August 26. Whether they camped on the flat, north of the pond, or among the trees on the south edge is unknown. But just imagine fifteen hundred horses coming down to the pond for a drink.

Not long after the Nez Perce left, Howard's scouts rode into the almost-empty camp.

> *Right in the center of an Indian camp I rode up to a poor helpless old squaw.... She laid on a few ragged robes, and suddenly closed her eyes as if expecting a bullet but not wanting to see it come. She seemed rather disappointed when instead of shooting her I refilled her water-bottle. She made signs that she had been forsaken by her people, and wanted to die, and from a couple of shots I heard ten minutes later as I followed the trail down the creek, one of our wild Bannack scouts acceded to her wishes and put her out of her misery.*—John W. Redington (scout)[40]

Four days later, General Howard's aide-de-camp issued a memorandum prohibiting the killing of Nez Perce people left behind in camp. The memo, however, had no effect in changing the traditional Bannock custom.

> *General Howard has given me orders that no prisoners shall be killed by the [Bannock] scouts but brought safely and unharmed into our camp. See that this is carried out, he was much annoyed to learn of the killing of that old woman.*—Lt. Robert Fletcher, August 31, 1877[41]

0.1 mile past Indian Pond, turn east onto a dirt service road for 0.2 mile to the Pelican Creek trailhead.

Pelican Creek Trail

Leaving Indian Pond, the Nez Perce headed east along Pelican Creek on August 27. Four days later, Howard's advance scouts unexpectedly ran into someone along Pelican Creek.

> We have just met an escaped prisoner from Joseph's band, his name is James C. Irwin, lately discharged from Co. G 2d Cavalry, Ft. Ellis [Bozeman]. He says he left the hostile camp about 8 o'clock this morning…. This man Irwin will come to your camp and explain the situation. It will be very important to keep this man with you.—S. G. Fisher (scout), September 1, 1877

After spending a week with the Nez Perce, Irwin was able to furnish General Howard with reliable information. He knew the camp was headed for the Clarks Fork River and that the terrain between here and there was quite rough.

> They evidently had a hard struggle to get through this place for the trees and logs was smeared with blood from their horses cut on the sharp stones and pine knots.—S. G. Fisher (scout), September 3, 1877[42]

Because the Pelican Creek Trail goes through bear habitat, this guide does not recommend hiking the trail.

Return, via Fishing Bridge, to the Grand Loop Road.

Rejoin the Mainstream Traveler at the Fishing Bridge junction.

For the Mainstream Traveler

Fishing Bridge to Tower Junction

This next 6-mile section of the road follows the Nez Perce Trail in the reverse order they took it. They came across the Central Plateau, emerged near Mud Volcano, forded the Yellowstone, and headed south toward Yellowstone Lake on the east side of the Yellowstone River. So, drive north, away from Yellowstone Lake, for 4.9 miles to a sign for Nez Perce Ford Picnic Area. Turn east and drive for 0.3 mile down to the river to see Nez Perce Ford.

Nez Perce Ford

Nez Perce Ford is the spot where the Nez Perce crossed the Yellowstone River on August 25. Just prior to that,

> *During the forenoon the Indians had captured a soldier.... He told them of the Helena tourists camped near the Falls, the number of the men and horses.*—Emma Cowan (tourist, Radersburg party)[43]

The soldier was J. C. Irwin, who escaped on September 1 and was discovered by Scout S. G. Fisher on Pelican Creek. The consequences of Irwin's telling the Nez Perce about the Helena party of tourists will be seen a few miles north of here.

> *The Indians plunged into the stream without paying much regard to the regular ford, and camped on the opposite shore.*—Emma Cowan (tourist, Radersburg party)[44]

After crossing the river, the camp halted for their mid-day break and the chiefs counseled with each other.

> *Before the council, Poker Joe saw me crying. He said, "Me no cry," and he lifted up his dirty old shirt and showed us a bullet wound through his chest and back— just a small hole in front and an ugly ragged one in the back. How he escaped blood-poisoning, I cannot say. There was no dressing on the wound, and all that covered it was his shirt, but it seemed to be healing in spite of the dirt and lack of care. How he could harangue the camp, so to speak, with such an injury, was a wonder to us. He could be heard for half-a-mile.*—Emma Cowan (tourist, Radersburg party)[45]

> *The council being over the chiefs arose and...joined the crowd that had surrounded us during the exciting proceedings of the council. Joe came to us and said:*
> *"Send home now. Send'm your sisters home now. You three go home now."...*
> *"Your sisters ride, you walk," to which I assented.*—Frank Carpenter (tourist, Radersburg party)[46]

> *The women were given horses, the man was made to go afoot. They must not travel too fast. Food was given for their living while going to some town or wherever they lived.*
> *We did not want to kill those women. Ten of our women had been killed at the Big Hole, and many others wounded. But the Indians did not think of*

that at all. We let them go without hurt to find their own people. —Yellow Wolf[47]

We were now ready to depart and…the girls mounted their horses. Joe now led his horse…and taking his gun bade me get on behind him. I did so and we started for the river.…

Having reached Mud Spring we stopped and Joe asked me if I had matches. I told him that we had not, and he gave me some. I dismounted and Emma and Ida joining us, Joe turned and said:

"Now my friends, good-bye. You go down river, way down. No stop. Go all night. No stop. You go three days, get'm Bozeman. You go all night.…

"You no get'm Bozeman three days, Injun catch'm you.…

"Me want you to tell'm people in Bozeman me no fight no more now. Me no want to fight Montana citizens. Me no want to fight Montana soldiers. Me want peace. Me no want to fight no more now. You tell'm Bozeman people." —Frank Carpenter (tourist, Radersburg party)[48]

Poker Joe spoke to Emma, Frank, and Ida at length on the subject of peace.

I thought he never would quit talking. —Emma Cowan (tourist, Radersburg party)[49]

> Return to the Grand Loop Road. 0.8 mile north of Nez Perce Ford is the entrance to the Mud Volcano area.

Mud Volcano

Although the Nez Perce had come by here on August 25, the cavalry and infantry didn't camp near here until September 1.

On the evening of this day a discharged soldier named Irwin came into my camp. He had been held a prisoner in the camp of the enemy for several days, but finally escaped to us. His communication to me of matters relating to the camp, organization, and discipline of the hostiles, and their mode of marching and scouting, was interesting. —Gen. O. O. Howard

Irwin…said that he had been honorably discharged from the Second Cavalry at Fort Ellis [Bozeman], and was exploring the Park alone when captured.…

Irwin told us that while he was a prisoner he acted as guide, and that Shively was boss packer for the squaw packtrain.…

Irwin's information to General Howard certainly did save many miles of marching, by taking the shortcut. —John W. Redington (scout)[50]

The shortcut was this: while the Nez Perce headed east from Yellowstone Lake along Pelican Creek and then over the Absaroka Mountains, General Howard went north to go out the Lamar River, up Soda Butte Creek to Cooke City and then across a pass in the Absarokas to the headwaters of the Clarks Fork. This route, although rough, was not nearly as tough as the trail taken by the Nez Perce through the mountains, which remain a wilderness area even today. Modern highways follow the route taken by Howard, so the remainder of this chapter follows Howard's route and the course of a Nez Perce raiding party.

While camped on the Yellowstone River, the soldiers had an opportunity they had not had all summer.

This afternoon I ordered the whole troop to disrobe and bathe in a middling hot spring, red flannels got a washing as did some choicer hides which had not seen water since leaving Wallula [Washington]. One of the sullen resentful dirtier troopers was sent cartwheeling into this mild caldron by eager hands; this prude left his underwear on. The boys tore this off, claiming that the seam squirrels needed an airing. —Capt. Robert Pollock, September 2, 1877

North of Mud Volcano, just after crossing Trout Creek in 2.1 miles, Sulphur Mountain lies on the west side of the road.

Sulphur Mountain

Rising only three hundred feet above the road level, Sulphur Mountain looks like just another hill. But as the highest point on this side of Hayden Valley, it makes a good lookout. On August 25, a group of tourists—ten men from Helena—had seen the Nez Perce from the top of Sulphur Mountain.

We were just on the point of leaving the [Sulphur] Springs, when Duncan came running down from the top of Sulphur Mountain, exclaiming, "There's a d—n big party of tourists, or else a big band of elk, ahead!" Wilkie said— "Yes, your elk will turn out to be trees, like all the rest of the game you see."
After traveling 3 or 4 miles the boys began to grow uneasy. We could see something alive coming, but did not know what it was....

We traveled on...and, on reaching the top of a small hill, saw a large camp across the Yellowstone. Duncan exclaimed: "Indians! Indians! My God, it's Indians!" He wanted us to backtrack....

We traveled back at a very lively rate for five or six miles to Sulphur Springs, where our scare seemed to subside a little.... We then found a beautiful and safe camp.—Ben Stone (tourist, Helena party), September 6, 1877

On September 2, Howard's command came by Sulphur Mountain, whose shoulder reaches down to the river.

Under our new guide, the discharged soldier brought in from Fisher, whose name was Irwin, we took our course across a mountain-range.... But, though the trail did lead in the right direction, it took us over such fearful steeps, and across such deep and rough ravines, with precipitous banks, that it seemed utterly hopeless for our train of supplies ever to get through.

These difficulties being in view, the troops gave up the wagon-train and took what provision they could carry with the pack-train, and went on to cross the Yellowstone at Baronet's Bridge.—Gen. O. O. Howard

3.2 miles north of Sulphur Mountain, notice the sign for the Mary Mountain Trail. From here, the Nez Perce went south, but Howard went north.

In 0.4 mile, pull into a tiny turnout on the bank of the Yellowstone River. On the hillside just above the turnout was the location of Spurgin's beaver slide.

Spurgin's Beaver Slide

Imagine, if you can, this country without roads. And then imagine trying to drive a wagon from Mud Volcano to this point. The wooded hill on the west side of the road was one of the "fearful steeps" mentioned by General Howard. A supply wagon driver described the descent.

A courier came from General Howard directing us to...make our way to Yellowstone Falls. Obeying orders, we passed over a high plateau of easy going [Hayden Valley].... Suddenly, we came up to a full stop on a timbered ridge that extended toward the river. Medium sized pine trees grew here. We took a survey of the whole situation and came to the conclusion that the only way to get down was to take a jump of some five hundred feet.

309

Someone suggested to prepare a slide and go downhill like a beaver. The pines were not thick and the ground was smooth, although about as steep as the roof of an ordinary house. We picked out a place that looked most suitable for our descent and commenced clearing a roadway.

We had with us a very large rope—one hundred feet long—for emergency cases and were not all ready to "go". The crowd called out, "Here, Buck, you take the lead and if you can make it we will try it". One end of the rope was fastened to the hind axle of my wagon then two turns were made around a substantial tree, with several men holding onto the end of the rope so that the wagon could not get away, they payed it out as fast as the descent was made. Nothing daunting, I climbed up into my spring seat and gathered up the lines—not even taking off my leaders.

I made the start downward and nearly stood up straight on the foot rest of the wagon, it was so steep. Slowly and carefully we went the length of the rope when a halt was called, and with the aid of a short rope made fast to the hind axle and securely tied to another tree, we then loosened the long rope and came down and made another two turns around a nearby tree and was then ready for a second drive; thence a third and so on until the bottom was reached in safety.

The rope was then carried up the hill and another teamster took courage to try his luck and his wagon too, was landed at the bottom of the hill.— Henry Buck (wagon-train driver)[51]

George Cowan, the tourist from Radersburg who had been shot three times, was in one of the wagons that descended the "beaver slide."

*Cowan suffered intensely, but bore it all bravely. Part of the time he was standing on his head, and then again he would be on his feet. It was enough to make a well man sick.—*A. J. Arnold (tourist, Radersburg party)[52]

The rope burns created by the ropes snugging on the trees were visible for years. The last rope-burned tree was burned in the fires of 1988.

> 1.0 mile north of Spurgin's beaver slide, the road crosses Otter Creek.

Otter Creek

310

Feeling they were a safe distance away from the Nez Perce and reassuring themselves that General Howard's troops would take care of these Indians, the Helena party of ten men had stopped and camped on Otter Creek after spotting the Nez Perce train from Sulphur Mountain. But General Howard would not pass this way for another week. And the Nez Perce were less than ten miles away. Irwin, the discharged soldier captured by the scouts, had told the warriors about the Helena tourists.

The three released Radersburg tourists traveled by here on August 26 as they headed toward Mammoth Hot Springs. They were hurrying to get away from the Nez Perce camp, yet their worn-out horses made slow progress. The Nez Perce hadn't wanted them to travel too fast and become informers for the army.

> *The poor old horses needed constant urging to make them travel as fast as my brother could walk.*—Emma Cowan (tourist, Radersburg party)[53]

Emma, Frank, and Ida didn't see the Helena group's camp when they passed it.

> *Our party consisted of Kenk, Stuart, Roberts, Foller, Weikart, Duncan, Detrich, Wilkie, Ben. Stone, the colored cook, and myself, and were on our way to visit the Geyser Basins. Yesterday we were encamped near Sulphur Mountain, and during the afternoon one of the boys said he had seen either a herd of buffalo or elk, or a band of Indians, about five or six miles above us on the other side of the Yellowstone river. Duncan took a spyglass and went up on the mountain to determine if possible, what they were. He soon returned and said they were Indians, and proposed that we get out of that as soon as possible. We accordingly packed up and moved back three or four miles, when one of the boys proposed that we go no farther, as Howard was after the Indians, and by tomorrow they would be gone, and we pitched our tents there. We camped for the night, but some of the boys wanted to go back home, but the majority was of the mind to go ahead to the geysers, as we had come thus far, and the journey was almost completed.* —Frederic Pfister (tourist, Helena party)[54]

In order not to appear unmanly, the fellows tried to ignore their queasiness. But then sleep didn't come as easily as usual.

> *We finally agreed to wait until the next day when two of us would go and ascertain if the camp had moved, and if so, which way, &c. We then went to bed. Duncan, not feeling safe, took his blankets and made his bed half a mile from camp in the timber, all of us laughing at him.*—Ben Stone (tourist, Helena party), September 6, 1877

311

Joe Roberts, Andrew Weikert, and Fred Pfister were members of the Helena tourist party whose camp was raided by Nez Perce scouts. (Photo courtesy of Montana Historical Society.)

I know one that did not close his eyes, and that was your humble servant. I felt as though someone ought to stay awake; if the truth was known, I felt pretty nervous.—Andrew J. Weikart (tourist, Helena party)[55]

After breakfast next morning Stewart wanted Kenck, if he did not feel safe, to take any two horses in the outfit, return to the Hot Springs and then take the wagon train from there home; said he was the only married man in the party and could not afford to take the risk the others would. Kenck refused, saying he would stay with them and see them through.—Ben Stone (tourist, Helena party), September 6, 1877

In denying his desire to get farther away from the Nez Perce, Charles Kenck unknowingly made a fatal decision.

We got up about six or seven o'clock this morning, and Andy Weikart and Wilkie took their horses and went out on a scout. They were to fire their guns if they saw Indians, and we waited three or four hours for them to return. It was nearing dinner time and I left the camp for the purpose of getting wood, leaving some of the boys asleep, and the remainder sitting about the camp fire. I was busy getting wood when all of a sudden, pop, pop, went the guns and I heard the Indians' yip! yip! I looked around and saw the camp full of Indians with the boys jumping and going in every direction. I saw two of the boys coming towards me and I lit out for the river. I reached the river and on looking back heard two shots and some one exclaim, "O, my God!" I don't know who these two were but think it was Jack Stuart and Kenk. —Frederic Pfister (tourist, Helena party)[56]

Pfister and Detrich jumped over an embankment and started for the Yellowstone River. Pfister jumped the creek at or near the camp, but Detrich was not so fortunate but fell in, and it happened to be in a hole so he laid quite still. The grass was high on either side. He stayed in the water for about four hours. The Indians did not see him, so he made good his escape after they, the Indians, had left the camp. Roberts and Foller did some tall running, according to their own account, while the Indians were blazing away at them most every jump, but finally got away all safe. They struck out for Virginia City which was about 150 miles. The first night they camped in the timber, they laid down beside a big log. One of the boys had a coat on and the other hadn't, so the one with the coat had to lay on the outside. They traveled the next day; they were getting pretty hungry, so they tried fishing. Caught two little fishes. They built a fire and roasted one; the other they saved for another meal. Those two fishes were all they had to eat for nearly three days. They met some soldiers in the afternoon of the third day; they got what they wanted to eat and got enough to last them to Virginia [City].... Duncan, he lit out from the camp like a scared wolf, and got where the timber was the thickest and stayed until dark...then struck out for the Mammoth Springs. Steward and Kenk did not fare so well. The Indians followed them up and shot Stewart in the side and in the calf of the leg. He fell. Then they followed Kenk up until they killed him. Shot him through the body; one ball struck him in the back of the neck and broke it. I suppose it killed him instantly. They raffled his pockets, then came back and was going to kill Stewart. He asked them to spare his life; they asked him if he had any money. They rolled him over and took 260 dollars and a silver watch.... **313**
After a time they told him he could live. So they left him; he dragged himself down to the creek and washed his wound.... He looked up and saw his mare coming toward him; he got a halter and put it on her and then he led her to a log and crawled onto her.... He rode her about 1 mile, but his wound pained him so that he had to get off her. About this time Stone came hobbling along. He was afflicted with rheumatism anyway, and laying in the water so long had done him no good. —Andrew J. Weikart (tourist, Helena party)[57]

A Nez Perce version of the raid was not recorded.

> *There were two other small scouting bands in the Yellowstone Park country besides mine. One was headed by Kosooyeen, the other by Lakochets Kunnin [Rattle Blanket]. I do not know which of these made attack on some hunters or visitors, but I have heard they killed one man. Each party did scouting every sun.*—Yellow Wolf[58]

Weikart and Wilkie were out doing some scouting of their own while their camp was being attacked. When they returned to Otter Creek,

> *We hollowed a couple times, but received no answer. Then rode into camp and found that the boys had got away in a hurry by the things were laying around promiscuously.... They, the boys, did not take time to take their outfits or anything except their clothes they had on their backs. The Reds did not want the shot-guns, so they smashed them around the trees so as to make them unfit for further use. They took what they needed in shape of blankets, tents, provisions, saddles and fourteen head of horses. What they did not want, they put on the fire and burned up. They gave the boys a complete surprise.*—Andrew Weikart (tourist, Helena party)[59]

Not wasting any time, Weikart and Wilkie immediately headed for Mammoth Hot Springs, hoping to find their friends there.

Proceed 2.7 miles north to Canyon Junction.

Canyon Junction

Today you're seldom more than a few minutes away from a snack or a meal. Food was not so accessible to the soldiers who were under orders to live off the land.

> *On the Yellowstone the army ran out of tobacco and most everything else, and filled up on lake trout without salt. These fat fish were lazily lolling around in the river, and luckily it was no trick to catch them. Most of them were wormy, but in those hungry days everything went. After Colonel Parker and I had filled up on them and were scouting around an outpost he said to the officer commanding it, who was just then eating a stand-up lunch, "Say, lieutenant, don't you know that those trout are full of worms?"*
>
> *The lieutenant finished swallowing a big mouthful and replied, "Well, if the worms can stand it, I can," and started in on another fish.*—John W. Redington (scout)[60]

September 1, 2, and 3, Howard's troops leisurely traveled down the Yellowstone River, seeing some of the sights along the way. The wagon pack-train was behind the troops and, due to the roughness of the terrain, couldn't catch up. So the decision was made to pack all the supplies on horses and the send the wagon- train home.

> *Our marches at this time averaged about fifteen miles a day; the object in making such small distances, being to enable certain supplies from Virginia City to overtake us.*—Thomas Sutherland (war correspondent)[61]

North of Canyon Village Junction 18.2 miles is Tower Junction. This road winds between Dunraven Peak and Mount Washburn.

Continue with the Mainstream Traveler at Tower Junction for a sidetrip to Corwin Springs. Or follow the Mainstream route to Yellowstone River and then on to Cooke City.

For the Mainstream Traveler

Sidetrip

Tower Junction, Wyoming, to Corwin Springs, Montana, via Mammoth and Gardiner

This sidetrip traces the route of the Nez Perce raiders as well as that of the rescue of the released captives. Proceed northwest from Tower Junction for the next 11.2 miles to Blacktail Deer Creek.

Blacktail Deer Creek

Near here Emma Cowan and her brother and sister, Frank and Ida Carpenter, plodding along on two worn-out horses, unexpectedly met up with another scouting party.

> *In rounding a point of timber, we saw in a little meadow not far beyond, a number of horses and men. At the first glance we thought them Indians. Frank drew our horses back into the timber and went forward to investigate. He returned in a very few minutes and declared them soldiers. Oh, such a feeling of relief!*
>
> *Imagine their surprise when we rode into the camp and my brother told them we were fleeing from the Indians, the only survivors of our party, as he believed then....*

315

> *This company of soldiers was a detachment from Fort Ellis [Bozeman], with Lieutenant Schofield in command. They were sent out to ascertain the whereabouts of the Nez Perces, and were returning in the belief that the Indians were not in that vicinity....*
>
> *The soldiers quickly prepared supper for us....*
>
> *As we were about to move off, a man came hurrying down the trail. He [Pfister] proved to be one of the Helena party. He said they were attacked at noon. Frank and I concluded that Poker Joe knew what he was talking about when he told us to travel all night. A horse was provided for this man, hurry orders given, and we set out for the [Mammoth Hot] Springs.—Emma Cowan (tourist, Radersburg party)[62]*

Emma, Frank,[63] and Ida were escorted out of the park by Schofield's detachment, and traveled on home by way of Bozeman. All ten of the Radersburg tourists had survived their encounter with the Nez Perce. However, they did not yet know that each one of the others was also safe. Nearly a month passed before Emma Cowan learned that her husband, George, was still alive.

> Continue driving west for 6.7 miles to Mammoth Hot Springs. From Mammoth, proceed 5.5 miles through the North Entrance to Gardiner, driving along the Gardiner River. Drive through town, and continue north on US 89 for 7.5 miles to the small town of Corwin Springs.

Corwin Springs

Having left the main camp back near Fishing Bridge, the Nez Perce raiding parties roamed this far north. Meanwhile Lieutenant Doane from Fort Ellis, near Bozeman, was heading toward the park with a large group of Crow scouts, and a company of cavalry. The two groups ran into each other at Bart Henderson's ranch, located near the present-day town of Corwin Springs.

> *The Indians came up behind the house, got the horses out of the corral, set fire to the house, and went back to join ten others who had stopped, watching from the hillside. Then the eighteen went back, driving the horses up the river. The white men put us on the Indian trail at once, and we pushed them hard enough to get back nineteen horses.—Lt. Hugh Scott*

As Doane's command followed closely on the heels of the Nez Perce raiders, the hundred or so Crow scouts suddenly dwindled to about twenty, possibly because the Crows and Nez Perce had a strong tribal friendship.

The Crows could not be induced to go ahead.—Lt. Hugh Scott

From Corwin Springs, return the 13.0 miles to Mammoth.

Mammoth Hot Springs

Five of the ten Helena tourists had converged on the hotel near the Liberty Cap at Mammoth Hot Springs. Here they awaited word as to the fate of their five other friends.

> *I turned my horse out to graze and waited until noon for the rest of the boys to come in, but none came. I then saddled my horse again and went back on the trail again about eight miles and from this point could see about four miles more, but could not see nor hear anything of them. I returned sad at heart but with a determination to go back and hunt for them if I could persuade someone to go with me.... No one volunteered to go with me.... So I concluded to start the next evening alone...but Jim McCarty, who owned an interest in the Springs and has lived on the frontier a long time, told me if I would wait until the next morning, he would go with me.... We started the next morning with two saddle horse and two pack-horses, leaving Detrich, Stewart and Stone at the Springs. The ambulance was coming up after Stewart that day and I begged Detrich to go with him and take care of him, but he wanted to wait until I came back.... When we started, Mack told him to look out for his hair; he said he would try to, adding, "Andy, you will give me a decent burial, won't you?" I told him jestingly that I would, never thinking that I would be called on to perform the reality so soon.*—Andrew Weikart (tourist, Helena party)[64]

One of the reasons Richard Dietrich wanted to stay at Mammoth was to await the return of eighteen-year-old Joe Roberts. Dietrich had promised Joe's mother that he would be responsible for him. Roberts, however, by this time was safe in Virginia City.

Why Dietrich was standing in the doorway of the hotel will never be known, especially since he had been warned the Nez Perce were close by.

> *It was coming towards sundown when we saw a white man standing in the doorway of a house. We stopped not far from him but did not dismount. We sat on our horses, six or seven of us, thinking. Chuslum Hahlap Kanoot [Naked-footed Bull] said to me, "My two young brothers and next younger brother were not warriors. They and a sister were killed at Big Hole. It was*

317

Richard Dietrich was shot by Nez Perce scouts while he was standing in the doorway of the hotel at Mammoth Hot Springs. (Photo courtesy of Montana Historical Society.)

just like this man did that killing of my brothers and sister. He is nothing but a killer to become a soldier sometime. We are going to kill him now. I am a man! I am going to shoot him! When I fire, you shoot after me."

Chuslum Hahlap Kanoot then fired and clipped his arm. As he made to run, another warrior, Yettahtapnat Alwum [Shooting Thunder] shot him through the belly.—Yellow Wolf[65]

Following closely behind the Nez Perce raiding party was Lieutenant Doane's detachment of cavalry.

We rounded a point and at McCartney's cabin in a side gulch found a white man lying dead at the door, not yet cold. He had been standing in the doorway, looking out, when one of the Indians we were chasing rounded the point and shot him. He had plunged forward on his face, and been shot again, the bullet going the length of his body.—Lt. Hugh Scott

Meanwhile, the only other man left at the hotel, Ben Stone, made a narrow

318 escape.

Stone made good his escape from the Springs when the Indians put in their appearance, by running out the back door and up a gulch. An Indian saw him and started after him, but while the Indian was behind the house, old

Ben climbed up a tree. It was getting dark and the Indian rode directly under the tree where Ben was and stopped under it. Old Ben said his heart beat so loud and fast that he was afraid that the redskin would hear it beat, but it seems that he did not for he soon rode off up the gulch. —Andrew Weikart (tourist, Helena party)[66]

From Mammoth, return to Tower Junction and join the Mainstream Traveler there.

For the Mainstream Traveler

Tower Junction, Wyoming, to Yellowstone River

Turn east at Tower Junction for 0.9 mile. After crossing the Yellowstone River, turn north onto a service road that leads to a small parking area near the site of Baronett's Bridge.

Baronett's Bridge

Baronett's Bridge was built in 1871 as a toll-bridge, and Jack Baronett profited more from miners on their way to and from the Clarks Fork than he did from tourists in Yellowstone.

On arriving at Barronet's bridge, we found that a small raiding party had been there and had made an unsuccessful attempt to burn the bridge. We were delayed here several hours in repairing the damage. —Thomas Sutherland (war correspondent)[67]

If your map of Yellowstone has enough detail that it shows Baronett's Bridge, chances are that the map locates it in the wrong place. Baronett's Bridge crossed the Yellowstone River, not the Lamar.

Join the Hiker to Baronett's Bridge. Or continue with the Mainstream Traveler to Cooke City.

Baronett's Bridge across the Yellowstone River was partially burned by a Nez Perce raiding party. (Photo courtesy of Montana Historical Society.)

For Hikers

Miles: 1.5, round-trip

On this 35–45-minute walk you will see the site of Baronett's Bridge and walk along a few hundred yards of the very road taken by the Nez Perce raiders and General Howard's cavalry.

Starting at the parking lot, on the trail closest to the river (GPS N44°55.337', W110°24.036'), walk north along the Yellowstone for 0.3 mile. Right after passing a boulder about 6 feet high, step closer to the edge and look down to the river. From this point you should be able to see the stonewall abutments for Baronett's bridge on this side of the river. They sit on top of a ledge at the narrowest part of the river.

As you continue to walk east, in another 0.1 mile you will be able to see traces of the wagon road switchbacking down the north bank of the Yellowstone River. Another 0.1 mile walk, staying close to the river, will bring you to the remains of the wagon road on the south side of the river. The hillside has eroded severely enough that the original roadbed is mostly covered with talus, which provides very unsure footing.

The Baronet's Bridge, a slight structure, stretched across the roaring torrent of the Yellowstone, had its further [south] end so much burned by the raiders that it had fallen out of place, and was not passable; so that we were allowed to rest three hours, long enough to repair the bridge....

The beams, shortened by the fire, were tied to some heavy timber that was fortunately on hand. Mr. Baronet's house, the only one we had seen since Henry Lake, stood a few hundred yards away, on Joseph's side of the river. It was appraised at three hundred dollars, and much of its lumber was brought to the river, for replanking. The bridge, which was probably fifty feet above the water, extended from bank to bank, had but one intermediary support, and that fearfully near to demolition. As the first animals were started across the patched-up structure it trembled, and swung laterally very perceptibly, but by a little setting of teeth, and what a Chicago orator called "clear grit" ...in the short space of half an hour the work was done; led horses, loaded pack-mules, and marching men had crossed the flood.—Gen. O. O. Howard

> Continue walking east for 3 or 4 minutes to the confluence of the Yellowstone and Lamar rivers. Now, keeping the Lamar River on your left, walk upstream about 0.2 mile. Then you can follow the traces of the wagon road back to the parking lot. The return trip should take about 15 minutes.
> Join the Mainstream Traveler for the trip to Cooke City.

For the Mainstream Traveler
Yellowstone River to Cooke City, Montana

> Proceed east on the Northeast Entrance Road through the gentle Lamar Valley for 19.2 miles to Icebox Canyon.

Lamar Valley

The Nez Perce scouts fled up the Lamar in advance of General Howard. At the confluence with Soda Butte Creek, the Nez Perce raiders probably followed the river, while the road follows the creek.

321

Icebox Canyon

The names of many of the landscape's features have changed since 1877. The Absaroka Mountains, which you are now entering, were originally called the Snow Mountains. The east fork of the Yellowstone is today called the Lamar River. According to the following excerpt from a letter, Icebox Canyon, which was called Clark's Pass, was supposed to have been renamed also.

> We marched down and crossed the [Yellowstone] river 30 miles from the lake, then followed up East Fork [respectively, the Lamar River and Soda Butte Creek] to its source, going through Clark's pass [Icebox Canyon] in the Snow [Absaroka] Mountains, soon reaching the headwaters of Clark's Fork, down which we are now moving. Clark's pass, a grand spot enclosed, by mountain walls two or three thousand feet high, almost equalling the Yosemite in magnificence, was named by Gen. Howard "Jocelyn Cañon" and will so appear on the official maps of the park in the future. Quite an honor for S.P. But it is getting so dark I cannot see to write.—Capt. Stephen P. Jocelyn, September 13, 1877[68]

> Continue for 12.1 miles to Cooke City.

Cooke City

When General Howard came through Cooke City, he found the miners here armed and stockaded. That was about the extent of the excitement, since the Nez Perce actually traveled about ten to fifteen miles south of Cooke City. An historical information sign on the south edge of town mentions the Nez Perce passage through the area.

> The soldiers fixed up the Baronet bridge, burned by a war-party, and marched on up Soda Butte creek and passed Cooke City, where several pioneer miners volunteered to serve against the Indians. Along here Captain Fisher and his little bunch of Bannacks rejoined the command and again rode out far in the advance, on the heels of the enemy. —John W. Redington (scout)[69]

322 But Chief Scout Fisher had been on the heels of the Nez Perce for almost two weeks already. By this time he was quite skeptical about the results of his efforts.

> Am tired of trying to get Soldiers & hostiles together. U.S. too slow for business. —S. G. Fisher (scout), September 5, 1877[70]

Join the Mainstream Traveler at Cooke City in the next chapter.

For Further Reading

The Yellowstone Story, Volume I, by former Park Historian Aubrey Haines, has one chapter on the Nez Perce in Yellowstone that further amplifies the account presented here.

The Yellowstone Association Institute, P.O. Box 117, Yellowstone National Park, Wyoming 82190, usually offers a course or two each summer on the Nez Perce route through Yellowstone, perhaps backpacking or horsepacking the trail in eastern Yellowstone. Check the current schedule at www.yellowstoneassociation.org.

The captured tourist and natural-born storyteller Frank Carpenter wrote *Adventures in Geyser Land* about his family's and friends' visit to Yellowstone. The 1935 reprint edition includes Emma Cowan's comments on the text and her own narrative and George Cowan's reminiscences. Because this is a rare and expensive book, it is available through inter-library loan.

A map of the *Nez Perce Trail Through Pelican Creek, East Fork Yellowstone, Crandall Creek Camp Area and Trail Creek Meadows Camp* (map 1 of 2) can be purchased at www.nezperce.com.

CHAPTER 10

Clarks Fork

A Daring Escape

Cooke City to Laurel, Montana

*Chases after indians in so vast a country where we must go with a limited quantity of supplies is but a chance in a thousand to hit the mark you are aiming at. "Tis terribly hard on horses and men—and but poor satisfaction at best should you gain the end.—*Capt. Frederick Benteen, August 11, 1877[1]

*But every attempt to communicate with Sturgis was, as we afterward found, unsuccessful. The bodies were found of every courier sent out, of every miner or white man caught in the mountains; for at this juncture the Indians spared nobody.—*Lt. C. E. S. Wood

*Every white man in those mountains could be counted our enemy.—*Yellow Wolf[2]

The Story

While the Nez Perce were leaving Yellowstone Park by going almost due east through the wild Absaroka Mountains, General Howard headed northeast to Cooke City and over a pass in the Absarokas to the headwaters of the Clarks Fork of the Yellowstone River. Following the Clarks Fork downstream, Howard converged with the Nez Perce trail at Crandall Creek. The fleeing bands were just thirty-six hours ahead of their military pursuers.

Near the top of the next pass, over Dead Indian Hill, the Bannock scouts lost the trail in the tracks of a great milling of horses. Chief Scout S.G. Fisher finally figured out the puzzle—the Nez Perce had not headed southeast toward the Shoshone River as originally expected. Instead they had pulled off a daring escape by descending a steep incline from Dead Indian Hill Pass into Clarks Fork Canyon. This incredible route was only twenty feet wide in some places.

Ten days earlier, on the first of September, Colonel Samuel D. Sturgis had parked his Seventh Cavalry near the mouth of the Clarks Fork Canyon. The plan was to squeeze the Nez Perce between his troops in front and Howard's

324

Colonel Samuel D. Sturgis parked several companies of the Seventh Cavalry on the Clarks Fork River, anticipating that the Nez Perce entourage would choose that exit from the Absaroka Mountains. (Photo courtesy of National Archives.)

behind. A week passed, and still the Nez Perce had not appeared. Sturgis' scouts told him there was no entry, other than the mouth, into the canyon. Fearing he had missed them completely, Sturgis moved south to the Stinking Water (now Shoshone) River, near Cody, Wyoming. When he also failed to find the trail of the Nez Perce down there, he realized he had been outwitted. Circling back through the mountains, Sturgis converged with the Nez Perce and Howard's trail near Dead Indian Pass. Scrambling down into the canyon on the route he thought did not exist, Sturgis caught up with Howard a few miles below the mouth of the Clarks Fork Canyon.

General Howard was gentlemanly in his chagrin at finding Sturgis behind him instead of in front of him. To make amends, Colonel Sturgis now rushed ahead with his nearly rationless troops in an effort to catch the Nez Perce.

Chronology of Events

1877

1 September	Colonel Sturgis parks his command near Clarks Fork Canyon.
6 September	Sturgis moves his camp closer to Heart Mountain.
7 September	General Howard passes Cooke City.
8 September	Howard's scouts meet Sturgis's couriers.
	Sturgis heads to the Shoshone River.
	The Nez Perce descend into Clarks Fork Canyon.
9 September	Howard camps at the foot of Dead Indian Hill.
	Sturgis reaches the Shoshone, near Cody, does not find the Nez Perce, and heads north into the Absarokas.
10 September	Howard descends into Clarks Fork Canyon.
11 September	Sturgis catches up with Howard near Belfry.

Travel Plan

Mainstream	Adventurous	Intrepid
Cooke City to Sunlight Creek	follow Mainstream	follow Mainstream
	Sidetrip Sunlight Picnic Area	follow Adventurous
Sunlight Creek to Wyoming 120	follow Mainstream	follow Mainstream
Wyoming 120 from Wyoming 296 to Park County 1AB	follow Mainstream	follow Mainstream
Sidetrip Park County 1AB to Clarks Fork Canyon	follow Mainstream	follow Mainstream
Park County 1AB to Laurel	follow Mainstream	follow Mainstream

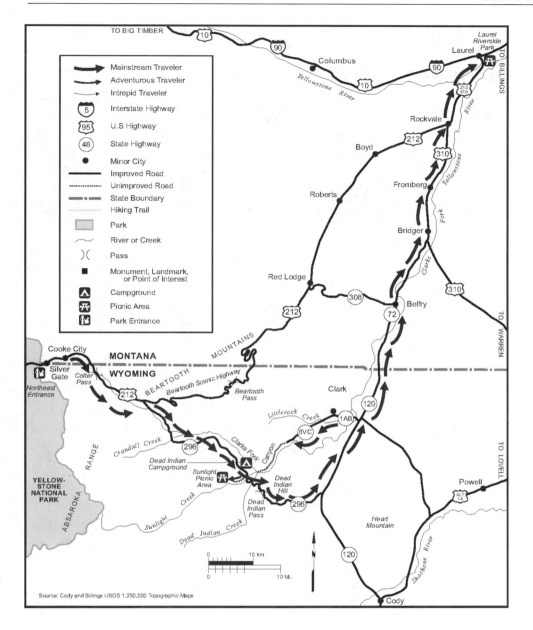

Source: Cody and Billings USGS 1:250,000 Topographic Maps

For the Mainstream Traveler

Cooke City, Montana, to Sunlight Creek

4.7 miles east of Cooke City you arrive at the Montana-Wyoming state line, which is also the boundary between the Gallatin and Shoshone national forests. Continue driving east on US 212 from the border for 8.8 miles to the junction with Wyoming 296, Chief Joseph Scenic Highway. Once you have crossed Colter Pass, you are in the drainage of the Clarks Fork River.

Headwaters of the Clarks Fork

The Nez Perce avoided this more-traveled and populated route, which was a main access for prospectors and miners going to and from Cooke City. General Howard, however, took this easier, although longer, journey. Meanwhile, the Nez Perce were struggling through the rugged Absaroka Mountains, about ten miles south of here.

Somewhere along this stretch of the Clarks Fork, an unexpected meeting occurred.

> *While our scouting outfit was on the headwaters of the Clark's Fork, Yellowstone River affluent, we saw a solitary white man some distance away. The discovery was mutual, and we watched each other rather suspiciously from high points, but soon got together. The stranger proved to be Roque, a French Canadian, scouting for Colonel Sturgis, 7th U.S. Cavalry. He was several miles from his command...and we were about six miles ahead of General Howard's army. When we told Roque about where the main hostile trail went...he dashed back to tell Sturgis, and one of our scouts started back to carry the news of our discovery of the Seventh Cavalry whereabouts.*—John W. Redington (scout)[3]

Anticipation must have been high among General Howard and his men. The Nez Perce were now between Howard's and Sturgis's troops. The trap was about to be sprung.

328

Turn southeast on Wyoming 296, Chief Joseph Scenic Highway. Stop at a Point of Interest in 2.4 miles that shows how the Nez Perce route closely parallels most of this highway, beginning at Crandall Creek in another 5.1 miles.

Crandall Creek

General Howard converged with the Nez Perce trail at Crandall Creek on September 8.

> *The Indians' big trail, now in plain view, swept down the valley, and not a soul was in sight for ten miles and more.*—Gen. O. O. Howard

> *Dead couriers, miners, and prospectors were found in this vicinity in fearful frequency, showing how difficult it had been for Sturgis and me to communicate.*—Gen. O. O. Howard

From the Crandall Creek Bridge, continue southeast on Wyoming 296. A pullout in 13.6 miles presents a picture-postcard vista of the landscape the Nez Perce and you will be traveling around—the Clarks Fork Canyon. Continue for 1.6 miles to Sunlight Creek.

Join the Adventurous Traveler for a short sidetrip to the Sunlight Picnic Area. Or continue with the Mainstream Traveler at Sunlight Creek.

For the Adventurous Traveler

Sidetrip
Sunlight Creek to Sunlight Picnic Area

Miles: 2.8, round-trip
Map: Shoshone National Forest

The highway bridges a 350-foot deep chasm created by Sunlight Creek. Since this gorge presented a formidable obstacle, a short sidetrip to the Sunlight Picnic Area suggests a more accessible crossing of the creek.

Backtrack by driving west on the Chief Joseph Scenic Highway for 0.5 mile. Turn south on Park County Road 7GR, which switchbacks down to cross Sunlight Creek in 0.7 mile. The Sunlight Picnic Area is just 0.1 mile farther on.

Howard's troops took the Lodgepole Trail from Crandall Creek and probably crossed the Sunlight, about 5 miles upstream from here.

Return to Chief Joseph Scenic Highway at Sunlight Creek and continue with the Mainstream Traveler there.

For the Mainstream Traveler

Sunlight Creek to Wyoming 120

From the Scenic Area east of the bridge over Sunlight Creek, continue east for 2.1 miles to Dead Indian Campground.

Dead Indian Campground

Located along Dead Indian Creek, the campground has always been a natural site to spend the night.

> On the 10th we came to a hostile camp which had just been abandoned, at the base of the last mountain necessary to climb before reaching the buffalo plains at Heart Mountain.—Frank Parker (scout and war correspondent), September 16, 1877

Two weeks previously a memorandum had been issued to the scouts, prohibiting the killing of prisoners (see page 304), but it appears to have had little effect.

> Just as I halted to go into camp for the night one of my Scouts…rode past me. Went up the creek a short distance. I was about to unsaddle when I heard him raise a war whoop and three shots was fired within a few seconds. I lit into my saddle and ran my horse up there. Got there just in time to see a Nez Perce breathe his last. He had been wounded in the hip and had been left by his comrads who had evidently left here this morning…. Sumner said he rode up near where he lay and the Indian threw the robe off that covered him and raised up in a setting posture. Sumner waited no longer but jerked his pistol and shot him through the chest. The Indian fell back but Sumner gave him two more shots. One of Wilbers Scouts came up and scalped the dead Indian. Madison John stretching and drying the scalp had it stuck up on a little willow stick when Gen. Howard and his aidecamp Lt. Fletcher rode up. Howard dismounted near the scalp. I didn't want Howard to see it so I winked to Jule (a Cheyenne half breed) and while I drew Howards attention in another direction Jule stepped around and got his toe against the stick with scalp down in the rye grass out of sight.— S. G. Fisher (scout), September 9, 1877[4]

That the Nez Perce were familiar with central Montana is demonstrated by this 1871 photo by W.H. Jackson, which shows a Nez Perce camp on the Yellowstone River near present-day Livingston. (Photo courtesy of Smithsonian Institution National Anthropological Archives, Bureau of American Ethnology Collection.)

From Dead Indian Campground, continue uphill on 7 percent grades. In 6.5 miles, pull over for a viewpoint of the Clarks Fork Canyon. Continue on for 0.9 mile to Dead Indian Pass.

Dead Indian Hill Pass

Having topped the last high mountain of the Absaroka range, at over eight thousand feet, the plains of Wyoming and Montana—buffalo country—lay just ahead. Heart Mountain, a frequently mentioned landmark, stands out on the eastern plains.

331

Interpretive signs at the summit of Dead Indian Hill Pass commemorate the passage of the Nez Perce and the Army through here. Just a mile or two beyond the pass, the Nez Perce played a trick that tested S.G. Fisher's excellent ability as a scout.

> *From the top of this divide the Enemys trail Bears off to the South East which my Indians tell me would take them to Stinking Water [Shoshone River] to the South of Hart Mountain which is in sight from the sumit we passed over this morning. After leaveing the summit the Enemy followed the Stinking Water trail about two miles then they turned back north driveing their horses around in every direction for the purpose of cacheing their trail which they done in good shape. The Scouts scattered out in every direction to hunt for their trail. I finaly stumbled on it. Instead of going out of the bason on the open plain, they had turned North, passing along the steep side of the Mountain through the timber for several miles.... The trail led us through a rough canyon very narrow in places.—S. G. Fisher (scout), September 10, 1877*[5]

The passage down into the narrow Clarks Fork Canyon from here is rough and steep.

> *My command, discovering Joseph's ruse, kept the trail which Sturgis had been so near, but had not seen, and, finally, slid down the canyon, many a horse, in his weakness, falling and blocking the way. The mouth of this canyon, which debouches into Clark's Valley, was not more than twenty feet across from high wall to high wall. And one may imagine the scene of cavalry, infantry and pack-mules crowding through it, and admire the quick wit of an Indian who had the hardihood to try the experiment, and break the almost impassable roadway.—Gen. O. O. Howard*

The sight and experience of the trail and descent to the canyon is available only to the most intrepid hikers. To pick up the next section, you will need to circle around and come into the Clarks Fork Canyon from the opposite side.

332

Proceed east on Chief Joseph Scenic Highway. If you happen to be traveling this road at dusk, you will be amazed at the distance at which you can see headlights out on the plains. Perhaps Nez Perce scouts saw Sturgis's campfires from up here. After Dead Indian Hill Pass, in 2 miles look north to Bald Peak. How did the Nez Perce get from here to there? Continue on 11.2 miles to the junction with Wyoming 120.

For the Mainstream Traveler
Wyoming 120 from Wyoming 296 to Park County 1AB

Proceed north on Wyoming 120 for 12.6 miles to the junction with Park County Road 1AB.

Sturgis's Camp

Between mileposts 123 and 124 on Wyoming 120, look to the west to see the mouth of the Clarks Fork Canyon. Colonel Sturgis camped about halfway between the highway and the canyon.

> *Just before leaving the [Crow] Agency, Col. Sturgis had employed a couple of prospectors who claimed to be thoroughly familiar with the country, to make a scout over in the approaches to the Canyon, with orders to report at a certain point on a certain day....*
>
> *We reached the camp at which our scouts were to report and went into camp in the timber at the base of a towering mountain, said to be about five miles from the exit of the canyon, and there settled down to await a report from our scouts.*—Pvt. Theodore Goldin

After waiting for a week—not long enough, as it turned out—Colonel Sturgis headed south to the Stinking Water (Shoshone) River, paralleling the route Wyoming 120 takes today. The terrain along this stretch of highway has some relatively smooth spots, but south, between the Sunlight Basin Road and Cody, the country is quite broken and rough. In his report, Sturgis complained that the scouts had not sufficiently advised him concerning the roughness of the terrain that his troops struggled through. His scouts hadn't given him accurate intelligence in other areas, either.

333

Continue with the Mainstream Traveler at Park County 1AB for the Sidetrip or for the trip to Laurel.

For the Mainstream Traveler

Sidetrip
Park County 1AB to Clarks Fork Canyon

> To see where the Nez Perce made their daring escape, turn west on Park County 1AB. In 3.3 miles, bear southwest on Park County 8VC. In 1.4 miles the road crosses Littlerock Creek.

Littlerock Creek

Two days after Colonel Sturgis had left his camp near here, Howard's command emerged from the canyon and found, to their dismay, that the Seventh Cavalry had disappeared.

> *We struck Clarks Fork about two miles below where it comes out of the canyon. Here the Command camped for the night at 5 p.m. The Scouts went on about 6 miles to little rocky creek. Charley Rainey, Jule and Indians found three dead bodies of white men a little off the trail on the River. They came on and overtook me telling me about it.... From the papers and letters the boys picked up near the dead men I think one of their last names was Olson and one Anderson. They were evidently Danish or at least two of them and were from the Black Hills. The Bodies were not stripped nor scalped.—S. G. Fisher (scout), September 10, 1877[6]*

Going into camp, Howard's men surely conjectured about what had happened to Sturgis. That question would not be answered for another twenty-four hours.

> Stop at the roadcut in another 2 miles to take a close look at the anticline of Bald Peak and make your own guess about how the Nez Perce exited these mountains. Some say the Nez Perce peeled off the east shoulder. Some think they should have gone down Paint Creek. The actual route is still a mystery.
>
> Continue 4.4 miles to the dead-end at the Clarks Fork Canyon. During the drive, look off to the east to find Heart Mountain, which dominates the eastern horizon.

Clarks Fork Canyon

On September 1, Colonel Samuel D. Sturgis had originally camped near here, although somewhat closer to the foot of Heart Mountain. He was waiting to squeeze the Nez Perce between his command at this end and Howard's forces behind the Nez Perce. But Sturgis' intelligence was mixed. Some scouts said the canyon was passable, but he found that it was not. Other scouts failed to return to camp. Two weeks had passed since Sturgis had heard from Howard, and a missive from Colonel Nelson Miles at the end of August had suggested that Sturgis station himself on the Stinking Water (Shoshone) River. Sitting, waiting, twiddling his thumbs, Sturgis felt he had probably missed the Nez Perce.

> *Waiting a full day longer than the time agreed upon for the return of our scouts, the Colonel became anxious, and dispatched two scouting parties…with orders to penetrate into the range and try and discover traces of our overdue scouts.*—Pvt. Theodore Goldin

> *About 3 o'clock p.m. Lieutenant Hare returned, reporting that when about 16 miles out he had come upon the two scouts previously sent out, one of them dead and the other in a dying condition; that these scouts had been attacked by about thirty Indians (as indicated by the pony tracks) who had come apparently from the direction of the Stinking [Shoshone] River. While Lieutenant Hare was making his report Lieutenant Fuller also returned, reporting that when about 18 miles out he had seen from the top of a high mountain what appeared to be the hostiles, moving on the Stinking River trail, and that they had disappeared behind a range of mountains…. The guide who accompanied him (and who had also been engaged in prospecting among these mountains) assured me that from the point where the Indians had disappeared behind the mountain range, it was altogether impossible for them to cross over to Clark's Fork, and that they must necessarily debouch on the Stinking River.*—Col. S. D. Sturgis

With this latest information, Sturgis concluded that the Nez Perce must be headed south to the Stinking Water (Shoshone). When he arrived at the Shoshone River and found no trace of the Nez Perce, he knew he had been on a wild goose chase. He then circled through the mountains back to this point.

335

Join the Hiker for a trip into the canyon. Otherwise, return the way you came and continue with the Mainstream Traveler at Wyoming 120.

For Hikers

Clarks Fork Canyon

Miles: 11, round-trip
Map: USGS quad, Deep Lake, Wyoming

A two-and-a-half-hour hike alongside the Clarks Fork River brings you to the end of the jeep trail. Intrepid types may be tempted to drive this trail. It's a good place to ruin your tires. Other deterrents include large rocks and small boulders on the path, sudden dips of gulches, and not much in the way of places to turn around—just in case you change your mind. Top speed on this jeep trail is 5 mph, only slightly faster than walking pace.

Descent into Clarks Fork Canyon

Once you have reached the end of the jeep trail, look east across the river and you can see where the Nez Perce descended into the Clarks Fork Canyon from Dead Indian Pass. Believe it or not, you are only 4 miles from the road over Dead Indian Pass.

> *During the day we travelled up a mountain [Dead Indian Hill] and through Box Canyon. It was on this night that we heard of the incident of General Sturgis' command.... He had six companies of the Seventh cavalry and had been ordered to some point on the Clark's Fork or Stinkenwater [Shoshone River]. At the point where he had been sent was a rockslide through which if Joseph passed over that particular divide he would have to go. No man with a horse could get down that slide on his horse. It was a point where troops could pick off the Indians as they came down slowly and in single file. Here, I suppose, Howard expected that Sturgis would intercept the Nez Perces....*
>
> *On the 11th we broke camp early and marched all day...during that time crossing the trail of Sturgis' men. We were laying our course easterly. The Sturgis trail crossed ours at right angles and away from the rock slide mentioned above. There was much discussion in the camp that night [September 11] as to why Sturgis had left the place originally assigned to him and gone away from Joseph, especially after a detail of his own troops had located the Indian camp in close proximity to his own.—Pvt. William Connolly[7]*

> Return to Wyoming 120 and continue with the Mainstream Traveler.

For the Mainstream Traveler

Junction of Wyoming 120 and Park County 1AB to Laurel, Montana

> From the junction of Wyoming 120 and Park County 1AB, proceed north for 18.5 miles on Wyoming 120, which becomes Montana 72 in Belfry.

Belfry

General Howard camped on the Clarks Fork a few miles south of Belfry on the evening of September 11. In the distance behind them, the troops could see a body of mounted men headed in their direction. Sturgis was finally joining forces with Howard, but not in the victorious manner they had originally hoped for.

> *Though Sturgis and I were disappointed, we formed at once a close combination. I was delighted to observe the elastic tread of his horses, which could in a very few minutes walk away from ours.*—Gen. O. O. Howard

> From the junction of Montana 308 with Montana 72 in Belfry, proceed north on Montana 72 for 10.8 miles to the junction with US 310. Turn north on US 310 for 1 mile to the highway historic sign in Bridger, which mentions the Nez Perce retreat.

Bridger

Having crossed the Absaroka Mountains, the Nez Perce and General Howard were now in Absaroka, or Crow, country. The Nez Perce had expected to take refuge with their old friends, the Crows. But the Crows allied themselves with the whites.

> *A few Crow Indian warriors joined us at a point on Clark's Fork thirty or forty miles above where it empties into the Yellowstone…. The Crows attached themselves to Fisher's little band of Bannock scouts. Other Crows arrived. Within a day or two they greatly outnumbered the Bannacks. The whole body of Indian special detectives were going here and there, in groups,*

337

presumably searching for the enemy. Most likely, they were searching for loose horses—or for anything else that was loose and desirable and conveniently transportable.—Pvt. William White[8]

From the highway historic sign in Bridger, continue north on US 310 for 7.2 miles to Fromberg.

Crow Country

Central and eastern Montana, spilling over into Wyoming, was the home of the Crows, long-time friends of the Nez Perce.

An old Indian woman and her daughter came across the trail of Joseph and his band and saw a horse tied in the brush and riding down there found a young woman had dropped out of Joseph's band and confined herself and was trying to wrap her baby up and join the band. The old woman and daughter coaxed the woman to go home with them and not try to overtake Joseph, which she did. Three or four years afterwards the government learned that there was a Nez Perce renegade Indian among the Crows and ordered her sent in exile with the others.—C. T. Stranahan (agent for Nez Perce Reservation)

Continue north for 9.5 miles to Rockvale, at the junction of US 212.

Rockvale

After joining forces near the Montana-Wyoming border, Colonel Sturgis dashed ahead of General Howard, making two days' worth of miles in one. His weary command finally went into camp near present-day Rockvale.

Well, early on the 12th, General Howard instructed General Sturgis to make forced marches and overtake the Nez Perces. He had but one medical officer and asked for another, and Merrill said they wanted me. I told them they would have to give me a good horse, as mine was worn out, and Merrill said I should have one of his. So I was ordered out. Marched from 6:30 A.M. until 9 P.M.—a long and weary ride. It rained all afternoon and my boots and everybody else's got full of water. Made a wet and disagreeable camp with but little to eat.—Dr. John FitzGerald, September 16, 1877[9]

Turn north on US 212 and US 310 for 10.5 miles to Laurel Riverside Park, on the south bank of the Yellowstone River.

Join the Mainstream Traveler at Laurel Riverside Park in the next chapter.

For Further Reading

"The Nez Perce in Yellowstone in 1877: a Comparison of Various Writers' Attempts to Deduce Their Route," by Yellowstone Park historian Lee Whittlesey, explores conflicting theories about the route the Nez Perce took between Yellowstone Park and the Clarks Fork. The article appears in *Montana: The Magazine of Western History.*

The map *Nez Perce Trail Through Trail Creek Camp, Dead Indian Gulch, Clarks Fork Canyon & Sturgis Route to Stinking Water & Return* (map 2 of 2), and a PowerPoint book on CD, *Nez Perce Triumph at Clarks Fork,* can be purchased at www.nezperce.com.

CHAPTER 11

Canyon Creek

General Howard's Last Gasp

Laurel to Lewistown, Montana

Poor Nez Perces! There are not more than perhaps 140 or 150 of them, while we had about 400 soldiers and nearly as many Crow Indians. I am actually beginning to admire their bravery and endurance in the face of so many well equipped enemies. —Dr. John FitzGerald, September 16, 1877[1]

I do not understand how the Crows could think to help the soldiers. They were fighting against their best friends!—Yellow Wolf[2]

Our Christian General [Howard] often forgets there should be a day of rest. One minute he is a happy man; the next he is worried, cross or pouty.... He is the first Professor I have had to follow and I hope he may be the last. He says that nobody likes him and this is truer than he thinks. Too timid a pursuer; pickets, patrols and flankers spread out all over the lines of march, likes to give us talks about the hostile peril in the day and evenings when he isn't lying on a blanket on clear nights looking at and studying the stars. After four months of this tomfoolery, we know the hazards by heart. A dedicated army man, everything done by the book down to the last period. We had an inspection this morning, as useless as this eternal marching. A domineering officer. I think him a good follower of Indians, but as an Indian fighter I fear he may prove a failure. As you have guessed, I am no longer a favorite.—Capt. Robert Pollock, September 16, 1877

The Story

To make amends for his tactical error in allowing the Nez Perce to slip by him at Clarks Fork Canyon, Colonel Samuel D. Sturgis took the lead in an attempt to catch up with the Nez Perce. Although General Howard's command had been constantly in pursuit for six weeks and was not well supplied, Sturgis' troops were scarcely in better condition. The Seventh Cavalry had been scouting in central Montana all summer and had very sparse rations themselves.

340

Lieutenant Guy Howard made this sketch of the troops crossing the Yellowstone River near present-day Laurel. (Photo courtesy of Dr. Norris Perkins.)

Crossing the Yellowstone River near present-day Laurel, Montana, the Nez Perce camp traveled about six miles east down the Yellowstone and then headed northwest up Canyon Creek. A couple of raiding parties forayed farther down the Yellowstone to a farm and to the small settlement of Coulson in present-day Billings. They burned some buildings and haystacks, stole a few horses, killed two men, and hijacked a stagecoach.

Just as this stolen stagecoach with its Nez Perce driver and passengers and their attached warhorses was bouncing along in the wake of the main entourage, Sturgis' scouts discovered the Nez Perce. By heading directly north from the Yellowstone at Laurel, the troops caught up with the rear of the Nez Perce caravan about nine miles from the river. The Battle of Canyon Creek began.

Nez Perce sharpshooters advantageously positioned themselves in the rocks of the bluffs above Canyon Creek. One company of cavalry did charge but, unsupported, quickly withdrew. Being overly cautious, Colonel Sturgis ordered his cavalry to dismount, much to the disgust of many of them. Afoot, the troops simply could not gain the upper hand. The long-distance skirmishing resulted in three dead and twelve wounded troopers. The Nez Perce claimed three wounded. It is said that, from the mouth of the draw, one Nez Perce sharpshooter held off all four hundred of Sturgis' troops for ten minutes.

While the Nez Perce continued their tired hurry north, Sturgis' command **341** had mule meat and buffalo wallow water for dinner on the battlefield that evening. A few hours later, a couple of hundred Crows arrived at the soldiers' camp, and the next morning they raced off to worry the rear of the Nez Perce train and to capture as many horses as they could. Sturgis also followed after the Nez Perce the next day but never got close to them. It was the last gasp for Sturgis' command. That night, troopers straggled into camp leading their horses behind them until well after dark. When the command finally reached the Musselshell River, near present-day Ryegate, a couple of days later, Colonel Sturgis gave up the chase and waited for Howard to catch up to him.

Having taken a roundabout route, General Howard caught up with Sturgis seven days later, on September 21. Since the Nez Perce remained well in advance even though Howard had pushed his troops at top speed, Howard decided to slow down on purpose. Howard knew that if he slowed down, the Nez Perce would also slow down. A slowdown might allow Colonel Nelson Miles, stationed at Fort Keogh (Miles City), enough time to cut across country and intercept the Nez Perce. Although Sturgis and Howard had spent their last burst of energy, strategy still offered one last opportunity to defeat the Nez Perce.

Chronology of Events

1877

12 September	The Nez Perce cross the Yellowstone River near Laurel.
13 September	Nez Perce raiders hijack a stagecoach. The Battle of Canyon Creek occurs when Colonel Sturgis catches up with the Nez Perce.
	Sturgis camps on the battlefield.
15 September	Sturgis camps on the Musselshell and decides not to continue pursuing the Nez Perce.
20 September	General Howard camps on the Musselshell.
	The Nez Perce camp near Judith Gap.
21 September	The Nez Perce camp near Lewistown.
	Howard joins Sturgis on the Musselshell.
22 September	Howard and Sturgis camp on Careless Creek.

Travel Plan

Mainstream Traveler	Adventurous Traveler I	Adventurous Traveler II	Intrepid Traveler
Sidetrip Laurel to Canyon Creek Battle monument	follow Mainstream	follow Mainstream	follow Mainstream
Laurel to Billings	Canyon Creek Battle monument to Broadview	follow Mainstream	follow Adventurous
Sidetrip Riverfront Park		follow Mainstream	
		Sidetrip Coulson Park	
Billings to Broadview		follow Mainstream	
Broadview to Ryegate	follow Mainstream	follow Mainstream	follow Mainstream
Ryegate to Judith Gap	Ryegate to Judith Gap	follow Mainstream or Adventurous I	follow Mainstream or Adventurous I
Judith Gap to Lewistown	Judith Gap to Lewistown	follow Mainstream or Adventurous I	follow Mainstream or Adventurous I
Sidetrip Lewistown to east Lewistown	follow Mainstream	follow Mainstream	follow Mainstream

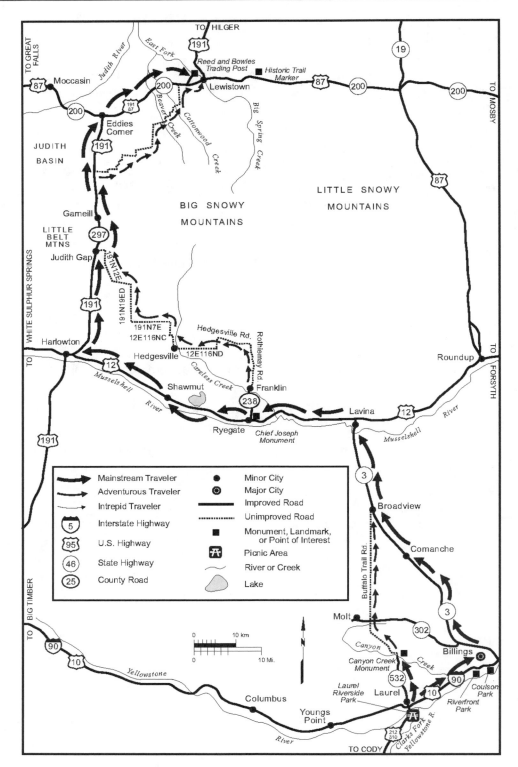

For the Mainstream Traveler

Sidetrip

Laurel to Canyon Creek Battle Monument

> Although this is a sidetrip for Mainstream Travelers because the pavement
> ends at the Canyon Creek Battle monument, Adventurous Travelers can
> continue past the Canyon Creek Battle monument on a gravel road with
> the scenic name of Buffalo Trail Road.

Laurel Riverside Park

The Clarks Fork flows into the Yellowstone River, two miles east of Riverside
Park. Somewhere between the park and the confluence, the Nez Perce and
Sturgis' troops crossed the river. The historical information sign in the park
commemorates the Nez Perce Trail.

> *Early in the forenoon we forded the river, where there was ample evidence
> that our wily foes had crossed, apparently many hours before.... The old
> colonel [Sturgis]...gave the order to go into camp....*
>
> *Captain Benteen...picked out the most desireable place possible, and we
> swung into line, dismounted and were just preparing to unsaddle, when one
> of our scouts came galloping into camp, shouting at the top of his voice:
> "Injuns, Injuns! Big fight and fire down river!" One hasty glance confirmed
> his report, as dark clouds of smoke could be seen rolling up, and now and
> then came the faint, distant sound of rifle shots to our ears.*—Pvt. Theodore
> Goldin

The Nez Perce had turned down river for six miles and now were traveling
northwest up Canyon Creek. Meanwhile, a Nez Perce raiding party had set fire
to some buildings and haystacks farther downstream.

> The Mainstream Traveler follows the route taken by the Seventh Cavalry as
> they headed due north to intercept the Nez Perce caravan. From Laurel's
> Riverside Park, proceed north on US 310 and 212 0.1 mile to the bridge
> over the Yellowstone, and another 0.6 mile to the junction with I-90.
> Continue north on US 310. In downtown Laurel, a statue of Chief Joseph
> stands on the southeast corner of First Avenue and Old US 10. Continue on
> First Avenue until it changes its name again to Montana 532. It is 8.3 miles
> from I-90 to the Canyon Creek pavilion and monument at the end of the
> pavement.

345

The Stolen Stagecoach

North of Laurel about four miles, as you crest a ridge and skirt a small hill, you see the flat of Canyon Creek stretched out before you, bordered by rimrock buttes. Perhaps it was from this vantage point that the troops first saw the Nez Perce caravan moving up Canyon Creek.

> *Although the hostile trail led down the Yellowstone, we saw Indian scouts watching us from the bluffs to the north, and soon they charged down. But our outfit sent them to charging backward, and when they had driven them over the bluffs we caught a sight of what was on the other side, and there was the whole hostile outfit right under us, strung along the benches and bottoms of Canyon Creek....*
>
> *Half a mile in their rear was a big stage coach with its four horses trotting along, and on the box was an Indian driver, with nearly half a dozen other Indians squatting on the roof, with their war horses hitched behind.*
>
> *When these hostiles saw us they quickly unhitched the stage horses, mounted their cayuses, and dashed into skirmish line flanking their outfit, which had what looked like more than 2000 head of horses. The old stage was abandoned in the sagebrush.*—John W. Redington (scout)[3]

The stagecoach had been stolen as it made a stop at a station near the junction of Canyon Creek and the Yellowstone. (See **Canyon Creek**, page 349.)

Canyon Creek Battle Monument

> *We rode about five miles at a good gait acrost an open country. We came to the raise about 2 p.m. There the Indians opened fire on us from the top of the hill. We kept on until we made the bench. The enemy had retreated acrost the bench and was now behind the break. They were string along for about one mile. Could onely see their heads as they raised up to shoot. Here the cavalry made a halt about five hundred yards from the Indians. I kept on thinking the cavalry would charge the enemey (which they had ought to have done) but instead of charging they were dismounted and deployed to right and left and comenced fireing rapidly which put me in rather a warm place as shots was comeing from bowth ways.*—S. G. Fisher (scout), September 13, 1877[4]

Colonel Sturgis had four hundred men at his disposal yet never committed more than half of them to the skirmish. Some thought that Sturgis' extreme caution was the result of having had his son killed with Custer at the Battle of the Little Big Horn the preceding year.

It was about one half hour from the time the fight comenced until we drove them from the brake. Here we got the first view of their Camp or rather their herd which was about one mile distant and scattered for a mile on the other side of Canyon Creek.... The soldiers drove the Indians slowly acrost the flat, or rather a gradual decent cut by small ravines and dry washes. Here the Indians fought entirely on horse- back, fireing mostly from their horses at long range, doing but little harm. During all this time their herd was moveing slowly acrost our front in the direction of the Canyon, evidentley being driven by the Squaws and children, the warriors keeping between us and their herd, Standing us off. As soon as their herd was in the Canyon the Indians got in the rocks and cottonwood timber along the Creek, dismounted in most cases concealing their war horses near them in ravines. Here the hardest fighting was done, the Indians haveing a great advantage of being in the rocks and timber while we were on an open grass bottom. I don't think there were more than two hundred Soldiers actualy engaged at any one time, the greater portion of them being held back on the bench as a reserve or to guard the Amunition train.—S. G. Fisher (scout), September 13, 1877[5]

While the Nez Perce women and boys drove their horses into the canyon, the warriors held off the cavalry at the mouth of the ravine. Captain Benteen did charge the Nez Perce position with one company of cavalry.

A Squad of Cavalry came up the gulch oposite where we were but did not stop long as the Indians opened a real hot fire on them and they retreated down the gulch. We still tried to hold the ground, but the reds got so thick in the rocks above us that we could not raise our head to shoot without a dozen shots being fired at us. I drawed lots of shots from them by raising my hat on the muzzle of my gun above the bank, dodging it down whenever they fired a volley at it.—S. G. Fisher (scout), September 13, 1877[6]

Other soldiers horseback, like cavalry, were off to one side. Away ahead of the walking soldiers. They tried to get the women and children. But some warriors, not many, were too quick. Firing from a bluff, they killed and crippled a few of them, turning them back.—Yellow Wolf[7]

The traveling camp had nearly been surprised. Soldiers afoot—hundreds of them....

We had our warrior ways. We did not line up like soldiers. We went by ones, just here and there, entering the canyon.

347

I came to one place at the mouth of the canyon. Only one warrior there doing the fight. His horse hidden, he was behind rocks, holding a line of dismounted soldiers back. He was shooting regularly, not too fast.—Yellow Wolf[8]

Behind one rock, occupied by an Indian, 50 empty shells were found after the battle.—Pvt. Jacob Horner

After the Nez Perce had withdrawn from the battlefield, the hungry troops fixed dinner for themselves.

After the battle was over and darkness had come on we had to cut steaks from the horses and mules shot during the day.... It was all the food we had.—John W. Redington (scout)[9]

When the battle closed for the day, it developed that three men had been killed and twelve wounded.... Because of the shortage of water, the wounded endured suffering beyond description. The relief train in the rear made very slow progress through the rough country and did not come up until the third day after the battle. The only water in the proximity of the troops was stagnant rain water which had collected in buffalo wallows, and in spite of orders to resist drinking the sickening contents, many of the men endeavored to quench their thirst, which action later resulted in summer complaint, rendering the men unfit for service.—Pvt. Jacob Horner

Making our wounded as comfortable as possible and posting a strong guard, the idea of making night march in pursuit of our enemy having been abandoned... we rolled up in our blankets..., and we were soon sleeping soundly, but were awakened some time in the night by sharp challenges and loud talking near one of the outposts. Soon some two hundred young Crow warriors came dashing into camp, shouting and singing, and from that time on until early dawn sleep was an impossibility, as between the beating of their tom- toms, their shrill war whoops as they danced their war dances, pandemonium raged, but at the first peep of dawn they were off, vowing to overtake and annihilate the enemy.—Pvt. Theodore Goldin

Join the Adventurous Traveler for the Canyon Creek to Broadview leg. Mainstream Travelers can return to Laurel and I-90 to continue with the Mainstream Traveler for the Laurel to Billings section.

For the Mainstream Traveler

Laurel to Billings

Turning east onto I-90 in Laurel, you will cross Canyon Creek in 8.8 miles, between mileposts 442 and 443.

Canyon Creek

Just a little south of where I-90 runs today, the stagecoach road from the Tongue River (Miles City) and points east passed on its way to Helena. A stage station was located between the interstate and the river, west of Canyon Creek. In fact, a stagecoach had pulled in just moments before the Nez Perce raiders appeared.

> The stage had just arrived, when the lookout discovered a hostile war party dashing down the river, and everybody made a run for the thick willows, with hostile bullets flying around them. There were half a dozen stage passengers, most of whom struck off afoot up the river, and eventually reached some settlement. One of the passengers was a dentist, and the hostiles scattered his gripsack full of store teeth and tools of torture all over the ground.—John W. Redington (scout)[10]

Six or seven of the Nez Perce raiders commandeered the stagecoach and drove it up Canyon Creek, following the main camp. The stage was abandoned about six miles northwest of here when the cavalry scouts discovered the Nez Perce just before the battle.

Another 4.6 miles brings you to exit 447, S. Billings Avenue.

Join the Mainstream Traveler for the sidetrip to Riverfront Park. Or continue to exit 450 to join the Adventurous Traveler for the sidetrip to Coulson Park. Or continue to exit 450 to join the Mainstream Traveler for the Billings to Broadview leg.

349

For the Mainstream Traveler

Sidetrip
Exit 447 to Riverfront Park

The purpose of this sidetrip is to visit the site of a ranch raided by the Nez Perce scouts. Turn south on S. Billings Ave. for 0.6 mile to Riverfront Park, which is on the bank of the Yellowstone River.

Drive into the park and, at the T, turn north and follow the road around little Josephine Lake for 0.6 mile to an information plaque.

Riverfront Park

In 1877, Joseph Cochran had just established a farm near here. He, himself, was upriver doing some logging. In his absence, two trappers were camped at his place. The two men, Dills and Summers, were sitting outdoors eating dinner when six Nez Perce raiders rode up. Supposing they were friendly Crows, the two unsuspecting diners made no move to protect themselves and were shot. The raiders then burned the new buildings on the small farm. By taking a walk along the southeast end of tiny Josephine Lake, you can see the area of the Cochran homestead.

> *The damage done by the Nez Perces on the Yellowstone is as follows: Stone & Rouse's stage station, hay and corrals burnt; Ed. Forrest's hay burned and stock stolen; at Josephine Tree two men killed (Clinton Dills and W.M. Sumner), camp burned and fourteen head of horses stolen; near McAdow's mill the houses of Egestone and Ralston were burned, no damage done the mill or property of McAdow excepting the loss of three ponies.—Rocky Mountain Husbandman, October 4, 1877*

Leaving Riverfront Park, turn north on S. Billings Ave for 0.5 mile. Turn east on South Frontage Road. In 2.1 miles it changes its name to Garden Avenue. Continue on Garden Avenue for 1.2 miles to 27th Street.

Join the Adventurous Traveler for the sidetrip to Coulson Park. Or join the Mainstream Traveler for the trip from Billings to Broadview.

For the Adventurous Traveler

Sidetrip
Coulson Park

Miles: 4.0, round-trip

Travelers who take this sidetrip will see the site of the town of Coulson where the Nez Perce raiders burned a saloon and a house.

From the junction of 27th Street and Garden Avenue (.1 mile south of exit 450), proceed north on Garden Avenue for 0.2 mile to Belknap Street. Turn west on Belknap for 1 block and then north on Charlene Street. In 0.3 mile the pavement ends at a railroad track beside the PP&L coal-fired electric generating plant, which is situated on the original old site of Coulson. Continue for 1 more mile, alongside the Interstate, to the park entrance. At the farther (east) end of the park, 0.4 mile away, sits a boulder with a plaque that marks the townsite of Coulson.

Coulson Park

Coulson was a very small, newly established logging settlement in 1877. The sawmill here was supplied by cottonwood logs floated down the Yellowstone River. P. W. McAdow, the owner of the mill, had ten men working for him as loggers farther upriver. After burning two houses and stealing three horses here, the Nez Perce raiders turned back to join the main column on Canyon Creek.

Return to the junction of 27th Street and Garden Avenue and turn west on 27th Street for 0.1 mile to the I-90 overpass.

Howard detoured to Pompey's Pillar, which is 28 miles east of here, at exit 23 of Interstate 94.

Join the Mainstream Traveler for the Billings to Broadview section.

For the Mainstream Traveler
Billings to Broadview

From the 27th Street exit of I-90 (exit 450), proceed north on Montana 3 (27th Street through downtown Billings) for 31.8 miles to Broadview. Montana 3 parallels the course of the Nez Perce as they hurried north from the Canyon Creek battle.

Join the Mainstream Traveler at Broadview.

For the Adventurous Traveler
Canyon Creek Monument to Broadview

Miles: 24.7
Maps: BLM–Billings and Roundup

From the Canyon Creek Monument proceed north on Buffalo Trail Road. As you drive up the narrowing canyon, imagine Nez Perce sharpshooters behind rocks, holding off the cavalry while the women, children, and horses fled into the protection of the ravine. In 7.9 miles you will cross Montana 302. Now that you've reached the plains and can see for miles in every direction, continue north on the wide gravel road for 16.8 miles to Broadview.

Buffalo Trail Road

Early on September 14, Sturgis resumed the pursuit, preceded by a large party of Crow scouts, who killed five more of the rear guard of the Nez Perces and captured four hundred of the entire number of ponies taken by Sturgis' command.—Record of Engagements with Hostile Indians

Some of us stayed back to watch the enemies. I looked one way and saw strange Indians....

I rode closer. Eeh! Crows! A new tribe fighting Chief Joseph. Many snows the Crows had been our friends. But now, like the Bitterroot Salish [Flatheads], turned enemies.

My heart was just like fire.—Yellow Wolf[11]

352

Sturgis' worn-out cavalry dragged along, well behind the Crow scouts.

> *When we reached the more level country at the top of the pass, our allies were nowhere to be seen, but we could hear the sound of distant firing, and passed several dead bodies along the trail, all of them those of the enemy.—* Pvt. Theodore Goldin

> *The approach of night found my command scattered for ten miles, and fully one-third on foot; and I was thus forced to go into camp after a weary march of 37 miles. Captain Bendire's detachment (of General Howard's command) did not arrive in camp until late at night, with every officer and man on foot. This detachment was so manifestly unable to continue further that I directed Captain Bendire to remain in camp next day to rest his animals, and afford his men an opportunity for securing some game (as they, as well as all the others, had been several days without rations) and then return to General Howard's command. With my own force I renewed the pursuit next morning.—*Col. S. D. Sturgis

Join the Mainstream Traveler at Broadview.

For the Mainstream Traveler

Broadview to Ryegate

Proceed north on Montana 3 for 14.8 miles to the junction with US 12.
Turn west on US 12.

Musselshell River

The Musselshell River, which runs parallel to US 12 on the south side, was a main thoroughfare through buffalo country.

> *On reaching the Musselshell River, I found that the distance between the Indians and my command had not been sensibly diminished. For the last seven or eight days both man and beast had been pushed to the utmost verge of physical endurance; what, with fatigue and a disease of the hoof which had suddenly broken out among my horses, most of them were unable to carry their riders, who, in turn, were growing so weak through long and weary marching without rations, as to be unable to walk and lead*

353

their horses. Under these circumstances I felt compelled to suspend further pursuit, in order that both men and animals might rest, and the troops provide themselves with game until our supplies should overtake us.—Col. S. D. Sturgis

Howard had taken a detour down the Yellowstone to Pompey's Pillar before cutting across country to the Musselshell. So Sturgis waited here for a week until Howard caught up to him.

The Musselshell where we struck it was certainly a lovely stream, with grassy meadows, shady trees and good running water. And there were millions of buffalo berries which we broke off in great clusters as we rode under the trees that bore them. The acid taste was very welcome after a long fast on fruit....

And those berries are certainly the best puckerers on earth. They put on a pucker that never comes off. —John W. Redington (scout)[12]

From Montana 3, travel west on US 12 for 12.3 miles to the bridge over Careless Creek.

Careless Creek

The Nez Perce and the army behind them left the Musselshell here and followed Careless Creek northwest to Judith Gap. Adventurous Travelers will be rejoining Careless Creek a few miles north of Ryegate.

Continue driving west for another 3.4 miles to the Chief Joseph Monument on the east edge of Ryegate.

Chief Joseph Monument

This simple granite monument commemorates the passage of the Nez Perce through this area. Their route from the Musselshell to Lewistown is not known exactly and is open to interpretation. The caravan probably broke into smaller groups to facilitate hunting and food gathering as the people headed toward Judith Gap.

Downtown Ryegate is 0.4 mile farther west.

Ryegate

Even when the troops were traveling at top speed, the Nez Perce stayed well in front of them. Utterly worn out, with no hope of catching the elusive Nez Perce, General Howard resorted to strategy. He deliberately slowed down his march.

> *After Howard's and Sturgis' commands had come together at the Musselshell river, the chase was kept up through the alkali plains and Judith Basin at comparatively slow marches. The reason being that General Howard had sent couriers ahead to Colonel Miles to look out for the Indians making towards the Upper Missouri. Miles sent back word that if eight days could be given him he would succeed in getting beyond the hostiles, and would strike them. To bring about so favorable a result our marches were "slowed," so that the Indians not finding us within a dangerous proximity, would slacken their pace too.*—Thomas Sutherland (war correspondent)[13]

Continue with the Mainstream Traveler, or join the Adventurous Traveler at Ryegate.

For the Mainstream Traveler
Ryegate to Judith Gap

This route goes along two sides of a right triangle, while the Nez Perce Trail makes up the hypotenuse. From the center of Ryegate, proceed west on US 12 for 28.6 miles toward Harlowton. At the junction with US 191, on the east side of Harlowton, turn north on US 191 for 17.6 miles, to Judith Gap.

Where the Buffalo Roamed

While this country does not look particularly prosperous now, in 1877 the prosperity and way of life provided by the buffalo were on the brink of changing. The government policy of killing off the buffalo in order to starve Native Americans into submission was just about to make its effects felt.

355

> *As we entered the Judith Basin I helped to kill several buffalo for the army. I killed many of these animals on the plains, but this was my last buffalo hunt.*—Alexander Cruikshank (scout)[14]

> Join the Mainstream or the Adventurous Traveler at Judith Gap.

For the Adventurous Traveler
Ryegate to Judith Gap

Miles: 52.6
Map: BLM — Harlowton, Big Snowy Mountains
Special considerations: These roads seem to create an above-average number of flat tires. Be sure your spare tire and jack are in working condition.

This route approximates the Nez Perce path to Judith Gap. In downtown Ryegate, turn north on county road 238. The pavement ends 4.9 miles out of town, after crossing over Careless Creek.

Careless Creek

Private Connolly had been marching with Howard for three months and seems to have lost all interest in the chase. His diary entries bespeak the monotony of the terrain and the routine of the pursuit.

> *Sept. 22nd. Broke Camp, traveled on prairie all day, went about 20 miles, with 7th Cav. Camped on Careless Creek. Saw some antelope. Plenty of wood & water.*
> *Sept. 23rd. In camp on Careless Creek. Saw more antelope and buffalo. Plenty of wood and water.*
> *September 24. Broke Camp, traveled on prairie about 8 miles. Camped on creek close to Judith Cuts. Saw some antelope and buffalo. Plenty wood and water.*—Pvt. William Connolly[15]

Continue north on the now-gravel Rothiemay Road for another 8.2 miles to Hedgesville Road. Turn west on Hedgesville Road, which is a narrow, dirt road. In 8.5 miles you will cross into Wheatland County, and the road name becomes 12E116ND. In another 5.1 miles the road jogs north and becomes 12E116NC. 5.3 miles farther on, after the road jogs west, north, and west again, 12E116NC turns north. However, you continue traveling west on 191N7E. In 5.0 miles turn north on 191N19ED. In 6.0 miles turn west on

191N12E. 2.9 miles farther on, the road jogs northwest and parallels the railroad tracks. In another 5.4 miles the 191N12E junctions with 191N19E, a paved road also known as county road 297. Turn west on 191N19E for 1.3 miles into Judith Gap.

Join the Mainstream Traveler or the Adventurous Traveler in Judith Gap.

For the Mainstream Traveler
Judith Gap to Lewistown

Continue north on US 191 for 21.3 miles to Eddie's Corners. Turn east on US 87 for 17.1 miles to downtown Lewistown.

Lewistown

Camp Lewis, a summer post for a single company of infantry, had been disbanded in 1875. In 1877, a trading post was all that stood in the geographical center of Montana. Reed and Bowles' cabins and stockade formed the lone outpost of civilization here, although the stories that survive about these two men are neither genteel nor indicative of a progressive, advanced culture.

Join the Mainstream Traveler in Lewistown.

For the Adventurous Traveler
Judith Gap to Lewistown

Miles: 44.7
Maps: BLM—Big Snowy Mountains and Lewistown
Special considerations: There's no turnaround for large vehicles at the Reed and Bowles Trading Post.

Judith Gap

Early in August, nearly six weeks before the Nez Perce arrived in central Montana, Lieutenant Gustavus Doane had been ordered to Judith Gap to burn grass and drive the game away in preparation for the arrival of the Nez Perce. This hardy veteran of the first Yellowstone expeditions was intimately familiar with this country. Leaving here with a hundred Crow scouts on August 21, Doane moved to Fort Ellis at Bozeman. While proceeding into Yellowstone Park, his detachment surprised a Nez Perce raiding party. (See **Corwin Springs** on page 316.)

Drive north on US 191 for 14.2 miles. About half a mile after milepost 32, at the electric substation, turn east onto Little Trout Creek Road for 1.4 miles. At the T, turn north and follow Little Trout Creek Road as it bends east and north for 4.0 miles. Turn east on Sipple Road for 4.0 miles. At the T, turn north on Rockford Road for 1.0 mile. At the next T, follow Rockford Road as it turns east for 1.6 miles. Turn east again, at your next opportunity, on Crystal Lake Road for 1.0 mile. At the T, turn north on the Carroll Trail and follow this winding road for 3.0 miles. At the T in the coulee, turn northwest along Beaver Creek Road for 0.7 mile. At the next crossroads, turn east on Beaver Creek Cutoff and follow the road up and out of the coulee for 2.6 miles. At the T, turn east on Cottonwood Cutoff for 4.2 miles. The road goes over Cottonwood Creek immediately and then heads due north to the junction with US 191, US 87 and Montana 200.

Turn east on the highway for 1.1 miles. Bear northeast onto the truck route of Alternate US 87, Alternate US 191, and Alternate Montana 200. Follow this truck route, which bypasses downtown, for 2.1 miles to the junction with county road 237. Turn north on Joyland Road. The pavement ends in 0.9 mile, and in another 0.5 mile a driveway enters from the north. Turn north into this driveway and cross the narrow wooden bridge across Big Spring Creek. Just beyond the bridge to the east is the Reed and Bowles Trading Post.

Reed and Bowles Trading Post

In 1877, the log cabin you see before you was one of four or five buildings inside a square stockade. "Major" Alonzo S. Reed and his partner, John J. Bowles, had bought the buildings of Fort Sherman, a trading post, in 1874, and moved them two miles down Big Spring Creek to this place where the Carroll Trail crossed Big Spring Creek. During the summers of 1874 and 1875, the Carroll Trail was guarded by a single company of the Seventh Infantry, which was stationed at Camp Lewis.

By locating their post a couple of miles away from Camp Lewis, Reed and Bowles had the best of both worlds. They were close to protection, should trouble arise. But they were just far enough away from watchful eyes to ply their illegal trade in alcohol, guns, and ammunition to passing Indians. Actually, any disturbance that arose was usually self-created by these alcohol-loving men. Reports of stabbings, beatings, and even murders were regular occurrences.

The Nez Perce had visited Reed and Bowles on other trips to buffalo country, and now was no exception. Camping a couple of miles away, the warriors came over to the post on the evening of September 21.

Return to the junction of Joyland Road with Alternate Routes US 87, US 191, and Montana 200. Turn east for 0.7 mile to the junction with US 191. Continue driving south on US 191, which is also named First Avenue North, for 0.3 mile to downtown Lewistown.

Join the Mainstream Traveler at downtown Lewistown in either this chapter or the next one.

For the Mainstream Traveler

Sidetrip

Downtown Lewistown to east Lewistown

At the junction of First Avenue North and Main Street, follow Main Street, which is US 87 and Montana 200, east. 0.5 mile from downtown, on the north side of the highway, the Chamber of Commerce offers an information center as well as a museum. 1.6 miles east of the museum, a historic sign along the roadside tells about the Nez Perce route through this area.

Judith Basin

It was nearly October and the mountains would soon be blocked with snow. Realizing the end of the chase was near, even though the final outcome was not yet known, Howard began detaching companies from his command so they could return to their home posts before the onset of winter.

> *After we had passed through the Judith Basin...General Howard resolved upon sending back the First Cavalry and the mule pack train.*—Thomas Sutherland (war correspondent)[16]

359

Return to downtown Lewistown and join the Mainstream Traveler there in the next chapter.

For Further Reading

The very readable *Tough Trip Through Paradise* by Andrew Garcia lives up to the reputation you might expect from a manuscript that was discovered in dynamite boxes. Long on story, it is a little short on historical accuracy. Beginning with Garcia's tenderfoot attempts to trade furs with the Indians in the Musselshell country in 1878, the book positively exudes frontier flavor. In the middle section, Garcia recounts the story of the 1877 retreat as he remembers his Nez Perce wife telling it.

CHAPTER 12

Across the Missouri to Bear Paw

Race to Canada

Lewistown to Chinook, Montana

Another Indian war, or, more strictly speaking, another cruel injustice, was to be enacted.—Col. Nelson Miles

We could have escaped from Bear Paw Mountain if we had left our wounded, old women, and children behind. We were unwilling to do this. We had never heard of a wounded Indian recovering while in the hands of white men.—Chief Joseph

I was too small to fight in the war, but I heard the bullets. I remember the hunger, the cold and freezing nakedness of us children.—Black Eagle[1]

The Story

General Day-After-Tomorrow Howard was nearly a week behind the Nez Perce and purposefully traveling slow. As he had expected, the Nez Perce also slackened their pace. The people were weary. The old and the sick who could not keep up dropped out of the race to Canada and were never heard from again. Meanwhile, Colonel Nelson Miles from the Tongue River Cantonment (Miles City) was rapidly marching northwest in an effort to intercept the Nez Perce before they reached the Canadian border.

After crossing the Missouri River at Cow Island, the Nez Perce raided the storage depot there. More important to the outcome of the story, leadership of the Nez Perce camp changed. Chief Looking Glass berated Poker Joe for hurrying the children and old people, and then he resumed the post of leader. Poker Joe had been pushing the Nez Perce along for almost two months now, ever since the Battle of the Big Hole.

On September 30, forty miles from the Canadian border, the trap was sprung. Colonel Miles charged the Nez Perce camp gallantly, lost twenty percent of his force, and settled down to a siege for the next five days.

General Howard and an escort of seventeen men arrived to support Miles on October 4. A courier had been sent to Sitting Bull, but his thousand Sioux

Black Eagle was a teenager during the flight. He escaped to Canada, then returned to Idaho in the summer of 1878. Rather than surrender to authorities and be shipped off to exile in Oklahoma, he returned to Canada. This photo was taken around 1900. (Photo courtesy of Smithsonian Institution.)

warriors did not arrive to support the Nez Perce. A truce was called. Conditions were negotiated: The Nez Perce would be allowed to keep their horses and go home in the spring. Chief Joseph surrendered his rifle, and 431 Nez Perce joined him. That night, Chief White Bird, disbelieving the words of a white man, left for Canada. Around 233 people joined Chief White Bird in the flight to Canada.

White Bird's suspicions were correct. The Nez Perce who had surrendered to Miles did not go home in the spring. By that time they were on their way to exile in Oklahoma.

Chronology of Events

1877

18 September	Colonel Miles leaves Fort Keogh (Miles City).
23 September	The Nez Perce cross the Missouri River at Cow Island. After negotiations fail, they attack the supply depot.
24 September	Major Ilges and thirty-eight citizen volunteers arrive at Cow Island.
25 September	Ilges skirmishes with Nez Perce on Cow Creek.
	Miles hears that the Nez Perce have already crossed the Missouri. He crosses the Missouri at the mouth of the Musselshell.
30 September	Miles charges the Nez Perce camp on Snake Creek.
1 October	General Howard and Colonel Sturgis arrive at Carroll on the Missouri River. Howard and seventeen men board the steamer *Benton* to go upriver.
3 October	Howard debarks the *Benton* at Cow Island.
4 October	Howard arrives at the Bear Paw Battlefield after dark.
5 October	Chief Joseph surrenders with 380 Nez Perce. Chief White Bird flees to Canada.
7 October	Miles leaves Bear Paw Battlefield with the Nez Perce who surrendered.

Travel Plan

Mainstream Traveler	Adventurous Traveler	Intrepid Traveler I	Intrepid Traveler II
Lewistown to Hilger	follow Mainstream	follow Mainstream	follow Mainstream
Hilger to Bear Paw Battlefield	Hilger to Stafford Ferry	follow Adventurous	Hilger to Cleveland
	Stafford Ferry to Cleveland	Stafford Ferry to Cleveland	
	Cleveland to Bear Paw Battlefield	follow Adventurous	follow Adventurous
Bear Paw Battlefield to Chinook	follow Mainstream	follow Mainstream	follow Mainstream

363

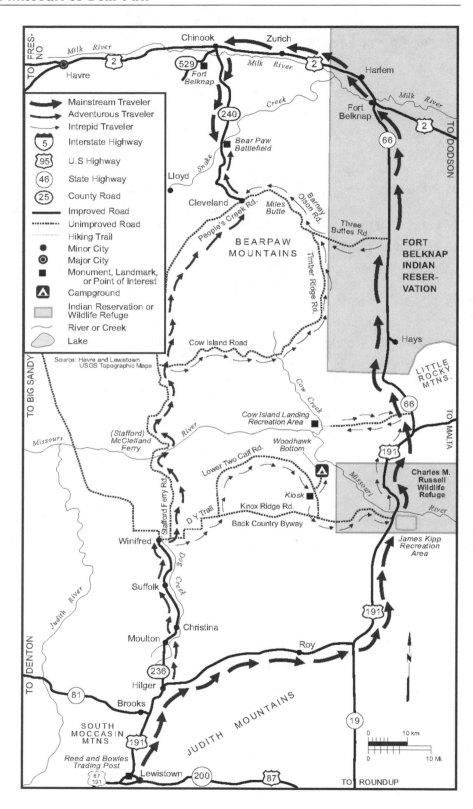

Mainstream Traveler
Adventurous Traveler
Intrepid Traveler

(5) Interstate Highway
(95) U.S Highway
(46) State Highway
(25) County Road
Improved Road
Unimproved Road
Hiking Trail
● Minor City
◎ Major City
■ Monument, Landmark, or Point of Interest
▲ Campground
Indian Reservation or Wildlife Refuge
River or Creek
Lake

Source: Havre and Lewistown USGS Topographic Maps

For the Mainstream Traveler

Lewistown to Hilger

> **Special considerations:** Adventurous and Intrepid Travelers will need a full tank of gas because it is 160 miles from Lewistown to Chinook.
>
> In downtown Lewistown, turn north on US 191 for 14.7 miles to Hilger. Leading between the South Moccasin Mountains to the west and the Judith Mountains to the east, this section of US 191 approximates the Carroll Trail. During the 1870s, the Carroll Trail was an important route for freight from the Missouri River on its way to Helena.

Hunger

Hungry, tired, always on the move, and without much time for hunting, the Nez Perce continued their marathon to Canada. Their friends, the Crows, had reneged on their promise to assist the Nez Perce if the latter were ever in trouble. Perhaps some Nez Perce scouts were just getting even when they raided a Crow village about twelve miles northwest of Lewistown.

> *In one part of the Judith we found the remains of a wrecked Indian camp, and wondered how it happened. From the way things were torn up around there, there had certainly been quite a little battle. George Huston figured out that the camp had been occupied by Dumb Bull's outfit of River Crow Indians, who were drying buffalo meat and were attacked by the Nez Perces.... We found by moccasin tracks that several Indians had skipped out afoot, and when we passed Reed's Fort later in the day we found that the scout's conclusions were correct. Dumb Bull was there, and was feeling pretty sore about the way the hostiles had cleaned him out of all his horses. But still he declined the invitation to come along with the scouts and get some sweet revenge.*—John W. Redington (scout)[2]

The stolen buffalo meat must have tasted as sweet as revenge to the famished Nez Perce.

Hilger

The divergence of county highway 236 and US 191 marks the spot where the Nez Perce went north while Howard's command continued northeast on the Carroll Trail. Howard had already started detaching troops from his command

and sending them home. Now he was a week behind the Nez Perce with no supplies, no food, and horses that could barely walk. Although never stated or implied, it appears that this was the point where he gave up the pretense of trying to catch the Nez Perce.

Continue with the Mainstream Traveler or join the Adventurous or Intrepid Traveler at Hilger.

For the Mainstream Traveler

Hilger to Bear Paw Battlefield

From Hilger, continue north on US 191 for 48.9 miles to the bridge over the Missouri River at James Kipp Recreation Area.

The Carroll Trail

US 191 continues to follow the route of the Carroll Trail for 28 miles past Hilger. Just after US 191 makes a right-angle turn to the north, the Carroll Trail continues on east, angling toward Carroll on the Missouri River.

The General's own command being now rationless, like ourselves, it was decided, temporarily at least, to abandon the chase and head for the little settlement of Carroll, Montana.—Pvt. Theodore Goldin[3]

Missouri River

The Nez Perce crossed the Missouri River at Cow Island, twenty-three miles west of the Fred Robinson Bridge.

On the 23d day of September the hostile Nez Perces came from the direction of Judith Basin, arrived opposite their camp [at Cow Island], and crossed to the north side of the Missouri River. They attacked this party (which had been increased to 12 enlisted men...joined by four citizens) about 6 p.m., charged seven different times upon their rifle-pits, but were repulsed with some loss. They wounded two of the citizens (Walter and Weimar). The Indians burned about 50 tons of freight during the night of the 23d, and at about 10 a.m. on the 24th left the vicinity in the direction of the pass between the Bear Paw and Little Rocky Mountains.—Col. John Gibbon, October 5, 1877

The Cow Island landing on the Missouri River as it appeared in 1880. (Photo courtesy of Haynes Foundation Collection, Montana Historical Society.)

The same day that the Nez Perce left Cow Island, Colonel Nelson Miles arrived at the Missouri River about forty miles east of here, near the mouth of the Musselshell River.

The next day, while Miles was still on the south bank of the Missouri preparing to scout for the trail of the Nez Perce, a small boat with three men floated by. They told Miles that the Nez Perce had already crossed the river at Cow Island. With the aid of a cannon, Miles got the attention of a passing steamboat.

> *September 23, 1877*
> *We reached Squaw Creek and traveled down it until we reached its mouth, where it empties into the Missouri 6 miles below the Musselshell River.... The steamer is unloading tonight and will take us over in the morning.*
>
> *September 24, 1877*
> *We crossed the river on the steamer Fontenelle & it was night before everything of ours was over.*
>
> *September 25, 1877*
> *Gen. Miles has been crossing his command all day...... A small boat with 2 men in it came down the river at dark. They report Nez Perces crossing the river at Cow Island...150 miles above us. The Indians are on their way to the British Possessions.—Pvt. William Zimmer[4]*

367

Miles angled northwest, knowing that at some point he would intersect the Nez Perce trail. During the march, he kept his men quiet. Hunting was forbidden because it might start a buffalo stampede. Running buffalo would alert the Nez Perce that people were close by.

Carroll was located about sixteen miles east of where US 191 crosses the Missouri today. When Howard's command reached Carroll on September 29, they found the steamer *Benton* waiting for them. The riverboat carried Howard and a detachment of seventeen men upstream to Cow Island.

From the Missouri River, continue north on US 191 for 14.3 miles to the junction with Montana 66. Turn north on Montana 66 for 50 miles to US 2. During most of this drive, you are traveling through the Fort Belknap Reservation, the home of the Assiniboine and Gros Ventre Nations. The highway leads between the Little Rocky Mountains to the east and the Bear Paw Mountains, where the final battle took place, to the west. The Nez Perce themselves actually traveled 10 to 15 miles west of Montana 66.

Little Rocky Mountains

Weather windy. We were up by 3 A.M. gathering buffalo chips to cook breakfast with & by 5 were on our way.... The country is a rolling prairie, but to our left & ahead there is a range of rough-looking hills called Little Rocky. When we got close to the foot of them we saw a herd of bear some 20 in number.... This evening we are camped on a bright stream running from these hills...where wood & grass is plenty. —Pvt. William Zimmer, September 28, 1877[5]

Turn northwest on US 2 for 24.8 miles to the junction with county highway 240 on the west side of Chinook. While you are in Chinook, you may want to stop at the Blaine County Museum (see page 398) before proceeding to the Battlefield. The Bear Paw Battlefield is reached by turning south on county highway 240 for 16.3 miles.

At mile marker 16, look to the east for a good view of the siege area. More than a thousand horses were pastured west of the road.

Join the Mainstream Traveler at the Bear Paw Battlefield.

For the Intrepid Traveler

Hilger to Cleveland

Miles: 179.7

Maps: Upper Missouri National Wild & Scenic River (maps 3 & 4), BLM, Lewistown, Winifred, Zortman, Dodson, and Rocky Boy

At Hilger, turn north on county highway 236 for 23.5 miles to Winifred. At the east edge of Winifred, follow the sign for Woodhawk Bottom by turning east on the D-Y Trail, a wide gravel road. In 1.9 miles, turn east, following the D-Y Trail, a Back Country Byway. In 2.9 miles, follow the Back Country Byway by turning east on E4 for 3.9 miles. The Back Country Byway continues by turning north on Knox Ridge Road. In 1.7 miles, a kiosk stands on the south side of the road. Stop here to see the route the Nez Perce took through this country. In 1.1 miles, turn north on the D-Y Trail, which changes to Lower Two Calf Road, for 15.0 miles.

Rain

A naturalist on an exploring trip through here in 1875 described the effect of rain on the terrain.

> In the absence of rain, it is dry and dusty, but thoroughly wetted, it becomes a greasy, slippery, fathomless mass of clinging mud.—William Ludlow, July 30, 1875[6]

Leave the Back Country Byway by turning north to the Woodhawk Bottom Recreation Area. In 1.0 mile, you will have your first view of the cottonwood-lined Missouri River. Another 1.0 mile brings you to another viewpoint, which is just a preview of the spectacular panorama of the oxbow of the river in 1.0 more miles. 0.6 mile farther on, you arrive at Woodhawk Bottom Recreation Area.

The right fork leads to a primitive campground with tables, firepits, and an outhouse. The left fork leads to another campsite in 1.1 miles before the track gives out in another 0.8 mile. Cow Island is about a mile-and-a-half upriver from here.

Return to Lower Two Calf Road, the Back Country Byway, and proceed east for 1.6 miles. Bear south on Middle Two Calf Road. In 8.3 miles, a very steep grade begins to go down to Two Calf Creek, which you will ford in another 1.6 miles. Continue on for another 2.9 miles, then turn east on Knox Ridge Road. In 0.1 mile, you enter the Charles M. Russell Wildlife Refuge. For the next 7.6 miles, the road parallels the Missouri River. Turn north on US 191 and cross the Missouri River in 0.4 mile.

Missouri River

General Howard and Colonel Sturgis eventually limped into Carroll, sixteen miles east of here.

> *Almost simultaneously with the arrival of the supply steamer, came a courier from General Miles, of whose exact location we had, up to this time, been unaware, telling us that he had the Indians corralled in the Bear Paw Mountains, and asking that all available troops be rushed forward to his assistance.*
>
> *Every horse and rider in the First and Seventh, believed capable of still bearing a rider, was rushed on board the steamer, ferried across the river and marched for the scene of action, while the dismounted men, and the disabled horses, remained in camp at Carroll for a few days until word was received that the Indians had surrendered.*—Pvt. Theodore Goldin[7]

"Every horse and rider" amounted to twenty-one men, including General Howard himself, his son, and two Nez Perce scouts. The riverboat carried this little detachment upstream to Cow Island, where, six days before, the Nez Perce had crossed the Missouri—twenty-three miles west of the Fred Robinson Bridge.

Continue north for 14.3 miles to the junction with highway 66. 1.7 miles north of the junction of 191 and 66, turn west on a dirt road. At any Y, always stick to the more traveled route. In 12.0 miles, continue straight ahead to Bull Creek. In 1.2 miles, you may use the pullout for your first glimpse of the Missouri River. Continue 0.6 mile farther on and park near the Y in the road at N47° 46.490', W108° 54.054'. Both forks become rugged from here on. The downhill road has half a mile of washouts.

From the Y, hike up the high road for 0.7 mile to N47° 46.363', W108° 54.877' for an excellent view of Cow Island. This vista gives a panorama of the landscape as you puzzle out how the Nez Perce may have come down to the river.

Cow Island

About the first of September, 1877, Col. George Clendennin appointed me as clerk to ship freight from Cow Island to points in Montana....

We were...camped...along the east bank of the river. To keep the water from running into their tent and supplies in case of rain they dug a ditch about 2-1/2 feet deep all around it. The dirt from the ditch they threw up on the outside. To that ditch and wall of dirt we 10 men, later on, owed our lives. For 30 hours we lay behind that little earthen breastwork and, with our Winchester, kept death and a howling horde of savages at bay.—Michael Foley (Cow Island clerk)[8]

After raiding the pile at Cow Island the white men had trenches already dug and that same night they had skirmishes, that is where one Indian was shot or piece of wood struck him on head caused by a shot. He was afterward named Shot-in-head.—Anonymous Nez Perce[9]

When everybody had what they wanted, some bad boys set fire to the remaining. It was a big fire! —Yellow Wolf[10]

The agent had a hospital tent there for his quarters with 500 sacks of bacon piled against it which they set on fire that lit the country up for miles. —Sgt. William Moelchert[11]

This guide recommends hiking down to Bull Creek because the road has half a mile of washouts and perhaps some cubic-foot-sized rocks. The walk will take about 2 hours with a loss in elevation of about 630 feet.

It is 1 mile to Bull Creek and another mile to the Missouri River bottomland, where actual cows may be grazing. In another 0.25 mile (N47° 46.864', W108° 56.235'), head toward the river on a sort of levee. You will reach the mouth of Bull Creek in 0.15 mile (N47° 46.950', W108° 56.428'). Cow Island is 0.3 mile downstream from here. Select a cowpath on the bench just above the river and begin walking.

Cow Island is a long, narrow island populated with cottonwood trees.

The Nez Perce left this area by going up the Cow Creek drainage. Cow Creek is 0.35 mile upstream from Bull Creek.

Bull Creek

> *After defeating the small guard at Cow Island, the Nez Perces had a picnic helping themselves to all the stores. They loaded every pack-horse they had with the best of groceries and canned goods, and for many miles up Cow Creek and Bull Creek we could trail them by the packages of finecut tobacco, beans and coffee that had trickled and dropped off their packs. But they refused to take the big stack of long Barrack-stoves that were going to steamheat Fort Walsh, so they set fire to the big pile they could not take along, and the stoves were warped and twisted most artistically.—John W. Redington (scout)[12]*

Return to highway 66 and proceed north for 26.0 miles. At mile marker 28, turn west on Three Buttes Road for 9.5 miles. Turn north on Barney Olsen Road for 12.5 miles as you circumnavigate Miles Butte.

Miles Butte

> *The country…changed to hilly and rocky. We went in camp at 3 P.M. on account of the weather…. It began to snow & by night several inches had fallen. (The worst of it was we had no tents….)*—Pvt. William Zimmer, September 29, 1877[13]

Turn west on Peoples Creek Road for 4.6 miles to Cleveland.
    Join the Adventurous Traveler at Cleveland.

For the Adventurous Traveler
Hilger to Stafford Ferry

Miles: 87.9
Maps: BLM maps—Lewistown and Winifred
Special considerations: Fill up on gas in Winifred, because the next opportunity for gas is Chinook, 120 miles away.

The ferry operates from May through October, depending on ice and flood conditions of the Missouri River. It runs from 7 a.m. to 7 p.m. and has a fourteen-ton, fifty-foot limit on the size of vehicles it can carry. Call 406-462-5513 for information.

Even a sprinkle of rain can turn the gumbo dirt roads of the Missouri Breaks into mud which clings to tires and collects in the wheel wells. If you have any reason to question road conditions, inquire locally before proceeding.

As you travel over a hundred consecutive miles on dirt and gravel roads through the rugged Missouri Breaks country, you'll come close to the still-wilder route taken by the Nez Perce. The badland-looking Missouri Breaks extend about six miles on either side of the Missouri River.

In Hilger, turn north on county highway 236, which follows along Dog Creek for much of the 23.5 miles to the town of Winifred. On the east edge of Winifred, turn east onto D-Y Trail, a wide gravel road that then becomes Stafford Ferry Road. It is 16 miles to the free Stafford Ferry.

Crossing the Missouri River

The Nez Perce crossed at Cow Island, twenty-four miles downstream from the Stafford Ferry. Although steamboats could travel as far upriver as Fort Benton during spring runoff, the lower water of summer and fall meant that Cow Island was the farthest upstream that boats could run. Freight was off-loaded at Cow Island and stored beside a bluff in an open-air depot. Bull trains then carried the freight on to Fort Benton. Guarding the freight at Cow Island in September 1877 were twelve soldiers and three civilians.

> *I think it was the first week of September when the last boat came down from Fort Benton, when we received orders to make out a detail of one none-commissioned officer and six privates to go down to Cow Island to guard the freight.... Before we started I reported to the Capt. and the last word he said to me "Sergt. be careful and keep a good lookout. I was advised that the Nez Perce are coming this way." Well, we went down the river, neither one of us being in Cow Island before didn't know exactly where it was till we came to a big bend in the river and saw some smoke coming up.... We pulled down and I proceeded at once to get the rations ready.... When I told the boys what the Capt had told me of course they, like all soldiers, got kidding about it and all said, "Well, let them come, we are here first." I walked down toward the freight pile when I heard the boys shouting, "They are coming—look across the river!" and sure enough there they were on the brow of the hill in single file on horseback....*
>
> *It wasn't long before 2 Indians came toward our camp when I stopped them and was going out to meet them when one of these civilians said to*

373

me, "Sergt. let me go out and see what they want, I have lived among Indians for many years and understand their ways." I said, "All right." He went out but hurried right back again and came back to the breastworks and said, "They won't have anything to do with me, they want to see the man in charge of the soldiers." I picked up my rifle to go when the civilian said, "You don't need that now, they won't harm you now." So I took his advice and left my gun behind and went out when to my surprise they spoke English as well as anyone could. They asked me for some of that freight; when I told them I could not give them any and walked away they went and came back the second time and I met them when they offered me money if I would sell them some of the freight as they were hungry and nothing to eat. I turned back to the breastworks and they came back the third time and pleaded with me for something to eat so then I went back to the breastworks and put a side of bacon in a sack filled about half full with hardtack, took it out to them and they very kindly thanked me for the same. Things went along for a while quietly till we saw an Indian coming between our breastworks and the foot hills stripped naked when we know this means fight.... This was sundown and from that time on till daybreak we were fighting for our lives. Of course the freight we could not save as it was piled right up against the bluff. —Sgt. William Moelchert[14]

The seven hundred people were hungry. They had politely asked for some of that fifty tons of supplies; they had even offered to pay. Native American custom was to share whatever food they had with guests and strangers. The parsimonious offer of a side of bacon and half a bag of hardtack must have been insulting. Once again the whites had unwittingly declared themselves as adversaries. The Nez Perce responded accordingly.

There was a coulee just north of the pile of freight that led back from the river and through this coulee the Indians were able to get at the pile of freight without us being able to see them. Working on the side of the freight pile furthest away from us they carried away everything they wanted and set fire to the rest.—Michael Foley (Cow Island clerk)

We took whatever we needed, flour, sugar, coffee, bacon, and beans. Anything whoever wanted it. Some took pans and pots for the cooking. We figured it was soldier supplies, so set fire to what we did not take. We had privilege to do this. It was in the war. —Peopeo Tholekt (Bird Alighting)[15]

374

Six days later, on September 29, General Howard arrived at Cow Island and headed north.

Cow Island was reached [by steamer] early the next day. With a small escort of seventeen mounted men, including the aides, I made a push along the large Indian trail, with the hope of reaching Miles, or communicating with him.—Gen. O. O. Howard

Join the Intrepid Traveler at Stafford Ferry or continue with the Adventurous Traveler.

For the Adventurous Traveler
Stafford Ferry to Cleveland

Miles: 48.4
Maps: BLM map–Winifred, Rocky Boy

Continue north from the Missouri River. At the T in 14.2 miles, follow the main road as it curves west on Lloyd Road. Continue north on Lloyd Road for 24.6 miles. At the intersection with Peoples Creek Road, turn east for 9.6 miles to Cleveland.

Continue with the Adventurous Traveler at Cleveland.

For the Intrepid Traveler
Stafford Ferry to Cleveland

Miles: 76.3
Maps: BLM map–Winifred, Rocky Boy
Special considerations: This route fords rather than bridges Cow Creek. The Timber Ridge Road can be quite rutted and holey or just two tracks running through the landscape.

Continue north from the Missouri River. At the T in 14.2 miles, follow the main road as it curves west on Lloyd Road. Continue driving north for 5.1 miles and turn east on Cow Island Road for 18.3 miles to the ford across Cow Creek.

375

Cow Creek

An abundance of rustling cottonwood trees, wild rose bushes, and grass contribute to the feeling of sanctuary provided by this western-style oasis. South of here, along Cow Creek, a small detachment of thirty volunteers from Fort Benton caught up with the Nez Perce just as the warriors were attacking a bull-train hauling supplies from Cow Island to Fort Benton. The command of Major Guido Ilges was too small to do anything other than worry the rear of the Nez Perce caravan briefly.

> I went, with thirty other Benton volunteers, under command of Major Ilgis, on horseback…. We then proceeded rapidly towards Cow Island, and arrived there just at night (after the Indians had left the island), and saw the goods still burning, but could at first see no men. Soon we saw a boat with three men in it. We hailed it and learned that eight men had kept the Indians at bay for forty-eight hours at that point, and finally had caused them to retreat, after firing the goods. We then sent by them, down the river, a message to Gen. Miles, who was forty miles below, and told them the directions the hostiles had gone, and what they had done at the island. We remained there that night, and, fearing the Indians might attack a train of wagons known to be on the north side of the river, early the next morning we crossed and went in pursuit. About nine miles from the crossing, we came upon the Indians just as they were stripping the canvas from the freight wagon. A half-breed along with us darted in advance of our party, and rode up to within two hundred yards of the hostiles, then suddenly wheeled his horse and ran back to us. Meantime, we had entrenched ourselves in a ravine, so that we could fire from under cover.
>
> About one hundred charged back after the half-breed, and when within range of our rifles, we opened fire upon them, and they fell back. They fought us at long range for about five hours, during which…they killed one of our men. They then left us, seeing that we were not strong enough to pursue and charge them. We returned to the crossing.—John Samples (Fort Benton volunteer)[16]

From the Cow Creek ford, continue north along Cow Creek. At the Y near a ranch in 2.0 miles, bear east for 4.5 miles. At the Y, bear northeast on the unmarked Timber Ridge Road for 15 miles. At the intersection, proceed straight ahead, north, on the Barney Olson Road for 12.5 miles. As you reach the next intersection, note Miles Butte to the west. Turn west on Peoples Creek Road for 4.7 miles to Cleveland.

> This section of the road enables you to parallel the route of the Nez Perce who traveled just slightly west of here. The Barney Olson is a wide gravel road.

The Nez Perce Slow Down

After crossing the Missouri, the leadership of the camp reverted to Chief Looking Glass.

> *Looking Glass upbraided Poker Joe for his hurrying; for causing the old people weariness; told him that he was no chief, that he himself was chief and that he would be the leader. Poker Joe replied, "All right, Looking Glass, you can lead. I am trying to save the people, doing my best to cross into Canada before the soldiers find us. You can take command, but I think we will be caught and killed."*—Many Wounds[17]

> Join the Adventurous Traveler at Cleveland.

For the Adventurous Traveler
Cleveland to Bear Paw Battlefield

Miles: 8.8
Map: Rocky Boy

Cleveland

In this vicinity, the scouts of Colonel Nelson A. Miles finally found the Nez Perce trail they had been aiming for.

> *We saw a bunch of them running buffalo, probably ten or twelve of them. They soon discovered us, as they had glasses. I soon noticed that they were the Nez Perces as they had striped blankets—the other tribes had solid colors. I sent another Indian back to tell the General [Miles] that we had found the Nez Perces and that they had better hurry up. The Nez Perces took what meat they wanted, as we did not crowd, not getting nearer than one-half mile.*—Louis Shambo (scout)

377

Weather thawing. There's not as much snow now as there was on going to bed last night.... We had marched about 2¹/₂ hours when we saw the scouts coming back full tilt. The command halted & we learned that the Nez Perces' camp was about 5 miles ahead.... Extra clothing were stripped & every man supplied himself with 100 rounds of ammunition. Cheyenne Indians were making themselves ready at the same time by doing away with their blankets & adorning themselves & ponies with feathers & their war hats. In a short time everything was in readiness & we started off at a brisk trot, leaving one co. of infantry with the pack train.—Pvt. William Zimmer, September 30, 1877 [18]

Turn north on county highway 240, Cleveland Road, for 8.8 miles to the Bear Paw Battlefield. This road parallels the route of the Nez Perce and the charge of Miles' command.

County Highway 240

On the morning of September 30th, 1877, the battalion...moved from its camp near the northeast end of Bear Paw Mountain, M.T., at 2:30 o'clock A.M.... The march was continued until about 8 o'clock A.M....when the trail of the Nez Perce Indians was discovered pointing in a northerly direction; it was pronounced by the Cheyenne Indian scouts who accompanied the command, to be two days old. After a short halt on the trail the march was resumed... The command had marched about five or six miles...when information was received from the Cheyenne scouts that the Nez Perces' village was located on a creek about seven miles in front. The command was immediately given for the column to take the trot, and subsequently the gallop was taken up.—Capt. Myles Moylan, August 16, 1878[19]

This gallop forward, preceding the charge, was one of the most brilliant and inspiring sights I ever witnessed on any field. It was the crowning glory of our twelve days' forced marching.—Col. Nelson Miles

378

Look over to the east around where mile marker 21 should be. The Nez Perce camped in this area on the night of September 28.

Join the Mainstream Traveler at the Bear Paw Battlefield.

For the Mainstream Traveler

Bear Paw Battlefield to Chinook

Bear Paw Battlefield

For those of you who have followed the Nez Perce (Nee-Me-Poo) Trail extensively, arriving at the Bear Paw Battlefield may be quite a moving experience. This site of the Nez Perce National Historical Park signifies the end. The end of the traditional sovereignty of the Nez Perce Nation. The end of the hope of escape. The end of your journey.

Remember the beginning of the Trail at Wallowa Lake and the utter grandeur of the scenery there. The contrast between that beauty and the bleakness of the landscape here at Snake Creek is a metaphor for the impoverishment of the Nez Perce People, Nee-Me-Poo. Their land, their horses, their caches of food, their lodges, their very own people—in just a few months, this wealthy tribe had lost almost all they valued.

For those who need to grieve for the loss, simply walking around, perhaps aimlessly, or just sitting and watching the grass and the sky and feeling the wind is the first thing to do. Then when you're ready, you can read the story here or contact a park ranger in Chinook at 406-357-3130 for a guided tour.

Scattered around the battlefield are 143 small metal stakes that locate rifle pits, tepees, and death sites. Paths meander from one stake to another, but there is no particular order in which to see the markers. If you would like to be organized in your approach to the battlefield, park in the upper area. Start your exploration at the wayside panels and monuments, east of the parking area. Pick up a trail guide. A one-and-a-quarter-mile trail begins, which leads across a footbridge.

The tired and unsuspecting Nez Perce camped here on willow-lined Snake Creek in brush shelters. Proper tepees had been left behind two months and seven-hundred-fifty miles ago at Big Hole. A few pieces of canvas salvaged then or taken from some cabin along the way were hung around willow twigs.

> *It was growing colder every day as we headed northward. On September 29 when we finally arrived in the Bear Paws at the place we called "Ali-Kos-Pah" (Place of Manure Fires), it was already started to snow. I helped to gather buffalo chips and before long many fires were burning.*—Suhm-Keen (Shirt On, ten years old)

> *During the sleep before General Miles' attack at Bear Paw Mountain battle, in a dream I foresaw all that came to us. I saw, and recognized where our*

379

Colonel Nelson Miles charged the Nez Perce camp on Snake Creek, then settled down to a five-day siege called the Battle of Bear Paw. (Photo courtesy of National Archives.)

camp was pitched. I saw the waters of the stream all red with blood of both Indian and Soldier. Everywhere the smoke of battle hangs dark and low. I awoke! That vision is strong on my mind. I put on leggins and moccasins, and with blanket walk all over the grounds. I note it just as seen in the dream. The level meadow, the creek, the washout-gully, the surrounding bluffs. Yes, it is true what I saw while sleeping.

I go back to my poor, torn canvas shelter and sleep. The same dream-vision, and more, again passed before me. The mingled blood on the running water; smoke-darkened air; but with it all came falling leaves, withered flowers; followed by spring-time grass, bursting buds, sunshine, and peace. These signs I understood, and knew we would be very soon attacked.

It was coming daylight but dimly when I awoke and went out from the broken, wind-break of canvas. Going through the camp, I called out everywhere: "My people, I have been delayed in this, my dream. In Idaho, when I joined in the war, I knew, and in vision I was directed before hand. Listen well to my words; to my dreams of last night. I dreamed! and when I woke up, here, where we are camped, is the very ground I saw in vision. Above was the thick smoke of battle. On the stream from which we drink was the blood of both Indian and white soldiers.

380

"Very soon now will we be attacked.

"I slept again, and the same dream came back to me, and more. I heard the voice of my power saying to me: 'My boy, do not worry about this war. Open your eyes!'

"Hearing, I opened my eyes. I saw falling from trees, frost-yellowed leaves; mingling with withered flowers and grass. In my own country, each snow I have seen this, and I know it is the end. Those leaves are dead, those flowers are dead. This tells of the end of fighting.

"Soon we are to be attacked for the last time. Guns will be laid down."— Wottolen (Hair Combed Over Eyes)[20]

Few paid attention to Wottolen's warning. General Howard was days and days behind. So how could soldiers be close to them? The Nez Perce hadn't reckoned on another force pursuing them. Howard had sent a courier to Colonel Nelson A. Miles on September 12, and then he had slowed down. Miles received the dispatch on the evening of September 17 and departed from Tongue River (Miles City) the next day. Now, twelve days later, the stage was set.

While some were still eating breakfast, two scouts came galloping from the south, from the direction we had come. As they drew near, they called loudly. "Stampeding buffaloes! Soldiers! Soldiers!"

Some families had packs partly ready and horses caught. But Chief Looking Glass, now head of camp, mounted his horse and rode around ordering, "Do not hurry! Go slow! Plenty, plenty time. Let children eat all wanted!"

This slowed the people down....

It was about one hour later when a scout was seen coming from the same direction. He was running his horse to its best. On the highest bluff he circled about, and waved the blanket signal: "Enemies right on us! Soon the attack!"

A wild stir hit the people. Great hurrying everywhere. I...saw Chief Joseph leap to the open. His voice was above all the noise as he called, "Horses! Horses! Save the horses!"—Yellow Wolf[21]

The Nez Perce horse herd was grazing west of where highway 240 runs today.

We at once took the trot, and gallop and about 8:30 we came to the high ridge above the village, which lay in a grassy little bend of Snake Creek, surrounded on three sides by steep bluffs, some 50 feet high. Our line was deployed on the ridge, the 7th Cavalry (3 companies under Maj. Hale) on

381

*the right; the Mounted Battalion 5th Infantry in the center, and the 3 cos.
2nd Cavalry on the left.*

*We charged; the 7th Cavalry getting way ahead on the right [east], and
the 2nd losing ground by having to cross the creek. The 7th got into action
first, and had to withdraw and dismount, partly on account of the fierce
resistance, and partly the steep bluffs. At about 100 yards from the bluffs
our battalion dismounted and leading their ponies the men went right up to
the edge of the bluffs and settled down to work....*

*In the meantime the 2nd Cavalry had passed way off to the left [west],
and had cut off a greater part of the Indian herd of ponies; and two
companies of the 7th Cavalry had dismounted, whilst Maj. Hale with the
third company was being severely handled about a mile off on our right.—*
Lt. Thomas Mayhew Woodruff, October 15, 1877[22]

*When the camp was first descried, a portion of the lodges had been struck
and about one hundred ponies packed for the day's march. These, guided by
women and children and accompanied by fifty or sixty warriors, were at once
rushed out and started northward. An attempt was made to cut off their
retreat.... The Indians halted for fight after going about five miles from the
main body, and finding a large portion of their pursuers encumbered by the
care of the ponies they had secured, boldly assumed the offensive and forced
the soldiers back toward the main body.*—Capt. Henry Romeyn

The charge threw the Nez Perce into confusion. The people remaining in
camp panicked.

*The white army came on swiftly, their horses creating a great rumbling roar
with pounding hoofs.*

*My father told me to run out from there; to skip for my life. We ran for our
horses. Shooting began, and our horses became stampeded. Everybody
caught whatever horse they could. I got one horse, when only a little ways I
saw...the Cheyenne scouts coming ahead of the soldiers. They were getting
close, and I could not mount my horse fast enough. He was long-eared, and
tall, going round and round. I was short and could not jump to his back. But
the Cheyennes were shooting and I got to his back some way. Cheyennes
and horses were all mixed together, running.*

382

*I ran my horse about half mile when I thought of my little brother—that I
had left him. I turn my horse and go back fast to where I left him. I find
him, and getting him up behind me, we go. The Cheyennes and soldiers are
shooting at us as we pass.*

A Cheyenne warrior pursues a Nez Perce. (Photo courtesy of Idaho State Historical Society.)

One woman is ahead of us. I saw her shot and fall from her horse; the work of a bonneted Cheyenne on a spotted horse....

Soldiers continue sending shots at us but they can not stop us. My little brother, holding tight to me, has one braid of hair shot off close to his ear. Two soldiers pursue us but are driven back before they catch us.

I got away from that war alive, and never went back to any where near there again.... My father was killed in that battle.—Eelahweemah (About Asleep, fourteen years old)[23]

I, Two Moons, rode the circle of our camp, helping to hold the soldiers at a distance. There was fast shooting; horses running every where. Women and children helping the men endeavoring to catch their horses. Cheyenne and Sioux Indians leading the soldiers rounding up our horses; killing the women and children.

Looking back, I, Two Moons saw two little boys riding on one horse where bullets were flying fast. They were skipping for their lives, two cavalrymen closely pursuing, shooting at them. The horse ridden by the children, a long, leggy horse, was no longer going fast. He appeared winded. The soldiers were overtaking them, and I Two Moons rode forth meeting those enemies, driving them back. They would not face me with the gun. I now noticed the two boys on the horse. They were E-lah-weh-mah [About Asleep], and his little brother who was riding behind.—Two Moon[24]

The foremost thought in most minds was to catch a horse on which to escape.

383

Horses running in every direction. Women, old men, and young men were trying to capture saddle horses. The trying was vain.—Husis Owyeen (Shot in Head)[25]

It was morning, and we children were playing. We had hardwood sticks, throwing mud balls. I looked up and saw a spotted horse, a Cheyenne Indian wearing a war bonnet come to the bluff above me. He was closely followed by the troops. Some of the children ran back to the camps, some hurried to the gulch. I was with these last. Bullets were flying. We had to get away. I had no moccasins. I jumped in the creek and swam across maybe. When I got away I had only a shirt as clothing. Cold, wet, I was freezing. Some were on horses, and one woman showed pity for me. She took me up behind her.—White Bird (nine years old)[26]

Despite their success at surprising the Nez Perce and capturing the horse herd, the charging cavalry suffered severe losses.

Captain Hale and Lieutenant J.W. Biddle were killed at the first fire and Captains Moylan and Godfrey wounded immediately after, thereby leaving but one officer with the three troops. All the First Sergeants were also killed. Wherever the Indians heard a voice raised in command there they at once directed their fire.—Capt. Henry Romeyn

One historian reported that Lieutenant Eckerson, the lone surviving field officer of the charge, rushed up to Colonel Miles and shouted, "I am the only d— man of the Seventh Cavalry who wears shoulder straps alive." He was now in command of all three companies of the Seventh. The cavalry succeeded in driving off the Nez Perce horse herd. Those who did not or could not escape rushed to the defense of those left in camp.

We had no knowledge of General Miles' army until a short time before he made a charge upon us, cutting our camp in two, and capturing nearly all of our horses. About seventy men, myself among them, were cut off. My little daughter, twelve years of age, was with me. I gave her a rope, and told her to catch a horse and join the others who were cut off from the camp. I have not seen her since, but I have learned that she is alive and well.

I thought of my wife and children, who were now surrounded by soldiers, and I resolved to go to them or die. With a prayer in my mouth to the Great Spirit Chief who rules above, I dashed unarmed through the line of soldiers. It seemed to me that there were guns on every side, before and behind me. My clothes were cut to pieces and my horse was wounded, but I was not hurt. As I reached the door of my lodge, my wife handed me my rifle, saying; "Here's your gun. Fight!"—Chief Joseph

A Nez Perce warrior hands off a gun to a friend who has none. (Photo courtesy of Idaho State Historical Society.)

Since the horse herd had been driven off, those people who had not captured a horse on which to make their escape were now marooned in the camp.

> *Finally the Indians took refuge in the holes and ravines in the bluffs and kept up a constant fire on us. But we had them and their families hemmed in, in the village.*—Lt. Thomas Mayhew Woodruff, October 15, 1877[27]

> *The Indians occupied a crescent-shaped ravine, and it was apparent that their position could only be forced by a charge or a siege. The first could not be accomplished without too great a sacrifice.*—Col. Nelson Miles

And so the siege began.

> *The men behaved splendidly and the coolness of some was wonderful. To get a position from which their fire could be made more effective it was desired to deploy Company G of the 5th as skirmishers by the right flank, and the bugler was ordered to sound the deployment. "I can't blow, sir; I'm shot!" said the brave fellow, and a glance toward him showed him on the ground with a broken spine. Another man lay still when the movement began, his head toward the enemy. A Sergeant in his rear, creeping crab-wise toward his new position, was directed to have him move along. "He can't do it, sir; he's dead," was the reply.*—Capt. Henry Romeyn

During the first day of fighting, both sides suffered heavy losses.

> *A bad mistake was made by Husishusis Kute [Bald Head] during this sun's fighting. Three brave warriors, Koyehkown, Kowwaspo, and Peoppeop Ipsewahk [Lone Bird] were in a washout southeast of camp. They were too far toward the enemy line. Husishusis thought them enemy Indians killed*

385

them all. He had a magazine rifle and was a good shot. With every shot he would say, "I got one!" or "I got him!"

Lean Elk [Poker Joe] was also killed by mistake. A Nez Perce saw him across a small canyon, mistook him for one of the enemies, and shot him.

Four good warriors killed by friends through mistake. Four brave men lost the first day....

You have seen hail, sometimes, leveling the grass. Indians were so leveled by the bullet hail. Most of our few warriors left from the Big Hole had been swept as leaves before the storm. Chief Ollokot, Lone Bird, and Lean Elk [Poker Joe] were gone.

Outside the camp I had seen men killed. Soldiers ten, Indians ten. That was not so bad. But now, when I saw our remaining warriors gone, my heart grew choked and heavy. Yet the warriors and no-fighting men killed were not all. I looked around.

Some were burying their dead.

A young warrior, wounded, lay on a buffalo robe dying without complaint. Children crying with cold. No fire. There could be no light. Everywhere the crying, the death wail.

My heart became fire.—Yellow Wolf[28]

As the casualties in my command were twenty percent (20%) of the force engaged, the care of the wounded, owing to the absence of tents, the utter lack of fuel and the prevalence—from the evening of the 30th—of a cold wind and snow storm, became an exceedingly difficult matter.—Col. Nelson Miles, December 27, 1877

In this charge he [Miles] lost heavily in men and horses, but covered himself with glory.—Helena Weekly Independent, *October 11, 1877*

On the bluff to the south was the soldiers' camp. Apparently, being covered in glory wasn't enough to keep the soldiers warm.

The 7th and 2nd Cav. were withdrawn from their positions after sunset, and we encamped on the ridge where we had established the Hospital, keeping strong pickets out to watch the Indians and prevent them from escaping from the village. There was occasional firing during the night.—Lt. Thomas Mayhew Woodruff, October 15, 1877[29]

386

Behind the first line I saw a row of bodies covered with blankets.—Yellowstone Kelly (scout)

I remained to help care for the wounded and bury the dead. There were fourteen men killed and thirty wounded besides a great many horses were shot and crippled. A long trench was dug into which the dead were placed side by side, and covered over. Many of the men were literally shot to pieces, but no time was taken or effort expended in fixing or cleaning them up in any manner, but were put into the trench with spurs, belts or other wearing apparel upon them. An officer read the burial service and a shot fired over the graves. While I had been so anxious to get in this fight, yet the sights which I witnessed among the dead and wounded took a great deal of this notion out of me. One cannot realize the feeling engendered by taking part in such carnage as a battle produces until they have had the actual experience in warfare. It was a horrible and gruesome sight. —Alexander Cruikshank (scout)[30]

And the weather! All the accounts mention the weather.

To add to the discomfort a snow storm set in, and by night, four or five inches had fallen upon the combatants and disabled alike. —Capt. Henry Romeyn

It was snowing. The wind was cold! Stripped for battle, I had no blanket. —Yellow Wolf[31]

October 2nd.
Last night was a fearful one. It blew very hard & about 3 inches of snow fell. It snowed some during the day & it's been very cold.

October 3rd.
The weather has been disagreeable most of the day. It's snowing off & on until dark.

October 4th.
Weather some warmer.

October 5th.
It froze very hard last night, but the sun came out bright & warm this morning. —Pvt. William Zimmer[32]

While people on both sides of the battlefield were freezing, those Nez Perce who had escaped the fighting earlier in the day were also suffering a few miles north of the battlefield.

We mounted horses and left. Only one blanket, I rode bareback as did the rest. Going quite a distance, we stopped. We listened to the guns back where they were fighting. I cannot tell the distance. There we stayed till the evening drew on. The night darkness came about us, and still we do not travel further.... Chief Joseph's older wife and daughter are with us. But people are scattered everywhere, hungry, freezing. Almost naked, they had escaped from the camp when the soldiers came charging and shooting.

Thus we remained overnight. We must not build a fire. No bedding, cold and chilly, we stood or sat holding our horses. We cried with misery and loneliness, as we still heard the guns of the battle.—Penahwenonmi (Helping Another)[33]

The next day, October 1, the fighting continued.

As the hidden sun traveled upward, the war did not weaken.

I felt the coming end. All for which we had suffered lost!...

The sun drew on, and about noon the soldiers put up a white flag. The Indians said, "That is good! That means, 'Quit the war.'"

But in short minutes we could see no soldiers. Then we understood. Soldiers quit the fight to eat dinner!

No Indian warrior thought to eat that noon. He never thinks to eat when in battle or dangerous places. But not so the soldier. Those soldiers could not stand the hunger pain. After dinner they pulled down their white flag.

The flag did not count for peace.

The fight was started again by the soldiers after stopping their hunger. There was shooting all the rest of that second sun's battle. Stronger cold, thicker snow came with darkness.—Yellow Wolf[34]

Negotiations between the Nez Perce and Colonel Miles began that same day.

Tom Hill, Indian name: Whis-tool, a boy, could speak very good English. He was sent to General Miles' camp by the chiefs. Afterwards a smaller boy, George Washington, about thirteen years old was sent to help young Hill. They went to learn what was wanted by General Miles. They were our interpreters.—Yellow Wolf[35]

Under the flag of truce, young Tom Hill accompanied Chief Joseph to Miles' camp.

Tom Hill and Alex Hayes appear in this 1900 photo. (Photo courtesy of National Park Service, Nez Perce National Historical Park.)

General Miles, like many others, supposed Joseph to be the leader of the hostiles, and wanted his surrender in place of the real leader—Looking Glass. This suited the Indians exactly and they allowed Joseph to go to the camp of the soldiers.—Duncan McDonald (Nez Perce reporter)

On the morning of October 1st, I opened communication with the Nez Perces and Chief Joseph and several of his warriors came out under flag of truce. They showed a willingness to surrender and brought up a part of their arms (eleven (11) rifles and carbines) but, as I believe, becoming suspicious from some remarks that were made in English, in their hearing, those in camp hesitated to come forward and lay down their arms.—Col. Nelson Miles, December 27, 1877

389

The Nez Perce's reluctance to lay down arms was glossed over in Miles' official report. Witnesses, however, reported an event that delayed the cease-fire.

> *Gen. Miles said to Joseph, "Now, you go back across to your people and tell all your people to come over to me," and he advised me, Hill, to stay with him.... Just the moment when Joseph and his other two men left and had gone a few steps an officer came up to Gen. Miles and told me to call Joseph back, to come alone, and Joseph returned. Joseph came. General told Joseph to stay and told me to go to the Indian trenches and tell my people to come. I looked at Joseph's face, and tears were dripping from his eyes. Joseph said, "Now you are going to throw me away." He was addressing me. I said, "I can not do that. You will not die alone. If you die today, I shall die for you also," and I went across to my people. I told my people Chief Joseph was on the other side with the troop and we are going to quit fighting, and while I was making that announcement to the people, going from trench to trench.* —Tom Hill

> *I saw Chief Joseph taken to the soldier camp a prisoner!*
> *The white flag was pulled down!*
> *The white flag was a lie!* —Yellow Wolf[36]

Three Nez Perce warriors, seeing that Chief Joseph was taken hostage, took advantage of a situation that presented itself to them immediately afterward.

> *At that moment I saw Capt. Jerome on a brown horse coming along. Just then I saw two Indians meet Capt. Jerome, grabbed the reins of the horse's bridle. I noticed Yellow Bull was holding the reins of the bridle and another Indian...whose name is White Bull, seized Capt. Jerome and pulled him off the horse. Then some one holloed to me, "They are going to kill that captain." Then I ran toward them and I grabbed Capt. Jerome by the arm and took him away from the Indian. I took Capt. Jerome to the trench and kept him there overnight. This capture of Capt. Jerome was in the evening. Just then it got dark, the troops fired at us, and battle took place again. All of this time the Indians wanted to kill Capt. Jerome, and I said, "No," and I protected him. I said to the Indians, "If Joseph should be killed across on the other side, then this captain shall die."* —Tom Hill

The Nez Perce treated the captive Lieutenant Jerome as a guest.

> *We fed him on buffalo meat, the best we had. We treated him well. Letters passed between this officer and General Miles.* —Yellow Bull[37]

Yellow Wolf recalled the contents of those letters.

> *This is what the interpreter said the paper told: "I had good supper, good bed. I had plenty of blankets. This morning I had good breakfast. I am treated like I was at home. I hope you officers are treating Chief Joseph as I am treated. I would like to see him treated as I am treated."*
>
> *But Chief Joseph was not treated right. Chief Joseph was hobbled hands and feet. They took a double blanket. Soldiers rolled him in it like you roll papoose on cradle board. Chief Joseph could not use arms, could not walk about. He was put where there were mules, and not in soldier tent. That was how Chief Joseph was treated all night.*—Yellow Wolf[38]

The third day of the siege, October 2, began.

> *It came morning, third sun of battle. The rifle shooting went on just like play. Nobody being hurt. But soon Chief Looking Glass was killed. Some warriors in same pit with him saw at a distance a horseback Indian. Thinking he must be a Sioux from Sitting Bull, one pointed and called to Looking Glass: "Look! A Sioux!"*
>
> *Looking Glass stepped quickly from the pit. Stood on the bluff unprotected. It must have been a sharpshooter killed him. A bullet struck his left forehead, and he fell back dead.*
>
> *That horseback Indian was a Nez Perce.*—Yellow Wolf[39]

The man who had led the Nez Perce out of Idaho and who had promised peace to Montana settlers was now dead. The sandstone monument on the northeast side of the battlefield honors Chief Looking Glass. The rifle pit where he was killed is immediately south of the small obelisk.

Negotiations were resumed later that day.

> *Late in the afternoon of the second, Joseph raised a white flag. Cheers greeted its first appearance and soon under it the Nez Perce Chief, his clothing pierced with over a dozen bullets, although he was still unharmed, stood face to face with his opponent.*
>
> *While he was willing to treat he did not admit that his case was desperate, and his first proposition was to be allowed to march out armed and mounted, abandoning only the position to his foe. He was willing to fight still, but wished to save his women and children. So did the opposing commander, though refusing to entertain this proposition, and the Nez Perce went back to renew the battle....*

391

> *On the third another parley was held, the terms proposed being a surrender of persons, all property and arms to be held by the Indians. This was refused but afterwards modified to the surrendering of the property taken from the river, they to retain the stock and arms and to return to their own country. This is all the Chief would offer.*—Capt. Henry Romeyn

> *The Indians have split. Chief Joseph want to surrender & White Bird wants to fight it out.*—Pvt. William Zimmer, October 2, 1877[40]

In fact, the surrender terms would be very similar to those proposed on October 3. Meanwhile, the Nez Perce had literally dug in.

> *We digged the trenches with camas hooks, and butcher knives. With pans we threw out the dirt. We could not do much cooking. Dried meat and some other grub would be handed around. If not enough for all, it would be given the children first. I was three days without food. During the last fight I heard many make the remark: "I have not eaten since we were attacked!" Children cried with hunger and cold. Old people suffering in silence. Misery everywhere! Cold and dampness all around!*
> *In the small creek was water, but we could get it only at night. In traveling we had buffalo horns for purpose of water. With strings we could let them down while crossing streams horseback. We carried them with us all the time. They came handy here.*—Anonymous Nez Perce woman[41]

On October 4th, in one of these hand-dug pits, the final casualties of the war died.

> *It was towards noon that a bursting shell struck and broke in a shelter pit, burying four women, a little boy, and a girl of about twelve snows. This girl, Atsipeeten, and her grandmother, Intetah, were both killed. The other three women and the boy were rescued.* —Yellow Wolf[42]

That evening, General Howard arrived with his small escort, which included two Nez Perce scouts.

> *While I was talking to my people one Indian announced that Gen. Howard has overtaken the two Nez Perce scouts, Capt. John and George Me-yop-kar-wit. These two Nez Perce Indian scouts had a long pole; a white flag tied to their pole, they were coming across to see us. Just as these two scouts got near the trenches White Bull took up his gun and was going to kill both of these scouts. One Indian, who is dead now, grabbed White Bull's gun and told him to stop.*—Tom Hill

Captain John and George both had daughters with the fleeing bands and had been with General Howard since Idaho. Now they brought a message to the Nez Perce chiefs.

> *There was a council, and the main messenger talked this way: "Those generals said tell you: 'We will have no more fighting.... We...sent all our messengers to say to them, "We will have no more war!"'"*
>
> *Then our man, Chief Joseph, spoke, "You see, it is true. I did not say, 'Let's quit!'*
>
> *"General Miles said, 'Let's quit.'*
>
> *"And now General Howard says, 'Let's quit.'..."* ·
>
> *So when General Miles's messengers reported back to him, the answer was, "Yes."...*
>
> *We were not captured. It was a draw battle.*—Yellow Wolf[43]

The Nez Perce understood that the army was capitulating. After all, Colonel Miles was the one who offered to stop fighting. Chief Joseph believed he was agreeing to a cease-fire, the return of Nez Perce horses, and his people's return to their home.

> *General Miles had promised that we might return to our country with what stock we had left. I thought we could start again. I believed General Miles, or I never would have surrendered.*—Chief Joseph
>
> *White Bird then said: "Joseph, you do not know the white men as well as we do. Never in the world will Americans fulfill the promises made the Indians."*—Duncan McDonald (Nez Perce reporter)

Chief Joseph's agreement to terms in no way bound Chief White Bird. Each chief—indeed, each individual Nez Perce—now made his or her own choice: to give up their weapons to Colonel Miles with the promise of going home again in the spring, or to continue the flight to Canada. No person could speak for another; no one could make a decision for anyone else.

> *As soon as it was dawn our boys began to poor lead into their pits and by ten A.M. they squealed. White rags could be seen in all directions in their camp. Our officers met their chiefs half way & had a talk & soon after Joseph's people brought in their arms & ammunition.*—Pvt. William Zimmer, October 5, 1877[44]

393

Accordingly, on the following morning [October 5] at about eleven o'clock these Indians, Captain "John" and "George," were sent with a flag of truce to the enemy. After much parleying and running to and fro between the camps, Joseph being promised good treatment, sent the following reply.—
Gen. O. O. Howard

Tell General Howard I know his heart.
   What he told me before I have in my heart.
   I am tired of fighting.
   Our chiefs are killed.
   Looking Glass is dead.
   Too-hul-hul-sote is dead.
   The old men are all dead.
   It is the young men who say yes or no.
   He who led on the young men is dead.
   It is cold and we have no blankets.
   The little children are freezing to death.
   My people, some of them, have run away to the hills,
   and have no blankets, no food;
   no one knows where they are—perhaps freezing to death.
   I want to have time to look for my children
   and see how many I can find.
   Maybe I shall find them among the dead.
   Hear me my chiefs.
   I am tired;
   my heart is sick and sad.
   From where the sun now stands,
   *I will fight no more forever.—*Chief Joseph

The surrender was made about noon of the 4th [5th] day of October, and consisted of 113 guns which the Indians had taken from the soldiers.... The Indians then did not want to give up their own guns, and soon shooting was going forward on both sides, after the Government guns had been surrendered. About an hour before sundown.... Joseph then came forward with his own gun to where Howard and Miles were seated, side by side, and extended his gun as if to give it up. Howard extended his hand to receive it, but Joseph refused to let him have it, saying, in substance, that he, Howard, had followed him like an old squaw with his troops, that he, Joseph, at any time could have whipped him with one hundred of his own men, and that he would not surrender anything to him. He said that Gen. Miles had whipped

394

him, and that to him he would surrender, and extended to Miles his gun,
which Miles took.—John Samples (Fort Benton volunteer)[45]

Husishusis Kute [Bald Head], the Palouse chief, walked beside Chief Joseph, who was riding a horse. White Bird was the only other surviving chief, but he did not surrender.

The troops took possession of the Nez Perce camp, but apparently, security that night was lax. About a hundred people escaped under the cover of darkness.

It was in the night when I escaped with Chief White Bird and his band all
afoot. People were divided. Some would go with Joseph, some with White
Bird. The fight was over and nothing to stay for.... We left that night before
Joseph had given his gun to General Miles. We walked out, leaving many of
our friends. Some were too bad wounded to travel and had to stay. Only
about forty unwounded men stayed with Joseph and there were many
women and children. Many more of them than men, both wounded and
unhurt.

   Night drew on as we left. We had blankets but not too heavy for the
traveling. Not enough to keep us warm when camping. It was lonesome, the
leaving. Husband dead, friends buried or held prisoners. I felt that I was
leaving all that I had but I did not cry.—Wetatonmi[46]

I escaped with Chief White Bird. We left in the night while many of the
warriors were still giving up their arms. White Bird would not surrender! He
said Chief Joseph could do as he pleased. Wot-to-len [Hair Combed Over
Eyes] wanted to go on fighting. We followed those who had gone towards
the Sioux camp. They knew the country, and direction to travel. It was slow
going afoot, for we had some children. The Sioux received us as friends.—
Anonymous Nez Perce woman[47]

Search parties were sent out during the two days that Miles and Joseph remained at the battlefield.

During the surrender we were ordered to go out in the prairie and out
among the other tribes of Indians to look for Nez Perce Indians that were
kept during that five days' battle and I obeyed the order and I left for
good.—Tom Hill (thirteen years old)

395

October 6th.—Weather quite warm.
October 7th.—Weather windy & threatening. The Indian pony herd has
been on the increase ever since we came. Its number is now about 1500.
They were scattered about the prairie for miles around. White Bird has not

been heard of since his escape. Since the surrender the Indians say it was wholly his fault in their standing out as long as they did. Gen. Miles started for the Tongue River Post at 10 A.M.—Pvt. William Zimmer[48]

A body count was taken during the two-day stay at the battlefield.

The number of dead Indians is 43 & the number of wounded so far sas they have asked for [medical] atendance is 67. Our killed is 26, wounded 42. (I think some of our wounded have died since.)—Pvt. William Zimmer, October 7, 1877[49]

Our losses were 2 officers and 21 men killed, 4 officers and 42 men wounded. The Indians lost 23 killed and 51 wounded in the village; 5 Indians were killed outside and 11 more were killed over on Milk River by the Gros Ventres and Assiniboines, to whom these 11 had gone for assistance. We captured about 800 ponies.—Lt. Thomas Mayhew Woodruff, October 15, 1877[50]

These casualties brought the total for the war to 113 soldiers killed, 144 wounded, and 50 civilians killed. Nez Perce deaths numbered about 125 and about 90 wounded.

Although General Howard wrote the following directive to Miles on the battlefield, no part of it was destined to be carried out.

On account of the cost of the transportation of the Nez Perces prisoners to the Pacific coast, I deem it best to retain them all at some place within your district, where they can be kept under military control till next spring. Then, unless you receive instructions from higher authority, you are hereby directed to have them sent under proper guard to my department, where I will take charge of them, and carry out the instructions I have already received.—Gen. O. O. Howard, October 7, 1877

From the Bear Paw Battlefield, turn north on highway 240. In 14.8 miles, you will cross the Milk River.

Milk River

396

Those who escaped the battlefield headed north, going toward Canada. Several villages were scattered along the Milk River, including those of the Assiniboine and Gros Ventre, who live today on the Fort Belknap Reservation, just east of Chinook. Some Red River Metis, or mixed-blood French Chippewas as they were sometimes called, also lived along the river.

It was again snowing as I rode on to the north. Toward evening I crossed the Milk River which was almost dry. Here I stopped for the night; my horse was too tired to go on. I had no food, no blankets except the one I used for the horse's saddle-blanket. Along came an Indian, and when we "threw the signs", I discovered he was a friendly Cree. He was kind and generous, for he gave me a pair of moccasins and some food.—Suhm-Keen (Shirt On, ten years old)

There was some inches snow. With my moccasins bad worn, I thought, "This will kill me!" I kept going. Headed for a canyon where one horse was hid. A lot of Nez Perces were somewhere ahead of me. I must find them! I got the horse and went on.

Came full morning, but I saw no one anywhere. Later, I noticed signs of people. I came to the half bloods on Milk River. They treated me fine. Boys watched my horse while he grazed. Knowing I was hungry, they gave me food aplenty. They gave me new moccasins, for my feet were part naked. They directed me how to find my people.

I traveled on.—Yellow Wolf[51]

> Proceed north on county highway 240 for 0.6 mile. Turn southwest on county road 529, Clear Creek Road, for 1.3 miles. Just after you cross to the south side of the Milk River, you can see a few old buildings to the southeast. These are all that remain of Fort Belknap.
>
> The buildings are on private land, which is not open to public access.

Fort Belknap

Fort Belknap had been decommissioned in 1876, but some Gros Ventre and Assiniboine still lived near it.

Thirty-five of them went to the camp of the Gros Ventres and Assiniboines, who were adjacently camped near Fort Belknap, about twelve miles distant from the battleground.... They numbered about 200 or 300 lodges. They invited the Nez Perces into their lodges and gave them a feast. In the meantime, they took away their horses and arms, and then ordered them to leave on foot and without arms. After they had gone a short distance, the Gros Ventres and Assiniboines pursued them on horseback and shot down thirty-four of their number, one only escaping by concealing himself in a ravine. He succeeded in returning to the others, who were loitering around

397

*Miles, and that before the close of Miles' fight.—*John Samples (Fort Benton volunteer)[52]

*We reached the Milk River, also the mixed camp of 80 lodges of Indians.... This place is called Belknap.... The stockade & log warehouse are standing yet & occupied by a trader.—*Pvt. William Zimmer, October 9, 1877[53]

Return to county highway 240, Dike Road, and continue north for 0.8 mile to the junction with US 2 in Chinook. Turn east for 4 blocks. Then turn south on Indiana Street to the Blaine County Museum, on the corner of 5th and Indiana.

Blaine County Museum

The centerpiece of the museum's Nez Perce exhibit is a large mural that graphically depicts the Battle of the Bear Paw. Attended on one side by a painting of the incident at Cow Island and on the other side by a painting of Chief Joseph's surrender, these historically accurate depictions form a visually moving trinity. A video uses these painting to illustrate the final major events in the Nez Perce flight.

Comparative photos between Cow Island as it appeared in the 1870s and as it appears today show some of the detective work that has gone into researching exactly where the historical events took place. Altogether, the photos, paintings, and maps form an interesting and substantial collection for this small, active museum.

Join the Mainstream Traveler at Chinook in the next chapter.

For Further Reading

Robert Ege's *After the Little Bighorn* describes the military engagement at the Bear Paw Battlefield. This twenty-six-page tribute to the Seventh Cavalry details the charges and advances as well as some individual acts of heroism.

Every year, a commemoration ceremony is held at the Bear Paw Battlefield on the weekend nearest to October 5. Contact the Bear Paw Battlefield for more information, 406-357-3130.

CHAPTER 13

Aftermath

The Nez Perce Diaspora

Chinook, Montana, to Fort Walsh, Saskatchewan

Chinook, Montana, to Miles City, Montana, to Fort Leavenworth, Kansas, to Tonkawa, Oklahoma, to Nespelem, Washington

You know how you feel when you lose kindred and friends through sickness-death. You do not care if you die. With us it was worse. Strong men, well women, and little children killed and buried. They had not done wrong to be so killed. We had only asked to be left in our own homes, the homes of our ancestors. Our going was with heavy hearts, broken spirits. But we would be free. Escaping the bondage sure with the surrendering. All lost, we walked silently on into the wintry night. —Wetatonmi[1]

Thus has terminated one of the most extraordinary Indian wars of which there is any record. The Indians throughout displayed a courage and skill that elicited universal praise, they abstained from scalping, let captive women go free, did not commit indiscriminate murder of peaceful families, which is usual, and fought with almost scientific skill, using advance and rear guards, skirmish lines, and field fortifications.—General William Tecumseh Sherman (U.S. Army)

With women's hearts breaking, children weeping and men silent, we moved over the divide and closed our eyes upon our once happy homes. We were wanderers on the prairie. For what? For white man's greed. The white man wanted the wealth our people possessed; he got it by the destruction of our people. We who yesterday were rich are beggars today, made so by the order of a Christian white chief. We have no country, no people, no home. We do not desire longer life, and we pray day and night that the Great Spirit will remove us.—Chief White Bird, October 22, 1877

399

As these people have been hitherto loyal to the Government and friend of the white race from the time their country was first explored, and in their skillful campaigns have spared hundred of lives and thousands of dollars worth of property that they might have destroyed, and as they have, in my opinion, been grossly wronged in years past, have lost most of their warriors, their homes, property and everything except a small amount of clothing; I have the honor to recommend that ample provision be made for their civilization, and to enable them to become self-sustaining. They are sufficiently intelligent to appreciate the consideration which in my opinion is just due them from the Government. The Nez Perces are the boldest men and best marksmen of any Indians I have encountered, and Chief Joseph is a man of more sagacity and intelligence than any Indian I have ever met.— Col. Nelson Miles, December 27, 1877

My efforts will be to send the Nez Perces where they will never disturb the people of Oregon or Idaho again.—Gen. William T. Sherman, October 24, 1877

The Story

On behalf of the old people, the wounded, the women, and the children, Chief Joseph surrendered on October 5, 1877. With him were about three hundred-eighty Nez Perce.

The Nez Perce (Nee-Me-Poo) National Historic Trail ends at the Bear Paw Battlefield near Chinook, Montana. But the story of the Nez Perce flight for freedom does not end there. Rather, the Bear Paw marks the divergence of two paths. Although Chief Joseph surrendered along with about two-thirds of his people, Chief White Bird and the remaining third of the Nez Perce did succeed in reaching Canada.

About 150 people had left camp and headed north just as the battle began on the morning of September 30. They were joined, on the night of October 5, by most of the able-bodied warriors, plus a greater number of women and children. Chief White Bird, who refused to surrender, simply walked out of camp at Bear Paw. Some estimate that about 330 escaped the battlefield, but a Nez Perce source, Black Eagle, recalled 233 who actually reached the Sioux camp. Not all the fleeing small contingents of Nez Perce reached the safety of the Grandmother's Land. Some men, as noted in the previous chapter, were killed by some Assiniboine and Gros Ventre who lived along the Milk River.

Once in Canada, the Nez Perce found refuge with Sitting Bull and his five thousand Lakota (Sioux). The week following the Nez Perce arrival at Fort Walsh in Saskatchewan, the Sitting Bull Commission arrived. Their purpose was to induce Sitting Bull to return the Lakota people to their home in Dakota. The

Lakota had arrived in Canada between December 1876 and May 1877, fleeing the reprisals made against them in the wake of the Battle of the Little Big Horn.

However, the head of the delegation was General Terry, who had been Custer's superior. A less appropriate negotiator could hardly have been chosen. Another action also spoke louder than words: the same army that had just chased the Nez Perce out of the country wanted the Lakota to return. No wonder Sitting Bull distrusted the intent of the Commission.

Food was scarce to feed these thousands of people. Buffalo, although plentiful in 1878, didn't come north in 1879 because a prairie fire of suspicious origin had burned off the grass. Additionally, the U.S. government's policy of killing off all the buffalo in order to force Native Americans into submission was beginning to pay off. Native Americans had been displaced by so-called civilized people. Buffalo, the wild animals native to the plains, were being killed off and would soon be replaced by domesticated cattle.

In the spring of 1878, the first of many small Nez Perce groups started wandering back to Idaho. They drifted back slowly, some spending a year or two with the Salish (Flathead) or the Cree, before actually returning to Idaho. Once discovered in Idaho, many of the refugees were then shipped off to join Joseph in exile in Oklahoma. Eighty people were eventually added to the exiles in this manner. Some Nez Perce never returned to Idaho at all.

Those people with Chief Joseph went with Colonel Miles to Fort Keogh (Miles City) fully expecting to go home in the spring. Ten days later they were sent to Fort Lincoln at Bismarck, North Dakota. Next they were shipped to Fort Leavenworth, Kansas. In July 1878, they were shipped even farther away from their home, to northeastern Oklahoma. The following year they were moved once again to north central Oklahoma, near Ponca City. In Eekish Pah, the hot place, the people continued to die off rapidly. No newborn children survived this time.

Chief Joseph became a popular and sympathetic figure. He made a trip to Washington, D.C., in 1879 to plead his case with President Hayes. Easterners, Presbyterians, and the Indian Rights Association petitioned and wrote letters advocating for the Nez Perce return to their homeland. Westerners found this view sentimental and pitiless. People in Idaho remembered that twenty-one of their neighbors had been killed by these Indians.[2]

In 1885, the 268 Nez Perce remaining in Oklahoma were finally shipped to the Northwest. Of these, 118 elected to go to the Nez Perce Reservation in Idaho. Chief Joseph, however, was not given a choice. He was sent to the Colville Reservation in north central Washington; 149 of his people decided to go with him.

The Nez Perce Nation had been split by the Treaty of 1863 into a Christian, treaty faction and a traditional, nontreaty faction. The flight dramatically highlighted their differences as the nontreaty bands fled their home in search of freedom. In 1885, that division was further formalized, a split that continues to the present day, with Nez Perce people scattered among four reservations.[3]

Chronology of Events

1877	
17 October	Sitting Bull Commission meets at Fort Walsh.
23 October	Colonel Miles and the Nez Perce arrive at Fort Keogh (Miles City).
31 October	Chief Joseph and 430 Nez Perce leave Fort Keogh.
16 November	The Nez Perce arrive in Bismarck.
27 November	The Nez Perce arrive at Fort Leavenworth, Kansas.
July 1878	The Nez Perce are shipped to northeastern Oklahoma.
1879	
January	Chiefs Joseph and Yellow Bull visit President Hayes in Washington, D.C.
April	*The North American Review* publishes an article by Chief Joseph.
June	The Nez Perce are moved to the Oakland Reserve near Tonkawa, Oklahoma.
1882	Chief White Bird is killed in Canada.
1883	Twenty-three widows and orphans leave Oklahoma and go home to Idaho.
1885	The 268 surviving Nez Perce are shipped to Wallula, Washington, and are divided up: 118 return to the reservation in Idaho, and 149 go with Chief Joseph to the Colville reservation in north central Washington.
1899	Chief Joseph visits the Wallowas for the first time since 1877.
1904	
21 September	Chief Joseph dies.

Travel Plan

In this chapter, directions are given for travelers who would like to follow the approximate path taken by those with White Bird, who escaped to Canada. Directions are not given for the route that Chief Joseph and the majority of nontreaty Nez Perce took. However, major stopping places, directions for reaching historical sites, and events associated with the Nez Perce exile are noted.

Mainstream Traveler	Adventurous Traveler	Intrepid Traveler
Chinook to Havre	follow Mainstream	follow Mainstream
follow Adventurous	Havre, Montana, to Fort Walsh, Saskatchewan	follow Adventurous

Chief Joseph posed for this photo during his trip to Washington in January 1879. (Photo courtesy of Montana Historical Society.)

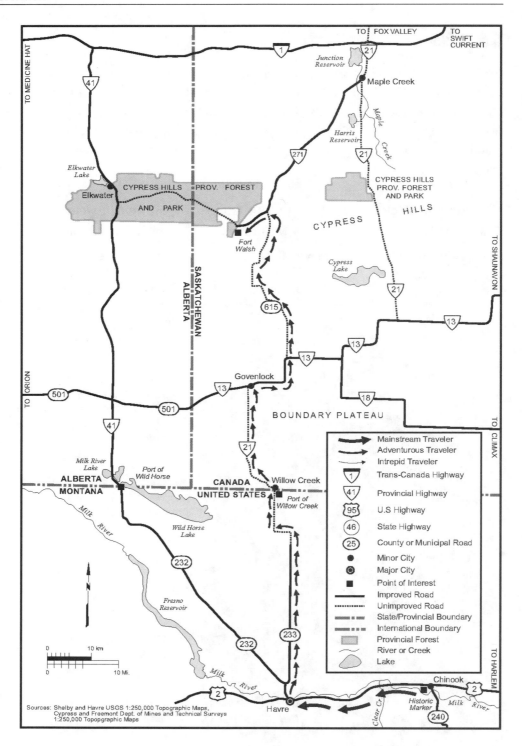

TO FOX VALLEY

TO SWIFT CURRENT

Junction Reservoir

Maple Creek

Harris Reservoir

Maple Creek

Elkwater Lake

CYPRESS HILLS PROV. FOREST AND PARK

Elkwater

CYPRESS HILLS PROV. FOREST AND PARK

HILLS

Fort Walsh

CYPRESS

Cypress Lake

TO MEDICINE HAT

SASKATCHEWAN
ALBERTA

TO SHAUNAVON

Govenlock

BOUNDARY PLATEAU

TO ORION

Milk River Lake

ALBERTA
MONTANA

Port of Wild Horse

CANADA
UNITED STATES

Willow Creek

Port of Willow Creek

Wild Horse Lake

TO CLIMAX

Mainstream Traveler
Adventurous Traveler
Intrepid Traveler
1 Trans-Canada Highway
41 Provincial Highway
95 U.S Highway
46 State Highway
25 County or Municipal Road
● Minor City
◉ Major City
■ Point of Interest
—— Improved Road
········ Unimproved Road
—·—·— State/Provincial Boundary
—··—··— International Boundary
▨ Provincial Forest
〰 River or Creek
▨ Lake

Milk River

Fresno Reservoir

N

Chinook

Historic Marker

Milk River

Havre

Clear Cr

TO HARLEM

0   10 km

0   10 Mi.

Sources: Shelby and Havre USGS 1:250,000 Topographic Maps,
Cypress and Freemont Dept. of Mines and Technical Surveys
1:250,000 Topopgraphic Maps

Chief White Bird's Journey

Chinook, Montana, to Fort Walsh, Saskatchewan

For the Mainstream Traveler

Chinook to Havre

> In Chinook, at the junction of highway 240 and US 2, turn west on US 2.
> 0.1 mile west, a roadside historic sign tells about the Battle of Bear Paw.
>   For the remaining 21.0 miles into Havre, US 2 parallels the Milk River. In
> 5.6 miles US 2 crosses the Milk River.

Milk River

Not all the escaping Nez Perce survived their encounters with the people of this country.

> *The Assiniboines are killing the Nez Perces as I sent them word that they could fight any that escaped and take their arms and ponies.*—Col. Nelson Miles, October 14, 1877

> *We went down Milk River…and…somewhere…near…Chinook…I ran across a naked Indian lying dead among the sage-brush, without a scalp. I searched about on the ground for a clue and soon found four more scalped Indians.…*
>
> *I went on down to the camp of a large number of Upper Assiniboines and asked them about it. They said that the five men and two others were Nez Perce scouts who had come to them, asking them to turn out and help them fight the whites. "What did you do about it?" I asked. They said, "We held a council and determined to tell them we had no cause to fight the whites, by whom we were well treated, and advised them to go over and see the Gros Ventres, who might want to fight. We said to each other, 'Give them a good dinner—give them the best you have got, for it is the last dinner they are ever going to eat.'"*
>
> *After their dinner, I was told, they started toward the Gros Ventre village, and were allowed to get some miles away, when the young Assiniboine braves saddled up and went out and killed them all, and their scalps were there hanging on a pole to dry in the wind.*—Lt. Hugh Scott

405

Of the approximately 330 Nez Perce who left the battlefield and headed north, only 233 actually reached Canada. Several were killed, but almost half were captured and returned to Colonel Miles.

Travel 1.7 miles to the bridge over Clear Creek.

Clear Creek

Father Genin's mission with the Metis was located at the confluence of Clear Creek and the Milk River.

> *Leaving the Assiniboine village, I soon encountered Lieutenant Maus with ten men of the infantry, mounted, who said he was hunting for Nez Perce fugitives from Miles's fight, and thought there might be a lot of them in the village of the Red River half-breeds [Metis] living on Milk River.*—Lt. Hugh Scott

Indeed, several Nez Perce had found refuge in the Metis encampment.

> *One very dark night, our camp was suddenly filled with Nez Perces Indians. Among them was White Bird, a Nez Perces chief. Nearly all except him were badly wounded. We had heard the cannon fire two days previous, but did not know anything about the Nez Perces' war. The fight could not have been over fifteen miles from us. I began at once the work usually performed in hospitals.... The good half-breeds [Metis] fed those poor Indians, whilst I washed and wrapped their wounds.... The action of the half-breeds and mine evoked a serious suspicion in army quarters. However, the cloud soon vanished, and the officers understood that we could not reason, at such a juncture, upon the merits or demerits of that so unexpected war.*—J. B. M Genin (Missionary Apostolic), December 13, 1877

Lieutenants Scott and Maus did not accuse Father Genin of aiding and abetting the enemy, but they did take the wounded Nez Perce with them.

> *We surprised the camp, and captured...forty-one or two Indians.... For three or four days after leaving the Milk River, I do not believe there was a time when hostile Indians could not be seen.*—Lt. Marion P. Maus

406

Milk River

In 1877 several villages were strung along the Milk River. Cree, Assiniboin, Gros Ventre, and Metis—in the camps of these peoples the fleeing Nez Perce found either respite or death.

A Metis (center) introduces a Nez Perce (right) to a Sioux (left). (Photo courtesy of Idaho State Historical Society.)

Four suns in all we are hiding, no food, starving and cold. No moccasins, I am barefooted.... After that time some other men came. They council and say, "Why do we stay here and nothing to eat? We better start for Sitting Bull right away."

Then we travel toward Sitting Bull's camp. Moving that fifth day, towards evening the men killed a buffalo bull. A fire is built. Meat is cooked by roasting, and we have supper, but my throat is dry. The meat sticks in my throat. I eat very little....

Next day we come to some Chippewa [Metis] Indians. They are nice people. They give us food. I am given a pair of moccasins. Then I felt better. But I never forget that I was five suns without food.— Penahwenonmi (Helping Another)[4]

I rode away in the darkness. I was freezing, with only the breechclout. All night I did not sleep. Coming the daylight, I saw a soldier approaching. I thought, "This is my chance. I will freeze without clothing." Then I killed that soldier and took all his clothes. Putting them on I felt more warm. Another soldier came riding to me thinking I was one of their men. I shot that soldier also, and gave his clothes to Indians who needed them. The Crees traded me some of their clothes for my soldier clothes. They told me I would be killed if found wearing soldier uniform. —Husis Owyeen (Wounded Head)[5]

407

In another 4.9 miles you enter Hill County.

Hill County

Hill County was named for James J. Hill, the railroad magnate who brought the Great Northern Railway, which parallels US 2, through here in 1887.

Hill paid for Chief Joseph's marble tombstone in Nespelem.

> Proceed on US 2 for 8.3 miles to Havre.
> Continue with the Adventurous Traveler at Havre.

For the Adventurous Traveler

Havre, Montana, to Fort Walsh, Saskatchewan

Miles: 91.1

Maps: Saskatchewan

Special considerations: The port of Willow Creek is open only from 9 a.m. to 5 p.m. Fort Walsh is open from May 15 to September 18. Daily visiting hours are 9 a.m. to 6 p.m.

Re-entry to the United States requires a passport or a birth certificate plus a photo I.D.

Although this is the most direct route today from Chinook to Fort Walsh, it probably lies west of the actual path taken by the various small groups of Nez Perce who fled north. In downtown Havre, turn north on county highway 232. After 3.2 miles, turn northeast onto county highway 233. The pavement ends in 21.3 miles, and 9.0 miles farther on is the port of Willow Creek.

United States-Canada Border

> *White Bird did not know whether or not it would be safe for him to go to Sitting Bull's camp, but after a consultation with his followers they came to the conclusion they might as well be killed by Indian enemies as by the whites.*—Duncan McDonald (Nez Perce reporter)

> *From this place we moved each sun for two suns. Stormy dark, we could not tell direction to go. Often traveled wrong way. It was the second sun, a little past noon, we crossed the border into Canada. In the evening we camped, and next morning, the third sun, we had not gone far when we saw Indians coming. At quite a distance one of those Indians threw a sign:*

> *"What Indians are you?"*
>
> *"Nez Perce," one of our men answered. Then he signed, "Who are you?"*
>
> *"Sioux," was the reply.*
>
> *"Come on," one of our men signed. "We will have smoke ready!"*
>
> *We knew that some time ago we had trouble with the Sioux, so we must smoke.*—Yellow Wolf[6]

Smoking a pipe refers to making peace between the peoples. The Nez Perce had never been friends of the Lakota (Sioux). In fact, in the alliance of nations on the plains, the Nez Perce were friends of the Crows, who were enemies of the Lakota. Doubtless, in aiding their friends the Crows, more than one Nez Perce warrior had killed or been killed by a Lakota warrior.

Upon their arrival, the Nez Perce were very unsure of the welcome they would receive from the Sioux. Would the Sioux offer them hospitality and then kill them, as the Assiniboine and Gros Ventre on the Milk River had done? Perhaps the Sioux would divide them up and kill them one by one?

> *But the Sioux mixed us up. They took us one by one. The women and children were separated from the men....*
>
> *When we came only a little ways from the camp, we saw smoke from many tepees of the Sioux. For eight or ten miles they seemed strung. I thought to myself, "There is quite a number of Sioux Indians!" Going closer, I could see down the canyon. Nothing but Sioux tepees.*
>
> *It was yet early morning when they took us scattering, in different tepees....*
>
> *They gave me everything I asked, just as if I were one of their children.*—Yellow Wolf[7]

From Willow Creek, proceed north on Saskatchewan 21, a gravel road, for 18.0 miles. Turn east on Saskatchewan 13 for 9.0 miles. Turn north on Saskatchewan 615, which is a gravel road, for the next 24.1 miles. Next, turn south on Saskatchewan 271, which is paved for most of the 6.5 miles to Fort Walsh.

Fort Walsh

409

Sitting Bull and five thousand Lakota had sought refuge in Canada just a few months previously to escape the reprisals by the U.S. Army resulting from the Battle of the Little Big Horn, in which Custer and his command were killed. Sitting Bull actually spent most of his four years in Canada near Wood Mountain, 150 miles east of Fort Walsh.

Fort Walsh as it appeared in 1878. (Photo courtesy of Montana Historical Society.)

Although Canada was willing to offer sanctuary to the Lakota, Major James Walsh of the North West Mounted Police (NWMP) had warned Sitting Bull not to cross the border to assist the Nez Perce. He would not harbor law-breakers.

The Visitor Center is a short walk from the parking lot. After looking at the exhibits, you can take a van down to the fort itself. But before you ride down, you might first like to walk around to the south side of the Visitor Center to the overlook.

At the time of the Bear Paw Battle, Sitting Bull was on his way to Fort Walsh to treat with the Sitting Bull Commission in mid-October of 1877. The commission's goal was to induce him to return to the Sioux reservation in the Dakotas. It was pure coincidence that the Commission arrived only a few days after the Nez Perce. A reporter accompanying the Commission described Fort Walsh as it appeared at that time.

Suddenly fort Walsh came into view, lying low in a charming valley. No more romantic spot, no wilder scene could impress a traveller at the end of a monotonous journey than the one that met our eyes. The fort, built by Major Walsh only two years ago, is notwithstanding its excellence of a form and aspect so quaint and old as to remind one of the stories of the early Kentucky stockades. It is in fact an irregular stockade of upright logs enclosing all the offices and buildings, which are likewise built of logs, necessary for the accommodation of a garrison. Whitewashed on every part except the roof, the fort nestles between the surrounding heights. A scraggly but picturesque little settlement adjoins it.—Jerome B. Stillson (newspaper reporter), October, 1877

A settlement had sprung up west of the fort, but no trace of it remains today.

After the departure of the Sitting Bull Commission, Major Walsh negotiated with Nez Perce on October 22 to ascertain their reasons for fleeing the United States. He told the Nez Perce that the North West Mounted Police could offer them protection only as long as they stayed in Canada. Nevertheless, shortly thereafter, a few Nez Perce returned to the Bear Paw battlefield.

> *The Nez Perces who went to Sitting Bull's camp are now for the second time on the old battle field near Bear's Paw mountain and have Sitting Bull and some of his Indians with them. They go after some supplies of ammunition, sugar, tobacco, etc., which they had concealed there after the war.—*J. B. M. Genin (Missionary Apostolic), December 13, 1877

Sitting Bull and five thousand Lakota had sought refuge in Canada in early 1877 to escape reprisals by the U.S. Army. (Photo courtesy of South Dakota State Historical Society.)

The following summer, Duncan McDonald visited the Nez Perce in Canada to gather the information with which he wrote his series of newspaper articles. So, while the rest of his reports were second-hand information, he actually participated as an interpreter in the July 1878 conference held at Fort Walsh. The purpose of the council was to induce White Bird and the one-hundred-twenty or so people remaining with him to surrender and join the other Nez Perce in exile.

> *It will be remembered that there were three Nez Perces sent direct from Fort Leavenworth. One of them was a brother-in-law of White Bird. The government thought best to send these men to White Bird, as they might possibly induce him to surrender.*—Duncan McDonald (Nez Perce reporter)

> *It was decided by the War Department to send a number of the reliable chiefs among the prisoners to their comrades [in Canada], and let them in person tell to the braves that they have not only escaped murder and hardship, but that they, on the other hand, have been treated well; well housed, well fed, well clothed and permitted every liberty in the power of the army to grant.*—The Daily Leavenworth Times , May 1, 1878

411

I do not want to go where Joseph is. The country is unhealthy. Let Joseph come back here, and together we will return to Idaho of our own accord.— Chief White Bird

Chief White Bird remained in Canada. During their first year in the Grandmother's Land, the Nez Perce camped at the east end of the Cypress Hills. But this country could not compare to home. Hungry, homesick, and in rags, some Nez Perce trickled back to Idaho beginning in the spring of 1878. Some went directly to Idaho. Some spent intervening years with Salish or Crees before returning to Idaho. A few stayed in Canada.

Eighty of those nontreaty people who were discovered on the Nez Perce Reservation and on other reservations were deported to Oklahoma to join the rest of the prisoners. One exception was Chief Joseph's adolescent daughter, Kapkap-ponmi (Sound of Running Feet). Separated from her father during the attack at the Bear Paw, she had escaped to Canada with her mother. The following year, she was among the first group that went back to Idaho. She, however, was not allowed to go to Oklahoma, and she died in Idaho a few years later before Chief Joseph returned from exile.

Due to widespread prairie fires in 1879, the buffalo did not come north that year. Starving Sioux began leaving for the Dakotas, band by band. Sitting Bull hung on until 1881, when he finally surrendered.

After the Sioux left Canada, the Nez Perce drifted westward toward Fort Macleod, settling at Pincher Creek, Alberta. Chief White Bird was killed near there in 1882 by one of his own people because his reputed shamanic powers had become too strong. His efforts to heal two sick Nez Perce children had failed. When the second was on his deathbed, he called for White Bird. This apparently was proof to the children's father that White Bird's powers as a medicine man were out of control.

Chief Joseph's Route

Chinook, Montana, to Nespelem, Washington

Chinook to Miles City, Montana

After staying at the battlefield for a couple of days after the cessation of hostilities on October 5, Colonel Miles headed back to his home base at Fort Keogh (Miles City), at the junction of the Tongue and Yellowstone rivers.

> *Several of our wounded died on the way before reaching the Missouri and had to buried beside the trail.*—Col. Nelson Miles

The forty-one Nez Perce who had been captured at the Metis village on the Milk River followed behind.

> *Hiring some Red River [Metis] carts, we loaded them with women and children and started for Miles's camp on the Missouri near the mouth of the Musselshell....*
>
> *The weather had become quite cold by that time, especially at night.... The children would cry all night until we killed some buffalo and wrapped them up in the green hides, and fed them and our men with meat without salt, cooked without utensils.*—Lt. Hugh Scott

Mouth of the Musselshell River

Miles crossed the Missouri River near where the Musselshell River feeds into it. Today the exact crossing lies under the waters of Fort Peck Lake, in the Charles M. Russell National Wildlife Refuge.

> *As the force moved across the rolling prairie it appeared like a great caravan. There were three battalions of well-equipped, hardy, resolute soldiers, with artillery, besides upward of four hundred prisoners; and on the opposite flank, some distance away, were driven over six hundred of the captured stock, while in the rear were the travois and ambulances, bearing the wounded, followed by the pack trains and wagon trains, and all covered by advance guards, flankers, and rear guards.*—Col. Nelson Miles

While Colonel Miles recalled the splendor of the procession, one of the privates remembered something much more simple.

413

> *The wounded Indians and wounded troopers played poker together around the campfire.*—Pvt. Jacob Horner

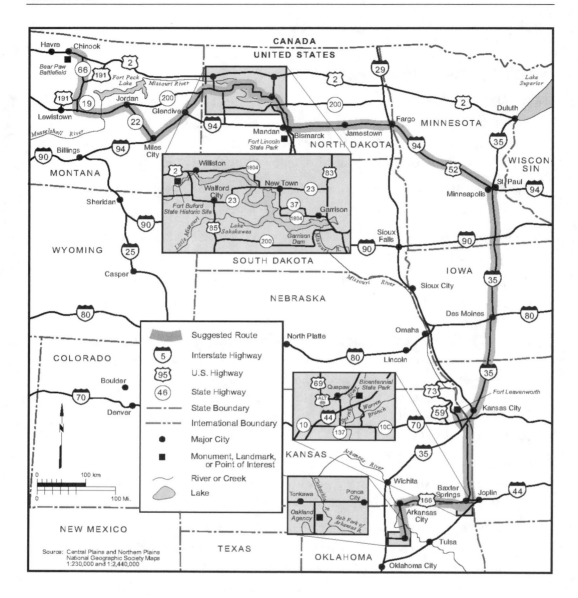

Miles City, Montana

I was down to Miles City. It has improved wonderful. There is about 2 log houses there now and more underway, besides quite a number of tents. Out of one a doctor has his shingle hung. Another one has the sign of Literature & Stationery. There is now 5 or 6 drinking places in the evenings.—Pvt. William Zimmer, September 13, 1877[8]

Fort Keogh was located on the west edge of Miles City, just 1.4 miles north of exit 135 off of I-94. The same site is now the home of the Fort Keogh Livestock and Range Research Station. All that remains of the original fort is two dilapidated officers quarters and an unkempt parade ground. To see the deteriorated fort that was just beginning to be built in 1877, drive west into the main entrance of the Research Station for 1.1 miles. Looking west of the office, you can see the few buildings that remain.

Half of an officers' quarters was moved to the Range Riders Museum 0.8 mile east of Fort Keogh. This private museum with a commitment to the preservation of local history is located on the site of the Tongue River Cantonment, the predecessor of Fort Keogh.

The parade grounds of Fort Keogh in 1878. (Photo courtesy of Montana Historical Society.)

Tongue River Cantonment

415

I directed General Miles to keep the prisoners till next Spring, it being too late to send them to Idaho by direct routes this Fall and too costly by steamer or rail.—Gen. O. O. Howard, October 10, 1877

But,

> *They remained in that place [on the Yellowstone] for ten days or two weeks,*
> *when I received an order from the higher authorities to send them down the*
> *river to Bismarck, Dakota. They were therefore placed in boats and sent*
> *down the Yellowstone to its junction with the Missouri, thence down the*
> *Missouri to Bismarck.* —Col. Nelson Miles

Both Miles' superior, General Phil Sheridan, and the General of the Army, William Tecumseh Sherman, overruled General Howard. They thought that sending the Nez Perce to Indian Territory would teach them a lesson.

Yellowstone River

About half the captured Nez Perce, consisting of the wounded, aged, and several women and children, were sent down the Yellowstone River by boat. The remainder of the adult men, women, and children were escorted overland by the military. The story of one boatload of prisoners was told very engagingly by its boatman.

> *There was also a fleet of flat boats tied up at Miles City.... I looked the boats*
> *over and found there was some fourteen of them large and small. Being the*
> *first to select my choice from this flat bottom fleet, I picked out one that*
> *appeared to be the swiftest runner.... After picking out my boat I reported to*
> *the quarter master who told me to make out a list for rations for 23 persons*
> *also a cooking and serveing outfit. The rations list was composed of dried*
> *salt port, Rio green coffee, Brown sugar, Hard tack, Rice, Navy Beans, Flour,*
> *Bakeing powder.*
>
> *Everything was now ready to start on a 400 mile trip. 22 Nez Perce*
> *Indian prisoners was turned over to be delivered to...Fort Buford, Dekota....*
> *The Nez Perce prisoners was devided all those that was strong was to go*
> *over land by wagon train. The sick[,] wounded[,] woman[,] and children was*
> *to go by river in the flat bottom boats.... Having much surply's and Indian*
> *baggage aboard, and was gliding along with fair speed till we came in view*
> *of the Buffalo rappids just a few miles below Miles City. The fall season had*
> *been a very dry one and the water in the river very low making it appear*
> *very dangerous to shoot the rapids but I had been over them befor and I*
> *knew where the deep water channel was....*
>
> *We had arrived about half-way down the rapids, I noticed Gen. Miles and*
> *the Doctor looking back up the rapids. I glanced up that way just in time to*
> *see one of our fleet boats comming over the rim of the rapids sideways and I*

said God "help them" for I knew they would perish.... We soon overtook the overland wagon train party that had halted and had formed a correll.... I made a touch and go landing. Gen. Nelson Miles and Doctor Reed...sprang ashore with a hasty good bye....

I whent in camp about a mile run after sun set, camping on the south side of the river just arround a bend of the river were there was an Island hid our camp from view form the north shore. The reason I did so was to be hid from any scout or Indian runner that may be sent out by Gen. Miles with some new order's.... I handed to the aged Chief [Washington] my gun also an extra cairadge and pointing to the fringe of bush along the river I said we must eat.... The aged Chief had not been goen long before we heard the gun report and the aged Chief came along the river shore towards our Camp. The indians who by now was making coffee and frying dried salt pork look up at me so I sign three of the women to go, meet him and he pointed back the way he came. He came into camp and wipped out the gun and handed it to me with the unused caretiridge.... Soon the Indian women returned with a fine three year old male white tail deer that was skined and ready for cooking quicker than meat was made ready in old Washington market in New York City.

Just at the streak of dawn the Indians now my people began to move arround. Coffee Hardtack with a peice of boiled salt port was the food for our breakfast. The evening befor I had them place stones filled between with sand to build a fire on the bottom of the boat to cook at any time and keep coffee hot for the weather was cool showing that winter was near.... Each day at mid sun I tied up for an hour giving my people time to releive their limbs my mooving around on mother earth. The boy's shaped bows and arrows from the young groth of ash to shoot bank beaver that was plentyfull....

We had now been running six suns and I found we was running a little over four miles per hour by water pressure only, so we was making about forty miles per sun on an avage.—Fred G. Bond (boatman)[9]

Fort Buford State Historic Site, North Dakota

Located where the Yellowstone meets the Missouri River, Fort Buford stands just two miles east of the Montana border, on North Dakota route 1804. Only three buildings remain from the hundred or so that were here in 1877.

417

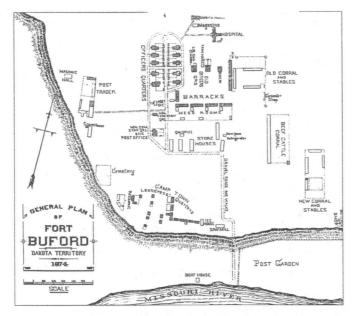

The layout of Fort Buford in 1874. (Photo courtesy of State Historical Society of North Dakota.)

Once you've arrived at Fort Buford, drive straight through the site and follow the signs to the confluence of the Yellowstone and Missouri rivers. Position yourself near the boat ramp as you read the next section of Fred Bond's story.

We was by now getting well down near the Government hay camp just above the mouth of the Yellowstone river. This summer hay camp was located near where the Missouri river and Yellowstone came togeather.... Befor long we came down so near we could see the mighty Missouri plunging along. My people all stood up giving a sigh for the water of that mighty river was the color of poor coffee and I could hardly convince them they had seen that river before at Bear Paw Mountain range. I must now hug the north bank of the Yellowstone...or be swept down the rivers where the two currants met foarming foaming whirpool with speed and dangerous suction. The Missouri river was one mass of slush ice traveling from seven to eight miles per hour and I must cross that river as quickly as possible for Fort Buford was on its north banks and I only had about five miles to cross this raging torrent....

We had now entered the Missouri river that was pushing us down river very fast. We had to do all in our power to get out of the suction of those two large rivers.... Slowly we was crossing the river but could we get near the landing to tie up. If we passed the landing we have to portage back. At

Fred Bond was twenty-five years old when he navigated the Missouri River. (Photo courtesy of Ward Hill Press.)

last I could see we could make the landing if we had shore help to tak our line and snub us up. For the river was very swift at that place it causing a cut bank. We now was about half mile from the landing so I told Washington to shoot gun three times to attract river guards to come to our help. He did so and I could see soldiers running it appeared from all corners of the Fort or Garrison. I got my snubline ready and warned my people to be ready for the jerk that we was bound to receive. I cast my line in a group of five soldiers who held us and our stern swong down stream. —Fred G. Bond (boatman)[10]

Chief Joseph and the group that had come overland arrived on November 7. The Nez Perce stayed at Buford for two or three days.

Now drive back to the fort.

While Joseph, the warriors, and their families, accompanied by the military escort, went overland, half of the Nez Perce prisoners continued their journey by water.

Fort Buford, D.T., Nov., 9th, 1877. Some two hundred of the Nez Perces prisoners left here last evening on board the mackinaws, escorted by two companies of the 1st infantry....

Quite a crowd had collected on the river bank to see the captives leave, and also to interview those who remained. These last were very busily engaged—the bucks in keeping themselves warm around the fires they had started in the open air, the squaws in putting up tepees, chopping wood, etc....

Over two hundred Nez Perce prisoners will leave here sometime tomorrow for Bismarck, going overland. They will be escorted by five companies of the 7th cavalry and two companies 1st infantry. I believe the train escort is a company of the 2d cavalry.—The Bismarck Tri-Weekly Tribune, November 16, 1877

419

The mackinaw boats were racing with time. Typically, ice closed the river at Fort Buford around November 17.

> *Once more we was drifting drifting on that vast muddy river that would put weak coffee to shame by its color....*
>
> *Day after day we sailed, drifted, and pushed ice packs from our bow and at times the ashpoles acting like runners to slip over some half hidden cake of ice that now was wirling in a jam crouding and crushing on their voige to perish in the warm waters of the South. Once in a while a deer or antelope would fall befor the never failing shot of Washington and the twang of the youth Indian bow with steel pointed arrows would furnish a beaver tail for replenish our feast, for beaver tail is good food if it cooked proper. And yet among my people I noticed a blank "now and anon" a blank turned up face to mine. Try as I could I could not find a spark of who had sown a word of evel among my people. What was it? they appeared all alike. Gloom "at times".... Their gloom was growing.*—Fred G. Bond (boatman)[11]

Fort Berthold, North Dakota

Halfway between Fort Buford and Bismarck, the Nez Perce stopped at Fort Berthold. The actual site of Fort Berthold has been covered by Lake Sakakawea behind the Garrison Dam, so nothing remains to be seen of the original location. The closest you can come to Fort Berthold is to drive toward White Shield, which is between Garrison and Parshall on the north side of the Missouri River. When North Dakota 1804 junctions with the paved road to White Shield, turn south (White Shield is north) for 6.5 miles to the end of the road. Fort Berthold was about 3 miles south-southeast of this point.

Fort Berthold was a trading post located at the Like-a-Fishhook village of the Mandan, Hidatsa, and Arikara peoples. The fifteen-hundred people here were all that remained after smallpox epidemics of the 1830s and 1840s decimated the villages of these sedentary, agricultural peoples. For mutual protection against their enemy—the much more powerful and mobile Lakota—the remnants of these tribes had banded together in this single village.

> *The night we camped at old Fort Berthold, the agency of the Arikaras, Mandans and Gros Ventres [Hidatsas] of the village, many individuals of those tribes came out to see the Nez Perces, whom they had heard of as fighting all summer, but had never seen before. At a big council held at our*

Fort Berthold as it appeared in 1871. (Photo courtesy of State Historical Society of North Dakota.)

camp, Joseph stood up in the middle of a great circle, containing about fifteen hundred Indians, whom he addressed in the sign language. There were representatives there from eight languages including mine, Nez Perce, Sioux, Cheyenne, Crow, Arikara, Mandan, Gros Ventre of the Village, and English. Joseph related his trials and tribulations entirely by gestures, without opening his mouth, and he was completely understood by all that vast concourse.—Lt. Hugh Scott

When the captives left, at least one boat was given a pesky farewell.

We pushed off safely except the small Mandan boys pelted us with rocks on our way till I got my gun. That bluff them away.

I had a terrible chill…. I left the boat in command of Washington and soon fell into the land of dreams…. And it came to me like a dream that my people believed they all died (be killed) when they arrived at…Fort A Lincoln [Bismarck]. —Fred G. Bond (boatman)[12]

No wonder they were gloomy! The Nez Perce believed they were being taken to their execution.

Bismarck and Mandan, North Dakota

Fort Abraham Lincoln is reached by taking I-94 exit 153 if you're coming from the west, or exit 155 if you're coming from the east. Once you're in downtown Mandan, turn south on North Dakota 1806, also called Sixth Avenue. As you're leaving town, note the Trail of Tears monument on the southwest corner of Sixth Avenue and Third Street. Continue for 7 miles to Fort Abraham Lincoln State Park. Proceed to the cavalry post at the south edge of the park (N46° 45.194', W100° 51.121').

Fort Abraham Lincoln

When F.J. Haynes took this photo of Fort Lincoln in June 1877, Colonel Sturgis and the Seventh Cavalry had already left for the summer to scout in central Montana. (Photo courtesy of Haynes Foundation Collection, Montana Historical Society.)

Fort Lincoln was the home of the Seventh Cavalry. The ill-fated Custer expedition had set out from here the preceding year. In May 1877, Colonel Samuel D. Sturgis had left here with his troops to scout in central Montana. The Seventh Cavalry had failed to catch the Nez Perce at the Clarks Fork, at Canyon Creek, and at the Musselshell and had given up the pursuit. Three companies of the Seventh were at the Bear Paw. And now the Seventh Cavalry was escorting the defeated Nez Perce from Fort Buford to Fort Lincoln.

422

Saturday forenoon Major Bates and two companies of the First infantry arrived in mackinaws with two hundred Nez Perces, comprising, the wounded, women and children. They were quartered at Fort A. Lincoln....

The balance of the captives, 240, with the Seventh cavalry are expected in this evening or to-morrow.—The Bismarck Tri-Weekly Tribune, November 19, 1877

By now all the flat boat fleet had reported to commanding officer of the Fort. The Main Street of Bismark of only three blocks was crouded with scouts, trappers, miners, gamblers and river men....

The little city was by now on the buzz getting ready to give a grand ball and supper in honor of Chief Joseph. The ladies at the Fort joined in. There was no printed tickets. The tickets was a $10.00 gold coin, ladies free and oppen to all. A runner came in from the West and reported that Gen. Miles and his command had camped the night befor in the Painted Woods. The NPRR agent had wired on the now single wire to Fargo N.D. 200 miles away for a full train of passenger cars to take the Nez Perce prisoners to the Indian Teritory.... The next day Washington and I had just got seated to breakfast in the restaurant when the Irish waitress and the cook rushed out of the Restaurant saying they comming they comming we joined the anxious croud and shore enough at the head of 4th Street comming down its slope was the Gen. Miles command. Early that morning they had sent a body of troops with the fort band to meet Gen. Miles. These troops had now formed a hollow squar arround the entire command protecting all flanks. The band was playing star spangle banner. Gen. Miles with Chief Joseph on is left was in the advance. The appearence of all was heart rending very sad. At the corner of Main and 4th Street the stampeed commenced. Women children and even men rushed the hollow square with all kinds of cooked food. I seen our restaurant waitress beating her way through the hollow squar with one half of a boiled ham. They beat the guards back to the center line and the wagons. The command had to halt till each Nez Perce prisoner and even the over land Guard was furnished with food of good kind. The officers of the command said nothing till all was given.... Satisfied the women and children drew back and the command passed on to the Fort. We went in to finish breakfast but Washington was too sad to eat and the Irish waitress said ["]The Divels to put those poor people under soldiers guard.["]—Fred G. Bond (boatman)[13]

423

The American public had been reading about Chief Joseph for over five months. They had heard how a small group of Native Americans had repeatedly bested the same army that had won the Civil War just twelve years earlier. They had been impressed with the honor and strength with which the Nez

This photo of downtown Bismarck was taken from the Sheridan House in 1877. (Photo courtesy of Haynes Foundation Collection, Montana Historical Society.)

Perce fought, while General Howard and his troops came across in the newspapers as a group of tired and incapable bunglers. No doubt about it, the sentiment of the American public was for the underdog, and the underdog Nez Perce were just about to encounter the American public.

The following invitation was issued this morning to Chief Joseph:

Bismarck, D.T., Nov. 21, 1877

To Joseph, Head Chief of Nez Perces.

Sir: Desiring to show you our kind feelings and the admiration we have for your bravery and humanity, as exhibited in your recent conflict with the forces of the United States, we most cordially invite you to dine with us at the Sheridan House, in this city. The dinner is to given at 1 1/2 P.M. to-day.

Respectfully,

Geo. W. Sweet, H .R. Porter, Wm. A. Bentley

Com.

At the Sheridan House the above invitation was interpreted to Joseph, Yellow Bull, Shaved Head [Husishusis Kute], and Yellow Wolf. They all accepted it and said they were glad to see the good feeling upon the part of the white people.

Joseph, and the other chiefs named, about twelve o'clock, held a reception in the Sheridan Parlors, and was presented to a number of the ladies of the house. They were told that this respect was on account of their humanity to our soldier prisoners.—Bismarck Tri-Weekly Tribune, November 21, 1877

424

A few hours after being told how generous his captors were, Chief Joseph learned of yet another broken promise.

Joseph, on Wednesday evening in his tepee down in the wood, was told by interpreter Chapman…that another movement had been ordered by the government. Joseph's head dropped and he murmured in his mother tongue, "When will those white chiefs begin to tell the truth?"—Bismarck Tri-Weekly Tribune, November 23, 1877

On November 23, a train pulled out of Bismarck headed east to St. Paul and then south for Fort Leavenworth.

And Chief Joseph stood on the rear platform of the train to wave good bye.—Fred G. Bond (boatman)[14]

Fort Leavenworth, Kansas

In Leavenworth, Kansas, turn off of Metropolitan Avenue, which is US 73 and Kansas 7, north into Fort Leavenworth. You will be stopped for a security search at the information booth in 0.1 mile. Ask for a map while you are there.

Tourism

The Nez Perce arrived at Fort Leavenworth on November 27, 1877. They numbered 431 persons: 79 men, 178 women, and 174 children. As soon as they arrived, tourists thronged to see them.

The number of people who visited the camp during the day did not fall short of 5,000.—The Leavenworth Daily Times, December 11, 1877

Since Joseph was brought to Fort Leavenworth last November it is estimated that at least one hundred thousand people have looked upon his dusky face.… Joseph took all this kindly, in fact seemed to enjoy being looked at being made a hero of, while his warriors, and the squaws and papooses made bushels of nickels by selling moccasins, bows and arrows and other Indian trinkets dear to the civilized heart.—The Leavenworth Daily Times, July 21, 1878

425

Proceed north on Grant Avenue for 1.8 miles. After passing a statue of General Grant, turn east on Riverside Avenue as it circles around. In 0.2 mile, turn east on Chief Joseph Loop and cross the railroad tracks. Just before the Y, turn south on a one-lane dirt road for 1.5 miles. In 1877, the cottonwoods north of the road in 0.6 mile were an island in the Missouri River. Continue circling the airfield. 0.9 more mile will bring you to the approximate location of the old racetrack where the Nez Perce camped west of the road, just before a flat place on the east side of the road.

Old Racetrack

Chief Joseph was found to be snugly quartered in the rear of a floored hospital tent surrounded by a number of his chiefs and reclining gracefully on a huge couch made of furs of wild animals. His appearance was much more attractive than when he was seen getting off the train Monday evening.... Another tent near by was occupied by the remainder of the wounded, who seemed to bear their afflictions quietly, all having a pleasant smile of welcome for any visitor. The two tents referred to were situated at some distance from the camp, which consisted of over a hundred tents arranged in convenient positions inside the circle of the race- track, but under the eye of the guard, who is constantly on duty in the place known as "the Judges' stand." Near the guard's beat are the tents occupied by the officers and soldiers who are detailed every day from the garrison to guard the prisoners.

A new tent has been erected for the exclusive use of Chief Joseph, near the officers' tent. It is being made better than the others and will be floored and a stove put in. The remainder of the occupants of the camp, consisting of a few men and about 200 women, were a picture worth remembering. Five car-loads of "Tepees" and other traps having arrived and being hauled in wagons were being hastily unloaded and each package taken care of by the women, some of whom carried their papooses on their backs and at the same time lugged away bundles that would make a stout white man tremble....

Many of the large number of children belonging to the party, who were big enough, were engaged in frolicking around among the trees while their mothers were busy at work.—The Leavenworth Daily Times, November 29, 1877

426

Near each lodge was stacked a huge pile of wood, some of the "stacks" being covered, to keep them dry.

...The prisoners have everything they need.—The Leavenworth Daily Times, December 11, 1877

The Nez Perce captives are fed on fresh beef, pickled pork, bread and beans, as they desire. One of the chiefs issues the rations every day.—The Leavenworth Daily Times, December 12, 1877

Mosquito season began in May, when the incidence of malaria, cholera, and yellow fever increased.

I cannot tell how much my heart suffered for my people while at Leavenworth. The Great Spirit Chief who rules above seemed to be looking some other way, and did not see what was being done to my people.—Chief Joseph

Follow the road on top of the levee for another 1.4 miles, then follow it as it turns south for 0.8 mile to a stop sign. Turn west across the railroad tracks for one block to the intersection of Sheridan Drive and USDB Road. Near the "Welcome to Sherman Army Airfield" sign, in a small grove of pines, stands a plaque commemorating the Nez Perce imprisonment at Fort Leavenworth and a sign noting Fort Leavenworth as part of the Nez Perce National Historic Trail.

Turn around and proceed east for 1 block, then turn south on Chief Joseph Loop for 0.8 mile. Turn northwest on Riverside Avenue for 0.3 mile. At the top of the loop, turn west on Kearney for 1 block and then north on Sumner Place. Sumner encircles the old parade grounds. The area here, which has several historic buildings, was the center of the post in its early days where the soldiers and their families lived.

Parade Grounds

Quite a large number of squaws and papooses were at the post yesterday, the latter frolicking on the parade ground and having a good time generally.—The Leavenworth Daily Times, June 2, 1878

Turn south on McClellan for 1 block, then east on Kearney for 2 blocks. Having completed the circle, head south on Grant Avenue back to US 73 and Kansas 7.

For the Adventurous Traveler

Baxter Springs, Kansas, to Tonkawa, Oklahoma

From US Alternate 69 in downtown Baxter Springs, turn west on 12th Street, US 166. In 0.4 mile, just before the railroad tracks, turn north on Ottawa Street for 2 blocks.

Baxter Springs, Kansas

During the hot days (July, 1878) we received notice that we were to be moved farther away from our own country. We were not asked if we were willing to go. We were ordered to get into the railroad-cars. Three of my people died on the way to Baxter Springs. It was worse to die there than to die fighting in the mountains.—Chief Joseph

The Nez Perce were shipped by train from Fort Leavenworth to Baxter Springs, Kansas, the southeastern-most town in the state. The train spur to Baxter Springs ended a block or two south of here because no trains were allowed to enter Indian Territory (Oklahoma). The train depot and freight yards were located west of Ottawa Street.

One train a day chugged into Baxter Springs. On July 31, 1878, it carried the Chief Joseph band of Nez Perce.

Train Depot

The Nez Perces lost five or six children on account of the heat in coming down from Leavenworth. They were buried near the depot, but not deep enough. They were rooted out and ate up by the hogs.—Columbus, Kansas, *Border Star,* August 23, 1878

Turn east on 10th Street for 0.4 mile. Return to US Alternate 69. Turn south for 6.1 miles to Quapaw.

Quapaw, Oklahoma

428

From Baxter Springs, the Nez Perce were moved by wagon across the border into Oklahoma to the Quapaw Agency, where they stayed for eleven months.

Today this northeastern-most county of Oklahoma is named Ottawa County. In 1878, this little area of 470 square miles was already crowded with Native

Americans who had been relocated to Kansas or Arkansas and then relocated again to Indian Territory: Miamis from Michigan, Ohio, and Indiana; Quapaws and Peorias from Illinois; Ottawas and Wyandots from Michigan; Senecas from New York; Shawnees from Ohio; Cherokees from the Carolinas and Tennessee; the recently arrived Modocs from southwestern Oregon; and Poncas from Nebraska. Anyplace the Nez Perce camped was bound to be on someone else's land. They first camped on the border of Modoc/Shawnee land, then moved a few miles away onto Peoria land. Peorians complained they were never paid for their land. No one was happy.

The Nez Perce first camped near the Modocs. To see a bit of the 6-square-mile Modoc reservation, follow Alternate US 69 south out of Quapaw for 0.3 mile. At the junction with Oklahoma 137, bear south for 5.2 miles. At the junction with Oklahoma 10, turn east for 5.1 miles, then continue due east on 10C for 1.9 miles. Turn south on S679 Road with a sign pointing to the Modoc cemetery, which is 0.4 mile away.

Modoc Cemetery

Although the Modocs were from Oregon, their home was in southwestern Oregon/northern California, so they did not have anything culturally in common with the Joseph band of northeastern Oregon. The Modoc camp was just under a mile from the cemetery.

Continue south past the cemetery for 1.7 miles. The Modoc Reservation was east of the road and the Shawnee reservation west of the road. Turn east on E120 Road. Now the Modoc Reservation was north of the road and the Shawnee south of the road. In 0.3 mile, as you cross Lost Creek, notice the flat area north of the road which would have made a good, though small and overtaxed, campsite for 450 people.

Lost Creek

Quapaw Agency
Indian Territory

429

We found the Nez Perces in a deplorable condition. Some fifty were sick, most with fever & ague and no medicine. ...The agent was requested to telegraph immediately for a supply of quinine which is expected tonight.

We visited their encampment which is pleasantly located in a grove by a running stream, but their filthy habits & generally unsettled condition render them a prey to disease. Besides, we found them discontented and evidently expecting any day to receive permission to return to Idaho.—William Stickney, August 13, 1878

Nearly all the excursionists to this country take in the Nez Perce and Modoc camps as objects of interest, taking care always to make inquiry as to the safety of their scalps before venturing over the territorial line.—Baxter Times, October 17, 1878

Continue east for 0.6 mile. Turn north on S689 Road.

Modoc Valley

As you descend into the Modoc Valley, imagine horse races on Sundays. The Quaker agent Hiram Jones punished the Nez Perce for drinking, gambling, and horse racing by withholding their rations.

The quantity of variety of the Official crookedness of Agt. Jones can only be measured by the length & breadth of his opportunities. He stands not only charged but convicted of stealing everything that he could lay his hands on.—H. H. Gregg, Seneca, Missouri, September 13, 1878

After a protracted letter-writing campaign by Gregg and by Ad Chapman, interpreter, Jones was released from duty in April 1879.

At the junction with E100 Road (10C) in 1.9 miles, turn west to complete your circumnavigation of the Modoc Reservation in 1.0 mile.

After one month on the too-small Modoc Reservation, the Nez Perce moved onto Peoria land. Continue west on E100 Road (10C) for 2.8 miles. Turn north on S650 Road for 2.7 miles to where the road bridges Warren Branch. In this abundant oak country along Warren Branch, the Nez Perce lived during the winter of 1878–79.

At the T in 1.2 miles, turn west on E69 Road for 0.3 mile. Turn north on S652 Road for 0.7 mile. Turn west on E60 Road for 3.0 miles and cross Interstate 44, Spring River at the Devil's Promenade Bridge and the Quapaw Tribal Headquarters. Turn east on E50 Road for 0.7 mile. Turn north on S630 Road for 0.9 mile. Then turn east on E40 Road for 1.0 mile to Bicentennial State Park. An interpretive sign here marks this site as part of the Nez Perce (Nee-Me-Poo) National Historic Trail.

Spring River

In late April 1879, after Indian agent Jones had been dismissed, and while no one was looking, the Nez Perce unexpectedly changed campsites.

> *The Nez Perce Indians having moved to the west bank of Spring River they are now located about 10 miles south of town. A number of them come to town almost every day. Last Saturday they came in force and made sundry little purchases.—Baxter Times, April 24, 1879*

> After looking around the picnic area and Spring River, return to the junction of E40 Road and S630. Turn north on S630 Road for 2.0 miles. Turn west on E20 Road for 5.0 miles into Picher. Turn north on US 69 for 3.0 miles. Turn west on US 166.

US 166

In June 1879 the Nez Perce were moved to near Ponca City, Oklahoma, along a route that is taken by US 166 through southern Kansas today. Traveling by wagon, the trip took nine days, with overnights on Tar Creek near Picher, Chetopa, Coffeyville, Sedan, Cedarvale, Dexter, and Arkansas City.

Arkansas City

Skipping to the end of the exile in Oklahoma, the Nez Perce departed from Arkansas City.

> *The promise of the Indian Department to Chief Joseph and his band of Nez Perce, so long unfulfilled, of returning them to their former home in Idaho has at length been redeemed, and on Friday the rejoicing redskins started off to the number of 268 souls....*

> *...Some few women with their young children rode; but most of the tribe tramped through the deep mud, and arrived in town late the same night or early the following morning.*

> *Here they spent the early forenoon, disposing of the few ponies they had brought along, and making necessary purchases. By ten o'clock they were mustered at the depot, where a special train of seven emigrant cars...was waiting to receive them. Some little trouble was caused by the children from the Chilocco School...being refused transportation by the special agent.... But Dr. Minthorn's deputy...who had the children in custody urged upon Dr. Faulkner [the chaperone] the moral obligation that rested upon him to take them....*

Only 124 of the band go to [Lapwai], the remainder accompany Chief Joseph to Eastern Washington.—Arkansas City Traveller, May 27, 1885

In Arkansas City, take US 77 south toward Ponca City, Oklahoma.

At the junction with US 60 and US 177, turn west for 12.1 miles to the Business 60 exit to Tonkawa. Turn south across the overpass, then head west on US 60 for 0.9 mile.

Chief Joseph Roadside Historical Marker

The monument here commemorates the six years of Nez Perce exile in this area.

Proceed east on US 60 for 0.1 mile. Turn south on Allen Drive for 0.9 mile to the Nez Perce Burial Ground. Continue south, passing Fort Oakland, for 1.6 miles.

Fort Oakland

At the hour for services (10:30 a.m.) the house [church] was filled to overflowing. The seats were occupied and a number squatted on the floor....

Let us look at them for a moment. Here on a front seat is Chief Joseph, the Head chief of this band. He believes the great Spirit created him chief. He is not yet converted, and at our former visit could not be induced to enter the church, but today he is here.... He has just donned citizens' clothes, is not at ease in the suit, yet is proud of it.

Near the door stands Tom Hill,...Lieut. of police.... In him is embodied firmness and honesty, a terror to all evil doers on the reservation.

On the left are more of their prominent men: Bald Head, Three Eagles, Jim Horn, Yellow Bull, Yellow Bear, etc. Most of these have been converted....

Every convert has put on the white man's clothes.... Some few are still robed in the blanket. The women are dressed very much alike; about the only difference is in the color, but red predominates. Their dresses are neat and becoming, and all of the same style. Each one of them has a shawl which covers her from the shoulders to the feet, and their head dress in most cases is a silk handkerchief tied tightly over the head....

Nearly all, male and female, wore moccasins, most of them ornamented with bead work, a few with silk. The little boys and girls are dressed similar to their seniors, and are squatted on the floor close in front of the preacher's stand. There were quite a number of infants in the congregation, some bound to a board, and could be passed around without any danger to their spines....

After the sermon, twenty-two presented themselves for admission and baptism....

Rev. Mr. Fleming was about to administer the baptismal ordinance, when Tom Hill...stepped forward and...made a wonderful confession of what he had been during his savage life. He said he thought then that the braver he was and the more he could do to overcome his enemies, the better he was, but now his heart was changed and he wanted to live at peace with all men. He hoped his sins were pardoned, and that he would be saved through Christ. This is but an outline of his words. He was then baptized....

Some of the others also made a public confession. Bald Head spoke of how ignorant and wicked he had been; of how he had worshipped spirits among the mountains of Idaho, and how he had been brought from darkness into the light of the Gospel, and now how he had learned of the true Spirit and of the Savior Jesus Christ....

Jim Horn, Jim Natt, and Red Wolf, after being duly elected, were ordained Ruling Elders, and the Presbyterian Church of Oakland, Indian Territory, regularly constituted with ninety-three members....

This people are already letting their light shine. When visitors come from other tribes, instead of entertaining them with a dance as formerly, they entertain them with a prayer meeting.—Arkansas City Traveler, February 9, 1881

At the T, turn east on E250 Road. In about 1.5 miles, after bending south, the road leads between the Chikaskia immediately to the east and the Salt Fork, just west of the road.

Confluence of Chikaskia River and Salt Fork of the Arkansas River

The Nez Perce located their camp at the confluence of the Chikaskia River and Salt Fork of Arkansas on the west bank of Chikaskia, two miles from the junction with Salt Fork.

The Ponca agent didn't even know they were coming and had no supplies, food, or quinine for them.

433

Only the climate killed many of us. All the newborn babies died, and many of the old people too. It was the climate. Everything so different from our old

homes. No mountains, no springs, no clear running rivers. We called where
we were held Eeikish Pah [Hot Place]. All the time, night and day, we
suffered from the climate.—Yellow Wolf[15]

Annual reports from the Oakland agents—a different man every year—
repeated the same themes: the Nez Perce were melancholy and homesick, and
there were fewer of them each year.

The Nez Perces located at Oakland comprise three hundred and twenty eight
souls and I am sorry to be compelled to report that there has been a large
amount of sickness and many deaths among them during the last year. This
arises from the fact that they have not become acclimated, and are to a
great extent compelled to live in teepees, the cloth of which has become so
rotten from long wear and the effects of the weather as to be no longer
capable of keeping out the rain, by which they were soaked during the last
spring. The tribe, unless something is done for them, will soon become
extinct.—Thomas J. Jordan (Oakland Agent), September 6, 1881

The ever-busy women continued to provide for their families as best they
could.

The Nez Perce Indians have almost stopped the glove trade for our
merchants, by the gloves of their own make. During the past year they have
disposed of more than one thousand pair of gloves, besides moccasins and
numerous other Indian trinkets.—Arkansas City Traveler, October 5, 1881

They are extremely anxious to return to their own country. They regard
themselves as exiles. The climate does not seem to agree with them; many of
them have died; and there is a tinge of melancholy in their bearing and
conversation that is truly pathetic.—John W. Scott (Oakland Agent),
August 15, 1884

> Continue south for 0.7 mile to the T and turn around. Retrace your route to
> US 60.

Wallula Junction, Washington

The town of Wallula, at the junction of the Walla Walla and Columbia rivers,
was built on the remains of old Fort Walla Walla, which was built on top of
even-older Fort Nez Perces. All that history now lies under Lake Wallula, which
was impounded by the McNary Dam in 1953 when the town moved uphill to
Wallula Junction.

Eight years after the Nez Perce had fled their homeland, they were given permission to return home. On May 22, 1885, the Nez Perce entrained at Arkansas City, Kansas. Traveling through Denver, Cheyenne, and Pocatello, the group of 268 people arrived at Wallula Junction on the Columbia River in eastern Washington, about twenty-nine miles west of Walla Walla.

> *When we reached Wallula, the interpreter asked us, "Where do you want to go? Lapwai and be Christian, or Colville and just be yourself?"* —Yellow Wolf[16]

One hundred eighteen Nez Perce opted to go home to Idaho to be with families and friends on the reservation there. Husishusis Kute (Bald Head) acted as the chief for this group. Joseph, however, was not given a choice. Sentiment in Idaho was still strongly against him, indictments were still out on him, and it was feared that he would be killed if he lived in Idaho. So Chief Joseph was banished to the Colville Reservation in north-central Washington. One hundred forty-nine people chose to retain their traditional ways and went with Chief Joseph.

Just thirty years earlier, when Joseph was fifteen, the strong and wealthy tribe of Nez Perce and a few thousand of their cultural cousins had arrived here at Wallula, then called old Fort Walla Walla, to make their first treaty with the Americans. Joseph and his people had made a complete circle; in 1855 they had been many and rich, in 1885 they were few and poor.

435

Gustavus Sohon drew this picture of the Nez Perce, Cayuse, Palouse, Walla Walla, Umatilla, and Yakama arriving at the Walla Walla Treaty Council in May 1855. (Photo courtesy of Washington State Historical Society.)

Fort Spokane, Washington

From Davenport, Washington, on US 2, drive 22.5 miles north on Washington highway 25. Fort Spokane is open from mid-June to Labor Day.

Fort Spokane is located on Lake Roosevelt, at the confluence of the Spokane River with the Columbia River. The fort was opened in 1880 to buffer settlers from the Indians.

The Chief Joseph band stayed here from May until December 1885, when they finally moved to Nespelem.

> *In spite of all protests, against the wishes of the people of eastern Washington and northern Idaho, in the face of the dire threats of vengeance that have been so frequently and openly expressed..., the government insists upon returning the remnant of the Nez Perce Indians to this country.... This action is a serious mistake and may result in the most serious consequences .... The government has done a cruel and unwise thing.... It is too late now to hope for redress through the hands of a government that should be ever ready to protect its people against a foreign foe or savage enemies.... There will be a force of soldiers on hand to protect the Indians.—Spokane Evening Review, May 26, 1885*

Fort Spokane. (Photo courtesy of University of Washington.)

Nez Perce Encampment at Nespelem, c. 1903. (Photo courtesy of Nez Perce National Historical Park.)

437

Chief Joseph's winter camp at Nespelem using longhouses and tipis, c. 1901. (Photo courtesy of Nez Perce National Historical Park.)

I visited Fort Spokane, where these Indians [the Nez Perce] were located, and found the military were subsisting them. The amount of supplies I had...was not sufficient to issue them one-fourth rations.... After considerable writing and telegraphing to the Department as to the condition of these Indians, I received authority to issue half rations.... when some months later I was permitted to contract for supplies to issue to these Indians full rations.— Benjamin P. Moore (agent, Colville Indian Agency)

Coulee Dam, Washington

> Just after crossing the bridge below Grand Coulee Dam, do not turn north on state road 155 but continue driving east for two blocks, turn north for one block, then turn east to the Colville Confederated Tribes Museum.
>
> After visiting the museum, return to Washington 155 and proceed north for 16 miles to Nespelem.

Nespelem, Washington

Nespelem is a tiny town on the Colville Reservation where the Nez Perce settled in 1886.

> On state road 155, halfway between mile markers 44 and 45, just beside the turnoff to Republic and Keller, a Heritage Marker tells the story of Chief Joseph.
>
> From the Heritage sign, head east on the road to Republic and Keller (D Street).

Encirclement Camp

The camp shown in the photo circled the area now bounded by C and D streets between 8th and 9th streets.

Nez Perce Cemetery

The Nez Perce National Historic Trail is a trail of graves. It began, symbolically, at the grave of Chief Old Joseph at Wallowa Lake and it ends at the Nez Perce Cemetery in Nespelem. There lie the bones of the survivors of this tragedy.

One obelisk stands in this cemetery and marks the grave of Chief Joseph. Although people have left items of remembrance here, the Nez Perce themselves do not want to call the spirits back. Please honor both the dead and living children and grandchildren of these people by not visiting and not walking on these marked and unmarked graves.

For Further Reading

Flatboating on the Yellowstone, by Fred G. Bond, tells the story of taking the Nez Perce from Miles City to Bismarck. Although the book was written forty-five years after the fact, Bond's frontier flavor adds zest to his poignant tale.

With One Sky Above Us: Life on an Indian Reservation at the Turn of the Century, by Mick Gidley, presents many photos by Dr. Edward Latham, who was the Agency Physician on the Colville Reservation from 1890 to 1910.

Lt. C.E.S. Wood, who recorded Chief Joseph's surrender speech at Bear Paw, sent his twelve-year-old son to live with Chief Joseph for eight months in 1892. *Days with Chief Joseph*, by Erskine Wood, is the diary of three of those months.

Epilog

Thus ends the heart-rending story of the Nez Perce flight and their exile in Oklahoma and Canada. An honorable people, fighting for a just cause, lost. But their loss does not feel like our gain. The unfairness of this terrible wrong sits uneasily with our American sense of justice. We find little to be proud of in this account of our Euro-American legacy, but much to admire in that of the Native American.

If we read the story again, and perhaps yet again, we search for some understanding, some clue that will make it all make sense. We want so much for the underdog Nez Perce to win their independence. Yet they never do.

The story leaves us stranded. There's nothing we can do about that long-passed situation. Guilt over those actions of our great-great-grandfathers feels distant and inappropriate; after all, *we* didn't cause either the problem or the bitter solution. We are left with the cold comfort of facts.

Some of us would prefer not to think any further about the wrongs perpetrated back then. Others of us fantasize about how it might have happened differently if we had been alive in 1877. We imagine what we might have done in a particular situation; we hope we would have acted differently.

Yet, do we, more than 125 years later, even now comprehend this story? When our government today deals with other nations, does it avoid the pitfalls that it made with the Nez Perce? As we look at current U.S. policies toward minorities in this country and developing countries around the world, we might well wonder whether our country has learned from its past. As we review the turning points that led up to the United States-Nez Perce War, we see that the U.S. makes similar choices at similar decision points in its relationships with other nations today. The same kinds of injustices perpetrated against the Nez Perce Nation continue to be committed by the United States.

Our hearts ache when we read the century-old Nez Perce story. But, in comparable modern-day situations, many of us support our government when its policies are parallel to those that generated the United States-Nez Perce War.

The news we hear on television or radio or read in the newspaper provokes strong feelings.

> *Too much praise cannot be placed to the credit of Gen. Miles and the officers and men who crushed out the power of the Nez Perces to do evil.—Bozeman Times,* November 8, 1877

For the words "Gen. Miles" substitute our current president, and for the words "Nez Perce" substitute "Middle East," "North Korea," or "terrorists." Today the media still demonize the opposition and declares government actions to be patriotic. Miles and Howard and Gibbon were patriotic; do we admire them?

If we look into the background of the conflicts of the 21st century, we find the same ingredients that were listed in the "Recipe for War," Chapter 2.

The first major turning point in Nez Perce-United States relations was the 1855 Treaty. Until the 1850s, the Nez Perce Nation and the United States existed as two sovereign nations. But the Nez Perce Treaty, along with its kindred 370 other Indian treaties, was made with a view to extinguishing Native American title to their land—a necessary precursor to settling and exploiting the very land we all occupy today. By participating in the treaty process, the Nez Perce, and Native Americans across the continent, were asked to view land as a commodity to be bought and sold—a view essentially at odds with their belief about and experience of the earth as mother. After all, how can anyone sell his or her mother?

The assumption that other nations see things the way we do or that the American approach is the only point of view is really an attitude of cultural superiority. Since the powerful United States is seldom on the butt end of someone else's cultural supremacy, it's a particularly difficult quality to be aware of. We don't really know what it's like to be in the position of the Nez Perce, negotiating with such a powerful country that it doesn't have to understand or respect our beliefs and laws. We don't know what it's like to have someone else's laws forced on us and our own legal system made irrelevant.

During the U.S.-Nez Perce treaty negotiations in 1855, the treaty negotiators designated a head chief, even though the Nez Perce themselves recognized no head chief. A president or head chief makes perfect sense in a federalist context. But the bands of Nez Perce were what might be called the ultimate states-righters. Each band had its chief, and the chiefs and bands were not required to agree among themselves. Designating a head chief made about as much sense as it would make to us to designate one governor to head all the states. The U.S. pulled a coup by appointing the head chief of another nation. Interference with the governments of other nations did not stop with the appointment of a Nez Perce head chief. The coups have continued as the U.S. still intervenes in foreign governments today.

This intrusion onto another nation's sovereignty is called imperialism. A century or two ago, imperialism was justified on the grounds that Native Americans were uncivilized savages who did not use their land anyway. Today, "terrorist" inspires as strong a gut reaction in us as the term "heathen savage" did in our ancestors. Just as the American government of the 19th century made the country safe for "civilized" people by eradicating or fencing in the

441

land's original keepers, today the U.S. takes on the responsibility for making the world safe by trying to crush terrorists. The rationale has been modernized, but the underlying intent remains the same. The United States has continued to believe its manifest destiny is the right to intervene in the governing of other nations.

Another ingredient in the Nez Perce recipe was greed itself. Gold was discovered in Nez Perce territory, and miners moved into the Nez Perce Nation without regard to treaty stipulations. The corollary to the discovery of mineral wealth was that a new treaty had to be drawn up to legalize the land grab that was in fact going on. The American viewpoint is that exploitation of land for economic benefit takes precedence over other viewpoints that emphasize land as the focus of self-determination, land as sacred, land as home, land as a base for tribal/communal life styles. Today, for instance, the "black gold" of the Arctic National Wildlife Refuge threatens to make a "refuge" into an environmental refugee.

"War is made to take something not your own," said Yellow Wolf, whose home, land, food supplies, cattle, horses, and other possessions all "disappeared" during the conflict. Behind the military were civilians cashing in on Nez Perce possessions and gaining stock. The Nez Perce War cost the U.S. government over $900,000.

During the two decades between the first treaty in 1855 and the war in 1877, when whites and Nez Perce lived together on the same land, white settlers killed over thirty Nez Perce. In not a single instance were the perpetrators punished; if brought to trial they were acquitted. Yet the war was ignited when warriors took their revenge by killing four white men, at least one of whom was an unpunished murderer. The higher value placed on white lives is a racial ethnocentrism that continues today.

About equal numbers of Nez Perce and whites were killed in the actual conflict. The sorrow of the Nez Perce story is that three-hundred more people, including all the newborn children, died during the exile. This is the price they paid for seeking retribution by killing fourteen Idaho citizens. This twenty-to-one ratio still applies today. Compare the number of Americans killed on September 11, 2001, to the number of Afghanis killed. Or the number of American troop casualties in Iraq to the number of Iraq civilians killed.

442   During the year preceding the war (1876), several councils were held between the nontreaty Nez Perce and government representatives. Although the whites believed they were seeking a peaceful solution, the Nez Perce felt provoked. Their concerns were never addressed, and the whites kept using threats. Finally, General Howard delivered an ultimatum—to move onto the reservation within thirty days—which was very difficult to meet. The effect of this council process was to force the Nez Perce into a nearly untenable position. And indeed, under the pressure, three Nez Perce warriors sought revenge for previous wrongs done to them.

Even by our own American rules of the game, we cannot generally justify an intrusion into another nation until it has resisted us. The strategem of forcing countries into a tight political corner generally leaves them with one response: expressing their patriotism by defying the U.S. Today, Third World nations, faced with economic domination by multinational corporations, may retreat to a position of fundamentalism just to escape U.S. influence. Once the offending country has declared its determination to govern itself without U.S. "assistance," the U.S. then feels very justified in sending arms and economic aid to that country's enemies or neighbors. The result is to attempt to subvert a country's expression of nationalism.

Taking the offensive, as Howard's troops did when they attacked the Looking Glass band on Clear Creek, has the effect of radicalizing people who are otherwise trying to keep the peace. As a result of being attacked, the Looking Glass band joined the nontreaty flight. Recipients of attacks by the U.S. are driven to radical responses.

While suffering our share of national shortcomings, our country's greatest strength is the belief in personal liberty. The rights of the individual is a truly American concept, an idea borrowed by the founding fathers of the United States from the Americans native to this continent. Learning to actually live this concept is the challenge we—personally and nationally— still face. Do we have the courage to allow individual nations to express their own self-determination?

If we choose to honor the memory of the valiant Nez Perce, if we are to redeem our own variegated history and perhaps mitigate our own self-created karma, let our country not waste the lessons given to us by the Nez Perce. A century later, we do not feel proud of the cultural superiority and racial ethnocentrism our grandfathers perpetrated on the Nez Perce, we do not feel proud of our grandfathers' greed or imperialism. May our personal actions and those of our nation be those that our grandchildren can be proud of.

Chief Joseph summed it up well. Although referring to his own race, his comments can be applied to Africans, Asians, Latins, Arabs, and indigenous peoples the world over.

443

> *Whenever the white man treats the Indian as they treat each other, then we shall have no more wars. We shall be all alike—brothers of one father and*

one mother, with one sky above us and one country around us, and one government for us all. Then the Great Spirit Chief who rules above will smile upon this land, and send rain to wash out the bloody spots made by brothers' hands upon the face of the earth. For this time the Indian race are waiting and praying. I hope that no more groans of wounded men and women will ever go to the ear of the Great Spirit Chief above, and that all people may be one people.—Chief Joseph

Sources of Maps

GPS map software (whether or not you have a GPS device) is a great way to view maps on a laptop or personal computer.

State, Provincial, and County

The *Atlas and Gazetteer* for Oregon, Washington, Idaho, Montana, or Wyoming can be found in many outdoor stores or ordered from www.delorme.com.

Idaho Division of Tourism Development
700 West State Street
P.O. Box 83720
Boise, ID 83720-0093
208-334-2470
1-800-VISITID (800-847-4743)
www.visitid.org
info@tourism.idaho.gov

Kansas Travel & Tourism
1000 S.W. Jackson Street, Suite 100
Topeka, KS 66612-1354
785-296-3481
1-800-2KANSAS
www.travelks.com
travtour@kansascommerce.com

Montana Department of Commerce
301 South Park Avenue
P.O. Box 200533
Helena, MT 59620-0533
406-841-2870
1-800-VISITMT (800-847-4868)
visitmt.com

North Dakota Tourism Division
Century Center
1600 E. Century Ave. Suite 2
P.O. Box 2057
Bismarck, ND 58503-2057
701-328-2525
800-HELLO-ND (800-435-5663)
www.ndtourism.com
tourism@state.nd.us

McLean County (south third)
North Dakota State Highway Department
600 E. Boulevard Avenue
Bismarck, ND 58505-0700
701-224-3534

Fort Buford
Fort Buford State Historic Site
15349 39th Lane, NW
Williston, ND 58801
701-572-9034

Oklahoma Tourism and Recreation Department
Travel & Tourism Division
120 N. Robinson, 6th floor
P.O. Box 52002
Oklahoma City, OK 73152-2002
405-230-8400
1-800-652-6552
www.travelok.com
information@TravelOK.com

Oregon Tourism Commission
775 Summer St. NE
Salem, OR 97301-1282
503-986-0000
1-800-547-7842
www.traveloregon.com
info@traveloregon.com

Tourism **Saskatchewan**
1922 Park Street
Regina, SK S4N 7M4
CANADA
306-787-9600
1-877-2ESCAPE (877-2273)
www.sasktourism.com

Washington State Department of Trade and Economic Development, Tourism Division
P.O. Box 42525
Olympia, WA 98504-2525
1-800-544-1800
www.experiencewashington.com
tourism@cted.wa.gov

445

Asotin County
Clarkston Chamber of Commerce
502 Bridge Street Clarkston, WA 99403
509-758-7712
800-933-2128

Wyoming Travel & Tourism
I-25 at College Drive
Cheyenne, WY 82002
307-777-7777
1-800-225-5996
www.wyomingtourism.org

Bureau of Land Management

Idaho State Office
1387 South Vinnell Way
Boise, ID 83709
208-373-4000
www.id.blm.gov
    Map to Request: Orofino (Office:
    Cottonwood, 208-962-3245)

Montana State Office
5001 Southgate Drive
Billings, MT 59101
406-896-5000
www.mt.blm.gov
    Maps to Request: Billings, Roundup,
    Harlowton, Big Snowy Mountains,
    Lewistown, Winifred, Rocky Boy,
    Zortman, Dodson, Upper Missouri
    National Wild & Scenic River (maps
    3 & 4)

District Offices:
Dillon, 406-683-2337
Fort Benton, 406-622-3839
Havre, 406-265-5891
Lewistown, 406-538-7461
Miles City, 406-232-4333

National Forests

Forest Service maps can be ordered
on-line at:
    www.fs.fed.us
    store.usgs.gov
    www.rockymtnmaps.com

**Beaverhead-Deerlodge National
Forest**
420 Barrett Street
Dillon, MT 59725
406-683-3900
www.fs.fed.us/r1/b-d

Bitterroot National Forest
1801 North First Street
Hamilton, MT 59840
406-363-7100
www.fs.fed.us/r1/bitterroot

    Ranger District Offices:
    Darby, 406-821-3913
    Stevensville, 406-777-5461
    Sula, 406-821-3201

Caribou-Targhee National Forest
499 North 2400 East
St. Anthony, ID 83445
208-624-3151
www.fs.fed.us/r4/caribou-targhee

    Ranger District Offices:
    Dubois, 208-374-5422
    Island Park, 208-558-7301

Clearwater National Forest
12730 Highway 12
Orofino, ID 83544
208-476-4541
www.fs.fed.us/r1/clearwater

    Ranger District Offices:
    Kamiah, 208-935-2513
    Kooskia, 208-926-4274
    Powell, 208-942-3311

Gallatin National Forest
Box 130
Federal Building
Bozeman, MT 59715
406-587-6701
www.fs.fed.us/r1/gallatin

    Ranger District Offices:
    West Yellowstone, 406-823-6961

Lolo National Forest
Building 24
Fort Missoula
Missoula, MT 59801
406-329-3750
www.fs.fed.us/r1/lolo

Nez Perce National Forest
Route 2, Box 475
Grangeville, ID 83530
208-983-1950
www.fs.fed.us/r1/nezperce

Ranger Districts:
Slate Creek, 208-839-2730

Salmon-Challis National Forest
50 Highway 93 North
Salmon, ID 83467
208-756-5100
www.fs.fed.us/r4/sc

Ranger District Offices:
Leadore, 208-768-2500

Shoshone National Forest
808 Meadow Lane
Cody, WY 82414
307-578-1200
www.fs.fed.us/r2/shoshone

Wallowa-Whitman National Forest
P.O. Box 907
1550 Dewey Avenue
Baker, OR 97814
503-523-6391
www.fs.fed.us/r6/w-w

Ranger District Offices:
La Grande, 541-963-7186
Wallowa Valley, 541- 426-4978

Other Very Useful Maps

Hells Canyon National Recreation Area
88401 Hwy. 82
Enterprise, OR 97828
541-426-4978
Clarkston, WA
509-758-0616
www.fs.fed.us/hellscanyon

Yellowstone National Park
P.O. Box 168
Yellowstone National Park, WY 82190
307-344-7381
www.nps.gov/yell

USGS topographical maps can be downloaded from www.topozone.com

Other Resources

Following the Nez Perce Trail: A Guide to the Nee-Me-Poo National Historic Trail with Eye-witness Accounts
www.nezpercetrail-guide.com

Nez Perce (Nee-Me-Poo) National Historic Trail
www.fs.fed.us/npnht

Nez Perce Trail Foundation
www.nezpercetrail.net

Nez Perce National Historical Park
39063 US Highway 95
Spalding, ID 83540-9715
208-843-2261
www.nps.gov/nepe

Big Hole National Battlefield
P.O. Box 237
Wisdom, MT 59761-0237
406-689-3155
www.nps.gov/biho

Bear Paw Battlefield
P.O. Box 26
Chinook, MT 59523
406-357-3130

Friends of Bear Paw, Big Hole and Canyon Creek Battlefields
www.friendsnezpercebattlefields.org
info@friendsnezpercebattlefields.org

The Appaloosa Horse Club
2720 West Pullman Road
Moscow, ID 83843
208-882-5578
www.appaloosa.com

Confederated Tribes of the Colville Reservation
P.O. Box 150
Nespelem, WA 99155
509-634-2200
www.colvilletribes.com

Confederated Tribes of the Umatilla Indian Reservation
P.O. Box 638
73239 Confederated Way
Pendleton, OR 97801
541-276-3165
www.umatilla.nsn.us

Nez Perce Tribe
P.O. Box 365
Lapwai, ID 83540
208-843-2253
www.nezperce.org

Wallowa Band Nez Perce Trail Interpretive Center, Inc.
P.O. Box 15
Wallowa, OR 97885
541-886-3101
www.wallowanezperce.org
tamkaliks@eoni.com

Cast of Characters[1]

Five nontreaty bands fled from Idaho in the summer of 1877. Of the estimated eight hundred people, approximately one hundred twenty-five were warriors. Over two thousand military men were involved in chasing the Nez Perce at some point between June and October of 1877. This cast of characters includes the major personalities involved in conflict. Also included are people who wrote about their experiences and who have been quoted frequently in the text.

Nez Perce Names

Different sources often spell the same Nez Perce name several different ways. Wilhautyah, for example, is spelled variously as Welotyah and Willatyiah. Epigrams contain the spelling as it originally occurs in the source material; the text of the book uses the spelling and translation given by L.V. McWhorter.

Bald Head—See Husishusis Kute.

Big Thunder (Hin-mah-tute-ke-kaikt or James)—Also known as Thunder Eyes, this chief and shaman signed the Treaty of 1855. Although his home territory included Lapwai, he refused to sign the Treaty of 1863. In this manner he challenged the authority of Lawyer. His daughter was the wife of William Craig. Big Thunder died in 1867 while on a buffalo hunt in Montana.

Bond, Fred—Bond left home in Brooklyn at age thirteen to become a buffalo hunter. At age twenty-five, he skippered a flatboat of twenty-two Nez Perce from Miles City down the Yellowstone and Missouri rivers to Bismarck. His booklet *Flatboating on the Yellowstone, 1877* is fun to read.

Brooks, Bernard—A bugler for Captain Jackson's company, Brooks was killed and buried at Camas Meadows. Some of his letters are published in *Snake River Echoes*.

Buck, Henry—A merchant in Stevensville, Buck joined Howard's command as a supply-wagon driver from the Big Hole to Yellowstone National Park. His very interesting recollection is contained in a 125-page manuscript at the Montana Historical Society.

Carpenter, Frank—Brother of Ida Carpenter and Emma Cowan, he was part of the Radersburg tourist party in Yellowstone that was captured by the Nez Perce. He wrote the story of his friends and family in *Adventures in Geyserland*.

Charlot—Chief of the Salish (Flathead) Indians who lived in the Bitterroot Valley. The Salish were long-time friends of the Nez Perce.

Comba, Captain Richard—Led "D" Company during the Battle of the Big Hole.

Connolly, William—As a private with Howard's command, Connolly kept an abbreviated daily diary. Later in his life,

449

---

[1] For a more thorough list of Nez Perce, see *The Last Stand of the Nez Perce: Destruction of a People*, by Harvey Chalmers, II.

he expanded his recollections into a manuscript.

Cowan, Emma—The sister of Frank and Ida Carpenter and wife of George Cowan, twenty-four-year-old Emma was captured by the Nez Perce in Yellowstone on the day of her second anniversary.

Cowan, George—Emma Cowan's husband, George was shot and left for dead on the Mary Mountain Trail. He crawled fourteen miles in five days and was finally rescued by Howard's command on August 30.

Doane, Lt. Gustavus—This experienced officer is best known for the initial exploring expeditions into Yellowstone. In August 1877 he was ordered to Judith Gap to burn the grass so that when the Nez Perce came through, there would be no game. He rounded up a hundred Crows as scouts and left for Fort Ellis at Bozeman. His scouting expedition into Yellowstone on August 31 surprised a Nez Perce scouting party.

Eagle From the Light—Chief of a band from the Salmon River country, Eagle From the Light became so disgusted with the results of the Treaty of 1863 that he moved his band to the Bitterroot Valley of western Montana to live among the Flatheads (Salish) there. He personally did not join the nontreaty bands when they passed through the Bitterroot, although some families in his band did.

Eagle Robe—A member of White Bird's band who lived along the Salmon River. His murder in 1875 by Larry Ott was avenged by his son Wahlitits in the killings that ignited the Nez Perce war.

Eelahweemah (About Asleep) (David Williams)—Was a child in 1877.

Fisher, Stanton G.—Agent for the Fort Hall reservation near Pocatello, Idaho, Fisher acted as Chief Scout of fifty

Bannock scouts for General Howard from Henry's Lake through Yellowstone to the Clark's Fork. His diary, now at the Idaho Historical Library, is the main source of information for the Nez Perce route through Yellowstone.

FitzGerald, Emily—The wife of Captain John FitzGerald, she chronicled her daily life through letters to her mother, which are now collected in *An Army Doctor's Wife on the Frontier*. Emily lived at Fort Lapwai, and her letters home tell the personal side of the historic events that happened there.

FitzGerald, Captain Jenkins (John)—One of the surgeons accompanying General Howard's troops. A few of his letters from the field are contained in *An Army Doctor's Wife on the Frontier*. As a result of the soaking rain on the Clarks Fork, an old Civil War lung inflammation returned. He died two years later.

Gibbon, Colonel John (1827–1896)—During the Civil War, Gibbon received the rank of brevet major general. In 1877 he was the commander of the Seventh Infantry at Fort Shaw, near present-day Great Falls, Montana. He led the attack on the sleeping Nez Perce camp on the Big Hole.

Hahtalekin (c. 1843–1877)—Chief of the Palouse band whose home was at the junction of the Snake and Palouse rivers. He was killed at the Battle of the Big Hole.

Howard, Brigadier General Oliver Otis—Commander of the Department of the Columbia from 1874 to 1880, this veteran officer had lost his right arm during the Civil War. After the war, he was commissioner of the Freedman's Bureau. Howard was a member of the committee that formed a college for blacks and named it Howard University.

Husishusis Kute (Bald Head)—Chief and spiritual leader of the Palouse band who lived on the Snake River at Wawawai. He was thirty-seven years old in 1877. Husishusis Kute was one of the three chiefs who survived the flight. He surrendered with Chief Joseph. The following year he was sent on a mission to Canada to try to induce White Bird to return to the U.S. He became a Christian and, in 1885, led the contingent that returned to the Nez Perce Reservation in Idaho. Later he moved to the Colville reservation.

Husis Owyeen (Wounded Head)—Rreceived his name as a result of the Big Hole Battle.

Joseph, Chief Old (Tuekakas) (c. 1785–1871)—Chief of the Wallowa band of Nez Perce. Tuekakas was baptized by Spalding as Joseph. He is called Old Joseph to distinguish him from his more famous son, Chief Joseph. Tuekakas signed the Treaty of 1855 but refused to sign the Treaty of 1863. Indeed, he was so upset at the second treaty that he tore up his Gospel of Nez Perce and reverted to his native Dreamer religion.

Joseph, Chief (Heinmot Tooyalakekt [Thunder Traveling to Loftier (Mountain) Heights]) (1840–1904)—The civil or peace chief of the Wallowa tribe after his father's death in 1871. His younger brother, Ollokot, took on the responsibilities of war chief. Because of his leadership in negotiation prior to the war and his surrender after the war, he was the Nez Perce most well- known to the American public. For many years it was incorrectly assumed that Joseph was also the military leader of the retreat. In actuality, his role was more that of a guardian—rounding up the horses and preparing the camp to move.

Lawyer (Hallalhotsoot) (c. 1794–1876)—A buffalo hunter as a young man, his way with words earned him his English name. After learning to speak English and converting to Christianity, he was designated by the Americans as the head chief of the Nez Perce. He signed the Treaty of 1863, thus causing a deep rift in the tribe, the effects of which continue today.

Looking Glass, Chief (Allalimya Takanin) (c. 1832–1877)—This chief had inherited the English translation of his father's and grandfather's names—Apash Wyakaikt, meaning Flint Necklace. His home territory was around Kooskia, with winter grounds near Asotin. A warrior and buffalo hunter, Looking Glass had spent much time with the Crows. After the murders on the Salmon River, he retreated to his home on the reservation. When that was attacked by soldiers and volunteers two weeks later, he converted to the side of the other nontreaty bands. Because he was familiar with the buffalo country, he led the nontreaty Nez Perce out of Idaho.

McDonald, Duncan (1849–1937)—The son of a Scottish trader on the Flathead reservation, Angus McDonald, and a Nez Perce woman. In 1878, McDonald was hired by the Deer Lodge newspaper, *The New North-west*, to write a series of articles about the Nez Perce war. McDonald traveled to Canada to interview Chief White Bird and other survivors.

Miles, Colonel Nelson A.—During the Civil War, Miles had been General Howard's aide-de-camp. In March 1877 Miles wrote to Howard asking for a recommendation that he be promoted to general. Miles was married to General Sherman's niece. Miles was the commander of Fort Keogh at present-day Miles City, Montana, where the Tongue River converges with the Yellowstone.

451

Ollokot, Chief (c. 1842–1877)—Chief Joseph's younger brother was the war chief of the Wallowa band. He participated in the negotiations prior to the war and was, undoubtedly, his brother's strongest counselor.

Ott, Larry—Settled on land at Horseshoe Bend on the Salmon River that originally belonged to Eagle Robe. In 1875, while Ott was fencing in Eagle Robe's garden as his own, Eagle Robe dissented and threw a rock at him. Ott responded by shooting Eagle Robe. Although Ott was Wahlitits' intended victim on June 13, 1877, he was in Florence rather than at home and thus escaped revenge.

Pahkatos Owyeen (Five Wounds)—See the story of Rainbow.

Penahwenonmi (Helping Another) (1840–1938)—Was married to Husis Owyeen (Wounded Head).

Peopeo Tholekt (Bird Alighting)—A young warrior of the Looking Glass band, Peopeo told his story to McWhorter, who recorded it.

Poker Joe (Lean Elk)—A French-Nez Perce half-blood and sub-chief of the Bitterroot band. Poker Joe guided the Nez Perce from Big Hole to the crossing of the Missouri River. He was killed at the Battle of the Bear Paw.

Rainbow (Wahchumyus)—One of the great buffalo hunters, he and his warmate Pahkatos Owyeen (Five Wounds) had just returned from Montana at the time of the White Bird Battle. He was killed at the Big Hole.

Red Heart, Chief—Journeying back from Montana, Red Heart's band was arrested on July 16, 1877, and sent to Fort Vancouver as prisoners. In April 1878 they were released and returned to Idaho.

452   **Red Owl, Chief (Koolkool Snehee)**—A sub-chief of the Looking Glass band, his home territory was the camp on the South Fork of the Clearwater, near present-day Stites, where the Battle of the Clearwater took place.

Redington, John Watermelon—An itinerant printer, Redington was anxious to join the campaign against the Nez Perce, and he finally wangled his way into the action as a scout for General Howard. His articles and his letters to McWhorter are great fun to read.

Sarpsis Ilpilp (Red Mocassin Tops)—A warrior of the White Bird band, he was allegedly wounded by Samuel Benedict in 1875. On June 13, 1877, he went with his cousin Wahlitits to seek revenge. Between them, they killed Richard Devine, Henry Elfers, Robert Bland, and Robert Beckrodge and wounded Samuel Benedict. This incident ignited the Nez Perce war. Sarpsis was killed at the Battle of the Big Hole.

Sherrill, Tom—Tom and his brother, Bunch, were citizen volunteers from the Bitterroot Valley who participated in the attack at the Big Hole. Later, Tom Sherrill became the attendant of the Big Hole Battlefield.

Spalding, Henry (1803–1874)—Henry and Eliza Spalding arrived as missionaries among the Nez Perce in 1836 and settled at Lapwai. Henry was allegedly abused as a child and could be somewhat mean-tempered, despite his strong Presbyterian convictions. After the Whitmans were killed in 1847, the Spaldings left their mission. Eliza died in 1851, and Henry remarried. Spalding returned to the Nez Perce as a schoolteacher in 1863.

Spurgin, Captain William F.—Spurgin commanded the engineering company of fifty axemen who accompanied Howard's command, improving and building roads as they went.

Stevens, Isaac I. (1818–1862)—Appointed as governor of the newly formed Washington Territory in 1853, Stevens also landed the job of directing the survey for a northern route across the continent. He negotiated treaties with the Nez Perce and the Flatheads (Salish) and many other tribes in 1855. Stevens died during the Civil War.

Sturgis, Colonel Samuel D. (1822–1889)—Participating in several Indian campaigns in the 1850s, Sturgis was promoted to lieutenant colonel during the Civil War. After Custer's death, he succeeded to the command of the Seventh Cavlary at Fort Lincoln, Dakota Territory. His son died with Custer. Sturgis waited for the Nez Perce to emerge from the Clarks Fork, but moved before they had arrived. He then pursued them and engaged them at the Battle of Canyon Creek.

Sutherland, Thomas—The journalist who traveled with Howard, Sutherland's articles appeared in the *San Francisco Chronicle* and the *Portland Daily Standard.*

Toohoolhoolzote—Chief of the nontreaty band, whose home was between the Snake and Salmon rivers. At the final Lapwai council in May 1877 he was designated to speak for the five nontreaty bands. Although he was an old man, he led the young men in battle. He was killed at the Battle of the Bear Paw.

Two Moon—Two Moon was one of McWhorter's informants regarding his experiences during the events of 1877 in which he participated as a warrior. Two Moon was recognized as having strong medicine power.

Tuekakas—See Chief Old Joseph.

Wahlitits (Shore Crossing)—Son of Eagle Robe and a warrior of the White Bird band, Wahlitits sought revenge for the murder of his father. On June 13, 1877, he gathered his cousin, Sarpsis Ilpilp, and his nephew, Wetyetmas Wahyakt, for the purpose of killing Larry Ott. Not finding Ott at home, the trio proceeded to kill Richard Devine, Henry Elfers, Robert Bland, and Robert Beckrodge. He was one of the

three warriors who wore red coats at the White Bird Battle. Wahlitits and his pregnant wife were killed at the Battle of the Big Hole.

Wetatonmi—The widow of Ollokot, she remarried and became Mrs. Susie Convill.

Wetyetmas Wahyakt (Swan Necklace)—The seventeen-year-old nephew of Wahlitits acted as horseholder for Wahlitits and Sarpsis Ilpilp while those two took their revenge by killing white men who had wronged them. After the exile, he was known as John Minthon. His role in the initial Salmon River killings was kept secret from whites until after his death in the 1920s.

White Bird, Chief (c. 1827–1882)—One of the nontreaty Nez Perce chiefs, White Bird was a buffalo hunter and warrior. He led the group of Nez Perce who escaped from the Bear Paw Battlefield up to Canada. He was killed in 1882 near Fort Macleod by one of his own people because his shamanistic powers had become too strong. Read *White Bird: The last great warrior chief of the Nez Perces*, by Bob Painter.

Whitman, Marcus and Narcissa—The Whitmans arrived as missionaries among the Cayuse in 1836 and were colleagues of Henry and Eliza Spalding. After being unsuccessful in their attempts to convert the Cayuse, the Whitmans were murdered in November 1847. The Whitman Mission, west of Walla Walla, is a national historic site.

Wilmot, Luther P. (Lew)—A teamster from Mount Idaho, Wilmot was elected a lieutenant of the Mount Idaho volunteers in June 1877. He was one of The Brave 17 and did scouting from Misery Hill. He wrote several manuscripts and articles about his experiences. He later moved to the Colville reservation.

453

Wood, Charles Erskine Skinner—A lieutenant with Howard's command, Wood recorded Chief Joseph's alleged surrender speech. Wood later became a writer. In the 1890s his son, Erskine, spent two summers with Chief Joseph. His diary is published by the Oregon Historical Society.

Wottolen (Hair Combed Over Eyes)—Wottolen was a warrior in 1877 and later a tribal historian. He became one of McWhorter's major informants regarding the Nez Perce side of the story.

Yellow Bull—Father of Sarpsis Ilpilp, he led the young men on the second raiding party along the Salmon. He accompanied Chief Joseph to Washington, D.C., in 1879. After Oklahoma he settled on the Colville, but he moved back to Lapwai in 1890.

Yellow Wolf (1856–1935)—A young warrior during the flight of 1877. His uncle, Yellow Wolf, was a sub-chieftain of the Wallowa band. L.V. McWhorter recorded Yellow Wolf's recollections in *Yellow Wolf: His Own Story*.

Bibliography

Books and Manuscripts

Adkison, Norman. *Indian Braves and Battles with More Nez Perce Lore.* Grangeville, Idaho: Idaho Country Free Press, 1967.

Adkison, Norman. *Nez Perce Indian War and Original Stories.* Grangeville, Idaho: Idaho Free Press, 1967.

Aegerter, Mary and Steve F. Russell. *Hike Lewis and Clark's Idaho.* Moscow, Idaho: University of Idaho Press, 2002.

Alcorn, Rowena Lung. *Timothy: A Nez Perce Chief.* Ye Galleon Press, 1985.

Anglin, Ron. *Forgotten Trails: Historical Sources of the Columbia's Big Bend Country.* Pullman, Washington: Washington State University Press, 1995.

Annual Report of the Commissioner of Indian Affairs to the Secretary of the Interior for the Year 1877. Washington: Government Printing Office, 1877.

Armstrong, Virginia I. (ed.) *I Have Spoken.* Chicago: Swallow Press, 1971.

Arnold, R. Ross. *Indian Wars of Idaho.* Caldwell, Idaho: Caxton Printers, 1932.

Asotin County Historical Society. *Anatone and Alpowa-Silcott: Early Beginnings.* Twin City Printing.

Ault, Nelson A. *The Papers of Lucullus Virgil McWhorter.* Friends of the Library: State College of Washington, 1959.

Axtell, Horace and Margo Aragon. *A Little Bit of Wisdom. Conversations With A Nez Perce Elder.* Lewiston, Idaho: Confluence Press, 1997.

Bailey, Robert Gresham. *Hells Canyon.* Lewiston, Idaho: R. G. Bailey Printing Co., 1943.

Bailey, Robert Gresham. *River of No Return.* Lewiston, Idaho: R. G. Bailey Printing Co., 1947

Baird, Dennis, Diane Mallickan, and W.R. Swagerty. *The Nez Perce Nation Divided: Firsthand Accounts of Events Leading to the 1863 Treaty.* Moscow, Idaho: University of Idaho Press, 2002.

Baird, Lynn and Dennis. *In Nez Perce Country: Accounts of the Bitterroots and the Clearwater after Lewis and Clark.* Moscow, Idaho: University of Idaho Library, 2003.

Bancroft, Hubert Howe. *The Works of Hubert Howe Bancroft.* Volume 31. San Francisco: The History Company, Publishers, 1890.

Barklow, Irene Locke. *Gateway to the Wallowas.* Wallowa, Oregon: Enchantments Publishing of Oregon, 2003.

Bartlett, Grace. *From the Wallowas.* Enterprise, Oregon: Pika Press, 1992.

Bartlett, Grace. *The Wallowa Country, 1867–1877.* Fairfield, Washington: Ye Galleon Press, 1984.

Bartlett, Grace. *Wallowa: The Land of Winding Waters.* privately printed, 1979.

Beal, Merrill D. "I Will Fight No More Forever." Seattle: University of Washington Press, 1963.

Bennett, Robert A. comp. *We'll All Go Home In The Spring.* Walla Walla, Washington: Pioneer Press Books. 1984.

Boas, Franz. *Folktales of the Salishan and Sahaptin Tribes.* Lancaster, Pennsylvania: American Folklore Society, 1917.

Bond, Fred G. *Flatboating on the Yellowstone 1877*. New York: New York Public Library, 1925.

Bond, Fred G. *Flatboating on the Yellowstone, 1877*. Staten Island: Ward Hill Press, 1998.

Bonney, Orrin H. and Lorraine. *Battle Drums and Geysers*. Chicago: The Swallow Press Inc., 1970.

Brady, Cyrus Townshend. *Northwestern Fights and Fighters*. Williamstown, Massachusetts: Cornerhouse Publishers, 1974.

Brooks, Charles E. *The Henry's Fork*. Piscataway, New Jersey: Winchester Press, 1986.

Brown, Mark Herbert. *Flight of the Nez Perce*. New York: Putnam, 1967.

Burdick, Usher Lloyd. *Jacob Horner and the Indian Campaigns*. Baltimore: Wirth Brothers, 1942.

Burns, Robert Ignatius. *The Jesuits and the Indian Wars of the Northwest*. New Haven: Yale University Press, 1960.

Byrne, P. E. *Soldiers of the Plains*. New York: Minton, Balch & Company, 1926.

Carpenter, Frank D. *Adventures in Geyserland*. Caldwell, Idaho: The Caxton Printers, 1935.

Carpenter, John Alcott. *Sword and Olive Branch*. Pittsburgh: University of Pittsburgh Press, 1964.

Carroll, John M. *Camp Talk: The Very Private Letters of Frederick W. Benteen of the 7th U.S. Cavalry to His Wife, 1871-1888*. Mattituck, New York: J. M. Carroll & Company, 1983.

Chaffin, Glenn. *The Last Horizon*. Somerset, California: Pine Trail Press, 1971.

Chalmers, Harvey. *Last Stand of the Nez Perce*. New York: Twayne Publishers, 1962.

Chittenden, Gen. Hiram Martin. *The Yellowstone National Park, Historical and Descriptive*. Cincinnati: Robert C. Clarke Co., 1895.

Clark, Ella. *Indian Legends from the Northern Rockies*. Norman, Oklahoma: University of Oklahoma Press, 1977.

Coburn, Walt. *Pioneer Cattleman in Montana: The Story of the Circle C Ranch*. Norman, Oklahoma: University of Oklahoma Press. 1968.

Coleman, Michael C. *Presbyterian Missionary Attitudes Toward American Indians 1837–1893*. Jackson, Mississippi: University Press of Mississippi, 1985.

Collections of the State Historical Society of North Dakota. Vol. I. Bismarck, North Dakota: Tribute, State Printers and Binders, 1906.

"The Commissioners of the Royal North-west Mounted Police." *Opening Up the West*. Toronto: Coles Publishing Company, 1973.

Coutant, C. G. *History of Wyoming* (3 volumes). Laramie, Wyoming: Chaplin, Spafford and Mathieson, 1899.

Cox, Ross. *The Columbia River or Scenes and Adventures during a Residence of Six Years on the Western Side of the Rocky Mountains Among Various Tribes of Indians Hitherto Unknown*. ed. E. I. and J. R. Stewart. American Exploration and Travel Series, 24. Norman, Oklahoma: University of Oklahoma Press, 1957.

Curtis, Edward S. *The North American Indian Volume 8*. Norwood, Massachusetts: The Plimpton Press, 1911.

DeHaas, John N., Jr. ed. *Historic Buildings in Bannack and Dillon.* Bozeman: Montana Ghost Town Preservation Society, 1976.

Drury, Clifford M. *Chief Lawyer.* Glendale, California: A. H. Clark, 1979.

Drury, Clifford M. *The Diaries and Letters of Henry H. Spalding and Asa Bowen Smith.* Glendale, California: Arthur H. Clark, 1958.

Drury, Clifford Merrill. *Henry Harmon Spalding.* Caldwell, Idaho: The Caxton Printers, 1936.

Drury, Clifford Merrill. *A Teepee in His Front Yard.* Portland, Oregon: Binsford & Mort, 1949.

Dunn, J. P., Jr. *Massacres of the Mountains: A History of the Indian Wars of the Far West.* New York: Harper & Brothers, 1886.

Ege, Robert J. *After the Little Bighorn.* Greeley, Colorado: Fred H. Werner, 1982.

Etulain, Richard W. *Idaho History: A Bibliography.* Pocatello, Idaho: Idaho State University Press, 1974.

Evans, Lucylle H. *Good Samaritan of the Northwest: Anthony Ravalli, S. J., 1812–1884.* Stevensville, Montana: Montana Creative Consultants, 1981.

Evans, Lucylle H. *St. Mary's in the Rocky Mountains.* Stevensville, Montana: Montana Creative Consultants, 1976.

Evans, Steven Ross. *Voice of the Old Wolf: Lucullus Virgil McWhorter and the Nez Perce Indians.* Pullman, Washington: Washington State University Press, 1996.

Finerty, John Frederick. *Warpath and Bivouac.* Norman, Oklahoma: University of Oklahoma Press, 1961.

Fitzgerald, Emily. *An Army Doctor's Wife on the Frontier*, ed. Abe Laufe. Lincoln, Nebraska: University of Nebraska Press, 1986.

Garcia, Andrew. *Tough Trip Through Paradise.* Sausalito, California: Comstock Editions, 1976.

Gay, E. Jane. *With the Nez Perces: Alice Fletcher in the Field, 1889–92.* Lincoln, Nebraska: University of Nebraska Press, 1981.

Gibbs, George. *Indian Tribes of Washington Territory.* Fairfield, Washington: Ye Galleon Press, 1978.

Gidley, Mick. *Kopet.* Seattle: University of Washington Press, 1981.

Gidley, Mick. *With One Sky Above Us.* New York: Putnam, 1979.

Gilman, Carolyn and Mary Jane Schneider. *The Way to Independence: Memories of a Hidatsa Indian Family, 1840–1920.* St. Paul: Minnesota Historical Society Press, 1987.

Glassley, Ray Hoard. *Indian Wars of the Pacific Northwest.* Portland, Oregon: Binfords & Mort, 1972, 1953.

Goldin, Theodore W. *A Bit of the Nez Perce Campaign.* Bryan, Texas: Privately Printed, 1978.

Greene, Jerome A. *Nez Perce Summer 1877: The U.S. Army and the Nee-Me-Poo Crisis.* Helena, Montana: Montana Historical Society Press, 2000.

Gulick, Bill. *Chief Joseph Country.* Caldwell, Idaho: The Caxton Printers, 1981.

Hagemann, E. R. ed. *Fighting Rebels and Redskins: Experiences in Army Life of Colonel George B. Sanford 1861–1892.* Norman, Oklahoma: University of Oklahoma Press, 1969.

Haines, Aubrey L. *An Elusive Victory: The Battle of the Big Hole.* Helena, Montana: Falcon Press Publishing, 1999.

Haines, Aubrey L. *The Yellowstone Story: A History of Our First National Park*. 2 vols. Mammoth, Wyoming: Yellowstone Library and Museum Association, 1977.

Hamilton, James McClellan. *From Wilderness to Statehood: A History of Montana, 1805–1900*. Portland, Oregon: Binford & Mort, Publishers, 1957.

Hampton, Bruce. *Children of Grace: The Nez Perce War of 1877*. New York: Avon Books, 1994.

Hansen, Virginia and Al Funderburk. *The Fabulous Past of Cooke City*. Billings, Montana: Billings Printing Company, 1962.

Hathaway, Ella E. *Battle of the Big Hole*. Seattle: Facsimile Reproduction, 1967.

Hatley, George B. *Riding the Nez Perce War Trail Twice: 1965–1990*. Privately printed, 2004.

Heady, Eleanor B. *Tales of the Nimipoo from the Land of the Nez Perce*. New York: World Publishing Co., 1970.

Hendrickson, Borg and Linwood Laughy. *Clearwater Country!: The Traveler's Historical & Recreational Guide: Lewiston, Idaho–Missoula, Montana*. Kooskia, Idaho: Mountain Meadow Press, 1999.

Highberger, Mark. *The Death of Wind Blowing*. Wallowa, Oregon: Bear Creek Press. 2000.

Highberger, Mark, ed. *Looking Back at Wallowa Lake: A Photographic Portrait*. Wallowa, Oregon, Bear Creek Press, 2001.

History of Montana 1739–1885. Chicago: Warner, Beers & Company, 1885.

Howard, Helen Addison. *Saga of Chief Joseph*. Caldwell, Idaho: Caxton Printers, 1965.

Howard, Oliver O. *My Life and Experiences Among Our Hostile Indians*. New York: Da Capo Press. 1972.

Howard, Oliver Otis. *Nez Perce Joseph, An Account of His Ancestors*. Boston: Lee and Shepard, 1881.

Hungry Wolf, Adolf. *Charlo's People: The Flathead Tribe of Montana*. Invermere, British Columbia: Good Medine Books. 1974.

Hunt, Elvid. *History of Fort Leavenworth: 1827–1927*. New York: Arno Press, 1979.

Hunter, George. *Reminiscences of an Old-Timer*. Battle Creek, Michigan: Review and Herald, 1888.

An Illustrated History of North Idaho. Spokane: Western Historical Publishing Company, 1903.

An Illustrated History of Union and Wallowa Counties. Spokane: Western Historical Publishing Company, 1902.

Ingram, Patricia M. *Historic Transportation Routes Through Southwestern Montana*. Boulder, Colorado: Western Interstate Commission for Higher Education, 1976.

Irving, Washington. *The Works of Washington Irving: The Adventures of Captain Bonneville*. New York: The Co-Operative Publication Society, Inc.

Jackson, Helen Hunt. *A Century of Dishonor*. Boston: Robert Brother, 1887.

Jackson, W. H. *Descriptive Catalogue of The Photographs of the United States Geological Survey of the Territories for the Years 1869 to 1875, Inclusive*. Washington, D.C.: Government Printing Office, 1875.

Jackson, William H. *The Pioneer Photographer*. Yonkers-on-Hudson, New York: World Book Company, 1929.

Jocelyn, Stephen Perry. *Mostly Alkalai.* Caldwell, Idaho: The Caxton Printers, Ltd., 1953.

Johnson, Virginia Weisel. *The Unregimented General.* Boston: Houghton, Mifflin Company, 1962.

Joseph. *Chief Joseph's Own Story: A Story of the Nez Perce: How They Lost Their Home, Why They Fought a War.* Wallowa, Oregon: Bear Creek Press. 2003.

Joseph. *An Indian's View of Indian Affairs.* Kirkwoody, Missouri: The Printery, 1973.

Josephy, Alvin. *Chief Joseph's People and Their War.* Yellowstone National Park: Yellowstone Library and Museum Association, 1964.

Josephy, Alvin M. *The Nez Perce and the Opening of the Northwest.* New Haven, Connecticut: Yale University Press, 1965.

Judson, Katharine Berry. *Myths and Legends of the Pacific Northwest.* Chicago: A.C. McClurg & Co. 1916.

Kip, Lawrence. *Indian War in the Pacific Northwest: The Journal of Lieutenant Lawrence Kip.* Lincoln, Nebraska: University of Nebraska Press, 1999.

Kip, Lawrence. *Sources of the History of Oregon.* Eugene, Oregon: Star Job Office, 1897.

Kirkwood, Charlotte M. *The Nez Perce Indian War Under War Chiefs Joseph and Whitebird.* Grangeville, Idaho: Idaho County Free Press, 1953.

Knight, Oliver. *Following the Indian Wars: The Story of the Newspaper Correspondents Among the Indian Campaigners.* Norman, Oklahoma: University of Oklahoma Press, 1960.

Koury, Michael J. *Guarding the Carroll Trail...Camp Lewis—1874–1875.* Fort Collins, Colorado: The Old Army Press. 1969.

Lambert, Major Joseph I. *One Hundred Years with the Second Cavalry.* Fort Riley, Kansas: The Capper Printing Company Inc., 1939.

Lane, Harrison. *The Long Flight: A History of the Nez Perce War.* Havre, Montana: H. Earl Clack Memorial Museum, 1982.

Liljeblad, Sven. *Indian Peoples of Idaho.* Pocatello, Idaho: Idaho State College, 1957.

Lolo History Committee. *Lolo Creek Reflections.* Lolo, Montana: 1976.

Loveridge, D. M. and Barry Ptoyondi. *From Wood Mountain to the Whitemud: A Historical Survey of the Grasslands National Park Area.* Ottawa: Environment Canada, 1983.

Ludlow, William. *Exploring Nature's Sanctuary: Captain William Ludlow's Report of a Reconnaissance from Carroll, Montana Territory, on the Upper Missouri to the Yellowstone National Park, and Return Made in the Summer of 1875.* Washington, D.C.: Government Printing Office, 1985.

McAllister, James W. *Into the Valley: A Homesteader's Memories of the 1870s.* Wallowa, Oregon: Bear Creek Press, 2003.

McBeth, Kate C. *The Nez Perces Since Lewis and Clark.* New York: F.H. Revel, 1908.

McConnell, W. J. *Early History of Idaho.* Caldwell, Idaho: The Caxton Printers, 1918.

McDermott, John Dishon. *Forlorn Hope.* Boise, Idaho: Idaho State Historical Society, 1978.

MacEwan, Grant. *Sitting Bull: The Years in Canada.* Edmonton: Hurtig Publishers, 1973.

McLaughlin, James. *My Friend the Indian*. Boston and New York: Houghton Mifflin Co., 1910.

McLaughlin, James. *The Superior Edition of My Friend the Indian*. Seattle: Superior Publishing Co., 1970.

Macleod, R. C. *The NWMP and Law Enforcement, 1873–1905*. Toronto: University of Toronto Press, 1976.

McWhorter, Lucullus V. *Hear Me, My Chiefs! Nez Perce History and Legend*. Caldwell, Idaho: The Caxton Printers, Ltd., 1983.

McWhorter, Lucullus V. *Yellow Wolf: His Own Story*. Caldwell, Idaho: The Caxton Printers, Ltd., 1983.

Malone, Michael P. and Richard B. Roeder. *Montana As It Was: 1876*. Bozeman, Montana: The Endowment and Research Foundation of Montana State University, 1975.

Marquis, Thomas. *Custer, Cavalry & Crows*. Ft. Collins, Colorado: The Old Army Press, 1975.

Marquis, T. B. *Memoirs of a White Crow Indian*. New York: The Century Co., 1921.

Marshall, Alan Gould. *Nez Perce Social Groups: An Ecological Interpretation*. Ann Arbor, Michigan: University Microfilms, 1978.

Matulka, Robert D. *The Battle of the Bear's Paw Between the US Army and the Nez Perce Indians, 30 September–5 October, 1877*. Research paper, US Naval Academy, 1960.

Merriam, H. G. ed. *Frontier Woman: The Story of Mary Ronan*. Missoula: University of Montana, 1973.

"Message from the President of the United States communicating in answer to a Senate resolution of November 13, 1877, information in relation to the cause and probable cost of the late Nez Perces war." 45th Congress, 2d session, Ex. Doc. No. 14.

Miles, Gen. Nelson A. *Personal Recollections and Observations*. Chicago: Werner Co., 1896; New York: DaCapo Press, 1969.

Miles, Nelson A. *Serving the Republic*. New York: Harper & Brothers Publishers, 1911.

Moeller, Bill and Jan. *Chief Joseph and the Nez Perces: A Photographic History*. Missoula, Montana: Mountain Press Publishing Company, 1995.

Monahan, Glenn and Chanler Biggs. *Montana's Wild and Scenic Upper Missouri River: A Guidebook for the Upper Missouri National Wild and Scenic River and the Upper Missouri River Breaks National Monument*. Anaconda, Montana: Northern Rock Mountains Books, 2001.

Mulford, Ami Frank. *Fighting Indians!* Fairfield, Washington: Ye Galleon Press, 1972.

Nez Perce Indians. New York: Garland, Publishing, 1974.

Nez Perce Tribe. *Treaties: Nez Perce Perspectives*. Lewiston, Idaho: Confluence Press, 2003.

Nieberding, Velma. *The History of Ottawa County*. Marceline, Missouri: Walsworth Pub. Co., 1983.

Norris, P. W. *Report Upon the Yellowstone National Park to the Secretary of the Interior*. Washington, D.C.: GPO, 1877.

The North Face of Yellowstone National Park. Bozeman, Montana: Montana Travel, Inc., 1981.

Noyes, A. J. *In the Land of the Chinook.* Helena, Montana: State Publishing Company, 1917.

Noyes, A. J. *The Story of Ajax: Life in the Big Hole Basin.* Helena, Montana: State Publishing Company, 1914.

Olson, Rolf Y. H. *The Nez Perce, the Montana Press and the War of 1877.* M.A. thesis, Montana State University, 1964.

Painter, Bob. *White Bird: The last great warrior chief of the Nez Perces.* Fairfield, Washington: Ye Galleon Press, 2002.

Phillips, James W. *Washington State Place Names.* Seattle: University of Washington Press, 1971.

Phillips, Richard. *Yellowstone Country.* Midland, Michigan: n.p., 1973.

Phinney, Archie. *Nez Perce Texts.* New York: Columbia University Press, 1934.

Pinkham, Ron. *100th Anniversary of the Nez Perce War of 1877.* Lapwai, Idaho: Nez Perce Printing, 1977.

Place, Marian. *Retreat to the Bear Paw.* New York: Four Winds Press: 1969.

Pollock, Robert Westly. *Grandfather, Chief Joseph, and Psychodynamics.* Baker, Oregon: Privately published, 1964.

Prucha, Francis P. *A Bibliographical Guide to the History of Indian-White Relations in the U.S.* Chicago: University of Chicago Press, 1977.

Ray, Verne F. *Ethnohistory of the Joseph Band of Nez Perce Indians.* Indian Claims Commission Docket No. 186. New York: Garland, 1974.

Ray, Verne F. *Lewis and Clark and the Nez Perce Indians.* Washington, D.C.: Potomac Corral of the Westerners, 1971.

Record of Engagements with Hostile Indians Within the Military Division of the Missouri, from 1868 to 1882. Washington, D.C.: Government Printing Office, 1882.

Redfield, Ethel E. ed. *Reminiscences of Francis M. Redfield.* Pocatello, Idaho: Privately printed, 1949.

Replogle, Wayne F. *Yellowstone's Bannock Indian Trails.* Yellowstone Park, Wyoming: Yellowstone Library and Museum Association, 1956.

Report of the Secretary of War. Washington, D.C.: Government Printing Office, 1877.

Ronan, Peter. *Historical Sketch of the Flathead Indian Nation From the Year 1813 to 1890.* Helena, Montana: Journal Publishing Co., 1890.

Russell, Charles Marion. *Back-Trailing on the Old Frontiers.* Great Falls, Montana: Cheely-Raban Syndicate, 1922.

Sayre, Robert F. *Thoreau and the American Indians.* Princeton: Princeton University Press, 1977. (first chapter)

Schmitt, Martin Ferdinand. *Fighting Indians of the West.* New York: C Scribners Sons, 1948.

Scott, Douglas D. *A Sharp Little Affair: The Archeology of the Big Hole Battlefield.* Lincoln, Nebraska: J & L Reprint Company, 1994.

Scott, Hugh Lennox. *Some Memories of a Soldier.* New York: Century Co., 1928.

Shaw, Janet. *1764: Meet Kaya: An American Girl.* Middleton, Wisconsin: Pleasant Company Publications. 2002.

Shawley, Stephen D. *Nez Perce Trails.* University of Idaho Anthropological Research Manuscript Series, No. 44. Moscow, Idaho: Laboratory of Anthropology, 1977.

Shield, George O. *The Battle of the Big Hole*. Chicago and New York: Rand-McNally, 1889.

Slickpoo, Allen P. Sr. *Noon Nee-Me-Poo: Culture and History of the Nez Perces*. Lapwai, Idaho: Nez Perce Tribe, 1973.

Slickpoo, Allen P. Sr. *Nu-Mee-Poom-Tit-Wah-Tit: Nez Perce Legends*. Lapwai, Idaho, Nez Perce Tribe, 1972.

Smith, G. Hubert. *Like-A-Fishhook Village and Fort Berthold, Garrison Reservoir, North Dakota*. Washington, D.C.: U.S. Dept. of the Interior, 1972.

The Soldiers' Side of the Nez Perce War: Eyewitness Accounts of "The Most Extraordinary of Indian Wars." Wallowa, Oregon: Bear Creek Press, 2003.

Space, Ralph S. *The Lolo Trail*. Lewiston, Idaho: Printcraft Printing, 1984.

Spalding, Henry Harmon. *The Diaries and Letters of H.H. Spalding and Asa Bowen Smith*. Glendale, California: H.H. Clark Co., 1958.

Spinden, Herbert Joseph. *The Nez Perces*. Lancaster, Pennsylvania: The New Era Printing Co., 1908.

Stadius, Martin. *Dreamers: On the Trail of the Nez Perce*. Caldwell, Idaho: Caxton Press. 1999.

Stanley, Edwin J. *Rambles in Wonderland or a Trip Through the Great Yellowstone National Park*. Nashville: Publishing House of the Methodist Episcopal Church, South, 1898.

Stevens, Isaac Ingalls. *A True Copy of the Record of the Offical Proceedings at the Council in the Walla Walla Valley 1855*. Fairfield, Washington: Ye Galleon Press. 1996.

Stevensville Historical Society. *Montana Genesis*. Missoula, Montana: Mountain Press Publishing Company, 1971.

Strachan, John. *Blazing the Mullan Trail*. Rockford, Illinois (1860–61): Privately printed, 1952.

Stranahan, C. T. *Pioneer Stories*. Lewiston, Idaho: Privately published, 1947.

Stuart, Granville. *Forty Years on the Frontier*. Vol. I. Cleveland: The Arthur H. Clark Company, 1925.

Sutherland, Thomas. *Howard's Campaign Against the Nez Perce*. Fairfield, Washington: Ye Galleon Press, 1980.

Swanton, John Reed. *Indian Tribes of Washington, Oregon & Idaho*. Fairfield, Washington: Ye Galleon Press.

Taylor, Marian W. *Chief Joseph: Nez Perce Leader*. New York: Chelsea House Publishers, 1993.

Tchakmakian, Pascal. *The Great Retreat: The Nez Perces War in Words and Pictures*. San Francisco: Chronicle Books, 1976.

Thomas, Anthony E. *The Life History of a Nez Perce Indian*. Ann Arbor, Michigan: University Microfilms, 1970.

Thomasma, Kenneth. *Soun Tetoken: Nez Perce Boy Tames a Stallion*. Jackson, Wyoming: Grandview Publishing Company, 1993.

Travis, Helga Anderson. *The Nez Perce Trail*. Yakima, Washington: Franklin Press, 1967.

Turner, C. Frank. *Across the Medicine Line*. Toronto: McClelland and Stewart Limited, 1973.

Turner, John Peter. *The North-West Mounted Police, 1873–1893*. Vol. 1. Ottawa: Edmond Cloutier, 1950.

462

United States Department of the Interior, National Park Service. *General Management Plan: Nez Perce National Historical Park and Big Hole National Battlefield.* Spalding, Idaho: Nez Perce National Historical Park, 1997.

Vestal, Stanley. *New Sources of Indian History 1850–1891.* Norman, Oklahoma: University of Oklahoma Press, 1952.

Walgamott, C. S. *Reminiscences of Early Days.* Twin Falls, Idaho: n.p., 1926.

Walker, Deward E. *Conflict and Schism in Nez Perce Acculturation.* Pullman, Washington: Washington State University Press, 1968.

Walker, Deward E., Jr. *Indians of Idaho.* Moscow, Idaho: University Press of Idaho, 1978.

Warren, Eliza Spalding. *Memories of the West.* Portland, Oregon: Marsh Printing, 1916.

Warren, Robert Penn. *Chief Joseph of the Nez Perce, Who Called Themselves the Nimipu—"The Real People."* New York: Random House, 1983.

Weatherford, Mark V. *Chief Joseph: His Battles, His Retreat.* Corvallis, Oregon: Lehnert Printing Company, 1958.

Wellman, Paul Iselin. *Death of the Prairie.* New York: The Macmillan Co., 1934.

Western Guide Publishers. *Maps of Early Idaho.* Corvallis, Oregon: Western Guide Publishers, 1972.

Wilson, Charles Banks. *Quapaw Agency Indians.* Afton, Oklahoma: Buffalo Publishing Co., 1947.

Wilson, Eugene Tallmadge. *Hawks and Doves in the Nez Perce War.* Helena: Montana Historical Society, 1966.

Wolle, Murield Sibell. *Montana Pay Dirt.* Athens, Ohio: Sage Books, 1983.

Wood, Charles Erskine Scott. *The Pursuit & Capture of Chief Joseph: A Story of the End of the Nez Perce War.* Wallowa, Oregon: Bear Creek Press, 2003.

Wood, Erskine. *Days With Chief Joseph.* Vancouver, Washington: Rose Wind Press, 1992.

Wood, H. Clay. *The Treaty Status of Young Joseph and His Band of Nez Perce Indians.* Portland, Oregon: pPrivately published, 1876.

Worcester, Donald. *Forked Tongues and Broken Treaties.* Caldwell, Idaho: The Caxton Printers, 1975.

Zimmer, William F. *Frontier Soldier: An Enlisted Man's Journal: The Sioux and Nez Perce Campaigns, 1877.* Helena, Montana: Montana Historical Society Press, 1998.

Articles

Alcorn, Rowena L. and Gordon D. Alcorn. "Aged Nez Perce Recalls the 1877 Tragedy." *Montana, the Magazine of Western History.* October 1986, pp. 54–67.

Alcorn, Rowena L. and Gordon D. Alcorn. "Old Nez Perce Recalls Tragic Retreat of 1877." *Montana, the Magazine of Western History.* January 1963, pp. 66–74.

Alcorn, Rowena and Gordon Alcorn. "Oldest Nez Perce Reaches Century Mark." *The Tacoma Sunday Ledger-News Tribune.* 26 November 1961.

Alcorn, Rowena L. and Gorden D. Alcorn. "Summer Carpet, Winter Food." *Frontier Times.* December-January, 1968. pp. 38 ff.

Allard, William Albert. "Chief Joseph." *National Geographic.* March 1977, pp. 409–434.

Aoki, Haruo. "Nez Perce and Proto-Sahaptin Kinship Terms." *International Journal of American Linguistics.* 32(1966):357–368.

Baird, G. W. "The Capture of Chief Joseph and the Nez-Perces." *International Review.* 7(1879):209–215.

Ballou, Howard Malcolm. "The History of the Oregon Mission Press." Hawaiian Historrical Society Annual Report, Portland: 1922.

Bennett, Eileen, ed. "The History and Legend of Bugler Bernard A. Brooks in the Saga of the Nez Perce War in Clark County." *Snake River Echoes: A Quarterly of Idaho History* 12, no. 2 (1984).

Brimlow, George Francis. "Nez Perce War Diary—1877 of Private Frederick Mayer, Troop L, 1st. United States Cavalry." *Idaho State Historical Society Seventeenth Biennial Report 1939–1940.* Boise, Idaho: 1940.

Brown, Mark H. "The Chessmen of War." *Idaho Yesterdays.* Winter 1966–1967, pp. 22–29.

Brown, Mark H. "Chief Joseph and the 'Lyin' Jack Syndrome." *Montana, the Magazine of Western History.* October 1972, pp. 72–73.

Brown, Mark H. "The Joseph Myth." *Montana, the Magazine of Western History.* January 1972, pp. 2–17.

Brown, Mark H. "Yellowstone Tourists and the Nez Perce." *Montana, the Magazine of Western History.* July, 1966, pp. 30–43.

Buck, Amos. "Review of the Battle of the Big Hole." *Montana Historical Society Contributions.* 7(1910):117–130.

Burns, Robert Ignatius, SJ. "Coeur d'Alene Diplomacy in the Nez Perce War of 1877." *Records of the American Catholic Historical Society.* 63(1952):37–60.

Burns, Robert Ignatius. "The Jesuits, the Northern Indians, and the Nez Perce War of 1877." *Pacific Northwest Quarterly.* Volume 42, January 1951, pp. 40–76.

Butterfield, Grace. "Old Chief Joseph's Grave." *Oregon Historical Quarterly.* 46(1945):70–73.

Butterfield, Grace and J. H. Horner. "Wallowa Valley Towns and Their Beginnings." *Oregon Historical Quarterly.* 41(1940):382–385.

Carpenter, John A. "General Howard and the Nez Perce War of 1877." *Pacific Northwest Quarterly.* Volume 49, October 1958, pp. 129–145.

Cataldo, J. M., S. J. "Sketch of the Nez Perce Indians." State Library, Olympia, Washington, *MSS.* 9(1880):43–50, 109–18, 191–199; 10(1881):71–77, 198–204.

Cataldo, J. M., S. J. "Sketch of the Nez Perce Indians." *Woodstock Letters.* Woodstock College, 10(1881):71–77, 198–204.

Chaffee, Eugene B. "Nez Perce War Letters to Governor Mason Brayman." *Fifteenth Biennial Report of the Board of Trustees of the State Historical Society of Idaho for the Years 1935–1936.* Boise, Idaho: 1936.

Cebula, Larry. "Filthy Savages and Red Napoleons: Newspapers and the Nez Perce War." *The Pacific Northwest Forum.* Cheney Washington: VI (1993), pp. 3–13.

Chapman, Berlin B. "Nez Perces in Indian Territory: An Archival Study." *Oregon Historical Quarterly.* 50(1949):98–121.

"Chief Joseph's Own Story." *March of Events*, Butte, Montana, 2 December 1923.

Clark, J. Stanley. "The Nez Perces in Exile." *Pacific Northwest Quarterly.* 36(1945):213–232.

Coale, George L. "Ethnohistorical Sources for the Nez Perce Indians." *Ethnohistory.* 3(1956):246–255, 346–360.

Coale, G. L. "Notes on the Guardian Spirit Concept Among the Nez Perce." *International Archives of Ethnography.* 40(1958):135–148.

Cobblestone: the history magazine for young people. September 1990. 11 (9).

Cowan, Mrs. George. "Reminiscences of Pioneer Life." *Contributions to the Historical Society of Montana.* 4(1903):156–187.

D'Aste, Jerome. "Woodstock Letters," 7(1878):180–184.

Davis, H. J. "An Incident of the Nez Perce Campaign." *Journal of the Military Service Institution of the United States.* 36(1905):560–564.

"Documents from the Cornerstone of the Nez Perce and Ponca Indian School." *Chronicles of Oklahoma.* 12(1934):359–364.

Dozier, Jack. "1885: A Nez Perce Homecoming." *Idaho Yesterdays.* Fall 1963, pp. 22–25.

Dusenberry, Verne. "Chief Joseph's Flight Through Montana: 1877." *The Montana Magazine of History.* October 1952, pp. 43–51.

Elliot, T. C. "The Mullan Road: Its Local History and Significance." *Washington Historical Quarterly.* 14(1923):206–209.

Fletcher, Alice C. "The Nez Perce Country." Proceedings of the American Association for the Advancement of Science, for the Fortieth Meeting held at Washington, D.C., August 1891, 40(1892):357.

Gibbon, John. "The Battle of the Big Hole." *Harper's Weekly.* 39(1895):1215–16, 1235–36.

Gibbon, John. "The Pursuit of Joseph." *American Catholic Quarterly Review.* 4(1879):317–344.

Goodenough, Daniel, Jr. "Lost on Cold Creek: Modern Explorers Track the Nez Perce." *Montana, the Magazine of Western History.* October 1974, pp. 16–29.

Gregory, V. J. "Sunset on the Lolo Trail." *Military Review.* April 1961, pp. 39–50.

Haines, Francis. "Chief Joseph and the Nez Perce Warriors." *Pacific Northwest Quarterly.* Volume 45, January 1954. pp. 1–7.

Haines, Francis. "The Nez Perce Tribe versus the United States." *Idaho Yesterdays.* Spring 1964, pp. 18–25.

Haines, Francis, ed. "The Skirmish at Cottonwood." *Idaho Yesterdays.* Spring 1958, pp. 2–7.

Harbinger, Lucy Jane. *The Importance of Food Plants in the Maintenance of Nez Perce Cultural Identity.* Unpublished M.A. thesis, Washington State University, Pullman, Washington.

Horner, J. H. "Early Wallowa Valley Settlers and How They Lived." *Oregon Historical Quarterly.* 43(1942):215–227.

Horner, J. H. and Grace Butterfield. "Enterprise: Its Background and Beginnings." *Oregon Historical Quarterly.* 39(1938):180–185.

465

Horner, J. H. and Grace Butterfield. "The Nez Perce-Findley Affair." *Oregon Historical Quarterly*. 40(1939):40–51.

Howard, O. O. "The True Story of The Wallowa Campaign." *North American Review*. July 1879, pp. 53–64.

Huegel, Tony. "An 1877 battle, slain Cavalry bugler fascinate an Idaho amateur historian." *Spokesman-Review and Spokane Chronicle*. 16 October 1986, p. ID7.

Hunt, Garrett B. "Sergeant Sutherland's Ride: An Incident of the Nez Perce War." *The Mississippi Valley Historical Review*. Vol. 14(1927):39–46.

"Indian Affairs." *The Daily Times*. Portland, Oregon. July 15, 1862.

Jackson, James P. "On the Trail of Chief Joseph." *American West*. May/June 1984, pp. 10–11.

Johanson, Dorothy O. "The Nez Perce War: The Battles at Cottonwood Creek, 1877." *The Pacific Northwest Quarterly*. Volume 27, April 1936, pp. 167–170.

Joseph, Chief. "An Indian's View of Indian Affairs." *North American Review*. 128(1879). Reprinted *North American Review*. Spring 1969, pp. 56–64.

Josephy, Alvin M., Jr. "The Last Stand of Chief Joseph." *American Heritage*. Volume 9, February 1958, pp. 36–43, 78–81.

Josephy, Alvin M., Jr. "The Naming of the Nez Perces." *Montana, the Magazine of Western History*. October 1955, pp. 1–18.

Koch, Elers. "Lewis and Clark Route Retraced Across the Bitterroots." *Oregon Historical Quarterly*. June 1940, vol. 41, no. 2, pp. 160–163.

Laird, Floy. "Reminiscences of Francis M. Redfield: Chief Joseph's War." *The Pacific Northwest Quarterly*. Volume 27, January 1936, pp. 66–77.

Lang, William. "Where Did the Nez Perces Go in Yellowstone in 1877?" *Montana, the Magazine of Western History* 40 (Winter 1990), pp. 14–29.

McDonald, Duncan. "The Nez Perce Indian War." *The New Northwest*. Deer Lodge, Montana, 26 April 1878–28 March 1879.

May, Allen J. "The Courage of Alice Fletcher." *The West*. January 1965, p. 16 ff.

Moody, Charles Stuart. "The Nez Perces Indians." *American Journal of Clinical Medicine*. 17(1910):1067–1072, 1180–1185, 1306–1312; 18(1911): 184–188, 406–410, 507–512, 1036–1041, 1176–1181.

Moore, Jean M. "The Escape of Nez Perce Jones." *Real West*. July 1967, p. 32 ff.

Morrill, Allen and Eleanor Morrill. "Talmaks." *Idaho Yesterdays*. Fall 1964, pp. 2–15.

Mueller, Oscor O. "The Nez Perce at Cow Island." *Montana, the Magazine of Western History*. April 1964, pp. 50–53.

"The New Indian War." *Frank Leslie's Illustrated Newspaper*. July 28, 1877. pp. 353–4.

Nieberding, Velma. "The Nez Perce in the Quapaw Agency, 1878–1879." *Chronicles of Oklahoma*. Spring 1966, pp. 22–30.

"Notes on the Nez Perce Indians." *American Anthropologist*. N.S., 23, 1922, pp. 244–246.

Owhi, Ben. "Owhi: Nez Perce Warrior." Okanogan County Heritage. September 1964, pp. 3–12.

Osborne, Alan. "The Exile of the Nez Perce in Indian Territory, 1878–1885." *The Chronicles of Oklahoma*. 56(1978–1979):450–471.

Park, Edwards. "Big Hole: still a gaping wound to Nez Perce." *Smithsonian.* May 1978, pp. 92–98.

Parker, Frank J. "Recollections of the Nez Perce War." *The Northwest.* July 1895, pp. 3–6.

Partoll, Albert J. "Angus McDonald, Frontier Fur Trader." *Pacific Northwest Quarterly.* 42(1951):138–146.

Phillips, Paul C. "Battle of the Big Hole." *Frontier: A Magazine of the Northwest.* Volume X, No. i. November 1926, pp. 63–80.

Redfield, F. M. "Reminiscences of Francis M. Redfield: Chief Joseph's War." *Pacific Northwest Quarterly.* 27(1936)66–77.

Redington, J. W. "Scouting in Montana in the 1870s." *Frontier.* Volume 13, No. 1. November 1932, pp. 55–68.

Rhodes, Charles D. "Chief Joseph and the Nez Perce Campaign of 1877." *Proceedings of the Annual Meeting of the Order of Indian Wars of the United States.* February 18, 1938, pp. 19–48.

Romeyn, Capt. Henry. "Capture of Chief Joseph and the Nez Perce Indians." *Montana Historical Society Contributions.* 2(1896):283–291.

Rothermich, A. E. "Early Days at Fort Missoula." *Sources of Northwest History* No. 23. Missoula: Montana State University, 1938.

Ruby, Robert H. "Return of the Nez Perce." *Idaho Yesterdays.* Spring 1968, pp. 12–15.

Sass, Herber Ravenel. "The Man Who Looked like Napoleon." *Collier's.* September 21, 1940, pp. 23, 60, 62.

Scrimsher, Leda Scott. *Native Foods Used by the Nez Perce Indians of Idaho.* Unpublished M.S. thesis, University of Idaho, Moscow, 1967.

Schulmeyer, Alfred W. "Presenting Company K, 7th U.S. Infantry, August, 1877." *By Valor & Arms.* Volume 3, Number 2, 1977, pp. 42–51.

Schwede, Madge L. "The Relationship of Aboriginal Nez Perce Settlement Patterns to Physical Environment and to Generalized Distribution of Food Resources." *Northwest Anthropological Research Notes.* 1970(4):129–135.

Skeels, Dell. "A Classification of Humor in Nez Perce Mythology." *Journal of American Folklore.* 1954(67):57–63.

Stewart, Edgar, ed. "Letters from the Big Hole." *The Montana Magazine of History.* October, 1952, pp. 52–56.

"Swan Song of the Nez Perces: Why Joseph, Friend of the White Race, Made Hopeless War in Defense of His People." *The Western News.* 9 August 1917, p. 7.

Thompson, Erwin N. "Thirteen U.S. Soldiers." *Frontier Times.* Spring 1962, p. 47 ff.

Titus, Nelson C. "The Last Stand of the Nez Perces." *Washington Historical Quarterly.* 6(1915):145–153.

Victor, Frances Fuller. "The First Oregon Cavalry." *The Quarterly of the Oregon Historical Society.* 3(1902):140–141.

Walker, Deward E., Jr. "Nez Perce Sorcery." *Ethnology.* 6(1967):66–96.

Walker, Deward E., Jr. "The Nez Perce Sweat Bath Complex: An Acculturational Analysis." *Southwestern Journal of Anthropology.* 22(1966):133–171.

Warren, D. E. "The Story of 'Two Others'." *Frontier Times.* December–January 1964, p. 34 ff.

Wells, Merle. "The Nez Perce and Their War." *Pacific Northwest Quarterly.* 55, January 1964, pp. 35–37.

Whalen, Sue. "The Nez Perces' Relationship to Their Land." *Indian Historian.* Fall 1971, pp. 30–33.

Wilmot, Luther P. "Pioneer's Story of Nez Perce War." *The Spokesman-Review.* Spokane, Washington: February 7, 14, 21, 1904.

Wilson, Bruce. "The Story of Chief Joseph." Omak, Washington: *Omak Chronicle,* 1960.

Wood, C. E. S. "Chief Joseph, the Nez Perce." *Century Magazine.* 28(1884),. pp. 135–142.

Newspapers

Arkansas City Traveler
Bismarck Tri-Weekly Tribune
Caldwell Tribune
Grande Ronde Mountain Sentinel
Helena Daily Herald
Helena Daily Independent
Idaho Tri-Weekly Statesman
Leavenworth Daily Times
Lemhi Herald
Lewiston Teller
New Northwest
New York Sun
New York Times
The Northerner
Rocky Mountain Husbandman
The Semi-Weekly Idahoan, Boise
Weekly Independent, Helena, Montana

"The Birch Creek Massacre." *The Tribune*, Dillon, Montana. 11 July 1930.

"Indians Are Coming." *Dillon Examiner.* 8 October 1958, p. 10.

"Mrs. Julia Schulz Recalls Nez Perce War Incidents." *Philips County News.* 8 September 1955.

"Warriors Found Whiskey in Wagons and Fight with Whites Started After Reds' Drinking Bout." *The Jordan Tribune.* 21 April 1941.

Banfill, W. H. "Canyon Creek." *Judith Basin County Press.* 13 February 1930.

Banfill, W. H. "Yellowstone." *Judith Basin County Press.* 28 February 1930.

Clarke, Samuel Asahel. Letters from Oregon to the New York Time and Sacramento Union. 18 June 1877, 29 June 1877, 10 July 1877, 27 July 1877, 17 August 1877.

Johnson, Bob. "Joseph's Camp Believed Discovered." *Missoulian.* 28 December 1965.

Jordan, Grace E. "Fred Noyes, 89 Year Old Indian War Veteran Still Concerns Himself Deeply about Nez Perce War." *Winners of the West.* 28 June 1943.

Plassman, Martha E. "When White Bird, Fighting Nez Perce Chief, fugitive in Canada, Refused to Surrender to U.S. Authorities." *The Park County News.* 13 August 1925.

Shoebotham, H. M. and R. H. Scherger. "We're Going to Fight Joseph." *The Billings Gazette.* 11 May 1963.

Watson, Elmo Scott. "Death of 91-Year-Old California Author...." *The Park Record.* 16 March 1944.

Manuscripts, Letters, and Diaries

Anderson, LeRoy and Rena. Cow Island Trail Project.

BLM, Idaho Falls. Archeological Survey Material Review.

Barrett, Alice F. "Reminiscences of Mrs. Alice F. Barrett." MHS Manuscript. 1908.

Barrett, Martin. "Sketch of the Life of Martin Barrett." MHS Manuscript. 1905.

Bessette, Amede. "Visit to the Big Hole Battlefield." MHS Manuscript, ca. 1908.

Bosler, E. R. MHS Manuscript. n.d.

Buck, Henry. "The Story of the Nez Perce Indian Campaign During the Summer of 1877." MHS Manuscript, 1922, 1925.

Catlin, Col. J. B. "The Battle of the Big Hole." MHS Manuscript. 1915.

Chatters, Roy M. "An Account of the Birch Creek Massacre of 1877." Washington State University MASC Manuscript, n.d.

Comba, Capt. Richard. "Reports to the Assistant Adjutant General, District of Montana, of the operations of his Company during the Nez Perce Campaign of 1877." 16 September 1877.

Cone, H. W. "White Bird Battle." Unpublished manuscript, Idaho Historical Library.

Connolly, William. Diary. Eastern Washington State Historical Society.

Connolly, William. "Recollections." Eastern Washington State Historical Society MS.

Cruikshank, Alexander. "The Birch Creek Massacre." MHS Manuscript.

Cruikshank, Alexander. "Chasing Hostile Indians: The Historical Narrative." Unpublished manuscript. Idaho Historical Library.

Davis, Mary Ann. Letter. July 22, 1877.

Deveny, Betty. "Slate Creek History." White Bird, Idaho: Salmon River Ranger District, Slate Creek Ranger Station. 1974.

Farrow, E. S. Letter. MHS. July 16, 1877–September 27, 1877.

Fisher, Don C. "The Story of the Nez Perce War in Idaho." Unpublished manuscript, Washington State University.

Fisher, S. G. "Journal of Mr. S. G. Fisher, Chief of Scouts, to Gen. O. O. Howard During His Campaign Against the Nez Perces, in Montana Territory, in the Summer of 1877." MHS Manuscript, n.d.

Gibbon Trail. USFS files.

Gilbert, C. C. "Report of His March and Unsuccesful Effort to reach General Howard's Command." 23 September 1877. Bowdoin College manuscript.

Governor's Letterbook 1859–62; 1870–78.

Hall, Mrs. Joseph. Letter. 1877.

Hardin, Second Lt. Edward E. Diary. MHS. 25 July 1877–31 October 1877.

Heuer, Karen. Camas Meadows segment. USFS—Missoula.

Hill, Mary Kearney. "Some Memories of Early Days in Idaho." St. Gertrude's Museum, Cottonwood, Idaho.

"History of Fort Missoula, Montana." MHS Manuscript. n.d.

Howard Trail. USFS files.

Howard, Gen. O. O. Incoming Correspondence, 1877.

Howard, Gen. O. O. Incoming Correspondence, 1877. Bowdoin College special collections.

Howard, O. O. "Journal of Expedition against Hostile Nez Perce Indians." Bowdoin College manuscript.

Johnson, Henry C. "Some Reminiscences of the Nez Perce Indian War." University of Idaho unpublished manuscript. 1927.

Jones, J. H. "The Rock Creek Massacre." MHS Manuscript. 1904.

Kuykendall, Elgin Victor. "The Contribution of the American Indian to Democracy." Unpublished manuscript.

Bibliography

Kuykendall, Elgin Victor. "Discussion of Nez Perce Ceremony of Koyit, the Spring Festival." Unpublished manuscript.

Lord, Herbert W. "Early Recollections." USFS—Missoula Regional Office files.

Luce, Edward S. "Chief Joseph, The American." MHS Manuscript. 10 July 1955.

McDonald, Angus. "Nez Perces Campaign." MHS Manuscript.

McDonald, Duncan. "The Old Nez Perce Woman." MHS Manuscript. n.d.

Martens, John P. MHS Manuscript.

Meany, Edmond Stephen. "Chief Joseph, The Nez Perce." University of Wisconsin Masters thesis. 1901.

Miles, Nelson A. "Report to the Assistant Adjutant General, Department of Dakota, December 27, 1877."

Moelchert, William. Letter. MHS. November 13, 1927.

Monteith Letters. Spokane Public Library.

Mudiman, T. E. Transcript of Tape Recording made by Gabriel Leveille, 1957.

Myers, Andrew. MHS Manuscript. 1915.

Noyes, A. J. "Louis Shambow." MHS Manuscript. December 17, 1916.

Owhi. "Statement on the Nez Perce War by Owhi." Unpublished manuscript. (is this the same as in Okanogan County Heritage?) <?>

Peopeo Tholekt. "Reminiscences." Unpublished manuscript.

Pouliot, Gordon L. and Thain White. "The Clearwater Battlefield: The Nez Perce War - 1877, A Preliminary Survey." Unpublished manuscript. Washington State University, 1960.

Pouliot, Gordon L. and Thain White. "The Possible Site of the Rains Scouting Party Tragedy." Unpublished manuscript. Washington State University, 1960.

Redington, J. W. "Scouting in Montana." Manuscript. Spokane Public Library.

"Route of the Utah and Northern Railway, 1882." from Heritage Hall, Dubois, Idaho.

Samples, John. Letter describing the battle of Cow Island. 25 November 1927.

Shearer, George. Correspondence. Idaho Historical Library.

Sherrill, Bunch. MHS Manuscript. 1916.

Sherrill, Thomas. "The Battle of the Big Hole As I Saw It." MHS Manuscript. 1916.

Sutherland, George W. "Statement." Manuscript, Eastern Washington University, 1946.

Wallace, Thomas S. "Report to Post Adjutant, July 27, 1878, Fort Missoula, Montana."

Walsh, Helen Julia Mason. Unpublished manuscript. Washington State University.

White, Thain. "Relics from Misery Hill: Nez Perce War, 1877." Manuscript. Washington State University.

Weikert, Andrew J. "Journal of Tour of the Yellowstone National Park in August and September, 1877." Manuscript. Big Hole Battlefield Library.

Weilger, David. "An Interview with James Boyd at Wolf Point." MHS manuscript. 1925.

White, Donny. "Indians of the Cypress Hills." 1980.

Wilmot, Luther P. "Narratives of the Nezperce War." University of Idaho library. Manuscript.

Wilmot, Luther P. "Narratives of the Nezperce War: The Battle of the Clearwater - 1877." Manuscript. University of Idaho Library.

Wilmot, Luther P. "Narratives of the Nezperce War: Misery Hill." Manuscript. Washington State University.

Wilson, Eugene T. "How Wily Chief Joseph of Nez Perces Was Captured." Manuscript.

Woodruff, C. A. "Battle of the Big Hole." Manuscript. MHS. 1912.

Woodruff, Lt. Thomas Mayhew. Letter. MHS. October 15, 1877.

Maps

Hill, R. G. Post Map, Fort Assinniboine, Montana. 1887.

Snyder, J. A. Map of the U.S. Military Reservation of Ft. Assinniboine, Montana Territory. 1879.

Acknowledgments

Thanks are extended to the following publishers and institutions for permission to reprint material copyrighted or controlled by them:

Caxton Printers, Ltd., for gracious permission to quote extensively from Lucullus V. McWhorter's *Hear Me, My Chiefs!* and *Yellow Wolf*,; from Frank Carpenter's *Adventures in Geyserland*; from Stephen Perry Jocelyn's *Mostly Alkali*; and from R. Ross Arnold's *Indian Wars of Idaho*.

Idaho State Historical Society, Boise, Idaho, for permission to quote from the library collections: S.G. Fisher's diary; H.W. Cone's "White Bird Battle"; Helen Mason Walsh's manuscript; Alexander Cruikshank's "Chasing Hostile Indians"; George Shearer's correspondence; Fletcher's letter to S.G. Fisher; Eugene B. Chaffee's "Nez Perce War Letters to Governor Mason Brayman" in the *Fifteenth Biennial Report of the Board of Trustees of the State Historical Society of Idaho for the Years 1935—1936*; and George Bromlow's "Nez Perce War Diary—1877 of Private Frederick Mayer, Troop L, 1st. United States Cavalry," in the *Idaho State Historical Society Seventeenth Biennial Report 1939–1940*.

University of Idaho Library, Moscow, Idaho, for permission to quote from "Some reminiscences of the Nez Perce Indian War," by Henry C. Johnson, 1927; and "Narratives of the Nezperce War" and "Narratives of the Nezperce War : The Battle of the Clearwater—1877," by Luther P. Wilmot, 1922.

Idaho County Free Press for permission to quote from Charlotte Kirkwood's *The Nez Perce Indian War Under War Chiefs Joseph and White Bird*, copyright 1953; and Norman Adkison's *Indian Braves and Battles with More Nez Perce Lore* and *Nez Perce Indian War and Original Stories*, both copyright 1967.

Montana Historical Society for permission to quote from E.S. Farrow's letters, Henry Buck's "The Story of the Nez Perce Indian Campaign During the Summer of 1877"; John P. Martens' diary; Col. J.B. Catlin's "The Battle of the Big Hole"; Thomas Sherrill's "The Battle of the Big Hole As I Saw It"; Bunch Sherrill's manuscript; Alice F. Barrett's "Reminiscences"; Martin Barrett's "Sketch of the Life of Martin Barrett"; C.A. Woodruff's "Battle of the Big Hole"; Andrew Myers' manuscript; Moccasin's and Speak Thunder's sworn statements; William Moelchert's letter to Hilger; General O.O. Howard's 1877 incoming correspondence; Eugene Tallmadge Wilson's *Hawks and Doves in the Nez Perce War*, copyright 1966; and William F. Zimmer's *Frontier Soldier: An Enlisted Man's Journal: Sioux and Nez Perce Campaigns, 1877*, copyright 1998.

Washington State University Archives for permission to quote from the McWhorter Collection, Don Fisher's "The Story of the Nez Perce War in Idaho," and Luther P. Wilmot's "Narratives of the Nezperce War: Misery Hill."

Ye Galleon Press for permission to quote from *The Wallowa Country 1867—1877*, by Grace Bartlett; *Howard's Campaign Against the Nez Perce*, by Thomas Sutherland; and *Indian Tribes of Washington Territory*, by George Gibbs.

Eastern Washington Historical Society for permission to quote from William Connolly's "Recollections" and diary.

Spokane Public Library for permission to quote from John W. Redington's "Scouting in Montana."

Bear Creek Press for permission to quote from *The Death of Wind Blowing.*

Oklahoma Historical Society for permission to quote from Alan Osborne's "The Exile of the Nez Perce in Indian Territory, 1878–1885," from *The Chronicles of Oklahoma.*

Wallowa County Chieftain for permission to quote from "Pioneer Woman Tells of Attack by Chief Joseph in Nez Perce War."

Hastings House for permission to quote from "Tragic Retreat," by Rowena and Gordon Alcorn.

Big Hole Library for permission to quote from Andrew Weikart's "Journal of Tour of the Yellowstone National Park in August and September, 1877."

All efforts have been made to contact copyright holders of material quoted in this book. However, if we have unwittingly infringed copyright in any way, we offer our sincere apologies and will be glad of the opportunity to make appropriate acknowledgment in future editions.

Notes

Chapter 1

1. Lucullus V. McWhorter. *Yellow Wolf* (Caldwell, Idaho: The Caxton Printers, Ltd., 1983), p. 18.
2. *YW*, p. 35.
3. Travelers coming in from the southeast may want to skip ahead to the Intrepid Traveler section, which leads from Joseph to Dug Bar, picking it up at Imnaha.
4. Highberger, Mark. *The Death of Wind Blowing: The Story of the 1876 Murder that Helped Trigger the Nez Perce War.* (Wallowa, Oregon: Bear Creek Press, 2000), pp. 39–41.
5. The most consolidated source of information about the Palouse is the book *Renegade Tribe*, by Clifford Trafzer and Richard D. Scheuerman, published by Washington State University Press in 1986.

Chapter 2

1. *YW*, p. 18.
2. Monteith to Howard, 19 March 1877, Howard collection, Montana Historical Society, Helena, Montana.
3. Frances Fuller Victor, "The First Oregon Cavalry," *The Quarterly of the Oregon Historical Society*, 3 (1902):140.
4. Emily FitzGerald, *An Army Doctor's Wife on the Frontier*, ed., Abe Laufe (Lincoln: University of Nebraska Press, 1986), pp. 222–224.
5. Oliver Otis Howard, *Nez Perce Joseph, An Account of His Ancestors* (Boston: Lee and Shepard, 1881), p. 35.
6. FitzGerald, p. 247.
7. Oliver Otis Howard, *My Life and Experiences Among Our Hostile Indians* (New York: DaCapo Press, 1972), p. 250.
8. Howard, *Nez Perce Joseph*, p. 59.
9. Ibid.
10. Ibid.
11. The traditional, non-Christian Nez Perce believed that dreams were a source of wisdom. Thus, whites called their belief system the Dreamer religion.
12. *YW*, p. 39.
13. *YW*, p. 39.
14. *YW*, pp. 39–40.
15. *YW*, p. 40.
16. L.V. McWhorter, *Hear Me, My Chiefs* (Caldwell, Idaho: The Caxton Printers, Ltd., 1983), pp. 229–230.
17. YW, p. 41.
18. *HMMC*, p. 168.
19. *HMMC*, p. 168.
20. *HMMC*, p. 200.
21. FitzGerald, p. 251.

Chapter 3

1. *YW*, p. 42.
2. Henry C. Johnson, "Some Reminiscences of the Nez Perce Indian War" (Manuscript, University of Idaho, 1927), p. 8.
3. *HMMC*, p. 230.
4. Norman Adkison, *Indian Braves and Battles with More Nez Perce Lore* (Grangeville, Idaho: Idaho County Free Press, 1967), p. 7.
5. FitzGerald, p. 266.
6. Robert Westly Pollock, *Grandfather, Chief Joseph, and Psychodynamics* (Baker, Oregon: 1964), p. 70.
7. Luther P. Wilmot, "Narratives of the Nezperce War," University of Idaho, Moscow, Idaho, p. 1.
8. Bennett, pp. 339, 341.
9. Dorothy O. Johansen, "The Nez Perce War: The Battles at Cottonwood Creek, 1877," *Pacific Northwest Quarterly*, 27(1936):167.
10. *YW*, p. 70.
11. *HMMC*, p. 283.
12. *YW*, p. 71.
13. *YW*, pp. 72–74.
14. *HMMC*, p. 286n.
15. George Francis Brimlow, "Nez Perce War Diary—1877 of Private Frederick Mayer, Troop L, 1st United States Cavalry," Boise, Idaho: 1940, pp. 28–29.
16. Ibid., pp. 29–30.
17. *HMMC*, p. 288.
18. FitzGerald, p. 274.
19. Norman Adkison, *Nez Perce Indian War and Original Stories* (Grangeville, Idaho: Idaho Free Press, 1967), pp. 38–39.
20. R. Ross Arnold, *Indian Wars of Idaho* (Caldwell, Idaho: The Caxton Printers, Ltd., 1932), pp. 158–161.
21. Adkison, *Nez Perce Indian War*, p. 25.
22. *HMMC*, pp. 234–235.

23. Luther P. Wilmot, "Narratives of the Nezperce War," p. 6.

24. *HMMC*, p. 200.

25. *HMMC*, pp. 201–202.

26. Johnson, p. 2.

27. Howard to Shearer, 18 July 1877, Shearer Collection, Idaho Historical Library, Boise, Idaho.

28. Oliver Knight, *Following the Indian Wars: The Story of the Newspaper Correspondents Among the Indian Campaigners* (Norman, Oklahoma: University of Oklahoma Press, 1960), p. 295.

29. "Pioneer Woman Tells of Attack By Chief Joseph in Nez Perce War," *Wallowa Co. Chieftain*, 9 July 1959.

30. *HMMC*, pp. 213–214.

31. "Pioneer Woman Tells of Attack."

32. *HMMC*, p. 217.

33. "Pioneer Woman Tells of Attack."

34. Robert A. Bennett, comp., *We'll all Go Home in the Spring* (Walla Walla: Pioneer Press Books, 1984), p. 340.

35. *HMMC*, p. 241.

36. McWhorter Collection, Washington State University, Pullman, Washington.

37. *YW*, pp. 54–55.

38. *HMMC*, p. 246.

39. Ibid., pp. 248–249.

40. *YW*, p. 56.

41. *HMMC*, p. 249.

42. Ibid., p. 233n.

43. Ibid., p. 249.

44. Ibid., p. 247.

45. McWhorter Collection.

46. *HMMC*, pp. 239–240.

47. Ibid., pp. 251–252n.

48. FitzGerald, p. 273.

49. McWhorter Collection.

50. *HMMC*, p. 247.

51. Charlotte M. Kirkwood, *The Nez Perce Indian War Under War Chiefs Joseph and Whitebird* (Grangeville, Idaho: Idaho County Free Press, 1953), p. 6.

52. *YW*, pp. 61–62.

53. Stephen Perry Jocelyn, *Mostly Alkali* (Caldwell, Idaho: The Caxton Printers, Ltd., 1953), p. 227.

54. *HMMC*, p. 258.

55. *HMMC*, p. 124.

56. Ethel E. Redfield, ed., *Reminiscences of Francis M. Redfield* (Pocatello, Idaho: 1949), p. 99.

57. Kirkwood, pp. 50–52.

58. *HMMC*, p. 240.

59. Kirkwood, pp. 50–52.

60. *YW*, p. 278.

61. Kirkwood, pp. 28–29.

62. *HMMC*, p. 201.

63. Helen Julia Mason Walsh, Manuscript, Idaho Historical Library, Boise, Idaho, p. 8.

64. *HMMC*, p. 212.

65. Ibid., p. 192.

66. McWhorter Collection.

67. *HMMC*, p. 228.

68. H. W. Cone, "White Bird Battle," unpublished manuscript, Idaho Historical Society, Boise, Idaho, p. 3.

69. Cone, pp. 6–7.

70. Ibid., p. 3.

71. *YW*, p. 62.

72. Ibid., pp. 68–69.

73. *HMMC*, p. 276.

74. Jocelyn, p. 228.

75. *YW*, p. 69.

76. Jocelyn, p. 229.

77. Howard, *Nez Perce Joseph*, p. 102.

78. Helen Julia Mason Walsh, unpublished manuscript, Washington State University, Pullman, Washington, pp. 18–26.

79. Eugene B. Chaffee, "Nez Perce War Letters to Governor Mason Brayman." Fifteenth Biennial Report of the Board of Trustees of the State Historical Society of Idaho for the Years 1935–1936 (Boise: 1936), pp. 73–74.

80. Eugene Tallmadge Wilson, *Hawks and Doves in the Nez Perce War of 1877* (Helena: Montana Historical Society, 1966), p. 6.

81. *YW*, p. 41.

82. Thomas Sutherland, *Howard's Campaign Against the Nez Perce* (Fairfield, Washington: Ye Galleon Press, 1980), p. 9.

83. Howard, *Nez Perce Joseph*, p. 150.

84. Sutherland, p. 11.

85. Brimlow, pp. 29-30.

86. Wilmot, pp. 8–9.

87. Kirkwood, p. 11.

88. Luther P. Wilmot, "In a Hot Fight with Chief Joseph," *The Spokesman-Review*, 14 February 1904.

89. *YW*, p. 76.

90. Johnson, p. 6.

91. Wilmot, "Hot Fight with Chief Joseph."

92. *YW*, pp. 76–77.

93. Shearer to Mason, 26 July 1877, Shearer Collection.

475

94. Wilson, p. 7.
95. Shearer to Mason.
96. Actually, two were killed and three were wounded.
97. Brimlow, pp. 29–30.
98. *YW*, p. 76.
99. Kirkwood, pp. 17–18, 21.

Chapter 4

1. *HMMC*, p. 304.
2. McDonald, 6 December 1878, p. 3.
3. This date is approximate.
4. Adkison, *Nez Perce Indian War and Original Stories*, pp. 42–43.
5. *HMMC*, p. 300.
6. *YW*, pp. 86–87.
7. *HMMC*, pp. 298–299.
8. McWhorter Collection.
9. *YW*, p. 100.
10. *YW*, pp. 88–89.
11. *HMMC*, p. 307.
12. *YW*, p. 101.
13. Peopeo Tholekt, "Reminiscences," 1935, Washington State University, Pullman, Washington, p. 3.
14. *YW*, p. 91.
15. Lt. E. S. Farrow to Gray, 16 July 1877, Montana Historical Society, Helena, Montana.
16. Jocelyn, p. 232.
17. Eileen Bennett, ed., "The History and Legend of Bugler Bernard A. Brooks in the Saga of the Nez Perce War in Clark County," *Snake River Echoes: A Quarterly of Idaho History* 12 no. 2 (1984), p. 39.
18. *HMMC*, p. 314.
19. *HMMC*, pp. 315–316.
20. *YW*, p. 96.

21. *YW*, pp. 100–101.
22. *YW*, pp. 96–97.
23. *HMMC*, p. 317.
24. *HMMC*, p. 322.
25. FitzGerald, p. 290.
26. *Snake River Echoes*, p. 39.
27. Sutherland, p. 15.
28. Luther P. Wilmot, "Thrilling Incidents of the Nez Perce War," *The Spokesman-Review*, 21 February 1904.
29. *HMMC*, p. 299.
30. Sutherland, p. 12.
31. Interview with Spud Dahler.
32. *HMMC*, pp. 265–267.
33. *HMMC*, p. 269.
34. *HMMC*, pp. 270, 272.
35. *HMMC*, p. 273.
36. *YW*, p. 103.
37. Sutherland, p. 15.
38. Luther P. Wilmot, "Narratives of the Nezperce War: The Battle of the Clearwater—1877," Special Collections Department, University of Idaho, Moscow, Idaho, p. 3.
39. FitzGerald, p. 278.
40. Wilson, p. 10.
41. *YW*, pp. 103–104.
42. Wilson, p. 10.
43. *HMMC*, p. 329.
44. Wilson, p. 10.
45. Sutherland, p. 18.
46. F. M. Redfield, "Reminiscences of Francis M. Redfield: Chief Joseph's War." *Pacific Northwest Quarterly*, 27(1936):75.
47. *YW*, p. 104.
48. William Connolly, "Recollections," Eastern Washington Historical Society, Spokane, Washington.

49. FitzGerald, p. 279–280.
50. Ibid., p. 285.
51. Luther P. Wilmot, "Narratives of the Nezperce War: Misery Hill," Washington State University, Pullman, Washington.
52. Eugene B. Chaffee, "Nez Perce War Letters to Governor Mason Brayman." *Fifteenth Biennial Report of the Board of Trustees of the State Historical Society of Idaho for the Years 1935–1936*. (Boise, Idaho: 1936), pp. 66–67.
53. Wilmot, "Misery Hill."
54. These were horses taken from the Looking Glass band on July 1.
55. Chaffee, pp. 66–67.
56. Wilson, pp. 8–9.
57. Chaffee, pp. 66–67.
58. Wilson, pp. 8–9.

Chapter 5

1. George Gibbs, *Indian Tribes of Washington Territory* (Fairfield, Washington: Ye Galleon Press, 1978, p. 11.
2. *HMMC*, p. 335.
3. Chaffee, p. 68.
4. Chaffee, p. 69.
5. FitzGerald, p. 291.
6. FitzGerald, p. 291.
7. Edwin Mason letters, Mss. No. 80, Montana Historical Society, Helena, Montana.
8. Connolly, p. 5.
9. Mason letters.
10. Sutherland, p. 24.
11. FitzGerald, p. 296.
12. Mason letters.
13. *HMMC*, p. 347.
14. *YW*, p. 107.

15. *HMMC*, p. 353.
16. Sutherland, p. 28.
17. Diary of John P. Martens, Martens Collection, Montana Historical Society, Helena, Montana, p. 55.
18. *YW*, p. 107.
19. Henry Buck, "The Story of the Nez Perce Indian Campaign During the Summer of 1877," Montana Historical Society, Helena, Montana, p. 22.
20. Mason letters.

Chapter 6

1. Buck, p. 1.
2. FitzGerald, p. 296.
3. *YW*, p. 108.
4. Buck, p. 5.
5. Buck, p. 26.
6. Lolo History Committee, *Lolo Creek Reflections* (1976), p. 9.
7. A.E. Rothermich, *Early Days at Fort Missoula*, Sources of Northwest History, no. 23 (Missoula: Montana State University, 1938), p. 4.
8. Buck, p. 11.
9. Buck, pp. 27–33.
10. Gibbon actually had 17 officers and 132 enlisted men. Seventy volunteers joined him in the Bitterroot but half of these returned home before reaching the battlefield. He therefore had 183 men at the beginning of the battle.
11. Col. J.B. Catlin, "The Battle of the Big Hole," Montana Historical Society, Helena, Montana, p. 2.

12. Tom Sherrill, "The Battle of the Big Hole As I Saw It," Montana Historical Society, Helena, Montana, p. 2.
13. *YW*, p. 108–109.
14. Sutherland, p. 29.
15. C.A. Woodruff, "Battle of the Big Hole," Montana Historical Society, Helena, Montana, p. 9.

Chapter 7

1. Gibbs, p. 11.
2. *HMMC*, p. 371.
3. *YW*, p. 109–110.
4. McWhorter Collection, Washington State University, Pullman, Washington.
5. *YW*, p. 110.
6. Richard Comba, "Reports to the Assistant Adjutant General, District of Montana, of the operation of his Company during the Nez Perce Campaign of 1877." 16 September 1877. Montana Historical Society, Helena, Montana.
7. *YW*, p. 115.
8. Sherrill, p. 4.
9. Comba.
10. *YW*, p. 123.
11. *YW*, p. 132.
12. *YW*, p. 135.
13. McWhorter Collection.
14. Wyakin refers to an individual's protective spirit power.
15. *HMMC*, p. 386–388.
16. *YW*, p. 138.
17. *YW*, p. 119.
18. *HMMC*, p. 373.
19. *YW*, p. 136.
20. McWhorter Collection.

21. McWhorter Collection.
22. McWhorter Collection.
23. Tom Sherrill, p. 7.
24. *HMMC*, p. 374.
25. J. B. Catlin, pp. 3–4.
26. *YW*, p. 120.
27. McWhorter Collection.
28. Tom Sherrill, pp. 6–8.
29. Comba.
30. *YW*, p. 121.
31. *YW*, p. 142.
32. Bunch Sherrill, manuscript, Montana Historical Society, Helena, Montana, p. 4.
33. Tom Sherrill, p. 9.
34. Tom Sherrill, pp. 11–15.
35. Catlin, pp. 4–5.
36. Tom Sherrill, p. 17.
37. McWhorter Collection, 110.
38. *YW*, p. 132.
39. *HMMC*, p. 393.
40. *YW*, p. 159.
41. *YW*, p. 155.
42. Tom Sherrill, p. 17.
43. *YW*, pp. 149–151.
44. *YW*, pp. 155–156.
45. *YW*, p. 156.
46. *YW*, p. 158.
47. *YW*, p. 158.
48. Comba.
49. J. W. Redington, "Scouting in Montana," Spokane Public Libraries, p. 1.
50. Tom Sherrill, pp. 19–23.
51. Catlin, p. 5.
52. Tom Sherrill, p. 23.
53. FitzGerald, pp. 303–304.
54. Redington, p. 1.
55. *HMMC*, p. 406.
56. *YW*, p. 159.
57. Redington, p. 3.

477

58. Jocelyn, p. 244.
59. Sutherland, p. 32.
60. Alice Barrett, "Reminiscences of Mrs. Alice F. Barrett," Montana Historical Society, p. 3.
61. Alice Barrett, p. 4.
62. Alice Barrett, p. 5.
63. Alexander Cruikshank, "Chasing Hostile Indians," p. 2.
64. McWhorter Collection, pp. 157–171.
65. Martin Barrett, Montana Historical Society, p. 5.
66. "Story of Andrew Meyers," Montana Historical Society, pp. 2–3.
67. Cruikshank, p. 5.
68. Mark Brown, "The Joseph Myth," *Montana The Magazine of Western History* 22 (winter 1971), p. 9.
69. *YW*, p. 165.
70. Cruikshank, p. 6.

Chapter 8

1. *YW*, p. 169.
2. *HMMC*, pp. 414–415.
3. *HMMC*, p. 417.
4. Sutherland, p. 34.
5. *YW*, pp. 166–167.
6. *HMMC*, p. 419.
7. Ibid., p. 419n.
8. Sutherland, p. 34.
9. *YW*, p. 167.
10. *HMMC*, p. 419.
11. *HMMC*, p. 419.
12. *YW*, p. 168.
13. To read an excerpt from a letter written by Brooks, see page 139 in Chapter 4.
14. *YW*, p. 168.
15. *YW*, p. 169.
16. *HMMC*, p. 423.
17. *HMMC*, pp. 423–424.

18. *YW*, p. 168.
19. *HMMC*, p. 424.
20. Ibid., p. 425.
21. Ibid., p. 424.
22. Sutherland, p. 36.
23. Frank D. Carpenter, *Adventures in Geyserland* (Caldwell, Idaho: The Caxton Printers, Ltd., 1935), pp. 35–36.
24. Connolly, pp. 8–9
25. Sutherland, p. 36.
26. Lt. E. S. Farrow to Gray, 24 August 1877, Montana Historical Society, Helena, Montana.
27. FitzGerald, p. 307.
28. Mark Brown, *The Flight of the Nez Perce* (Lincoln: University of Nebraska Press, 1982), p. 306.
29. Henry Buck, pp. 71–72.

Chapter 9

1. Jocelyn, p. 255.
2. *YW*, p. 26.
3. Carpenter, p. 45.
4. S. G. Fisher, Diary, Idaho Historical Library, Boise, Idaho, p. 4.
5. Henry Buck, pp. 72–73.
6. Carpenter, pp. 201–203.
7. Ibid., pp. 68, 87–88.
8. Ibid., p. 281.
9. *YW*, pp. 171–172.
10. Carpenter, pp. 286–287.
11. *YW*, pp. 172–173.
12. Carpenter, p. 287.
13. *YW*, pp. 173–175.
14. Don C. Fisher, "The Story of the Nez Perce War in Idaho," Washington State University, Pullman, Washington, p. 35.
15. Carpenter, pp. 287–288.

16. D. C. Fisher, p. 35.
17. *YW*, p. 175.
18. Carpenter, p. 97.
19. Ibid., p. 100.
20. Ibid., p. 289.
21. Ibid., p. 100.
22. *YW*, p. 175.
23. D.C. Fisher, p. 36.
24. Carpenter, p. 289.
25. Ibid., pp. 112–113.
26. Ibid., pp. 217–221.
27. *YW*, p. 175.
28. Carpenter, p. 291.
29. *YW*, p. 176.
30. Carpenter, p. 229.
31. Ibid., p. 258.
32. Ibid., p. 317.
33. Accounts of Meyers' rescue is on page 279; Mann's and Oldham's rescues are on page 287.
34. Carpenter, p. 294.
35. Ibid., p. 282.
36. Ibid., p. 231.
37. Carpenter, p. 224.
38. Ibid., pp. 208–215.
39. Ibid., pp. 222–224.
40. Redington, p. 17.
41. Fletcher to Fisher, 31 August 1877, Idaho Historical Library, Boise, Idaho.
42. S. G. Fisher, p. 7.
43. Carpenter, p. 297.
44. Ibid., p. 297.
45. Ibid., p. 262.
46. Ibid., p. 162.
47. *YW*, pp. 176–177.
48. Carpenter, pp. 163–164.
49. Ibid., p. 262.
50. Carpenter, pp. 312–313.
51. Buck, pp. 87–88.
52. Carpenter, p. 225.
53. Ibid., p. 300.
54. Ibid., pp. 183–184.

55. Andrew J. Weikart, "Journal of Tour of the Yellowstone National Park in August and September, 1877," Big Hole Battlefield Library, Wisdom, Montana, p. 4.

56. Carpenter, pp. 184–185.

57. Weikart, pp. 6–7.

58. *YW*, p. 177.

59. Weikart, p. 6.

60. Redington, pp. 13–14.

61. Sutherland, p. 38.

62. Carpenter, pp. 300–301.

63. Frank Carpenter visited the Nez Perce at Fort Leavenworth on June 16, 1878.

64. Weikart, pp. 8–9.

65. *YW*, p. 177.

66. Weikart, p. 9.

67. Sutherland, p. 38.

68. Jocelyn, p. 255.

69. Redington, p. 5.

70. S.G. Fisher, p. 9.

Chapter 10

1. John M. Carroll, *Camp Talk: The Very Private Letters of Frederick W. Benteen of the 7th U.S. Cavalry to His Wife, 1871–1888* (New York: J. M. Carroll & Company, 1983), p. 85.

2. *YW*, p. 184.

3. McWhorter Collection.

4. S. G. Fisher, p. 11.

5. Fisher, p. 12.

6. Fisher, p.12.

7. Connolly, pp. 10–11.

8. Thomas Marquis, *Custer, Cavalry & Crows* (Fort Collins, Colorado: The Old Army Press, 1975), p. 139.

9. FitzGerald, p. 311.

Chapter 11

1. FitzGerald, pp. 311–312.

2. *YW*, p. 194.

3. Redington, p. 6.

4. Fisher, pp. 13–14.

5. Fisher, pp. 13–14.

6. Fisher, p. 16.

7. *YW*, p. 186.

8. *YW*, p. 185.

9. Redington, p. 7.

10. McWhorter Collection.

11. *YW*, p. 187.

12. Redington, p. 8.

13. Sutherland, p. 43.

14. Cruikshank, p. 15.

15. Connolly, Diary.

16. Sutherland, p. 43.

Chapter 12

1. McWhorter Collection.

2. Redington, p. 10.

3. Goldin, p. 19.

4. William F. Zimmer, *Frontier Soldier: An Enlisted Man's Journal: Sioux and Nez Perce Campaigns, 1877* (Helena, Montana: Montana Historical Society Press, 1998), pp. 118–119.

5. Zimmer, p. 120.

6. William Ludlow, *Exploring Nature's Sanctuary: Captain William Ludlow's Report of a Reconnaissance from Carroll, Montana Territory, on the Upper Missouri to the Yellowstone National Park, and Return Made in the Summer of 1875* (Washington: Government Printing Office, 1985), p. 13.

7. Theodore W. Goldin, *A Bit of the Nez Perce Campaign.* Bryan, Texas: privately printed, 1978, p. 22.

8. "Ten Whites Withstood Attack," 8 January 1942.

9. McWhorter 150N-46.

10. *YW*, p. 199.

11. William Moelchert to Hilger, 13 November 1927, Montana Historical Society, Helena, Montana, pp. 2–3.

12. Redington, p. 11.

13. Zimmer, p. 121.

14. Moelchert, pp. 2–3.

15. *HMMC*, p. 471.

16. Kirkwood, p. 26.

17. *HMMC*, pp. 473–474.

18. Zimmer, pp. 121–122.

19. Robert J. Ege, *After the Little Bighorn* (Greeley, Colorado: Fred. H. Werner, 1982), p. 5.

20. McWhorter Collection.

21. *YW*, p. 205.

22. Thomas Mayhew Woodruff, "A Soldier Writes Home About the Final Battle," *Montana,* Autumn 1977, pp. 32–33.

23. McWhorter Collection.

24. McWhorter Collection.

25. *HMMC*, p. 482.

26. *HMMC*, p. 479–480.

27. T. Woodruff, pp. 32–33.

28. *YW*, pp. 209, 211.

29. T. Woodruff, pp. 32–33.

30. Cruikshank, p. 14.

31. *YW*, p. 210.

32. Zimmer, pp. 126–127.

33. *HMMC*, pp. 508–509.

34. *YW*, pp. 212–213.

35. McWhorter Collection.
36. *YW*, p. 215.
37. McWhorter Collection.
38. *YW*, p. 217.
39. *YW*, pp. 213–214.
40. Zimmer, p. 126.
41. McWhorter Collection.
42. *YW*, p. 220.
43. *YW*, pp. 224–5.
44. Zimmer, p. 128.
45. Kirkwood, p. 27.
46. *HMMC*, pp. 510–511.
47. McWhorter Collection.
48. Zimmer, pp. 128–130.
49. Zimmer, p. 129.
50. Woodruff, pp. 32–33.
51. *YW*, p. 230.
52. Kirkwood, pp. 27–28.
53. Zimmer, p. 130.

Chapter 13

1. *HMMC*, p. 511.
2. The fact that over thirty Nez Perce had been killed by whites prior to the outbreak of the war did not come into consideration.
3. The Colville Reservation in Washington, the Umatilla Reservation in Oregon, the Nez Perce Reservation in Idaho, and the Peigan Reserve in Alberta.
4. *HMMC*, p. 509.
5. *HMMC*, pp. 509–510.
6. *YW*, p. 233.
7. *YW*, p. 236.
8. Zimmer, p. 113.
9. Fred G. Bond, *Flatboating on the Yellowstone 1877* (New York: New York Public Library, 1925), pp. 4–9.
10. Bond, pp. 4–11.
11. Bond, pp. 11–12.
12. Bond, pp. 17–18.
13. Bond, pp. 19–22.
14. Bond, p. 22.
15. *YW*, p. 289.
16. *YW*, p. 290.

Index